S0-BBY-834

ISAIAH 46, 47, AND 48: A NEW LITERARY-CRITICAL READING

BIBLICAL AND JUDAIC STUDIES FROM THE UNIVERSITY OF CALIFORNIA, SAN DIEGO

Volume 3

edited by
William Henry Propp

Previously published in the series:

1. *The Hebrew Bible and Its Interpreters,* edited by William Henry Propp, Baruch Halpern, and David Noel Freedman (1990).
2. *Studies in Hebrew and Aramaic Orthography,* by David Noel Freedman, A. Dean Forbes, and Francis I. Andersen (1992).

ISAIAH 46, 47, AND 48: A NEW LITERARY-CRITICAL READING

by
Chris Franke

EISENBRAUNS
Winona Lake, Indiana
1994

Published for Biblical and Judaic Studies
The University of California, San Diego

by

Eisenbrauns
Winona Lake, Indiana

Printed in the United States of America.

Library of Congress Cataloging in Publication Data

Franke, Chris.
Isaiah 46, 47, and 48: a new literary-critical reading / by Chris Franke.
p. cm. — (Biblical and Judaic Studies ; v. 3)
Includes bibliographical references.
ISBN 0-931464-79-X (alk. paper)
1. Bible. O.T. Isaiah XLVI—Criticism, interpretation, etc.
2. Bible. O.T. Isaiah XLVII—Criticism, interpretation, etc.
3. Bible. O.T. Isaiah XLVIII—Criticism, interpretation, etc.
4. Bible. O.T. Isaiah XL-LV—Criticism, interpretation, etc.—History.
5. Bible as literature. I. Title. II. Title: Isaiah forty-six, forty-seven, and forty-eight. III. Series.
BS1515.2.F73 1994
224′.1066—dc20 94-1973
CIP

The paper used in this publication meets the minimum requirements of the American National Standard for Information Sciences—Permanence of Paper for Printed Library Materials, ANSI Z39.48-1984.♾™

CONTENTS

To my teacher and friend
David Noel Freedman

Acknowledgments

Let us now praise illustrious people . . . .

Here is a list of generous people, whose good works will not be forgotten. Some are intelligent advisors, others leaders by their studies and the wise words of their teachings, still others singers of songs, and writers of verses. All gave comfort and encouragement, faith and hope, each in her or his own way.

Without David Noel Freedman, this work would not have been completed. His generosity and enthusiasm, encouragement and counsel on several levels have surrounded and sustained me. His many timely and detailed communications were more than mere notes on the manuscript, or letters in response to questions. These communications in an uncanny way enabled me to engage in a sort of dialog with him and with the biblical text. His ideas were always stimulating, provocative and creative, sometimes overwhelming in their originality and vision. His sense of humor was always evident and made the going, when difficult, enjoyable nonetheless. No one could hope for a better director.

My other editor, Marianne Nold, read and reread the manuscript and made many helpful comments and corrections. In addition, she helped me to think about the nature of poetry and how the poet works. In many ways she reminded me that all the precedent is on my side, and the peeper's silver croak cannot be checked.

My colleague and friend, David Howard, was always available when I needed advice and support, and was helpful to me as I stumbled through the stages of the project.

The members of the theology department at the College of St. Catherine were instrumental in encouraging me to pursue my goal of completing this work. They were supportive throughout the project. The department chairs, Catherine Litecky and Shawn Madigan, arranged my teaching schedule in such a way as to allow me time to work on the project.

The librarians at the College of St. Catherine tracked down many of the obscure materials that I needed and saved me many hours of research time.

The coordinator of the dissertation committee at the Graduate Theological Union, Duane Christensen, was most gracious in agreeing to help me, and his involvement and assistance are appreciated.

Francis I. Andersen, another member of the committee, spent part of his sabbatical in the States carefully reading the manuscript, and made numerous comments on the manuscript, many of which have been incorporated.

Graduate students at the College of St. Catherine, Lucy Arimond and Susan Dingle, helped with editing and proofreading the manuscript.

Many other friends, with whom I wish to resume a more regular relationship now that every available moment need not be spent on the project, extended their hands in help in a variety of ways, and kept the process humane.

My parents initially provided the atmosphere to make accomplishment of the project possible. My mother led me to believe that I could do anything that I wanted to; my father offered unconditional support.

My family—my husband Mike and son Joshua—lived through the long winter of the project, allowing me the right amount of solitude I needed to concentrate on finishing, but not too much solitude, so that I had to keep one foot in the other world of trombone lessons, band concerts, long weekend vacations, trips to the theater. With them I can now enjoy the summer of its completion.

Abbreviations

References to standard commentaries on Isaiah cite only the author's name, not the page number, when the reference is to the commentator's treatment of the verse under discussion. When the reference from the commentator is to another verse or section, the full reference is given.

Abbreviations of Translations

JB	Jerusalem Bible
JPSV	Jewish Publication Society Version
NAB	The New American Bible
NEB	The New English Bible
RSV	Revised Standard Version

Abbreviations of Grammatical Terms

adv.	adverb	neg.	negative
art.	article	obj.	object
conj.	conjunction	part.	participle
def.	definite article	pass.	passive
f.	feminine	pf.	perfect
impf.	imperfect	pl.	plural
imv.	imperative	prep.	preposition
inf.	infinitive	pron.	pronoun
m.	masculine	s.	singular
n.	noun	syl.	syllable

Abbreviations of Books, Periodicals, and Serials

AB	Anchor Bible
AnBib	Analecta Biblica
ANEP	*The Ancient Near East in Pictures Relating to the Old Testament* (ed. J. B. Pritchard)
BDB	F. Brown, S. R. Driver, and C. A. Briggs, *Hebrew and English Lexicon of the Old Testament*
Bib	*Biblica*
BibOr	Biblica et Orientalia
BHK	Biblia Hebraica, ed. G. Kittel
BHS	Biblia Hebraica Stuttgartensia
BWANT	Beiträge zur Wissenschaft vom Alten und Neuen Testament
BZAW	Beihefte zur Zeitschrift für die Alttestamentliche Wissenschaft
CAD	The Chicago Assyrian Dictionary

CBQ	*Catholic Biblical Quarterly*
CBQMS	Catholic Biblical Quarterly Monograph Series
CHJ	Cambridge History of Judaism
CTA	A. Herdner (ed.), *Corpus des tablettes en cunéiformes alphabétiques découvertes à Ras Shamra–Ougarit*
CTM	Calwer Theologische Monographien
FRLANT	Forschungen zur Religion und Literatur des Alten und Neuen Testaments
FTL	Forschung zur Theologie und Literatur
GKC	E. Kautzsch, *Gesenius' Hebrew Grammar*
HDR	Harvard Dissertations in Religion
HKAT	Handkommentar zum Alten Testament
HTR	*Harvard Theological Review*
HUCA	*Hebrew Union College Annual*
IB	*Interpreter's Bible*
IDB	G. A. Buttrick (ed.), *Interpreter's Dictionary of the Bible*
IDBSup	*Interpreter's Dictionary of the Bible, Supplement*
Int	*Interpretation*
IRT	Issues in Theology and Religion
JAAR	*Journal of the American Academy of Religion*
JANESCU	*Journal of the Ancient Near Eastern Society of Columbia University*
JAOS	*Journal of the American Oriental Society*
JBL	*Journal of Biblical Literature*
JNES	*Journal of Near Eastern Studies*
JQR	*Jewish Quarterly Review*
JSOT	*Journal for the Study of the Old Testament*
JSOTSup	Journal for the Study of the Old Testament Supplement Series
JSS	*Journal of Semitic Studies*
JTS	*Journal of Theological Studies*
KAI	H. Donner and W. Röllig, *Kanaanäische und aramäische Inschriften*
NCBC	New Century Bible Commentary
OBO	Orbis biblicus et orientalis
Or	*Orientalia*
OTL	Old Testament Library
OTM	Old Testament Message
OTS	*Oudtestamentische Studiën*
PTMS	Pittsburgh Theological Monograph Series
RB	*Revue biblique*
SBLMS	Society of Biblical Literature Monograph Series
SBLSP	Society of Biblical Literature Seminar Papers
SBT	Studies in Biblical Theology
ScrHier	Scripta Hierosolymitana
UF	*Ugarit-Forschungen*
UT	C. Gordon, *Ugaritic Textbook*
VT	*Vetus Testamentum*
VTSup	Supplements to Vetus Testamentum
ZAW	*Zeitschrift für die Alttestamentliche Wissenschaft*
ZDPV	*Zeitschrift des deutschen Palästina-Vereins*

Introduction

The poem in Isaiah 47 on the downfall of Babylon has had a unique history in Deutero-Isaiah scholarship. While there are numerous opinions about the nature and length of sections within other chapters of DI, almost all scholars agree that this chapter is a lengthy poem of great literary merit. Most scholars, even those who segment the rest of DI into short form-critical units, agree that it stands as a unit, and further, that it is an "authentic" DI composition. However, critics have not sufficiently followed through on the ramifications of their assessments of this chapter as an "authentic" composition of DI and (at the same time) a unique composition by virtue of its length and coherency. It is not consistent to propose that DI is composed of short, somewhat unrelated form-critical units, while admitting that within the book there is a long, skillfully constructed poem by the same author (DI). Theories about the composition and unity or disunity of DI have not addressed the importance of this chapter to a study of the entire book.

The point of departure of this study is the poem in chapter 47. Since scholars generally recognize it to be a well-wrought poem, it can be studied with the goal of discovering more specifically what devices, techniques, and patterns are used to make it a superb literary piece. It can also be analyzed to see what structuring elements exist to demonstrate that it is a unity rather than a collection of short poems. My thesis is that if there is one such poem in DI, the book can be examined for evidence of other similar compositions. My method is to observe the phenomena of the text as it stands, and then to analyze these phenomena closely. This is preferable to imposing external divisions, such as theoretical form-critical or redactional units, upon the text.

Another aspect of this study of chapter 47 is to ask what its relationship to the surrounding material is and to define its larger literary context. This book includes analyses of the adjacent chapters 46 and 48. Scholars have noticed similarities among the three chapters, especially regarding the theme of the imminent downfall of Babylon and its gods. These two poems are analyzed in the same manner as chapter 47, with the aim of seeing what rhetorical devices are used and what the structure of each poem is. Comparisons are made among the three poems regarding literary construction, pattern and structure, theme and content. After this close reading some general observations are made about the composition of DI, the connection between these chapters and the larger unit of chapters 40–66, and the relationship of their form and structure to other poems in the Hebrew Bible.

Overview of Recent Studies of Isaiah 40–55

Historical Background

As long ago as the twelfth century, Ibn Ezra suggested the possibility that the book of Isaiah was not a unity. Most scholars credit the division of the book into two sections, chaps. 1–39 and chaps. 40–66, to Döderlein (1775) and Eichhorn (1783); Eichhorn also was the first to identify chaps. 40–66 as a product of the exilic period.

In 1892, B. Duhm suggested further divisions for the book.[1] Not only did he propose that chaps. 1–39 were a literary compilation rather than the work of one author, he also made a division between chaps. 40–55 and 56–66. Chaps. 40–55 were dated from around 540 B.C.E., while the servant songs and chaps. 56–66 reflected a later setting, the period after the return to Jerusalem. His methodology was similar to that of the source critics who analyzed the Pentateuch in the late 1800s.

Virtually all scholars today accept Döderlein's and Eichhorn's division in matters of the historical background of the text. Duhm's basic division also finds wide acceptance, though this acceptance is by no means universal.[2] A variety of methods is used to delineate the sections more precisely and account for the delineations. Form critics[3] separate genuine or authentic sections of chaps. 40–55 from material in these same chapters that they

1. B. Duhm, *Das Buch Jesaia* (Handkommentar zum Alten Testament 3/1; 3d ed.; Göttingen: Vandenhoeck & Ruprecht, 1914).

2. See the following, who develop in some detail the idea of the unity of authorship between chaps. 40–55 and 56–66: F. Maass ("Tritojesaja?" *Das ferne und nahe Wort: Festschrift L. Rost* [BZAW 105; Berlin: de Gruyter, 1967] 156–63); A. Murtonen ("Third Isaiah: Yes or No?" *Abr-Nahrain* 19 [1980–81] 20–42, cited by G. Polan, *In the Ways of Justice toward Salvation: A Rhetorical Analysis of Isaiah 56–59* [New York: Peter Lang, 1986] 11); N. Rabban (*Second Isaiah: His Prophecy, His Personality and His Name* [Jerusalem: Kiryat-Sepher, 1971] Heb.).

3. Pioneers in form-critical studies of DI include H. Gressmann ("Die literarische Analyse Deuterojesajas," *ZAW* 34 [1914] 254–97); Ludwig Köhler (*Deuterojesaja stilkritisch untersucht* [BZAW 37; Giessen: Alfred Töpelmann, 1923]); J. Begrich (*Studiën zu Deuterojesaja* [BZAW 77; Berlin: de Gruyter, 1938; repr. Munich: Chr. Kaiser,

attribute to a later hand, usually the author(s) or compiler(s) of chaps. 56–66. Recent redactional studies attempt to show that there are large-scale expansions of original oracles within chaps. 40–55, which come from a later time.[4] They usually attribute a significant number of these expansions to a school or group rather than to an individual prophet.

Most of these studies involve questions about authorship and attempts to identify different figures and historical periods. Some speak of Deutero-Isaiah and Trito-Isaiah as separate authors in their own right. Some characterize the relationship as one of author and compiler, or prophet and followers. Still others do not even speak of individuals, but of schools, disciples, or worshiping communities that were responsible for the composition, editing, and reediting of the work. In general, Deutero-Isaiah is associated with chaps. 40–55 and dated ca. 540 B.C.E. in Babylon; Trito-Isaiah (chaps. 56–66) is connected with the postexilic community in Jerusalem.

The evidence from historical data by which scholars make divisions between 40–55 and 56–66 is more varied (and more hypothetical) than the criteria scholars use in dividing Isaiah between chaps. 1–39 and 40–66. In chaps. 1–39 specific individuals from the eighth century are mentioned by name (e.g., Ahaz, Hezekiah), as are events of that period (e.g., the Syro-Ephraimite war).[5] The same holds true for chaps. 40–66, though to a lesser

---

1963]). For an excellent summary of the history of form-critical scholarship of DI, see Antoon Schoors, *I Am God Your Saviour: A Form-Critical Study of the Main Genres in Is. XL-LV* (VTSup 24; Leiden: Brill, 1973) 1–31. Cf. Yehoshua Gitay, *Prophecy and Persuasion: A Study of Isaiah 40–48* (FTL 14; Bonn: Linguistica Biblica, 1981) 3–24.

4. Rosario Pius Merendino, *Der Erste und der Letzte* (VTSup 31; Leiden: Brill, 1981); J. M. Vincent, *Studien zur literarischen Eigenart und zur geistigen Heimat von Jesaja, Kap 40–55* (Beiträge zur biblischen Exegese und Theologie 5; Frankfurt: Peter Lang, 1977); Klaus Kiesow, *Exodustexte im Jesajabuch: Literarkritische und motivgeschichtliche Analysen* (OBO 24; Fribourg: Editions Universitaires / Göttingen: Vandenhoeck & Ruprecht, 1979); J. H. Eaton, *Festal Drama in Deutero Isaiah* (London: SPCK, 1979); J. Vermeylen, *Du prophète Isaïe a l'apocalyptique: Isaïe I–XXXV, miroir d'un demi-millénaire d'expérience religieuse en Israël* (2 vols.; Paris: Gabalda, 1977–78).

5. J. H. Hayes and Stuart A. Irvine in *Isaiah the Eighth Century Prophet: His Times and His Preaching* (Nashville: Abingdon, 1987) have proposed that all of chaps. 1–33 are from the prophet of the eighth century. They do not question the thesis proposed by Duhm in 1892 that chaps. 34–35 are not part of First Isaiah. Most scholars agree that these chapters are from a later period, and many suggest that they are part of Second Isaiah. For a different view, see Joseph Jensen's recent commentary, *Isaiah 1–39* (OTM 8; Wilmington, Del.: Michael Glazier, 1984) 14, where he refers to Isaiah 1–39 as a "collection of collections" and distinguishes among at least six different sections, two of which (chaps. 24–27 and 34–35) are "wholly from later times."

degree (Cyrus the Persian is the historical figure mentioned in the context of liberation from the Babylonian exile).

No such specific events or figures are mentioned in chaps. 56–66 to clearly demonstrate a postexilic milieu.[6] However, references to temple and sabbath, the concern with liturgical matters, and the critical attitude the text takes toward certain elements in the community have led some to posit a postexilic Jerusalem–Judah source.[7] In order to develop this theory, a historical milieu is reconstructed by scholars. Once that historical context or framework is outlined, then chapters or sections of DI are placed within that framework. These reconstructions are highly speculative due to the paucity of information available on postexilic Judah.[8] Theories proposing a Jerusalem postexilic provenance are within the realm of possibility; indeed, they are attractive theories. However, since no specific events or historical figures are mentioned, it should be remembered that these are only possibilities that remain to be proven.

Another proposal further complicates the matter by attributing large portions of Isaiah 40–55 to the author of chaps. 56–66. Elliger's work has been influential on this point.[9] On the one hand, there are claims that the differences between the two sections are so marked that it is reasonable to propose a different author and time period for each. However, when similarities are noted, then the questionable sections of chaps. 40–55 are attributed to the author of chaps. 56–66. In the opposite direction, the similarities (especially the lyrical announcements of unconditional salvation) between chaps. 60–62 and 40–55 have been noted by many. Paul

6. For instance, one might expect a reference to Darius or to the construction or dedication of the temple.

7. See Paul Hanson, *The Dawn of Apocalyptic: The Historical and Sociological Roots of Jewish Apocalyptic Eschatology* (rev. ed.; Philadelphia: Fortress, 1979) 59ff. See also E. Achtemeier, who treats the matter on a more popular level in *The Community and Message of Isaiah 56–66* (Minneapolis: Augsburg, 1982) 80–81.

8. Elias Bickerman, "The Babylonian captivity," in *Introduction: The Persian Period* (CHJ 1; ed. W. D. Davies and Louis Finkelstein; Cambridge: Cambridge University Press, 1984) 342–57; Peter R. Ackroyd, *Exile and Restoration* (OTL; Philadelphia: Westminster, 1968); idem, "The History of Israel in the Exilic and Postexilic Periods," in *Tradition and Interpretation* (ed. G. W. Anderson; Oxford: Clarendon, 1979) 320–38; Bustenay Oded, "Judah and the Exile," in *Israelite and Judean History* (ed. John H. Hayes and J. Maxwell Miller; London: SCM, 1977) 435–88; E. Janssen, *Juda in der Exilszeit: Ein Beitrag zur Frage der Entstehung des Judentums* (FRLANT 69; Göttingen: Vandenhoeck & Ruprecht, 1956); J. Maxwell Miller and John H. Hayes, *A History of Ancient Israel and Judah* (Philadelphia: Westminster, 1986); John Bright, *A History of Israel* (3d ed.; Philadelphia: Westminster, 1981).

9. K. Elliger, *Deuterojesaja in seinem Verhältnis zu Tritojesaja* (BWANT 63; Stuttgart: Kohlhammer, 1933).

Hanson, for example, sees similarities in meter and internal structure, as well as theme, though he maintains that there is a difference in historical and geographic perspective.[10] It is necessary to comment on the relationship between chaps. 40–55 and 56–66 because of the way most recent scholars explain tensions within the text. The general tendency is to propose a variety of times, places, authors, and editors to account for conflicting ideas or differences within the entire section, chaps. 40–66. Thus, numerous passages in chaps. 40–55 (for instance, the servant songs and the polemics against idols) are attributed to another hand. I do not make such an assumption, but rather begin with the text in its present form and look for other explanations for tensions and difficulties in the text. It is important to examine these so-called difficult passages to see how they function in their present literary context.

Recent Form-Critical Studies

Among recent studies of Isaiah 40–55, the form-critical approach prevails. There is still a tendency to interpret the work as a collection of short, discrete, and relatively unrelated units.[11] Gunkel's assumptions about prophetic oracles being short, highly stylized poems continue to influence scholars to this day.[12] Schoors's recent study is a good example of this assessment of DI.[13] Other major works include those by C. Westermann, R. Melugin, and R. N. Whybray.[14] They see the material to be substantially the work of one author, but like Elliger are concerned with questions of "authenticity" and "genuineness" and attribute a sizable portion of material to the authors of chaps. 56–66.

10. Hanson, *The Dawn of Apocalyptic*, 56–73.

11. This tendency is not only evident in scholarly publications, but also persists in textbooks meant for introducing undergraduate students to the Old Testament, e.g., Lawrence Boadt, *Reading the Old Testament: An Introduction* (New York: Paulist, 1984) 419–22; and Philip Harner, *An Inductive Approach to Biblical Study* (Lanham, Md.: University Press of America, 1982) 47–51.

12. Gunkel's article, "Die Propheten als Schriftsteller und Dichter" (*Die Propheten* [Göttingen: Vandenhoeck & Ruprecht, 1923] 34–70) was reprinted in *Prophecy in Israel: Search for an Identity* (ed. David L. Petersen; IRT 10; Philadelphia: Fortress, 1987) 22–73.

13. Schoors, *I Am God Your Saviour.*

14. Claus Westermann, *Isaiah 40–66: A Commentary* (trans. D. M. G. Stalker; OTL; Philadelphia: Westminster, 1969) and *Sprache und Struktur der Prophetie Deuterojesajas* (CTM 11; Stuttgart: Calwer, 1981); R. F. Melugin, *The Formation of Isaiah 40–55* (BZAW 141; Berlin: de Gruyter, 1976); R. N. Whybray, *Isaiah 40–66* (NCBC; London: Marshall, Morgan & Scott / Grand Rapids: Eerdmans, 1981).

One of the main criteria used in the process of determining genuine or authentic passages is whether or not the verse or verses are harsh in tone or take a negative attitude toward the community. DI's message is interpreted as one that offers hope to a downtrodden community. Any verse or passage that has a tone critical of this downtrodden community is considered inappropriate and is seen to fit better into the historical setting reconstructed for Trito-Isaiah. For instance, the charge "stubborn and obstinate" leveled at the house of Jacob in 48:4 is excised from the text because it is not consonant with the proclamation of salvation and giving of encouragement to the exiles. The anti-idolatry sections, of which 44:9–20 is the most outstanding example,[15] are often eliminated from DI's authentic oracles,[16] again because of the negativity of the polemic as well as what some consider inferior literary style and unenlightened theology.

I do not interpret tensions, difficulties, and peculiarities in the text by assigning them to "another hand." There are other ways to interpret such difficulties. The relegation of harsh passages to a less enlightened postexilic figure turns DI into a superficial Pollyanna with a flat, one-dimensional view of the world.

Recent Literary Criticism of Deutero-Isaiah

There are some scholars—a minority—who have not been convinced by the form critics' divisions of chaps. 40–55. They have tried to demonstrate that the book is a unified construction and have applied different methods to the text. As early as 1928, Torrey referred to his ideas on Isaiah 40–66 as "a new view of the prophecy."[17] It was his opinion that these chapters, as

15. This chapter was arranged as prose in BHK and most translations followed suit, but the BHS edition has it arranged as poetry. The prose particle count of Francis I. Andersen and A. Dean Forbes (" 'Prose Particle' Counts of the Hebrew Bible," in *The Word of the Lord Shall Go Forth: Essays in Honor of David Noel Freedman in Celebration of His Sixtieth Birthday* [ed. Carol L. Meyers and M. O'Connor; Winona Lake, Ind.: Eisenbrauns, 1983] 174) shows it to have the lowest percentage of prose particles in all of DI (1.542%). This supports the text arrangement of the recent BHS edition and should invite more detailed investigation of the poetic structure of these verses.

16. H. C. Spykerboer, *The Structure and Composition of Deutero-Isaiah with Special Reference to the Polemic against Idolatry* (Frankener, Netherlands: Rijksuniversitet te Groninger, 1976) demonstrates that the passages against idolatry were authentic and an integral part of the work and that the book was a coherent whole. See also Richard Clifford, "The Function of the Idol Passages in Second Isaiah" (*CBQ* 42 [1980] 450–64).

17. C. C. Torrey, *The Second Isaiah: A New Interpretation* (Edinburgh: T. & T. Clark, 1928) 53.

well as chaps. 34–35, "formed a homogeneous group and were the work of a single hand."[18] His "new view" was that there were twenty-seven poems, composed and written down in the present order in Palestine near the end of the fifth century.[19] One of the strengths of his study is that it is sensitive to the literary features of each chapter on the level of the word and line, as well as on a larger scale. James Muilenburg[20] is considered the champion of the idea that DI wrote extended poems of high literary quality and that the book is a unified composition. He wrote his commentary well before the publication of his 1968 presidential address to the Society of Biblical Literature,[21] and the commentary is an excellent example of his rhetorical criticism in its early development. Since its publication, succeeding scholars have taken into account his analyses of the poems in their own studies. Many criticize his commentary for not devoting enough attention to form-critical methodology, even though Muilenburg defended and used findings of form critics when appropriate. Even Richard Clifford, whose recent commentary was very much influenced by Muilenburg's approach, claimed that Muilenburg ignored the findings of form critics and tended to "divorce the text from its context,"[22] though he admitted parenthetically that this tendency was only evident in the commentary proper, not in the introduction.[23]

Clifford, like Muilenburg, concluded that DI is composed of lengthy, complex speeches.[24] The two scholars differ from one another in that Muilenburg considered DI to be a prophet-poet, while Clifford sees DI as

18. Ibid.

19. In order to defend his thesis that DI is not a prophet of the return, he considers all references to Cyrus and Babylon to be interpolations. See his chapters 2 and 3, pp. 20–52. The positive aspects of his work have been overlooked by many, perhaps due to this idiosyncratic theory.

20. James Muilenburg, "The Book of Isaiah: Chapters 40–66," *IB* (ed. George A. Buttrick et al.; 12 vols.; New York: Abingdon, 1956) 5: 381–773.

21. James Muilenburg, "Form Criticism and Beyond," *JBL* 88 (1969) 1–18.

22. Richard J. Clifford, *Fair Spoken and Persuading: An Interpretation of Second Isaiah* (New York: Paulist, 1984) 35.

23. However, in his article "The Function of Idol Passages in Second Isaiah" (*CBQ* 42 [1980] 453), Clifford himself in practice shows these same tendencies. He is critical of the "controverted" discussions by form critics of the origin of the trial scene in DI. He says, "In my judgment, the prior question should be the rhetorical function of the trial in the particular passage. Investigation of the history of a form or motif remains, of course, highly important." Clifford admits the existence of findings and that they are important; however, the findings are not incorporated into his rhetorical analysis.

24. Clifford, *Fair Spoken,* 4–5.

an orator in the prophetic tradition.[25] In fact, in Clifford's judgment, an orator must weave speeches of sustained length in order to convince and persuade his audience to be moved to some specific action.[26] Conversely, he associates lyric poetry with short fragmented pieces that lift the spirit.[27]

The strengths of Clifford's approach are that, while he sees DI as one who stands in the prophetic tradition, he realizes that DI represents a departure from the tradition of preexilic prophecy.[28] Clifford sees the highly creative and original uses of forms in DI's work. He realizes that a single method for determining the boundaries of the compositions is not sufficient[29] and uses several criteria when making decisions about strophic divisions. He highlights strophic patterning in his analysis, since the aim of his book is to "stress the coherence of the thought."[30] Clifford's analysis has been important to my study of chaps. 46–48, though I do not agree with his statement that rhetorical criticism has "tendencies to mere aestheticism,"[31] nor with his theory that DI was an orator rather than a prophet. I am especially critical of his equation of lyric poetry with short units and oratory with long units.

Another scholar who views the book from the perspective of the features that unite it is Rémi Lack.[32] His approach to the text is informed by

25. Another study of oratory in DI was done by Y. Gitay in *Prophecy and Persuasion.* Gitay, like Clifford, views DI as an orator and emphasizes the aspect of persuasion and audience reaction in his study. He refers to his work as "a new literary approach" and discusses rhetorical approaches to the text. His methodology, however, is not to be confused with what Muilenburg refers to as rhetorical criticism. He judges DI's work by the rules of classical rhetoric.

26. Clifford, *Fair Spoken,* 5 and 36. At the same time, on p. 5 he admits that these speeches are "allusive and elliptical; their rhetoric and logic need elucidation." This sounds a good deal more like poetry than public oratory.

27. Ibid., 4. Clifford disagrees with those who fragment the chapters into short pieces because, he says, these short pieces do not allow for "genuine development of ideas. The pieces lift the spirit and expand the imagination through images and lyricism, not through argument. The view that Isaiah 40–55 is made up of brief and fragmentary pieces has the inevitable corollary that the author is a lyric poet rather than a national orator."

28. Ibid., 27. Opposing this is R. N. Whybray in *The Second Isaiah* (Old Testament Guides; Sheffield: JSOT Press, 1983) 21. His position on the relationship of the literature of DI to that of preexilic prophecy is that DI inherited a "long tradition of oral utterance" and that it has not been proven that DI broke away from that tradition.

29. Clifford, *Fair Spoken,* 39.

30. He specifically states that he does not consider the many other rhetorical techniques because they are not relevant to the aim of his work (Clifford, *Fair Spoken,* 40–41).

31. Ibid., 35; see also pp. 36–37.

32. Rémi Lack, *La Symbolique du livre d'Isaïe: Essai sur l'image littéraire comme élément de structuration* (AnBib 59; Rome: Pontifical Biblical Institute, 1973).

the methodology of French structuralism,[33] which analyzes the deep structure of the text, its interest being in the science of language and the way language functions.[34] He combines two disciplines, which he refers to as human science[35] and literary science[36] in his study. He demonstrates that the symbolism and imagery used throughout the book of Isaiah gives it an underlying unity transcending the conscious intentions of the editors or authors.

This does not mean, however, that he is not interested in the literary structure of individual sections. His analysis of individual poems enables him to demonstrate his thesis about the unity of the entire book. The poetry of chaps. 40–55, because of the repeated use of key words and the progressive development of imagery and vocabulary, is especially amenable to his methodology. Like Muilenburg, he reads a particular poem to discover what is unique to its structure, rather than reading it to discover features typical of a proposed literary genre.[37] Such analysis enables the critic to uncover the esthetic features of the text, what Germans call *das Kunstwollen.* This, according to Lack, is one of the goals of his analysis.[38]

After examining the individual poems in DI for key words and themes, Lack then compares the themes and vocabulary with the rest of DI. He describes the characteristic pattern of the first half of DI[39] as "développement par enveloppement":[40] each unit builds up a series or class of words, which is in turn intertwined with a new class or series of words in the following section. While this study investigates the surface structure of DI, not the

33. Ibid., 7. The work of the critic is not to explain the intent of the author or to interpret the work in terms of its milieu, but to show, in the manner of F. de Saussure, how the text exists as a connected system, an organized entity.

34. This analysis of structure is different from the structural analysis of rhetorical or literary criticism, which is discussed in this volume. Structuralism typical of the French school seeks to find underlying patterns of expression common to all human thought. My analysis, along the lines of rhetorical criticism, investigates structure on the surface level, not on the level of the deep structure.

35. He bases his work in this area on the theories of G. Durand, *Les structures anthropologiques de l'imaginaire: Introduction a l'archetypologie générale* (3d ed.; Paris: Presses universitaires de France, 1970).

36. Here he follows R. Ingarden, *Das literarische Kunstwerk* (2d ed.; Tübingen: Max Niemeyer, 1960) and R. Wellek and A. Warren, *Theorie der Literatur* (Berlin: Athenäum, 1966).

37. Lack, *Symbolique,* 104: " . . . *la* forme plus que *les* formes; l'oevre singulière—le poème—plus que les genres littéraires."

38. Ibid.

39. Based on his thesis of developing vocabulary, he divides chaps. 40–55 into chaps. 40:1–49:13 and 49:14–55:13. See *Symbolique,* 81–82.

40. Ibid., 81.

deep structure as Lack's work does, his conclusions on the use and development of certain themes and words, as well as his views on the structure and relationship of larger units within sections of DI, are incorporated where appropriate.

Methodology

This investigation builds on the work of Muilenburg and Clifford in that it analyzes the text from the perspective of rhetorical (literary) criticism. The goal of Clifford's rhetorical study was to demonstrate the coherence of thought in DI by showing the relationship of larger sections to one another; he therefore did not choose to do a close reading of the text. My study is limited to three chapters but goes beyond the work of Clifford (and Muilenburg) in that the chapters are examined in much greater detail on the level of word and line, as well as in larger units.

Literary /Rhetorical Criticism

Gunkel's comments about the form of the text and the way it affects content are important to biblical scholarship and they highlight one aspect of my study. In his work on the legends of Genesis, he discussed what he called the "artistic form" of the legends and the importance of incorporating it into a legitimate study of the text. He noted the hesitancy of scholars to express appreciation for the beauty of the Genesis narratives and suggested that this hesitation may have been due to the fact that "the aesthetic point of view seemed to them incompatible with the dignity of science."[41]

Almost seventy years later, Muilenburg alluded to a similar hesitancy on the part of scholars. In his address to the Society of Biblical Literature in 1968, Muilenburg discussed his approach to the text, which he termed "rhetorical criticism." He warned against a "too exclusive employment of form critical methods," especially in cases where there is an imitation of literary genres. When forms are imitated, not only by the prophets but also by historians and lawgivers, they undergo transformation. "In numerous contexts old literary types and forms are imitated, and, precisely because they are imitated, they are employed with considerable fluidity, versatility, and, *if one may venture the term, artistry*" (italics mine).[42] This can be read either as an apologetic remark or as an understatement, but in any case,

41. H. Gunkel, *The Legends of Genesis: The Biblical Saga and History* (trans. W. H. Carruth; New York: Schocken Books, 1901) 37.

42. Muilenburg, "Form Criticism and Beyond," 7.

both Gunkel in 1901 and Muilenburg in 1968 indicated that to venture into the area of artistry and esthetics is a touchy business.[43]

One of Muilenburg's strengths is that he stresses the importance of literary criticism,[44] or stylistics, while at the same time he is conversant with more traditional methods of biblical criticism.[45] He does not seek to undermine previous scholarship; rather, he opens up additional perspectives on the biblical text. Not all literary critics have the scope necessary to do justice to the peculiarities, vagaries, and unique features of the biblical text. Some scholars new to the field of literary criticism of the Bible have made extravagant claims in recent years about their contributions to the field and have reproached biblical scholars for ignoring the literary dimensions of the text. There are some rather heavy-handed treatments by these literary critics who dismiss biblical scholarship without adequate investigation of the field.[46] While some of the criticisms may be justified, to dismiss biblical scholars all at once betrays a lack of scope and an ignorance of the field, which does the critics no credit.

That many Bible scholars have ignored the literary dimensions of the Bible is granted. That biblical scholarship has ignored the question is

43. One of the strengths of Francis I. Andersen and David Noel Freedman's *Hosea: A New Translation with Introduction and Commentary* (AB 24; Garden City: Doubleday, 1980) is that, in addition to all their other observations, they clearly see evidence of artistry in the text. Their close work on the book of Hosea has uncovered a level of "artistry far more sophisticated than anything previously suspected" (p. 70). They do not eliminate esthetic considerations from their investigations. Therefore they are more likely to see them if they exist than are those who are suspicious of such considerations. M. O'Connor (*Hebrew Verse Structure* [Winona Lake, Ind.: Eisenbrauns, 1980] 20) moves in the opposite direction by refusing to consider esthetic functions in reading poetry. See S. Geller's critique of O'Connor in "Theory and Method in the Study of Biblical Poetry" (*JQR* 73 [1982] 65–77).

44. By this is meant the so-called "new literary criticism" of the Bible, not source criticism. I am in agreement here with W. Wuellner ("Where is Rhetorical Criticism Taking Us?" *CBQ* 49 [1987] 451–52) that rhetorical criticism and literary criticism have become indistinguishable, although I disagree with his characterization of theorists of this approach as "victims of the fateful reduction of rhetorics to stylistics." See his article for his definition of the term "rhetorical criticism," which goes beyond that of Muilenburg to include how communications transform and are transformed by the audience.

45. A collection of some of Muilenburg's articles has been gathered together in *Hearing and Speaking the Word: Selections from the Works of James Muilenburg* (ed. T. F. Best; Chico, Cal.: Scholars Press, 1984).

46. Meir Sternberg (*The Poetics of Biblical Narrative: Ideological Literature and the Drama of Reading* [Bloomington: Indiana University Press, 1985]) is known for his curt dismissals of biblical scholars and his opinion about the incompetence of these scholars in the area of literary criticism.

patently false. Muilenburg refers to the work of Lowth and Herder in the 1700s, to the metrical studies of Sievers in the early 1900s, and to the writings of Ewald, Budde, Duhm, and Cassuto as examples of the ongoing interest of biblical scholars in matters of style. Alonso Schökel[47] is cited by Muilenburg as the foremost representative of the field of stylistics, or esthetic criticism, in recent years because of his detailed discussion of stylistic phenomena in the Old Testament and his ample bibliography attesting to work in this area. Most of the recent scholarship that Muilenburg cites is in the field of Hebrew poetry rather than prose. His list includes the following scholars, all of whom have had a lively interest in literary criticism of the biblical text: W. F. Albright, F. M. Cross, D. N. Freedman, G. Gerleman, L. Krinetski, E. Good, R. A. Carlson, and W. Holladay.[48]

Almost twenty-five years after Muilenberg's survey, that list can be greatly expanded to include other scholars,[49] as well as the more recent work of those already mentioned. These scholars have varied interests in biblical poetry—meter, strophic and stanzaic divisions, gross structure of Hebrew verse, parallelism in its myriad manifestations, linguistic questions, questions dealing with structure from the level of the line to the overall structure of the entire poem, the relationship of form to content, the function of key words and themes, other literary devices, and the poetry/prose question. The proliferation of sections dealing with literary criticism of the Bible at regional and national meetings of the Society of Biblical Literature is another example of scholarly interest in this area.

Methodology

The method used in this book is best described as literary or rhetorical criticism,[50] so named by Muilenburg in his presidential address in

47. Alonso Schökel, *Estudios de poética hebrea* (Barcelona: Juan Flors, 1963).

48. Muilenberg, "Form Criticism and Beyond," 8.

49. For example, a nonexhaustive list includes the following: Andersen, Auffret, Barre, Berlin, Boadt, Ceresko, Christensen, Collins, Dahood, Damrosch, Exum, Fishbane, Fitzgerald, Gunn, Kessler, Kikawada, Kselman, Lundbom, O'Connor, Sasson, Trible, Watson. See the recent volume edited by R. Alter and F. Kermode, *The Literary Guide to the Bible* (Cambridge: Harvard University Press, 1987), which treats each book of the Bible from the perspective of its literary characteristics.

50. See the following for the development of the method of "rhetorical criticism," as outlined by Muilenburg: B. W. Anderson, "The New Frontier of Rhetorical Criticism: A Tribute to James Muilenburg" (*Rhetorical Criticism: Essays in Honor of James Muilenburg* [PTMS 1; ed. J. J. Jackson and M. Kessler; Pittsburgh: Pickwick, 1974] ix–xvii); R. Clifford, "Rhetorical Criticism in the Exegesis of Hebrew Poetry" (SBLSP; ed. P. Achtemeier [Chico, Cal.: Scholars Press, 1980] 17–28); D. Greenwood, "Rhetorical

1968.[51] The creative literature of Isaiah 40–66, in particular chaps. 46–48, can be examined from the perspective of rhetorical or literary criticism, with far more fruitful results than those from form-critical studies. Rhetorical criticism emphasizes the unique and the atypical in a text and is helpful in assessing material that bears evidence of a highly creative and original hand, a hand that transformed motifs, theologies, and genres. The process of rhetorical analysis is an inductive one.[52] Since the rhetorical critic pays attention to what is atypical, original, or unique, the critic cannot decide beforehand what to look for but must proceed on the basis of peculiarities in the text. Muilenburg's emphasis in his 1968 lecture was on determining the large units, that is, defining the limits of the pericope and the structure of the composition, discerning the "configuration of its component parts," and determining bicola and tricola, and clusters of bicola and tricola (stanzas or strophes).

In their commentary on Hosea, Andersen and Freedman take this investigation of literary structure further.[53] They discuss the structure of large units within the book but are also interested in operations on the level of word and line. They closely examine the language of the prophet in order to come to a better understanding of his meaning. They are interested in what they term "the peculiarities of the text," as well as in the possibilities of errors in the text. At times scholars respond to peculiarities by too quickly identifying them as errors, thereby missing the uniqueness of the message that the peculiarities may express. By examining the text on many levels (word, line, strophe) and from many perspectives (linguistic, thematic, prophetic), Andersen and Freedman have discovered numerous structural and rhetorical devices that point to a high level of unity, as well as evidence of sophisticated artistry on the part of the poet.

This study of the text of chaps. 46–48 takes into account the unity of the larger sections and divisions as well as the distinctive features on the level of word and line. Each chapter is analyzed as follows:

Criticism and *Formgeschichte*: Some Methodological Considerations" (*JBL* 89 [1970] 418–26); M. Kessler, "A Methodological Setting for Rhetorical Criticism" (*Semitics* 4 [1974] 22–36); idem, "An Introduction to Rhetorical Criticism of the Bible: Prolegomena" (*Semitics* 7 [1980] 1–27); I. Kikawada, "Some Proposals for the Definition of Rhetorical Criticism" (*Semitics* 5 [1977] 67–91).

51. Muilenburg, "Form Criticism and Beyond."

52. See W. L. Holladay, *The Architecture of Jeremiah 1–20* (Lewisburg, Pa.: Bucknell University Press, 1976) 20–21.

53. Andersen and Freedman, *Hosea*, 60–61.

1. *Text*: The transliteration of the text, indicating line and section (or strophic) divisions, and a schematic outline of syllable and stress count.
2. *Translation*: My translation of the chapter under study.
3. *Notes*: An analysis of the unusual features of the chapter on the level of the word and line. Peculiarities of grammar, style, vocabulary,[54] usage, syllable, stress, and count are discussed. The Masoretic Text is compared with 1QIsa[a] and other ancient manuscripts. Determining the limits of the line[55] is an important task in literary criticism. This is not always an easy task, as the works of M. O'Connor[56] and T. Collins[57] attest. Other questions also asked in the notes are: What kinds of devices does the author use on the level of the line? Is the poem constructed with line-pairs or line-trios (bicola or tricola)? How are these line-pairs or line-trios related? What kind of parallelism is used, and when is it used?[58]

54. A rhetorical analysis of Isaiah 56–59 was done by Gregory Polan, in which he demonstrated the stylistic devices used to structure the individual poems and the larger collection of poems. While he discussed in some detail the repetition of various key words, patterns of vocabulary, and chiasms achieved by arrangements of certain root words, he did not devote adequate attention to vocabulary. As a result he did not see other devices that were used in the poems and missed nuances in meaning that could perhaps have added to his thesis of the unity of the chapters (in *The Ways of Justice toward Salvation: A Rhetorical Analysis of Isaiah 56–59* [New York: Peter Lang, 1986]). In this volume, vocabulary is treated in some depth in order not to miss subtleties of expression.

55. This study uses the term "line" in the sense that it is used by O'Connor (*Hebrew Verse Structure*). This is equivalent to what is often called the "colon." There is no agreed-upon terminology in this area; other designations for the same unit include stichos or stich, verset, versicle, half-verse, or half-line. Instead of bicolon or tricolon, I prefer the terms line-pair and line-trio. See Watson, *Classical Hebrew Poetry: A Guide to Its Techniques* (JSOTSup 26; Sheffield: JSOT Press, 1984) 11–15, and Polan, *Ways of Justice*, 11 n. 30, on terminology.

56. O'Connor, *Hebrew Verse Structure.*

57. T. Collins, *Line-Forms in Hebrew Poetry: A Grammatical Approach to the Stylistic Study of the Hebrew Prophets* (Studia Pohl Series Maior 7; Rome: Pontifical Biblical Institute, 1978).

58. There are a variety of ways to describe parallelism and to explain how it works. A. Berlin, in *The Dynamics of Biblical Parallelism* (Bloomington: Indiana University Press, 1985), discusses it as a linguistic phenomenon. Literary critics J. Kugel (*The Idea of Biblical Poetry: Parallelism and Its History* [New Haven: Yale University Press, 1981]) and R. Alter (*The Art of Biblical Poetry* [New York: Basic Books, 1985]) point out some interesting features and examples of parallelism; however, in their generalizations about parallelism and how it functions, they fail to acknowledge the more complicated and intricate intralinear and interlinear relationships that exist.

4. *Microstructure*: A discussion of the main sections[59] (also called strophes or stanzas) of each poem. Once features on the level of the word and line are noted, larger structuring elements can be analyzed. Patterns can be observed in a variety of repetitions: repetitions of key words or themes; repetitions of grammatical, semantic, lexical or phonological patterns. Shifts or breaks in the writer's thought are also indications of breaks or divisions within the poem. It is important here to note that sometimes shifts in thought, or breaks, are obvious—for example, change of speaker or audience, change of theme, presence of a refrain, and so forth. Sometimes, the shifts are more subtle, and if close attention has been paid to the grammar and vocabulary of the line, it will be easier for the critic to notice subtle shifts. The determination of the unity of the larger sections (strophes or stanzas) can also be aided by examining division markers in the MT, 1QIsa[a], and to a lesser extent, the LXX.
5. *Macrostructure*: A discussion of the features that unify the whole poem. Again, key words and themes are important to macro-structure analysis, as well as larger patterns of repetition, such as the refrain, *inclusio*, or chiasm. Patterns of syllable and stress count are also noted.

Syllable and Stress Counting

The study of the three poems in Isaiah 46–48 includes assessing them in terms of their syllable and stress count. The method of syllable counting as a way to describe Biblical Hebrew poetry has been developed by David Noel Freedman[60] and has been adopted by others in their literary studies of individual poems in the Bible with beneficial results.[61] That same methodology is followed in this work.

59. See J. Kselman, "Psalm 3: A Structural and Literary Study" (*CBQ* 49 [1987] 573) on the use of the more neutral term *section.*

60. The practice of syllable counting has been described by Freedman in several articles, the most recent of which is "Acrostic Poems in the Hebrew Bible: Alphabetic and Otherwise" (*CBQ* 48 [1986] 408–31). Several of his articles are collected in *Pottery, Poetry, and Prophecy: Studies in Early Hebrew Poetry* (Winona Lake, Ind.: Eisenbrauns, 1980). In that volume, see especially "Acrostics and Metrics in Hebrew Poetry" (pp. 52–53); "Strophe and Meter in Exodus 15" (pp. 191–93); "Psalm 113 and the Song of Hannah" (p. 245); "The Refrain in David's Lament over Saul and Jonathan" (pp. 265–67); "The Structure of Psalm 137" (pp. 304–6). See also D. N. Freedman and C. Franke-Hyland, "Psalm 29: A Structural Analysis" (*HTR* 66 [1973] 239).

61. E.g., A. Ceresko, "The Function of Chiasmus in Hebrew Poetry," *CBQ* 40 (1978) 1–10; idem, "A Poetic Analysis of Ps 105, with Attention to Its Use of Irony,"

The Masoretic Text is used as the foundation. However, there are some changes from the system of the Masoretes, since it is recognized that their vocalization does not always reflect forms and pronunciations of the biblical period. Vocalization is changed wherever there were divergencies in the MT from classical Biblical Hebrew. Segolates are therefore read as single syllables. Secondary vowels, such as *ḥateps* associated with laryngeals, are not counted, including *pataḥ* furtive. This does not include the vocal *šewa*, which is counted. Resolved diphthongs of certain nouns, such as *mym*, are counted as one syllable. As a rule, the syllable count, using the above guide, is usually lower than the syllable count in the MT.

The reason for diverging from the MT is that the goal is to "recover and reproduce so far as is possible both the poetry and the meter of classical times."[62] Since it is impossible to represent perfectly the pronunciation of classical Hebrew poetry, it is admitted at the outset that these counts are only approximate and do not reflect precisely the pronunciation of the poems being studied. Consistency throughout in counting of syllables is important in order to gain an overall picture of the poem or poems under study. An advantage of syllable counting over stress counting is that it has more precision. Unlike some metrical systems, syllable counting has in its favor an objectivity that comes from describing observable phenomena. Whether or not poets themselves counted syllables is not the issue; what is important is that Hebrew poetry is quantitative, though not in the fashion of some rigid metrical systems. Syllable counting can be of assistance in an overall analysis of a poem and can be used in conjunction with other observations to come to a better knowledge about the structure of Hebrew poetry.

Stress counting is also used in this study as another way to describe poetic structure. In itself, stress counting reveals little about a given poem, but as with syllable counting, it can be helpful in understanding the structure of a given poem. Consistency in stress counting is important in order to avoid the excesses of previous scholars in this area. L. Köhler, for instance, in his stress counts of DI, began with certain preconceived notions about the meter of a given poem and proceeded to make wholesale emendations of the text to achieve the desired pattern.[63] He also was inconsistent in counting problematic shorter words, such as particles, negatives, and independent pronouns. Nor did he always count words joined by *maqqep* in the same

---

Bib 64 (1983) 20–46; L. Boadt, "Isaiah 41:8–13: Notes on Poetic Structure and Style," *CBQ* 35 (1973) 25; M. D. Coogan, "A Structural and Literary Analysis of the Song of Deborah," *CBQ* 40 (1978) 143–66.

62. Freedman, "Acrostic Poems," 411.

63. Köhler, *Deuterojesaja.*

fashion. When it suited the artificial pattern, he included or omitted them in his count. However, when there is no consistency in counting, the results yield little information about the text as it exists. This type of counting reveals only what the commentator had in mind before he began.

The goal in stress counting is to maintain a consistency in counting to see what it can reveal about the biblical text. The following is the procedure used in counting stresses in this book. Content words of one or more syllables, as well as any words[64] that regularly have at least two syllables, have one stress count.[65] Content words include independent personal pronouns and demonstratives such as *ʾny*, *ʾth*, and *zʾt*. Particles joined to another word by a *maqqep* are generally not counted.

One of the problems in counting stresses lies in the value given to one-syllable words such as prepositions, negatives, and other particles. While such words receive a stress if they are part of a two-syllable unit,[66] the general rule observed in this book is to consider one-syllable particles as unstressed. The matter is complicated when two such particles are present in one line. Isa 48:8b is an example of such a case. Should the two one-syllable particles (*gm* and *lʾ*) in this one line be given no stress counts, or should they be combined and given one count? The fact that the syllable count in the line in question is high (ten syllables) could tip the balance in favor of giving the line four stresses instead of three. A similar situation exists in 48:8a. Again the syllable count in the line is high, and even if the unit is considered two lines rather than one, the problem of how to count the two one-syllable particles still exists.[67] Other matters for consideration are whether to count one-syllable combinations, such as prepositions and suffixes,[68] and what to do with one-syllable particles that are unnecessary[69]

64. In this system, a word is whatever lies between two spaces; for instance, *wnpšm* 'and they themselves' (46:2c) is considered one word, as is *mnʿwryk* 'from your youth' (47:12c). When attached to another word, single-letter terms such as *w*, or prepositions as in the case of *m-* above, are part of the word and receive no extra stress. *Maqqep* is not automatically interpreted as joining two terms into one word. For example, in 47:2d–e, *ḥśpy-šbl* and *gly-šwq* receive two stress counts each.

65. In 48:1f, *lʾ* as a one syllable noncontent word would not be counted as a stress, but *wlʾ* with two syllables would be counted as one stress.

66. Such as *wlʾ* in 47:8f and 48:1f, *wʿl* in 48:2b, and *lk* in 48:5a.

67. Regarding *gm lʾ šmʿt*, if the rule to count only content words or words of two or more syllables is followed, the result is a one-stress line. Even reading *gm lʾ šmʿt gm lʾ ydʿt* as one line yields (according to the general rule) a very long line of only two stresses. In this case, the combination of two unstressed particles is considered the equivalent of one stress.

68. For example, *lk* in 47:1e and 5c.

69. Such as *nʾ* or *gm*.

or rare in poetry.[70] In such cases, decisions must be made taking other factors into account, and it must be admitted that the matter is unclear.

The reason for counting syllables and stresses is to have another way of determining patterns within a poem. While there is a certain amount of variation in individual lines, the patterns emerging from studies that involve syllable and stress counting point to the standard pattern in Biblical Hebrew poetry of a line-pair (or bicolon) having sixteen syllables and six stresses.[71] The study of these chapters in DI supports these findings.

Another approach to the study of Hebrew poetry that stresses the quantitative aspect has been proposed by Duane Christensen in a number of recent articles.[72] His system combines two complementary approaches—the counting of syntactic-accentual stresses and the counting of morae. The counting of syntactic units, a modification introduced by J. Kurylowicz,[73] differs from the traditional method in which word-stress is the focus. Rather than counting individual words, Kurylowicz counts syntactic units as indicated in the masoretic tradition, which means that in some cases independent nouns and verbs do not receive an accent.[74] The counting of morae differs from the counting of syllables in that the mora is the unit of metrical time equal to the short syllable.[75] In short, a mora is a subdivision of the syllable. The counting of both syllables and morae measures the length of a poetic line; the counting of syntactic-accentual stress units assesses the rhythmic manner of speaking or singing a line.[76] Recently Christensen discussed the relationship between music and language and posed the question: "Does the system of cantillation marks preserved by the

70. The sign of the definite direct object *ʾt* rarely occurs in poetry. When the poet uses it, it must be for a reason, and that reason may be metrical.

71. Freedman, "Acrostic Poems," 410–11. Chaps. 46 and 48 of DI fall into the standard pattern; however, chap. 47 will be shown to be similar to the acrostics in Lamentations 1–4, where the line-pair has a pattern of thirteen syllables and five stresses.

72. See the selected bibliography in this volume for a listing of Christensen's publications on biblical poetry and metrical questions.

73. J. Kurylowicz, *Studies in Semitic Grammar and Metrics* (London: Curzon, 1973) and *Metrik und Sprachgeschichte* (Wroclaw: Zaklad Narodowy im. Osslinskich, 1975).

74. The rules for counting syntactic-accentual units are listed in D. Christensen, "Narrative Poetics and the Interpretation of the Book of Jonah" (*Directions in Biblical Hebrew Poetry* [ed. E. Follis; JSOTSup 40; Sheffield: JSOT Press, 1987] 33). See also T. Longman, "A Critique of Two Recent Metrical Systems" (*Bib* 63 [1982] 240).

75. For the counting of morae as a method of scanning Hebrew poetry in the mid-seventeenth to the early-nineteenth centuries, see D. Christensen, "Two Stanzas of a Hymn in Deuteronomy" (*Bib* 65 [1984] 385).

76. See Christensen, "Narrative Poetics," 32, for the rules for counting morae.

Masoretes retain memory of the actual performance of the text?"[77] One of the strengths of Christensen's work is his emphasis on the importance of clarifying what is meant when scholars speak of meter, stress, accent, beat, rhythm, and determining how these factors affect the analysis of biblical poetry. My study of Isaiah 46–48 is limited to an analysis of the structure of the poems according to the methodology of counting syllables and stresses outlined above. Christensen's approach to the text represents another way of looking for patterns within a poem.

Limitations of This Study

Certain assumptions about authorship and composition are made in this book. First, the existence of an author/compiler, if only in the very last stage, is assumed.[78] I do not seek to distinguish between the original author and the final editor/compiler/author or to reconstruct different levels of authorship or editorial or redactional activity.[79] I also presume that the author/compiler used some principle of organization.

Diachronic exegesis seeks to answer questions about genre, *Sitz im Leben*, or stages of development. It looks for evidences of diversity within a text. This study, however, is synchronic; that is, it aims to examine the text as it exists in the MT. My interest is in the surface structure of the text. This study will emphasize features that bind the text into a unity.

Gunkel's notion, that prophetic literature is composed of short poems, is not taken for granted in this investigation. Rather, I use evidence from other biblical texts for the existence of lengthy poems as a point of departure. The acrostic poems of Lamentations 1–4(5) are an excellent example, since Lamentations and DI can be dated within approximately the same period. My assumption is that if there are poems of some length elsewhere in the Bible, it is possible that material in DI also may consist of lengthy poems. This approach is preferred to that of accepting without question the notion of hypothetical short units mentioned by Gunkel. This study begins

77. D. Christensen, "Prophets as Poet/Musicians in Ancient Israel: The Book of Nahum," a paper presented at the March 10, 1988 meeting of the Institute for Antiquity and Christianity.

78. See Andersen and Freedman, *Hosea*, 119–20, 315–16, on their methodological considerations in the interpretation of Hosea. M. Fishbane (*Text and Texture: Close Readings of Selected Biblical Texts* [New York: Schocken Books, 1979] xii), in his discussion of stylistic structuring, points to the fact that texts "reflect not only the creative impulse of their original composers, but that of . . . revisers and arrangers as well."

79. See Kessler, "Introduction," 8–16, on the movement away from the question of authorship in rhetorical criticism.

with the assumption that the poems in chaps. 46–48 are unified literary works. I use a number of criteria to test this assumption. The goals of this investigation are: to discover more about the poetic techniques and devices used by DI, to see how the poetry in chaps. 46–48 is related to other biblical poetry, and to make observations about patterns in biblical Hebrew poetry in general.

Isaiah 46

Text

		Syllable Count	*Total*	*Stresses*
Section I				
1a	krᶜ bl qrs nbw	2+1+2+2	7	4
b	hyw ᶜṣbyhm	2+4	6	2
c	lḥyh wlbhmh	3+5	8	2
d	nśᵓtykm ᶜmwswt	5+3	8	2
e	mśᵓ lᶜyph	2+4	6	2
2a	qrsw krᶜw yḥdw	3+3+2	8	3
b	lᵓ yklw mlṭ mśᵓ	1+3+2+2	8	3
c	wnpšm bšby hlkh	3+3+3	9	3
	8 lines		60	21
Section II				
3a	šmᶜw ᵓly byt yᶜqb	2+2+1+2	7	4
b	wkl-šᵓryt byt yśrᵓl	2+3+1+3	9	4
c	hᶜmsym mny-bṭn	4+2+1	7	3
d	hnśᵓym mny-rḥm	4+2+1	7	3
4a	wᶜd-zqnh ᵓny hwᵓ	2+2+2+1	7	4
b	wᶜd-śybh ᵓny ᵓsbl	2+2+2+2	8	4
c	ᵓny ᶜśyty wᵓny ᵓśᵓ	2+3+3+2	10	4
d	wᵓny ᵓsbl wᵓmlṭ	3+2+4	9	3
	8 lines		64	29
Section III				
5a	lmy tdmywny wtšww	2+4+3	9	3
b	wtmšlwny wndmh	5+3	8	2
6a	hzlym zhb mkys	3+2+2	7	3
b	wksp bqnh yšqlw	2+3+3	8	3
c	yśkrw ṣwrp wyᶜśhw ᵓl	3+2+4+1	10	4
d	ysgdw ᵓp-yštḥww	3+1+3	7	2

Translation

Section I

1a Bel knelt down, Nebo stooped.
b Their idols were
c on beasts and cattle.
d Your carried things were loaded things,
e a burden for the weary.
2a They stooped, they knelt down—together—
b they were not able to deliver a burden
c and they themselves into captivity went.

Section II

3a Listen to me, O house of Jacob,
b and all the remnant of the house of Israel,
c ones borne as a load from the womb,
d ones carried from birth,
4a and unto old age—I am he—
b and unto gray hair—I, I bear a heavy load.
c I, I have acted, and I, I carry,
d and I, I bear, and I deliver.

Section III

5a To whom will you compare me, and liken me,
b and equate me, that we will be compared?
6a Ones who lavish gold from a purse
b and silver in a balance they weigh out.
c They hire a smith and he makes it a god;
d they prostrate themselves, even bow down before it.

7a	yśʾhw ʿl-ktp ysblhw	4+1+2+4	11	3
b	wynyḥhw tḥtyw wyʿmd	5+2+3	10	3
c	mmqwmw lʾ ymyš	4+1+2	7	2
d	ʾp-yṣʿq ʾlyw wlʾ yʿnh	1+2+2+2+2	9	4
e	mṣrtw lʾ ywšyʿnw	4+1+4	9	2
	11 lines		95	31
Section IV				
8a	zkrw-zʾt whtʾššw	2+1+5	8	3
b	hšybw pwšʿym ʿl-lb	3+3+1+1	8	3
9a	zkrw rʾšnwt mʿwlm	2+3+3	8	3
b	ky ʾnky ʾl wʾyn ʿwd	1+3+1+2+1	8	3
c	ʾlhym wʾps kmwny	3+2+3	8	3
10a	mgyd mrʾšyt ʾḥryt	2+3+2	7	3
b	wmqdm ʾšr lʾ-nʿśw	3+2+1+2	8	3
c	ʾmr ʿṣty tqwm	2+3+2	7	3
d	wkl-ḥpṣy ʾʿśh	2+2+2	6	3
11a	qrʾ mmzrḥ ʿyṭ	2+3+1	6	3
b	mʾrṣ mrḥq ʾyš ʿṣtw	2+2+1+3	8	4
c	ʾp-dbrty ʾp-ʾbyʾnh	1+3+1+4	9	2/3
d	yṣrty ʾp-ʾʿśnh	3+1+3	7	2
	13 lines		98	38/39
Section V				
12a	šmʿw ʾly ʾbyry lb	2+2+3+1	8	4
b	hrḥwqym mṣdqh	4+4	8	2
13a	qrbty ṣdqty lʾ trḥq	3+3+1+2	9	3
b	wtšwʿty lʾ tʾḥr	5+1+3	9	2
c	wntty bṣywn tšwʿh	4+3+3	10	3
d	lyśrʾl tpʾrty	4+3	7	2
	6 lines		51	16
Totals				
	46 lines		368 syllables	135/136 stresses

Average syllables and stresses per line:
8 syllables/line; 2.93–2.96 stresses/line

7a They lift it on their shoulders, bear it up;
b then they set it in its place, and it stands;
c from its place it does not move.
d He even cries to it; it does not answer.
e From his distress it does not save him.

Section IV

8a Remember this, and stand firm.
b Bring to mind, O rebels,
9a Remember the first things of old:
b that I am El, and there is not another.
c Elohim, and there is none like me.
10a One who declares from the beginning the end time,
b and from time of old the things not yet made.
c One who says, “My plan will stand,
d and all my purpose I will accomplish.”
11a One who calls from the east a bird of prey,
b from a land afar the man of his plan.
c Indeed, I spoke; indeed I will bring it forth.
d I formed; indeed, I will do it.

Section V

12a Listen to me, O mighty of heart,
b ones far from justice:
13a I brought near my justice which is not far off,
b and my salvation which will not tarry.
c And I put in Zion my salvation,
d and give to Israel my glory.

Notes on Translation and Text

46:1a. *kr^{c} bl* "Bel knelt down"

This chapter begins abruptly, with no indication of speaker or audience. The reader is presented with a picture of the Babylonian gods Bel and Nebo stooping and kneeling while being carried on animals. The verb *kr^{c}* is used to indicate a variety of activities involving kneeling: kneeling down to drink (Judg 5:7), kneeling before a respected person (the captain before Elijah in 2 Kgs 1:13), or before God (Solomon before the altar in 1 Kgs 8:54). It sometimes is used in the context of humiliation of an enemy or a boastful person, as in Ps 22:30—"before him will kneel down all those who go down to the dust."[1] The verb *kr^{c}* is sometimes parallel to *hšt̲ḥwh* where the latter refers to worshiping God (Ps 95:6), but in Esth 3:2 both verbs are used for the people who bowed down and worshiped Haman. It is parallel with *rbṣ* when referring to a crouching lion (Gen 49:9, Num 24:9). Job 4:4 uses *kr^{c}* to refer to "crouching knees" and a stumbling person. Judges 5 repeats the parallel of *kr^{c}* with *npl* three times—Sisera kneels down, falls down between Jael's legs. The combination of *kr^{c}* and *npl* is also found in Ps 20:9, where those who boast of chariots and horses will "kneel down and fall," but those who boast in the name of Yahweh will rise and stand up. In Isaiah 46, the verbs portray the Babylonian gods in humiliating postures as they kneel down and stumble while they proceed on the backs of animals. The procession is not a glorious one.

"Bel"

Bel is the title for the god Marduk (Hebrew "Merodach"), protector of Babylon. Bel-Marduk was the Mesopotamian counterpart of Baal(Hadad).[2] His image, and the image of his son, Nebo (p. 29), were carried in a spring New Year festival procession in Babylon. For this reason, many scholars see features of that New Year procession in this description of Bel and Nebo.[3]

1. The motif of going down to the dust (*yrd* *^{c}pr*) is a key feature in chap. 47, where Babylon is to go down to the dust in defeat and humiliation.

2. Not only was Baal god of the storm, but he was also considered to be the ruler of heaven and earth and in this regard was similar to Marduk, the active head of the pantheon. See W. F. Albright, *Yahweh and the Gods of Canaan: A Historical Analysis of Two Contrasting Faiths* (Garden City, N.Y.: Doubleday, 1968; reprint, Winona Lake, Ind.: Eisenbrauns, 1978) 125.

3. For a description of this festival, which involved a solemn procession of the people and their god to an out-of-town sanctuary, see A. Leo Oppenheim, *Ancient Mesopotamia: Portrait of a Dead Civilization* (revised and completed by Erica Reiner; Chicago: University of Chicago Press, 1977) 187; and S. Pallis, *The Babylonian Akitu Festival* (Copenhagen: n.p., 1926). On processions in the Bible, see Paul Duff, "Processions," *Anchor Bible Dictionary* (Garden City: Doubleday, 1992) 5.469–73. C. Stuhlmueller (*Creative*

Others consider this to be a description of the transportation of these gods, borne on animals out of the destroyed city of Babylon. The flight of Merodach-Baladan at the approach of Sennacherib is similarly described—he gathered the gods in their shrines, placed them on vessels, and took himself off to a city.[4]

Another possible reason for this procession is the seizing of the figures of the gods along with the people by the conquering nation and taking all into exile.[5] Jer 48:7 and 49:3 describe the taking of Chemosh and Milcom into exile along with the priests and princes. Hos 10:5–6 describes a similar incident in which an idol is taken to Assyria as a tribute to the king. Amos 5:26 refers to the taking of Sakkuth and Kaiwan into exile beyond Damascus.

The name Bel occurs only here and in Jer 50:2 and 51:44, in the oracles against Babylon. A construction similar to that of Isa 46:1–2 is found in Jer 50:2. Short two-beat lines describe the downfall of Babylon and her gods:

nlkdh bbl	Babylon was taken
hbyš bl	Bel was shamed
ḥt mrdk	Merodach was dismayed.[6]

Redemption in Deutero Isaiah [AnBib 42; Rome: Pontifical Biblical Institute, 1970] 75–77) shows parallels between the Akitu festival and Isa 40:3–5 and 52:7–19.

4. See Eberhard Schrader, *The Cuneiform Inscriptions and the Old Testament* (trans. O. C. Whitehouse; 2 vols.; London: Williams and Norgate, 1885–88) 2.36; *ANEP*, 181, figs. 537–38.

5. J. Miller and J. J. M. Roberts (*The Hand of the Lord: A Reassessment of the "Ark Narrative" of I Samuel* [Johns Hopkins Near Eastern Studies; Baltimore: Johns Hopkins University Press, 1977] 10) describe the practice of carrying off divine images from as early as the old Babylonian period down to the end of the neo-Babylonian state and beyond. The motivation for the taking of the images was economic (precious metals and stones were overlaid on these idols), as well as theological. The capture of the gods was seen as evidence of the superiority of the victor's gods. Miller and Roberts refer to the practice of dedicating captured gods as booty to one's own gods—Esarhaddon boasts, "the gods in whom they trusted I counted as booty." They also cite texts in which Marduk claims that whenever he went away it was for business purposes, and that he was nevertheless in charge of history. These texts are compared to the claims in Second Isaiah that even though it seemed as though Yahweh was not in control of history, he was (ibid., 13). See also W. W. Hallo, "Cult Statue and Divine Image: A Preliminary Study" (*Scripture in Context II: More Essays on Comparative Method* [ed. W. W. Hallo, J. C. Moyer, and L. G. Perdue; Winona Lake, Ind.: Eisenbrauns, 1983], esp. 11–14), on the transporting of divine images.

6. Note the split-up of the customary pair, Bel-Marduk, in these lines, which is similar to the breakup of names of God elsewhere in Hebrew poetry. See E. Melamed, "Breakup of Stereotype Phrases as an Artistic Device in Biblical Poetry," *Studies in Bible* (ScrHier 8; ed. Chaim Rabin; Jerusalem: Magnes, 1961) 115–21, for examples of the breakup of Yahweh ᶜElyon, ᵓEl ᶜElyon, and ᵓElohim ᶜElyon.

hbyšw ᶜṣbyh	Her images were shamed.
ḥtw glwlyh	Her idols were dismayed.

The pattern in Isa 46:1 is similar:

krᶜ bl	Bel knelt down
qrs nbw	Nebo stooped
hyw ᶜṣbyhm	their idols were
lḥyh wlbhmh	on beasts and cattle.
nśᵓtykm ᶜmwswt	Your carried things were loaded things
mśᵓ lᶜyph	a burden for the weary.

The pattern of perfect verb/noun is continued throughout Jer 50:2. The same pattern begins Isaiah 46.[7] The rest of the verse, while maintaining the two-stress pattern, departs from the verb/noun arrangement and begins to pile up prepositional phrases and participles. Furthermore, the lines are loaded with syllables. It is not necessary to emend on account of the heaviness of the lines. Rather, this loading of syllables helps to define the meaning of the lines and emphasizes the heaviness of the load upon the beasts.

qrs nbw **"Nebo stooped"**

Qrs occurs only twice in the Hebrew Bible, both times in Isaiah 46, first in the participial form (according to the MT), then as a 3 m. pl. pf. verb. The two phrases (*krᶜ bl qrs nbw*) that make up this line are parallel. Casanowicz[8] cites this (along with 46:2a) as an example of paronomasia.[9]

7. See below on the participial form of *qrs* in the MT.

8. Immanuel M. Casanowicz, *Paronomasia in the Old Testament* (Boston: Norwood, 1894) 60. Casanowicz's basic notion of paronomasia (pp. 1, 5) is that it is a figure based on a similarity of sound that points out the mutual relation of two ideas, especially "similarity of sound and dissimilarity of sense" (p. 26). He lists 502 examples of paronomasia in the Hebrew Bible.

9. For more recent treatments of paronomasia in the Bible, see J. J. Glück, "Paronomasia in Biblical Literature," *Semitics* 1 (1970) 50–78, who states that "this phenomenon has enjoyed very little attention so far"; and J. M. Sasson, "Wordplay in the OT" (*IDBSup* [ed. Keith Crim et al.; Nashville: Abingdon, 1976] 968–70). Wilfred G. W. Watson (*Classical Hebrew Poetry: A Guide to Its Techniques* [JSOTSup 26; Sheffield: JSOT Press, 1984] 242–43) acknowledges the existence of wordplay in the Bible and states: "there is no shortage of such puns, though it must be admitted that many of them are quite weak." He cites a few cases from Ugaritic and Akkadian. In the Bible the majority of citations are from Isaiah 1–66 and Psalms, with a few others from wisdom literature. Watson defines paronomasia as "simply . . . the deliberate choice of two (or more) different words which sound nearly alike." The articles of Glück and Sasson are far more detailed and illustrate a variety of sophisticated examples of the phenomenon. Glück ("Paronomasia," 50) defines paronomasia as "the use of a word in such a manner as to imply a meaning and draw an image other than the one expected

The device of alliteration[10] in this introductory verse calls attention to the submissive state of these gods.

Instead of the participle, one might have expected, in light of Jer 50:2, a perfect verb form to follow the pattern of the previous verb. 1QIsa[a] reads *qrs*, without the *waw.*[11] Six of the verbs in vv. 1–2 are in the perfect form. The same pattern (all perfect verbs) is present in a similar passage in Jer 50:2. However, the more difficult reading, the participle, should be maintained. It is easier to understand why 1QIsa[a] and later manuscripts would change the text to reflect a more regular pattern. The presence of the unusual form of the participle is more difficult to explain.[12]

Nebo (Babylonian Nabu) is mentioned only here in the Hebrew Bible. However, there are names in the Bible with this element, including Nebuzaradan, Nebushazaban, Nebuchadnezzar, and Nebuchadrezzar. The royal names Nabonidus and Nabopolassar attest to the popularity of the cult of this deity during the period 612–538 B.C.E. The god Nebo was the son of Bel-Marduk and as the god of writing and wisdom was the keeper of the Tablets of Destiny. The function of Nebo was to write down, during the New Year celebration, the fates "decreed by the gods for the coming year."[13] These two most powerful deities are cast in an uncharacteristic light in this poem as they stumble and stoop.

---

in the context, or in addition to it as a secondary or tertiary idea." He and Sasson stress the ambiguity involved in wordplay.

The commentaries of Torrey, North, and G. A. F. Knight treat the phenomenon of wordplay in DI. D. F. Payne ("Characteristic Word-Play in 'Second Isaiah': A Reappraisal," *JSS* 12 [1967] 207–29) disagrees with the assessments of Torrey and North on wordplay as a special characteristic in DI. Payne is rightly critical of some of the examples Torrey uses to demonstrate his thesis. His conclusion is that since wordplay is found to a certain extent in all Hebrew poetry and the quantity of wordplay in DI is not unusual, it should not be considered a "special characteristic of this biblical writer" (p. 208).

10. Alliteration here means the recurrence of consonants, not just initial letter repetition of consonants. See note on v. 3cd for more on alliteration.

11. See G. R. Driver, "Linguistic and Textual Problems: Isaiah XL–LXVI," *JTS* 36 (1935) 399, for this reading (this is also the suggestion of Marti). However, see Torrey and Delitzsch, who repoint *kr*[c] as a participle to correspond with *qrs* here. Torrey also suggests the possibility that these verbs could be taken as imperatives. This would make a nice parallel with the imperatives used in regard to Babylon in 47:1ff.; however, there is no textual support for such a reading.

12. Notice a similar variation, or break in sequence, in Amos 4:4–5, which has six m. pl. imperative forms and one infinitive absolute, *qṭr*, used for the imperative.

13. C. R. North, *The Second Isaiah* (Oxford: Clarendon, 1964) 163.

46:1bc. *hyw ʿṣbyhm lḥyh wlbhmh*
"Their idols were on beasts and cattle"

Lines b–e of v. 1 pose difficulties. There are a variety of different renderings offered by ancient and modern translators. The LXX reads: the idols "have become beasts and cattle"; the Targum reads: they have "become the likeness of beasts and cattle," based on the idiom *hyh l* 'to become'. North reads *hyh l* 'to belong to' (on the model of Deut 10:9) and understands the passage to mean that the idols have become the property of the pack animals. Bewer reads "are consigned to beasts and cattle," a rendering favored by Muilenburg.

The Qumran MSS agree with the MT, but Clifford and Westermann emend the text. Clifford[14] considers *hyw ʿṣbyhm* to be a gloss taken into the text at an early stage and eliminates it from his translation. Westermann considers the text to the end of v. 1 to be in disorder and transposes the words based on his considerations of rhythm. He sees a "strong 2.2 rhythm" and, applying this opinion, reorders the text as follows:

hyw ʿṣbyhm mśʾ lḥyh
nśʾtykm lbhmh ʿmwswt lʿyph

Clifford reworks the same passage but he seems to read a 3+3 pattern, as can be seen from his reconstruction:

krʿbl [sic] *qrs nbw*
lḥyh wlbhmh nśʾt
ʿmwswt mśʾ lʿyph
qrsw krʿw yḥdw

A different suggestion from C. F. Whitley is to eliminate *mśʾ lʿyph* as a gloss.[15] His reconstruction is as follows:

krʿ bl qrs nbw	Bel bows down, Nebo stoops,
hyw ʿṣbyhm lḥyh	their idols are on cattle,
lbhmh nśʾtyhm ʿmwswt	their burdens loaded on dumb animals

He proposes a 3+3+3 pattern, eliminates the *waw* from *lbhmh*, and emends the 2 m. pl. suffix to 3 m. pl. Neither of these emendations is successful in eliminating perceived problems in the text. Especially unconvincing is the notion of a 3+3 pattern, when the first line of that supposed pattern is a line of four stresses.

14. Clifford, *Fair Spoken and Persuading*, and "Function of the Idol Passages in Second Isaiah," *CBQ* 42 (1980) 455.

15. C. F. Whitley, "Textual Notes on DI," *VT* 11 (1961) 459.

ʿṣbyhm **"their idols"**

This word only occurs in the plural (except for Jer 22:28).[16] In 1 and 2 Samuel it refers to the idols of the Philistines. In Isa 10:10–11, it is parallel with *ʾlyl* and *psyl*, other words for idols, where Assyria boasts of defeating nations with idols greater than those of Jerusalem and Samaria. Hos 8:4 also refers to the production of idols out of silver and gold, such as the production mentioned in Isa 46:6. In Hos 14:9 the idols are rejected, and Yahweh takes his place by asserting that "I, I answered [*ʿnyty*] (Ephraim)." This is what the idols in Isaiah 46 do not have the power to do (see v. 7).

Another passage dealing with idols (*ʿṣby*) is Isa 48:5ff.,[17] in which there is a danger of people attributing certain activities wrongly to idols. In chap. 48 Yahweh withholds his anger from people, so as not to "cut them off." The same combination of *lmʿn* and *krt* is found in Hos 8:4.[18] In Mic 1:7, *ʿṣb* is parallel with *psyl* and *ʾtnn* 'hire (of a harlot)'. The reference is to the destruction of idols, images, and the hires of a harlot.

Ps 106:38 refers to the idols of Canaan, *ʿṣby knʿn*, to whom child sacrifices were offered. Ps 135:15 and 115:4 speak of idols as the work of people's hands, made of silver and gold. The making of idols and the role of idols are important themes in chaps. 46 and 48 of this study, as well as elsewhere in DI (especially chap. 44). Psalms 115 and 135 emphasize one of the characteristics of the idols mentioned in DI: they are unable to act in any way. The idols are described in these psalms in a long series of negatives: they have mouths, but do not speak, eyes but do not see, ears but do not hear, and so forth. Their makers, and anyone who trusts in them, will be like them. Throughout DI the idols are characterized in a similar negative fashion.

46:1d. ***nśʾtykm*** **"your carried things"**

The 2 m. pl. possessive of the f. pl. noun[19] causes problems. Whybray calls the ending "clearly wrong" and reads *hm* ('their') instead. Clifford drops the ending altogether (see his reconstruction of v. 1, p. 30). Volz

16. F. I. Andersen and D. N. Freedman, *Hosea: A New Translation with Introduction and Commentary* (AB 24; Garden City, N.Y.: Doubleday, 1980) 378. However, BDB (p. 781) reads the *ʿṣb* in Jer 22:28 and the *ʿṣb* in Isa 48:5 as different nouns. According to Andersen and Freedman, the word in Hosea imitates the plural *ʾĕlōhîm* 'god' and may be a generic reference in Hosea 4:17, 8:4, and 13:2 to one pagan god, Baal. Freedman suggests (personal correspondence), based on the feminine forms *nśʾtykm* and *ʿmwswt*, that the noun *ʿṣby*(*hm*) is probably a feminine noun with a plural ending that is masculine in form. A similar example can be seen in *ʾšrhl ʾšrym*.

17. BDB considers this to be a different noun from the form in 46:1 (see above, n. 16).

18. See Andersen and Freedman, *Hosea*, 493, for this combination.

19. BDB 672.

reads *nś*ʾ*t kmw* ʿ*mwswt*; North suggests *nś*ʾ*t km*ʿ*mswt* 'carried like burdens'. The LXX reads "like a burden." It is especially important to determine exactly to whom the passage is being addressed. Because of the abrupt beginning of the passage,[20] the reader is thrown into the middle of the picture with little or no background. For whom is the description of the kneeling, bowing gods and animals intended? If 46:1 is a continuation of 45:20ff. (as suggested by Westermann), it may be that the addressees are the "survivors of nations," "the ends of the earth." Especially in 45:20–21, the survivors of nations are those who carry about wooden idols and pray to them, even though they cannot save. There are several places in DI that the nations, the islands, and others are addressed (41:1ff.—the coastlands, which engage in idol-making in 41:6–7; 49:1ff.—the coastlands, the peoples from afar). This audience, which prays to a god who cannot save, is encouraged to turn to Yahweh, who is the only god and savior.

The addressees could be those who hire idol-makers in vv. 6–7, by virtue of the continuation of the theme of idolatry. But who these individuals are is still undetermined. The 2 m. pl. form also appears in the poem at the beginning of each new section (lines 3a, 5ab, 8abc, and 12a), where it refers to "the house of Jacob / remnant of the house of Israel" (v. 3), to those who might compare Yahweh to other gods (v. 5), to the "rebels" (v. 8), and to those who are "mighty of heart / far from justice" (v. 12). The 2 m. pl. suffix in 46:1d refers to the same audience as in the rest of the poem, namely to the house of Jacob/Israel.[21] This clarifies the harsh accusatory tone of the addresses in lines 8ab and 12ab (see below on vv. 6–7 for a fuller discussion of idol-worship and the idolatry of Jacob/Israel). That at least some members of the community had idols is clear from Isa 48:5cd, where people were in danger of attributing certain activities to their own idols.

ʿmwswt **"loaded things"**

The f. pl. passive participle[22] of ʿ*ms*, a seldom-used word, is one of the many words used in this section to communicate the idea of carrying or bearing a load. The verb ʿ*ms* in Gen 44:13 and Neh 13:15 refers to loading sacks onto donkeys. Zech 12:3 describes Jerusalem as a "heavy [*m*ʿ*msw*] stone" and warns that all those who lift it [ʿ*msyh*] will be hurt. Ps 68:20 reads: *y*ʿ*ms lnw h*ʾ*l yšw*ʿ*tnw* 'He carries us; El is our salvation'. According

20. Muilenburg says it begins *in medias res.*

21. H. Leene sees the Israelites as guilty of idol-making by his interpretation of v. 8 ("Isaiah 46:8: Summons to be Human?" *JSOT* 30 [1984] 115). See below, on v. 8 (p. 50).

22. BDB 770.

to Dahood,[23] *ʿms* is quite frequent in Ugaritic and appears in an unpublished passage with El as subject.

The "loaded things" and "carried things" in chap. 46 could refer to the accessories that go along with the idols, including their attire, jewelry, and so forth, and even Bel and Nebo themselves.[24] Bel and Nebo are not the subjects that lift; rather, they are the things lifted. The use of the f. pass. part. of *ʿms* could refer more specifically to the idols (*ʿṣby*[*m*]) of line 1b.

One of the reasons poets sometimes use unusual words like *ʿmwswt* is to achieve an alliterative effect.[25] The repetition of the *m* and *s* sounds in lines 1de should be noted.

46:1e. *mśʾ* "a burden"

This is a noun formed from the root *nśʾ*,[26] and is the second occurrence in this verse of a word based on this root. This root is used to emphasize an important theme in DI, that of "bearing." The introduction to the book, 40:1–11, portrays Yahweh as both a powerful warrior ruling with his arm and a shepherd gathering lambs in his arm and bearing them in his bosom (*wbḥyqw yśʾ*).

The word *mśʾ* occurs in Num 11:11 and Deut 1:12, where it is a figure for the burden of the people Israel, which Moses complains is too heavy for him to bear. He asks rhetorically in Num 11:12, "Did I conceive this people and bring them forth that you should say, 'Bear (*nśʾ*) them in your bosom (*bḥyqk*) as a nurse bears (*nśʾ*) a nursing child' "? In Deut 1:12 the same question is asked by Moses: "Can I alone bear (*nśʾ*) your burden (*mśʾ*) . . . ?" Moses' remark to Yahweh is his way of putting the responsibility of bearing on the right party—Yahweh. It is he, not Moses, who should bear these people in his bosom.

23. M. Dahood, *Psalms II: 51–100* (AB 17; Garden City, N.Y.: Doubleday, 1968) 144.

24. The apocryphal letter of Jeremiah speaks of gods of silver and gold being clothed with robes, ornamented with golden crowns, and holding scepter, dagger, and axe. While this letter is from a later period, it has many similarities with anti-idolatry passages in Isaiah, esp. chaps. 44 and 46. The priests carry the gods on their shoulders. When they stand the gods upright, they cannot move; they cannot save themselves, nor can they save those in distress. See also A. Leo Oppenheim (*Ancient Mesopotamia,* 184–85), who discusses the paraphernalia of the images of the Babylonian deities, which included "sumptuous garments of characteristic style, crowned with tiaras and adorned with pectorals." The details of the paraphernalia and the divine attire were essential to establish the identity of the deity.

25. L. Boadt, "Intentional Alliteration in Second Isaiah," *CBQ* 45 (1983) 356.

26. BDB 672.

It is accepted by many scholars that Isa 40:1–11 introduces several key themes that are developed in greater detail in Isaiah 40–55.[27] One of the themes, "carrying" or "lifting," appears in chap. 46. In 46:1 it is not God who carries, but the reverse—the gods are carried by beasts and later, in v. 7, by people. The device of alliteration in v. 1 ties together the three synonymous words *nś*ʾ*tykm*, ᶜ*mwswt*, and *mś*ʾ and underscores the importance of these words to the development of the theme of the chapter.[28]

l*ᶜ*yph **"for the weary"**

The f. s. ᶜ*yph* refers here to the beasts of burden that carry the idols. The notion of "weariness" is important throughout DI, especially in connection with idol-making.[29] Elsewhere, in Isa 5:27, Assyria is portrayed as the opposite of weary. The nation that Yahweh calls out to accomplish his purpose comes swiftly, is not weary, does not stumble, and does not sleep or slumber. Babylon in DI is the antithesis of this powerful dynamic force. Especially in chap. 47, the image of Babylon is that of a city oppressed by her own powers, and overburdened and wearied (*yg*ᶜ) by her advisors, magicians, and sorcerers.

The word ᶜ*yp* is mentioned in an important section of First Isaiah, in 28:9–13. Yahweh has promised to give rest to the weary, but this promise is aborted by the people's refusal to hear the promise. The promise (v. 12) is imbedded between two sections (vv. 10 and 13), demonstrating that the word of Yahweh will be meaningless to his intransigent audience. Because they do not hear, they are doomed to be broken and ensnared. In DI the promise of rest and the revival of the weary is again brought to the people. But it is emphasized in 40:8 and 55:11 that the word *will* come to fruition.

46:2a. ***qrsw kr*ᶜ*w yḥdw*** **"they stooped, they knelt down—together"**

The verbs *qrs* and *kr*ᶜ are repeated from v. 1a in a chiastic arrangement. The subjects of the plural nouns are both the beasts that carry the idols and

27. John L. McKenzie, *Second Isaiah* (AB 20; Garden City, N.Y.: Doubleday, 1968) 16; C. Westermann, *Isaiah 40–66: A Commentary* (OTL; Philadelphia: Westminster, 1969) 33; R. Lack, *La symbolique du livre d'Isaïe: Essai sur l'image littéraire comme élément de structuration* (AnBib 59; Rome: Pontifical Biblical Institute, 1973) 83–86; R. F. Melugin, *The Formation of Isaiah 40–55* (BZAW 141; Berlin: de Gruyter, 1976) 85; David Noel Freedman, "The Structure of Isaiah 40:1–11," in *Perspectives on Language and Text: Essays and Poems in Honor of Francis I. Andersen's Sixtieth Birthday* (ed. E. W. Conrad and E. G. Newing; Winona Lake, Ind.: Eisenbrauns, 1987) 167–93. See also Eva Hessler, *Gott der Schöpfer: Ein Beitrag zur Komposition und Theologie Deuterojesajas* (Ph.D. diss., Greifswald, 1961; cited by Melugin, *Formation*, 78 n. 6). She sees 40:1–11 and 55:1–13 as prologue and epilogue for the structure of the chapters, imitating the form of a legal proceeding.

28. 1QIsa[a] reads *mšmy*ᶜ*yhmh* 'their announcers' instead of *mś*ʾ *l*ᶜ*yph*.

29. See Isa 44:12, where the idol-maker is wearied by the process of making an idol.

the idols Bel and Nebo. North is correct in his observation that the text describes a confusion of idols and exhausted animals.

yḥdw **"together"**

This adverb indicates unity of action or emphasis.[30] For examples of the former in DI, see 40:5, 41:1, 43:9; of the latter, see 41:19, 20, 23; 43:17. In DI, this word occasionally serves as a double-duty modifier. In 46:2 I read: "they stooped, they knelt down together," and "together they were not able." In 41:1 it modifies both the verbs that precede it and the verb that follows: "let them draw near, let them speak together" and "together let us draw near for judgment." See 43:9: "let all the nations gather together and all the peoples assemble" (*kl-hgwym nqbṣw yḥdw wyʾspw lʾmym*); 43:17: "bringing forth chariot and horse, army and warrior together" and "together they lie down, they cannot rise"; and 45:16: "the makers of idols go in confusion together." In each of these examples, the adverb is positioned between the lines it modifies.[31]

46:2b. ***lʾ yklw mlṭ mśʾ*** **"they were not able to deliver a burden"**

North sees the pack animals as the "logical subjects" here, since they are the ones who are unable to deliver the burden of the idols. But just as Bel and Nebo are included along with the animals as subjects of the verbs *qrsw* and *krʿw*, they are also implicit subjects of this verb. The burden of 46:2b is that of the idols. Bel and Nebo, in contrast with the picture of Yahweh (vv. 3–4), but similar to the idol of v. 7, are unable to deliver and bear the burden of the people who worship them and cry to them for help (v. 7). The emphasis of these lines is not only on the animals' inability to rescue the idols, but more importantly on the inabilities of Bel and Nebo.

The infinitive absolute *mlṭ* 'deliver' occurs also in Jer 39:18, where Yahweh promises "I will surely deliver you (*mlṭ ʾmlṭk*) . . . and you will have your life (*whyth lk npšk*)." In Ps 41:2 Yahweh delivers (*mlṭ*) the poor. In Jer 51:6 and 45, in the oracles against Babylon, all are urged to flee from Babylon to save their lives (*mlṭw ʾyš ʾt-npšw*). In DI there is no deliverance; v. 2c shows that the flight is into captivity.

46:2c. ***npšm*** **"they themselves"**

Several commentators see in this passage evidence of a distinction in DI between the gods themselves and the graven images made of them.[32]

30. BDB 403.

31. See M. Dahood, *Psalms III: 101–150* (AB 17A; Garden City, N.Y.: Doubleday, 1970) 439–44, for examples of this phenomenon.

32. See Thorkild Jacobsen, "The Graven Image," in *Ancient Israelite Religion: Essays in Honor of Frank Moore Cross* (ed. P. D. Miller, P. D. Hanson, and S. D. McBride;

Westermann states that "v. 2 clearly differentiates between the gods and their statues. . . . This passage constitutes the Bible's most profound utterance on the representation of a god by an image."[33] For Westermann, *lʾ yklw mlṭ mśʾ* has the meaning "the gods do not manage to save their statues." However, the subjects of the verb *lʾ yklw* are the animals carrying the gods, as well as the gods themselves. The word *npš* refers to the gods themselves, that is, their representations.[34] The m. pl. suffix refers back to the masculine verbs in line 1a. The gods themselves go into captivity.

***šby* "captivity"**

The expression *hlk bšby* occurs in Amos 9:4; Deut 28:41; Nah 3:10; Jer 20:6, 22:22, 30:16; Ezek 12:11, 30:17, 18; and Lam 1:18 (also v. 5). The word means 'state of captivity' or 'captives (coll.)'.[35] Usually the expression refers to Israel, Jerusalem, or the people going into captivity, but in Nahum and Ezekiel it is Egypt who walks into captivity, and in Jeremiah 30 it is Israel's foes. In this passage in DI, it is the Babylonian gods who go into captivity,[36] along with the animals who carry them. It may be implied that anyone associated with these deities will accompany them into exile.

46:2c. *hlkh* "they went"

For the 3 f. s. here, 1QIsa[a] reads the 3 pl., *hlkw*. The verb in the MT agrees with the f. s. *npš*; 1QIsa[a] appears to be connecting the verb to the nouns Bel and Nebo in v. 1a. As shown above, it is the gods (*npšm* 'their [m.] image') who go into exile.

46:3cd. *mny* "from"

This archaic form of the preposition (with the old *yod* of the genitive, according to BDB[37]) appears twice in these lines, in the same position.

Philadelphia: Fortress, 1987) 15–32, on the question of whether, in Mesopotamian worship, the god was identified with its own statue. There is evidence in Mesopotamian texts that in some cases the god and cult statue were identical with one another but in others that the two were distinct entities. He concludes that the significance of the image was that it represented a "promise, a potential, and an incentive to theophany, to a divine presence" (p. 29).

33. Westermann admits that the conception of the differentiation of gods from images is not part of the satire on the idols in 44:9–20, where the two are "identified without qualification."

34. *Npš* is used for a physical object and is also associated with the body. H. Donner and W. Röllig (*KAI* 2:133) state that the word is used for a burial monument or stele in Aramaic, Syriac, Palmyrene, Nabatean, and Arabic. This could be a statue or image of some kind. Here the word refers to the representation of the gods Bel and Nebo.

35. BDB 985.

36. See also 52:2, where Jerusalem is referred to as *šby*(*h*) 'captive' but is urged to throw off the bonds of captivity.

37. BDB 577; but see GKC §90 l.

Elsewhere the expression is *mbṭn // mrḥm* (Job 3:11; Ps 22:11, 58:4). The long form of the preposition, appearing twice, affects the syllable and stress count; the usage is for metrical purposes. L. Boadt explains the use of this unusual form as an example of the device of alliteration[38] used to underscore important moments in a poem.[39]

46:4a. *ʾny hwʾ* "I am (he)"

The same asseveration appears in 41:4; 43:10, 13, 25; 48:12; and 52:6. Muilenburg[40] interprets these as "covenant words" in DI and sees them as equivalent to "I am God" in an absolute sense. Torrey[41] suggests the possibility of translating "I am the same." Whybray finds it to be a characteristic

38. Boadt, "Intentional Alliteration," 358. Some scholars define alliteration as "the repetition of a consonantal sound at the beginning of a word" (see L. Alonso Schökel, *A Manual of Hebrew Poetics* [Rome: Pontifical Biblical Institute, 1988] 23). Alliteration here is defined as the recurrence of consonants (with L. Boadt, "Isaiah 41:8–13: Notes on Poetic Structure and Style," *CBQ* 35 [1973] 32–33; W. L. Holladay, "Form and Word-Play in David's Lament over Saul and Jonathan," *VT* 20 [1970] 157; R. Alter, *The Art of Biblical Poetry* [New York: Basic Books, 1985] 78; and Watson, *Classical Hebrew Poetry*, 225–28). It is not limited to consonants at the beginning of a word. A. Berlin (*The Dynamics of Biblical Parallelism* [Bloomington: Indiana University Press, 1985] 103–4) uses the term *consonance* for this phenomenon. She refines the definition of alliteration or consonance by stating that there must be at least two sets of consonants in close proximity in order to demonstrate a significant pattern (p. 105). Near alliteration is also to be taken into account. Casanowicz (*Paronomasia*, 28–29) has a section entitled "Consonants which alliterate with each other." He lists the following consonants: ʾ/ᶜ; *b/p*; *g/q*; *k/q*; *d/ṭ*; *d/t*; *ṭ/t*; *z/s*; *s/ś*; *s/š*; *ś/š*; *k/ḥ*. Berlin (p. 104) and Holladay both define consonance in terms of "the same or similar consonants." Vowel repetition is termed "assonance" (with Watson, *Classical Hebrew Poetry*, 222–23). This is not limited to final or stressed vowel assonance. Watson admits that there is some overlap between assonance and alliteration.

39. "The choice of this archaic form allows the poet to write out the whole preposition . . . thus (maintaining) a strong m/m/m/n/n//n/m/m/n/m pattern" (Boadt, "Isaiah 41:8–13," 32–33).

40. J. Muilenburg, "The Book of Isaiah: Chapters 40–66," *IB* (New York: Abingdon, 1956) 5.451.

41. Torrey, *Second Isaiah*, 315. Westermann reads with Torrey, translating 'I, the same'. Westermann refers to this as a "divine self-prediction." J. J. Scullion (*Isaiah 40–66* [OTM; Wilmington, Del.: Michael Glazier, 1982] 33) refers to it as a "self-assertion" or "self-presentation" formula. Melugin (*Formation*, 33–34) speaks of "self-predications" of Yahweh and finds that the "self-praise hymn style is not unique to Deutero-Isaiah" but is also found in Mesopotamian and Egyptian texts. In each case there is a "polemic edge" to these self-praises by the deities. See also N. Walker, "Concerning *hwʾ* and *ʾny hwʾ*" (*ZAW* 74 [1962] 205–6). I was unable to consult "The Divine Designation '*hū*' in Eblaite and the Old Testament" by M. Dahood (*Annali* 43 [1983] 193–99). In *Psalms III*, Dahood translates Ps 102:28 *ʾth hwʾ* 'you remain the same' and interprets this as a statement about the immutability of God (p. 22).

expression throughout DI, conveying the belief that Yahweh is the only God. Here the context of the assertion is that Yahweh is the one who carries, bears, acts on behalf of his people (in contrast with the Babylonian gods).[42] Isa 41:4 uses the verbs *ᶜśh* and *pᶜl* to describe Yahweh's activities; there are also assertions about Yahweh as first and last. Similar claims about Yahweh as first and last are found in 48:12, in the context of Yahweh as creator. That Yahweh is the only savior and there is none like him is the context of the assertions in 43:10, 13. In 43:25 Yahweh identifies himself as the one who forgives sins and offenses.[43] The emphasis in 52:6 is on identifying Yahweh by name as the one who speaks. The first-person pronoun is important in chap. 46, occurring in v. 4 five times, and once, later, in v. 9 (*ᵓnky*).

46:3cd, 4ab. ***mn . . . ᶜd*** **"from (birth) . . . to (old age)"**

The construction *mn . . . wᶜd* expresses idiomatically the idea of comprehensiveness.[44] The totality of Yahweh's deliverance of his people is expressed by these two extremes of birth/old age, an example of merismus.[45] Typical examples of this idiom join one object of comparison to the opposite, as in Gen 46:34: "From our youth until (now)" (*mnᶜwrynw wᶜd*). Isa 46:3cd and 4ab split up the elements of this idiom: *mny bṭn . . . mny rḥm* in 3cd; *wᶜd-zqnh . . . wᶜd śybh* in 4ab. Ps 71:17–18 has a similar expression[46] using the same word-pair, *zqnh śybh* of 46:4ab—"from youth . . . to now . . . to old age and gray hair. . . . "

The parallelism and patterning in 3cd and 4ab are very regular. Line 3cd has grammatical and lexical parallelism:

3c *hᶜmsym mny-bṭn*
3d *hnśᵓᶜyṭym mny-rḥm*

Grammatically, the pattern is m. pl. pass. part. / prep. / noun. Lexically, *ᶜms* and *nśᵓ* are a word-pair. *Mny* forms a parallel by repetition. *Bṭn* and

42. This is the idea behind the assertion *ᵓny ᵓny hwᵓ* in Deut 32:39. The other gods cannot rise up and deliver or help; there is no other god besides Yahweh—*ᵓyn ᵓlhym ᶜmdy.*

43. The phrase here is the variation, *ᵓnky ᵓnky hwᵓ*, which also occurs in 51:12.

44. BDB 581.

45. According to L. Alonso Schökel (*Hebrew Poetics*, 83), the reduction of a "complete series to two of its constituent elements" or the division of "a whole into two halves." Watson would further characterize this as an example of merism by means of polar word pairs in which the word pair expresses a totality in an abbreviated form (*Classical Hebrew Poetry*, 321–22).

46. The word pair *zqnh//śybh* is found in Ps 71:18. M. Dahood cites the occurrence in *UT* 51:v:66 of *šbt dqnk* 'the hoariness of your beard' in his discussion of this psalm (*Psalms II*, 175).

rḥm are lexically parallel as a word-pair, and morphologically parallel, both being segolates.

Line 4ab has lexical and partial grammatical parallelism. The grammatical parallelism could be diagrammed a b c d // a b c e.

And-unto	old-age,	I	am-he
a	b	c	d
And-unto	gray-hair,	I	bear
a	b	c	e

Lexical parallelism exists between the word-pair *zqnh* // *śybh* and the repetitions of *wʿd* and *ʾny*.[47]

At the same time, the sentence strung out among these verses is complex. The house of Jacob / remnant of the house of Israel are the ones who have been carried from the womb to old age; Yahweh is the one who has carried them from womb to old age. The phrases in 3cd and 4ab refer both to the previous verse, 3ab, as well as to the following, 4a–d.

46:4b. *ʾny ʾsbl* "I, I bear a heavy load"

Another verb for 'carry' is introduced into the text. This verb, unlike *nśʾ* and *mlṭ*, only occurs in Isaiah here in chap. 46 and in 53:4, 11.[48]

46:4c. *ʾny ʿśyty* "I, I have acted"

The verb *ʿśh* is part of a massing together of four verbs, three of which are synonyms for 'carry'. Some commentators feel *ʿśh* is "inappropriate" here and substitute *ʿmsty* or *nśʾty*. The absolute use of *ʿśh* is attested elsewhere with Yahweh as subject. The word is translated in BDB[49] 'act with effect'. 1 Kgs 8:32 calls for God to hear, act, and judge and in v. 39 to hear, forgive, act, and render. In Ezek 20:9, 14, 22, God acts for the sake

47. See Berlin, *Dynamics of Biblical Parallelism*, on the different types and aspects of parallelism.

48. J. Rabinowitz ("A Note on Isa 46,4," *JBL* 73 [1954] 237) draws attention to an Aramaic papyrus from 427 B.C.E., in which a man manumits his slaves if they promise to "serve and support him." The two words for 'support' used in this document are related to the Hebrew roots *sbl* and *nśʾ*. Rabinowitz concludes that the occurrence of these two words side by side points to legal terminology as the source of the phrase in Isaiah. He also comments on vv. 4a and b and compares them to the duty of slaves to support their master in old age, citing Greek manuscripts on manumission. He does not discuss the same occurrence of these two roots in 53:4, which has to do with the servant. His conclusion, that legal terminology is the source of the phrase in Isaiah, is not based on sufficient evidence. However, taking the pairing of these two words in Isa 46:6, 53:4 and the document to which Rabinowitz refers, it may be that these roots exist as a fixed word-pair, and that they emphasize the notion of slavery or service.

49. BDB 794.

of his name. Dahood[50] cites several psalms with the absolute use of the verb (Ps 22:32, 37:5, 39:10, 52:11, 118:24), as well as Isa 38:15. In addition, in vv. 10d and 11d, the identical root in the first singular is used. The verb *ʿśh* occurs elsewhere in DI in connection with God's activity, both in creating and in redeeming. Many scholars have noted the connection between Yahweh's creative and saving powers.[51] Furthermore, this verb is set apart from the other verbs, not only because it is not synonymous, but also because it is in the perfect tense ("I have acted") and the others are in the imperfect ("I carry" or "will carry").

The pattern of lines 4a–d is quite symmetrical:

wʿd-zqnh ʾny hwʾ
wʿd-śybh ʾny ʾsbl
ʾny ʿśyty wʾny ʾśʾ

Verse 4a corresponds to v. 4b with the repetition of a prepositional phrase and the first singular independent pronoun. The two verbs in 4c parallel two verbs in 4d. Overall, the fivefold repetition of the first singular independent pronoun corresponds with the five first-singular verb forms, totalling ten instances of the first-person singular. This symmetry is not achieved at the price of monotonous repetition, however. The poet has varied the pattern; in the beginning of the series, the pronoun appears with *hwʾ* and is not connected with a verb, as are the other four independent pronouns. In addition, the final verb is the only first-person verb in the series without the independent pronoun. Another variation is achieved by the use of the perfect verb *ʿśyty* amidst four imperfect verbs. The intertwining of these first-singular forms with the prepositional phrases in v. 4ab binds this verse to the previous passage, as described above.

The combination of the perfect *ʿśyty* with three imperfect verbs is a way of expressing the totality of God's activity. The verb *ʿśh*, as one of a long list of verbs, appears also in 46:11cd. There too the totality of God's activity is emphasized: he has acted in the past, and he will continue to do so in the future. Furthermore, the idea that Israel's God is active in making and doing is emphasized throughout chaps. 40–55, especially in contrast to the inactive gods of Babylon.

50. M. Dahood, *Psalms I: 1–50* (AB 16; Garden City, N.Y.: Doubleday, 1965) 144, 228, 241; *Psalms II*, 17.

51. G. von Rad, *Old Testament Theology: The Theology of Israel's Prophetic Traditions* (2 vols.; New York: Harper & Row, 1965) 2.238–62, has the classic treatment of this combination of Yahweh as creator-redeemer. See also Stuhlmueller, *Creative Redemption*, for the way DI combines creation and redemption.

46:5a. ***lmy*** **"To whom . . . ?"**

The expression *lmy* usually has to do with questions of belonging or possession: "whose maiden?" Ruth 2:5; "whose (servant)?" 2 Sam 16:19; "whose gold?" Exod 32:24; "whose land?" 2 Sam 3:12; "whose sorrows?" Prov 23:29. Only in Isa 46:5, Esth 6:6, and Lam 2:20 does the expression have a different sense. A similar question ("To whom can you liken God?") is asked in Isa 40:18. There the expression is *wʾl my.*

In his extensive treatment on the incomparability of Yahweh in the Old Testament, C. J. Labuschagne illustrates a variety of ways that this notion was developed in the Hebrew Bible.[52] Incomparability was expressed by the use of negation (e.g., "there is none like you") and other comparatives, by rhetorical questions (e.g., "who is like . . . ?"), and by verbs denoting equality and similarity. Chapter 46 uses a number of these expressions, here and in v. 9. The rhetorical question here is an example of one of them.

tdmywny **"(to whom) will you compare me?"**

In this Piel impf. of *dmh*, the *yod* has been retained.[53] The same form is found in Isa 40:18, 26,[54] where the same notion of comparison with Yahweh is expressed, the same rhetorical question is asked.[55] In 40:18 the verb *dmh* 'to compare' is parallel with *ʿrk* 'to arrange, set in order, compare'.[56] Ps 89:7 has the same word-pair in a set of rhetorical questions that point to the incomparability of Yahweh. The image called up by *ʿrk* is one of lining things in a row and comparing them.

In Isa 14:14, a taunt song against the king of Assyria/Babylon, the king in his arrogance claims that he will make himself like the most high. The form used is the Hithpael of *dmh*. In this taunt song, it is clearly shown that the king cannot make himself like God, and instead of ascending to the heights of the clouds, he is brought down to the depths.

52. C. J. Labuschagne, *The Incomparability of Yahweh in the Old Testament* (Leiden: Brill, 1966).

53. GKC §75dd / p. 214.

54. Frank Matheus ("Jesaja XLIV 9–20: Das Spottgedicht gegen die Götzen und seine Stellung im Kontext," *VT* 37 [1987] 312–26), on the basis of the repetition of certain words in Isa 40:18–46:8, sees a large chiasm ABC/C′B′A′, with 44:9–20 at the center. The root *dmh* in 40:18 is matched by the same root in 46:5–8; words of deliverance in 41:6–7 are echoed in 45:20; and the shame of those who trust in idols is mentioned in both 42:17 and 45:16–17. See also H. C. Spykerboer, *The Structure and Composition of Deutero-Isaiah with Special Reference to the Polemic against Idolatry* (Frankener, Netherlands: Rijksuniversitet te Groningen, 1976) 151 on the unity of 40:12–46:13.

55. The verb means "to resemble, be like in outward appearance, to look like" (Labuschagne, *Incomparability*, 28).

56. The verb *ʿrk* is one of the typical words cited by Labuschagne that are used to denote equality and similarity (ibid., 28).

The first-person suffix is a double-duty as a modifier, since it also modifies the following verb, *wtšww* 'and liken (me)'.

***wtšww* "and liken (me)"**

The *Hiphil* of *šwh* ('to be like'; *Hiphil* 'to make like') only occurs two times, here and in Lam 2:13. Both times it is parallel with *dmh*. In Isa 40:25, the *Qal* of *šwh* is parallel with *dmh*. These verbs are synonyms dealing with comparison, or more accurately, incomparability. In Lam 2:13 the object of incomparability is not Yahweh, but Jerusalem, because of her wretched condition. There will be no comforting Jerusalem, because her state is beyond comparison.

***wtmšlwny* "and equate me"**

This is the only occurrence of *mšl* in the *Hiphil*. All other uses of the root, which occur in the *Niphal* or *Hithpael*, make comparisons which have an unfavorable tone. Examples include Ps 28:1, 143:7: "If I become like those who go down to the pit . . . "; Ps 49:13, 21: man will be "like the beasts that perish"; Job 30:19: "I have become like dust and ashes"; Isa 14:10: all of the kings will say (to the king of Babylon) "you have become like us." The rhetorical nature of the questions in chap. 46 is enhanced even more by the use of this verb. No comparisons can be made between Yahweh and anyone or anything else.

Assyrian/Babylonian religion also speaks of the incomparability of its gods, and similar techniques are used to develop these ideas, such as rhetorical questions, the use of comparatives and negatives, and verbs denoting similarity.[57] The only term used in the biblical text that has a cognate in Assyrian/Babylonian is the verb *mšl*, related to Akkadian *mašalu*. Labuschagne concludes that most of the expressions for incomparability in Hebrew are significantly different from those used in Assyrian/Babylonian hymns. However, he refers to a fragment of a hymn to Nabu in which the incomparability of Nabu also rendered his temple, his city, and his district incomparable.[58] He says that gods were identified as incomparable if they conquered chaos and darkness.[59] In Isaiah 46, the poet asserts that Yahweh is beyond compare because he can help his people, and the comparison is made with the Babylonian gods Bel and Nebo (Nabu), who cannot do so.

***wndmh* "that we will be compared?"**

One technique or device used frequently by this author can be seen clearly here. Commentators refer to it as the "piling up" of words to make a point. Here is a line-pair (5a and 5b) of five stresses, four of which are verbs, all synonyms for 'to compare'. The pattern is a a′/a″ a, with the repetition

57. Ibid., 33–57.
58. Ibid., 44.
59. Ibid., 53.

of *dmh*, which forms an envelope (see Section III, p. 22). The device of alliteration and assonance can be seen in the threefold repetition of the 2 m. pl. impf. The line comes to an end with the chiasm of *dmh* and the change from a 2 to a 1st pl. impf. verb. The emphasis in this verse is on Yahweh, with the repetition of the first-person pronouns and first-person verbs.

According to Labuschagne,[60] the main reason that Israel called God incomparable was the fact of his miraculous intervention in history. He sees a close connection in the entire Old Testament between Yahweh's incomparability and his acts of redemption in history. The connection between incomparability and God's work as the upholder of justice and salvation is one of the main platforms of DI's teaching.[61]

46:6a. *hzlym* "ones who lavish"

The word is a *hapax legomenon*, a m. pl. participle of the root *zwl* 'to lavish'.[62] Duhm suggests that it is from the related root *zll* 'to throw away, squander'. Lam 1:8, 11 use *zll* to describe Jerusalem as one despised, or one who is made light of. Others (Cheyne, Marti) emend and read the root as *slh* 'to weigh' to achieve a parallel with *šql* in 6b and to pick up on the idol-making imagery. Another root, *nzl* 'flow, trickle', has been suggested by Kissane. He calls the form of the participle with an article "suspicious" and suggests reading a form of the verb used in Isa 48:21 (the *Hiphil* of *nzl*). On the contrary, the participle with the article is common in DI. In this poem, for instance, see lines 3cd, 12b. See also 47:8bc, 13d, 48:1bd, for examples in the other poems under study.[63]

Scholars are not in agreement about what is being described by *hzlym*. Some think that the poet is talking about the wages paid to the idol-maker.[64]

60. Ibid., 91.

61. Ibid., 102.

62. BDB 266.

63. There are five such forms in the poem in praise of Yahweh the creator in 40:12–31. In 40:22–23, 26 the form is used four times in the praise of Yahweh: *hyšb* ('he who dwells'), *hnwṭh* ('he who stretches out'), *hnwtn* ('he who brings'), and *hmwṣyʾ* ('he who brings out'). The notoriously difficult 40:20, *hmskn* ('he who is impoverished'?), is variously translated and emended. The form is a *Pual* participle, and the reference is to the idol-makers, to those who hire them, and to idols who do not move when they are set up. The poem in 40:12–31 contrasts the activity and might of Yahweh to the inactivity and powerlessness of all others. There are many similarities of vocabulary and grammar between these two poems (40:12–31 and chap. 46). Both show the incomparability of Yahweh to anyone or anything else and use a variety of devices to illustrate the comparisons and contrasts.

64. Clifford (*Fair Spoken and Persuading*) translates, "They who lavish gold from their purse, who weigh out silver on the scales."

Most, however, see this as the pouring out, weighing, or squandering of the materials from which the idol-maker will make the god.

The wealth of suggestions by modern commentators about possible meanings of the passage is instructive. The fact that so many people see so many different meanings in the passage may be a testimony to the skill of the poet in using a word to achieve just such a multiplicity of possible interpretations.[65] Paronomasia is a technique used elsewhere by this author, and we should not be surprised to find it here.

kys **"purse"**

This is a bag or purse in which money (Prov 1:14) or weights (Deut 25:13, Prov 16:11, Mic 6:11) are carried.

qnh **"beam, balance"**

The basic meaning of *qnh* is 'stalk, reed'.[66] But derived meanings refer to terms of measurement, such as "measuring rod" or a unit of measure in Ezek 40:3, 5. In Isaiah 46 *qnh* 'beam' is a synecdoche for the scales themselves. Other words used by DI for descriptions of measures are similarly rare and figurative: *šlš* 'third (measure)' and *pls* 'balance' in 40:12, in the description of God's incomparable power.

yšqlw **"they weigh out"**

The verb *šql* is used three times in DI (once elsewhere, in Isa 33:18) in significant locations: 40:12, 46:6, and 55:2. In 46:6 the subject is the lavishers, those who are hiring a smith to make an idol. In 40:12, a rhetorical question is asked: "who weighs out the mountains . . . ?" The answer to this question is: nobody but Yahweh can weigh out the mountains. In 55:2 the subject of the verb *šql* is Yahweh's people, of whom the question is asked: "Why do you weigh out money (*lmh tšqlw-ksp*) for what is not bread?" Three different subjects with the same verb (*šql*) are found in the beginning, the middle, and the end of DI (if chap. 55 is indeed the end). Yahweh (or nobody) weighs out the elements of the cosmos, the idol-worshipers weigh out money for their idols, and Yahweh's people weigh out silver for "what is not bread." The latter two payments are fruitless ventures, and the first weighing out is an incomparable act.

65. See David Gunn, "Deutero-Isaiah and the Flood" (*JBL* 94 [1975] 493–95), on poetic allusion in DI and the work of the critic in dealing with the possibility of multiple allusions. "One of the things that may least be said about Deutero-Isaiah's poetry is that it is obvious. . . . At its best it shares with other fine poetry an openness to interpretation, to which quality a certain initial opacity or ambiguity in the language often contributes significantly." On ambiguity, see Meir Weiss, *The Bible from Within* (Jerusalem: Magnes, 1984) 75–77, esp. n. 5; D. F. Payne, "Old Testament Exegesis and the Problem of Ambiguity," *Annual of the Swedish Theological Institute* 5 (1967) 48–81; G. Yee, "'Fraught with Background': Literary Ambiguity in II Samuel 11," *Int* 42 (1988) 240–53.

66. BDB 889.

"Ones who lavish . . . they weigh out"

These two lines are balanced in stress (3+3) and have parallel elements, with the pattern ABC/B′C′A′. *Gold* and *silver* are a common word-pair. The prepositional phrases "from a purse" and "in a beam" are grammatically parallel. However, none of the words is exactly parallel or synonymous. The subject of the two lines is "those who lavish" (m. pl. participle) and the verb is "they weigh out" (3 m. pl. impf.), so that the combined lines can be paraphrased: "the lavishers weigh out into a balance gold and silver from a purse."[67] The lines abound with alliteration: *he/zayin* and *zayin/he* in *hzlym* and *zhb*, the repetition of *kap/samek* in *mkys* and *wksp*, and the repetition of the *qop* in *bqnh* and *yšqlw*.

46:6c. *ṣwrp* "smith"

The *Qal* participle as a noun usually refers to smelters or refiners who fashion idols.[68] The verb *ṣrp* is usually used figuratively of God testing or refining his people. (See comment on 48:10 below.)

***wyᶜśhw ᵓl* "and he makes it a god"**

The construction is unusual and similar to the one found in Isa 44:15, *ᶜśhw psl* ('he made it a graven image'). We might expect the prepositional phrase *lᵓl*, as in Isa 44:17 (*lᵓl ᶜśh*) or Hos 2:10 (*wzhb ᶜśw lbᶜl*). The RSV and JPSV read, "He makes *it* into a god." The NEB translates the pronominal suffix "and fashion them into a god," presumably in reference to the gold and silver. The JB eliminates the pronoun from the translation, reflecting 1QIsa[a], which omits the suffix *-hw*. The 3 m. s. pronominal suffix occurs four times on the imperfect verb in vv. 6–7. In v. 7 it refers to the idol and what is done to it: they lift it, they bear it, they set it. Other texts can clarify what the object of the verb is here. In addition to the extended passage in 44:9–20, descriptions of the making of idols from Judges and Exodus shed more light on the process described here, as well as on the larger picture of anti-idolatry sections in DI.

In Judg 17:1–5 Micah's mother takes 200 pieces of silver to a smith (*ṣwrp*) and he makes it (*wyᶜśhw*) into a graven and molten image (*psl wmskh*). The object of the verb *ᶜśh* is the silver with which the smith makes

67. This is an example of synonymous-sequential parallelism, as described by P. D. Miller in "Synonymous-Sequential Parallelism in the Psalms" (*CBQ* 61 [1980] 256–60). Other terms applied to such a construction are *enjambment*, or *run-over line*, referring to a sentence or clause that does not end when the line ends but runs over into the next line. See Watson, *Classical Hebrew Poetry*, 333 for examples of different types of enjambment. This line-pair would fall into his definition of an "integral enjambment," occurring when two halves of a line form a single sentence.

68. See also Jer 10:9, 14; 51:17; Isa 40:19, 41:7; and Judg 17:4 for this usage. A more general sense is meant in Prov. 25:4 and Neh 3:8, 32.

the idol. The making of the golden calf in Exod 32:4 is described in the same way: the people take off their gold, give it to Aaron, and forming it with an engraving tool, Aaron makes it (*wyᶜśhw*) into a molten calf. In both cases the suffix refers to the material provided—by Micah's mother and by the people. In Isa 44:15, after the lengthy description of the planting and tending of trees, some of that material is taken and used by the smith to make an image (*ᶜśhw psl*).[69] In chap. 46, the object of the verb is the material which is used by the smith to make the idol.

There are other similarities between this section of chap. 46 and the satire on idol-making in chap. 44:9–20. In 44:15 and 17, as in 46:6, after the idol (*ᵓl*) or graven image (*psl*) is made, he falls down before it (*ysgd*), and worships it (*yštḥw*). In chap. 44, it is the idol-maker himself who worships the image he has made, not another group, as in chap. 46. The idol-maker in 44:17 also cries out to the image he has made and says, "Deliver me, for you are my god!" But it is not able to deliver him (v. 20); the outcome is the same in 46:7e.

The verb *ᶜśh* in 46:4 was unusual (as stated above, p. 39). It stood somewhat outside the pattern of the synonyms for 'carrying' and 'bearing' that formed that verse. There the subject was Yahweh. Here the subject of *ᶜśh* is the "smelter" or smith. This is another way of making a comparison and contrast between Yahweh as one who makes, and others who make things.

As will be developed further, the main activities described in these lines are not limited to the work of the goldsmith, but include those of the people who hire him to make a god. The following verbs are used in close succession to describe what they do: the word-pair *sgd* and *hštḥw* 'bow down, prostrate oneself' (found only in DI in chaps. 44 and 46); the verbs *nśᵓ* and *sbl* 'lift up, bear', repeated from vv. 1, 3, and 4; the verb *nwḥ* 'place, give rest to'. These are all 3 m. pl. impf. verbs. Of the seven 3 m. pl. impf. verbs used in 6c–7b, six are bound together by the device of alliteration in the repetition of the sibilants *śin*, *šin* and *samek* (notice also the sibilant *ṣade* in *ṣwrp*).

The subjects of these verbs are important to identify. Clifford states that all these are "the unified action of a single person hiring a smith at great cost and carrying the statue home." He states that the 3 m. pl. verbs are used for the passive, but oddly, his translation does not reflect this. He appears to be attempting to connect the subject of the 3 m. pl. verbs with the 3 m. s. verbs of lines 7d and 7e. As will be demonstrated below, this connection is incorrect and misleads the reader as to the identity of the parties involved.[70]

69. See also 2 Chr 24:14, where the workers bring silver to the king and to Jehoiada and make it (*wyᶜśhw*) into vessels for the temple.

70. See commentary on v. 7, p. 49.

46:7a. ***yś⁾hw ᶜl ktp ysblhw***
"they lift it on their shoulders, bear it up"

The line contains the usual three stresses but is long in respect to syllables—eleven in all. The expression *nś⁾ ᶜl ktp* occurs elsewhere: in Isa 49:22 kings will carry the daughters of Israel on their shoulders; Isa 30:6 refers to beasts of burdens (asses and camels) carrying treasures on their shoulders; Judg 16:3 has the expression in reference to Samson bearing the doors and posts of the city gates. The prepositional phrase *ᶜl ktp* can be read with the first verb of this line, *nś⁾* 'they carry it on (their) shoulders'. But it can also be seen to modify the following verb *ysblhw* 'on (their) shoulders they bear it'. *škm*, a synonym for *ktp*, appears with the verb *sbl* in Gen 49:15; it also occurs with the noun forms of the same root in Ps 81:7 and Isa 9:3; the prepositional phrase *mᶜl škm* occurs in Isa 10:27 and 14:25. Here in 46:7a, *ᶜl ktp* functions as a double-duty prepositional phrase, examples of which are found elsewhere in the poetry of DI. The verbs are identical to one another in syllable count. Alliteration in the use of the sibilants *šin* and *samek* also binds this long line together, as well as the assonance in the use of the 3 m. pl. ending with the 3 m. s. pronoun suffix on both verbs.

46:7b. ***wynyḥhw tḥtyw wyᶜmd***
"then they set it in its place and it stands"

According to BDB,[71] *tḥtyw* is an idiom meaning 'in one's place, where one stands'. The image is set in place by those who have carried it on their shoulders.[72] As above, here is another case where the verb *wynyḥhw*, the following *wyᶜmd*, or both. The arrangement of these lines in the MT indicates the ambiguity of the passage. Andrew Wilson[73] compares the formation of this word with that of *yḥdw*. He considers it to be parallel in this passage with "shoulder" and "its place."

46:7c. ***mmqwmw l⁾ ymyš***
"from its place it does not move"

Here is yet another prepositional phrase that could modify either the preceding or following verb. There are two *waw* conjunctions in v. 7abc and three impf. verbs without the *waw*. The presence and absence of *waws*

71. BDB 1065.

72. According to Oppenheim (*Ancient Mesopotamia*, 186), the image used in Babylonian processions resided in the sanctuary, where it rested on a pedestal above the level of human activities. The image "paralleled in all its essential aspects" the relationship of the king to his palace and to his city.

73. Andrew Wilson, *The Nations in Deutero-Isaiah: A Study on Composition and Structure* (Lewiston, N.Y.: Edwin Mellen, 1986) 155.

in the passage allow the reader latitude (and also cause some confusion) on how to read and arrange the lines. We would expect a *waw* on *ysblhw* if it were to be read apart from the prepositional phrase. Conversely, we might expect no *waw* on *yᶜmd* if it were modified by *tḥtyw.* The fact that there is no conjunction separating the last four words allows a variety of interpretations and arrangements of lines. This can be seen as a line-trio with a pattern 3+3+2, and a syllable count of 11, 10, 7. The lines are grammatically parallel in a pattern abc/abc/bc, except for the absence of a verb in the last line: verb/prep. phrase/verb; verb/prep. phrase/verb; prep phrase/verb. In the first two lines the prepositional phrase serves a double-duty purpose for the verbs preceding and following. In the last two lines, the verb *yᶜmd* serves as a double-duty verb for both the prepositional phrases preceding and following.

There has been a shift in these lines from the 3 m. pl. verb form "they lift, they bear, they set" to the 3 m. s. verb "it stands, it does not move." The emphasis in vv. 6–7b is on the action of the people who were manipulating their idol, and the profusion of verbs emphasizes the frantic activity in which these individuals were engaged—they squandered, they paid, they hired, they fell down, they worshiped, they lifted, they bore, they set in place. There are eight plural verbs or verb forms in vv. 6–7c. The flurry of activity on the part of the idol manipulators is contrasted with the verbs describing the idol's inactivity.

46:7b–e. *yᶜmd . . . lᵓ ymyš . . . lᵓ yᶜnh . . . lᵓ ywšyᶜnw* "it stands . . . it does not move . . . does not answer . . . does not save"

The verb *ymyš* from the root *mwš* or *myš* 'depart, remove' [74] is used mostly of inanimate things. Along with *ᶜmd* it is an effective contrast to the activities of the idol-makers, mentioned above. The idol does not depart from its place. The same root *mwš* appears in one other place in Isaiah 40–55, in 54:10,[75] where it is used as a figure of the immovability of God's steadfast love, *ḥsd.* Even if the mountains should depart (*ymwšw*), God's *ḥsd* will not depart (*ymwš*). A similar use occurs in Exod 13:22, where the pillar of cloud and pillar of fire (i.e., God's presence), do not depart from the people. The immovability of the idol is seen to be a negative feature in Isaiah 46, because it stresses inability to move. In Isa 54:10, and in Exod 13:22, immovability is a positive feature, stressing the fact that God's presence will not be removed from his people.

74. BDB 559.

75. See W. A. M. Beuken, "Isaiah LIV: The Multiple Identity of the Person Addressed," *Oudtestamentische Studiën* 19 (1974) 53–54.

These four verbs describe the stolid idol that has been made. It stands, but it does nothing—it does not move, does not answer, does not save. This is reminiscent of the idol passages in Jer 10:5ff. and Ps 115:3–7, in which the idols were characterized by their inability to act in any way.

ʾp yṣʿq **"he even cries to it"**

The same adverb (*ʾp*) was used above in 6d, where it had emphatic force. Here it has the same emphatic force as it describes the foolishness of calling upon the idol.

The verb form used here is 3 m. s., a change from the plural form used in vv. 6–7b. It is true that the indefinite personal subject ("they, one") can be expressed by the 3 m. s., as well as the 3 m. pl., and the plural of the participle,[76] all of which forms are found in vv. 6–7. The subject here is a person or persons who call upon the idol that has been made. The numerous plural verbs and verb forms have been discussed above; they refer to the people who have come to the smith with the request to make a god. The remaining singular forms refer either to the idol that stands still in its place, or to the smith who makes the idol (line 6c) and to the one who cries to the idol in line 7d. In 44:9–20 the person who made the idol also worshiped it, and cried out to it to save him.[77] In chap. 46, because of the shift from the plural to singular verb, it is also possible to identify the idol-maker with the one who cries to the idol for deliverance.

The similarity between chap. 46 and Exodus 32 has been noted above. In Exod 32:4 the person who makes the idols is Aaron;[78] he also proclaims a feast and afterwards leads the people in bringing offerings to the calf. Freedman[79] suggests that the activity of the idol-maker of chap. 46 can be compared with that of Aaron, the chief priest of Israel. Just as Aaron's action led the people to violate the covenant and jeopardize their existence, here too the actions of the idol-maker may have dire consequences.

The verb *ṣʿq* with the preposition *ʾl* is usually used for crying out to people or to God. Only here in Isa 46:8 is the object of the cry an idol.[80] The verb is used one other time in DI, in 42:2 in the description of the servant who does not cry, or lift up, or make his voice heard. Elsewhere in Isaiah (19:20, 33:7, 65:14), it is always a cry of distress. In 19:20, this cry of distress will be answered by Yahweh's sending a savior (*mwšyʿ*) to

76. GKC §53d, f, i / pp. 145–46.

77. See *Notes on Text and Translation* on line 6c, above (pp. 45–46).

78. Aaron is also identified as the idol-maker in Exod 32:35, though there is a difficulty with the translation, and the people themselves also may be implicated in this activity.

79. D. N. Freedman, private correspondence.

80. BDB 858.

deliver (*nṣl*). There is no one to save (*lʾywšyʿnw*) the idol-worshiper in his time of distress in Isa 46:7. All the actions in 6–7 are performed by those who deal with idols. The only verb referring to an idol that is not negated is *ʿmd*: the idol stands still, stops, is inactive. The utter ineffectiveness of the idols ends this section, in contrast to the previous section, which ended with the massing of verbs indicating the vitality and dynamic activity of Yahweh (lines 4cd).

46:8a. *whtʾššw* "stand firm"

Most commentators are in agreement here that "the meaning of this word has never been satisfactorily elucidated" (Whybray). The word is a *hapax legomenon.* Some scholars propose roots based on Aramaic loan-words, or Akkadian analogies. Others emend the text in their attempts to clear up the difficulties. The variety of suggested readings is listed below:

1. 'Found, establish, make yourselves secure, be steadfast' (suggested by Torrey, Volz, JPSV and others). According to Torrey, this "seems to have been the reading which all the old versions, except possibly the Greek, had before them." It may be derived from a semitic root meaning 'be founded, firmly planted' (Arabic *ʾassasa,* Akk. *ašāšu,* Rabb. Heb. *ʾšš,* Aramaic *ʾš*). Muilenburg considers Torrey's suggestion to be the best solution and prefers 'put yourself on a secure foundation' or 'be assured'. Volz rearranges this verse, placing the problematic word before *yʿmdw* in v. 7. He reads, "it is firmly planted, and it stands there."
2. 'Show yourselves obedient, attentive' (suggested by North). He cites a Sumero-Akkadian glossary in which *aššišu* is equated with Heb. *šmʿ* 'listening' and infers the meaning reflected in his translation. This equation is questionable, and his translation not convincing.
3. 'Show yourselves men' (Qimḥi, KJV, Leene, and others). This reading is based on the proposal of a denominative verb form *ʾyš.* Leene interprets the phrase to mean that Israelites are supposed to behave like human beings, that is, they are to move away from idol-making. He opposes the translation "stand firm," because in DI the making of images is not associated with instability, but with blindness and stupidity.[81]
4. 'Be ashamed' (Westermann reads with the Vulgate *confundamini* from a possible *htbwššw*).
5. 'Show yourselves intelligent, consider' (Syriac and RSV), from a reading of *htbwnnw.* Duhm suggests a similar translation, *verdet*

81. H. Leene, "Isaiah 46.8: Summons to be Human?" *JSOT* 30 (1984) 112–15.

vernunftig 'be sensible', based on the same root from which Hebrew *twšyh* is derived.[82] Gileadi translates 'come to your senses'.

6. 'Acknowledge your guilt' (Cheyne), based on a proposed emendation *htʾšmw.*
7. 'Groan' (LXX).
8. 'Be dismayed' or 'abandon hope' (NEB, JB). JB claims to be following the Syriac, but see #5 above. NEB rearranges the order of the words in 8ab, and reads as follows:

   Remember this, you rebels,
   consider it well, and abandon hope.

   This rendering, as well as the NEB's translation of v. 12, seems to assume a different audience from other translations.
9. "Remettez vous cela en memoire pour ranimer votre ardeur" (Bonnard). Bonnard imagines a root related to ʾš 'fire' and compares the word of God to a fire (citing Jer 23:29, 20:9; Ps 39:4).
10. Editors of BHS suggest that 8a be deleted entirely, perhaps to achieve a balance between vv. 8b and 9a.

In his discussion of intentional alliteration in Second Isaiah, L. Boadt[83] discusses the appearances of unusual or difficult words and grammatical forms in a given text and demonstrates how rhetorical criticism deals with these manifestations. He selects a number of passages from Second Isaiah and discusses the unusual or infrequent use of prepositions and the appearance of unusual word forms. While he does not directly discuss the word in question, he does comment on 46:8 from the point of view of the unusual use of the preposition ʿ*l* in combination with *hšybw.* He points out several alliterative links between 8a and b that serve to form a step-pattern through the line as a whole, including the repetition of *taw* and *he.* He fails to carry his thesis through (the use of unusual word forms to achieve alliteration) in treating *htʾššw,* because it also serves in the development of the step-pattern. Not only is the repetition of *he* and *taw* part of the pattern, but the repetition of *šin* as well, in *htʾššw, hšybw,* and *pwšʿym.* This strengthens the case against emending the text.

I have translated "stand firm" for the following reasons:

1. Most ancient versions seem to be based on this difficult reading.
2. None of the proposed emendations is compelling.
3. Alliteration is a frequent device used by this author, and the use of the unusual *htʾššw* emphasizes the alliterative pattern.

82. See BDB 444.
83. Boadt, "Intentional Alliteration."

4. It is typical of DI, in this poem in particular, to develop an idea by drawing comparisons and contrasts between various figures in the poem. Here a comparison is made between the motionless, powerless idols who "stand still" (and are not able to do anything) and the transgressors, who are commanded to be steadfast, to "stand firm." In the case of the idols, their standing still is a show of their incapacity. In the case of the transgressors, their standing still is of another sort. It is perhaps a demonstration of their return to faithfulness. Depending on who these transgressors are, it could be a command to them to stand in awe or fear of Yahweh who commands them. In any case, in view of the idolatry just mentioned and the serious charge against the people for being "rebels," the verb must be understood to have a forceful sense.

46:8b. *pwšᶜym* "O rebels"

Most scholars consider the rebels or "transgressors" to be the people who turned from Yahweh by practicing idolatry. Skinner points to a growing sense of antagonism between DI and at least a portion of his audience from 45:9 onwards. He also cites 46:12, 48:8, 53:12, and 66:24. Wade is more specific in identifying the listeners. He considers this term to be directed to Jews living in community in postexilic times rather than at the close of the exile, also citing Isa 57:3, 65:1, and 66:17. Beuken refers to the same term in 43:25, where it is obvious that Jacob/Israel is being addressed.

It is necessary to explore in more depth (1) the audience being addressed and (2) the nature of the crime or crimes that gave rise to labeling this audience as "rebels." The term *pšᶜ* has its origins in political life[84] (1 Kgs 12:19; 2 Kgs 1:1; 3:5, 7; 8:22) where it refers to revolt against a king. It is also often used in the Bible to mean a sin against God. Of the usage in Lam 1:5, Hillers says the word *pšᶜym* has connotations of breach of covenant. The acts of rebellion in Hos 7:13 and 8:1 involve, in 7:12–16, submission to Assyrian gods (and treachery against Yahweh), slandering Yahweh, involvement in Canaanite religion,[85] and in 8:1, transgression against the covenant, choosing kings without Yahweh's approval, making idols, and contracting treaties with other nations.[86] On the use of *pšᶜ* in Isaiah 56–66, Polan sees it in contexts of idolatry and sorcery in 57:3–5,[87]

84. D. Hillers, *Lamentations* (AB 7A; Garden City, N.Y.: Doubleday, 1972) 22.

85. Andersen and Freedman, *Hosea*, 471–72.

86. Ibid., 489.

87. G. Polan, *In the Ways of Justice toward Salvation: A Rhetorical Analysis of Isaiah 56–59* (New York: Peter Lang, 1986) 130–31. He also relates 57:4 to 58:1 (pp. 191–97). The root "carries the connotation of the nature behind sinful acts . . . points to

and in 59:12–13, suggests it is a "broad or more expansive word for sin"[88] involving, among other misdeeds, denying Yahweh and turning away from God. The rebellions of Jacob and the sins (*ḥṭʾh*) of Israel in Mic 1:5 will result in Yahweh's destruction of her images, her hires, and her idols. In Mic 3:8, Jacob's rebellion and Israel's sin (*ḥṭʾh*) are mentioned in the context of corrupt leaders: prophets, seers, and diviners (vv. 6–7); rulers, priests, and prophets (vv. 9–11). Those who turn aside the needy, trample the poor, or afflict the righteous are guilty of rebellion in Amos 5:12.

The grievous nature of these rebellions is alluded to by Dahood[89] in his discussion of Psalm 51, a prayer of contrition, which Dahood suggests may come from the sixth century because of similarities with P and DI. As covenant violations, rebellions of vassal against king, these acts are serious offenses. "We may accordingly assume that when *pšʿ* is mentioned in relation to God, a violation of one of the ten commandments is involved."[90]

The verb and noun that derive from it are used several times in chaps. 40–55. It first occurs in 43:25, where Yahweh promises to blot out and not remember (*zkr*) the rebellions and sins of Jacob/Israel. In 43:27 the statement is made that Israel's first father sinned, and the mediators rebelled. Most commentators suggest that the first father is Jacob but are undecided about the exact referents for mediators. Muilenburg suggests the possibility of Moses and the prophets. The charge against Jacob/Israel in 43:22ff. is that the people did not call upon Yahweh and did not bring offerings or sacrifices. The rebellions (*pšʿ*) and sin (*ḥṭʾt*), which God will sweep away in 44:22, are mentioned after the long section against idol-makers, a description Jacob/Israel is charged to remember.[91] The term *rebel* is applied to Israel in 48:8. Because of the rebellions of the people, they were sold and their mother was put away (50:1). The root appears several times in the servant song of chap. 53 (vv. 5, 8, 12).

The offenses of which the people are guilty on several occasions in DI are forgetting Yahweh, and/or idolatry, which would fit Dahood's understanding of *pšʿ* as a covenant violation or the breaking of one of the

---

the essential character of rebellion . . . what lies at the heart of a wicked deed" (p. 191). Rather than designating a particular fault in a list of sins, it represents the "heart of the revolt" (197).

88. Ibid., 284.

89. Dahood, *Psalms II*, 3.

90. Ibid. Dahood cites Rolf Knierim (*Die Hauptbegriffe für Sünde im Alten Testament* [Gütersloh: Gerd Mohn, 1965] 113–43) for an extensive treatment of the root and its connotations.

91. The expression in 44:21, *zkr ʾlh*, is similar to that in 46:8, *zkrw zʾt*. Both are imperatives charging Israel to bring to mind the worshiping of idols.

commandments.[92] The rhetorical question formula "who is like me?" is part of the context of these passages, and the charge to "remember this," after an extended discussion of idol-makers and idol-worshipers, is common to both vv. 44:9ff. and chap. 46.[93] The people are to remember not only the idol-making and idol-worship that are occurring in their midst, but also the infamous first idol-making event, which took place at the foot of Mt. Sinai and enraged Yahweh to the point of threatening extermination of the community.

The identification of the "rebellious ones" has wider ramifications for a study of DI. There is a consensus that the second half of the book of Isaiah (40–66) is further divided into Second Isaiah (chaps. 40–55) and Third Isaiah (56–66). This division is based on the theory that chaps. 40–55 are addressed to a community living in exile in Babylon on the eve of Cyrus's edict of liberation and that chaps. 56–66 are from a later period and different locale, the Palestinian community at the time of the rebuilding of the second temple. It is maintained that the Palestinian community was beset by problems of divisiveness and that two basic groups are portrayed in this section of Isaiah: the righteous ones who walk in the way of Yahweh and the children of transgression, who do not (see 57:1ff. for an example of this division). It is Paul Hanson's thesis[94] that chaps. 56–66 represent the views of a visionary group or community in opposition to the group of officials in charge of the restoration of Jerusalem.

In chap. 46 (as well as chaps. 43, 44, and 48) the rebels' offenses are forgetting God and worshiping other gods. If it can be shown that the rebellious ones, the transgressors of Isaiah 40–55, are identified with those of chaps. 56–66, there may be less reason to propose the existence of divided groups in Palestine during the period of the second temple. The mention of the procession involving Bel and Nebo at the beginning of the chapter suggests a setting in Babylon rather than in Israel or Judea. The fact that there is a danger of the Jews in exile being attracted to the worship of these deities may be an indication that the setting is at the end of the period of exile, rather than the beginning, when the people's memory of Yahweh and Zion was fresh in their minds, as in Psalm 137.

92. The parallel between *pšᶜ* and *ḥṭʾt* in 44:22 was mentioned above. The main characterization of the worship of the golden calf in Exodus 32 is *ḥṭʾh gdlh* (see Exod 32:21, 30). Exod 32:32 and 34 refer simply to *ḥṭʾh*.

93. Spykerboer (*Structure and Composition*, 151) also discusses the connection between 44:23 and 46:13. He is influenced by Lack, who also connects the larger units 42:18–44:23 and 44:24–46:13. The final verses are similar in that they both refer to the 'beauty' or 'glory' (*ytpʾr/tpʾr*) of Israel.

94. Paul D. Hanson, *The Dawn of Apocalyptic: The Historical and Sociological Roots of Jewish Apocalyptic Eschatology* (rev. ed.; Philadelphia: Fortress, 1979).

BDB indicates several objects of *pšᶜ*: nations, individuals, or God.[95] The verb *pšᶜ* and the m. noun are used several times throughout Isaiah, from chap. 1 through chap. 66, usually with the meaning of transgression against Yahweh. In fact, the book of Isaiah is framed by the notion of people in rebellion against God: 1:2, the introduction to the book, announces God's case against his sons who *pšᶜw by* 'rebel against me'. Isa 66:24 concludes with the grim punishment of those who 'rebel against me' *pšᶜym by.* Other than the additional appearance of the verb in 1:28, its use is restricted to chaps. 40–66.[96] The noun *pšᶜ*, except for one occurrence in 24:20, is also restricted to chaps. 40–66.[97] It should be observed that the word appears both in Second and Third Isaiah and does not necessarily point to the existence of divisive groups in a Palestinian setting during the reconstruction of the temple.

hšybw . . . ᶜl lb **"bring back . . . to mind"**

The Hiphil of *šwb . . . lb* with the preposition *ᶜl* is unusual; in fact, according to L. Boadt,[98] there are no other occurrences of the expression.[99] More common is the preposition *ʾl*, as in Lam 3:21 (*ʾšyb ʾl lby* 'I will bring it to my mind') and Deut 4:39 (*hšbt ʾl lbbk* 'you will bring to mind').[100] In Deut 4:39, the people are ordered to 'know and bring to mind' *ky yhwh hwʾ hʾlhym bšmym mmᶜl wᶜl hʾrṣ mtḥt ʾyn ᶜwd* 'that Yahweh is God—in heaven above and on the earth below there is no other'. The mourner in Lamentations brings to mind both his miseries and his belief in the steadfast love of God. It is the blessing and the curse ("all these things") that the audience is to bring to mind, in Deut 30:1, and in bringing them to mind the people will return to God and obey his voice.

46:8a, 9a. ***zkrw*** **"remember"**

There are four imperatives that begin this section of the poem. *Zkr* is repeated in 8a and 9a; a synonym, *hšybw ᶜl lb* (and the difficult *htʾššw*, discussed above) is placed between the two in 8b. Some of this language is identical to that of Lam 3:19–21. The three verses in Lamentations 3 make

95. BDB 833.

96. Isa 43:27, 46:8, 48:8, 53:12 (2 times), and 59:13.

97. 43:25; 44:22; 50:1; 53:5, 8; 57:4; 58:1; 59:12; and 59:20.

98. Boadt, "Intentional Alliteration," 359.

99. Whybray refers to this unusual construction. He draws a connection between its use here and in 44:19 and concludes that the verses might have come from the same hand. However, Whybray and Volz have incorrectly read the preposition as *ᶜl* in 44:19. According to BHS and BHK, the reading is *wlʾ yšyb ʾl* (not *ᶜl*) *bw.* This weakens Whybray's position even more on the questionable status of this verse in the poem.

100. See also Deut 30:1.

up the stanza in the acrostic poem beginning with the letter *zayin.* The words that initiate each verse of the tricolon are *zkr*, *zkwr*, and *zʾt.*

zkr . . .
zkwr tzkwr . . .
zʾt ʾšyb ʾl lby . . .
(Lam 3:19–21)

Isa 46:8–9 is also a line-trio and repeats a number of the same words, though there is no attempt at an alphabetic acrostic poem.

zkrw zʾt . . .
hšybw . . . ʿl lb
zkrw . . .
(Isa 46:8–9)

This may be an example of a word-trio (not just a word-pair), the combination of *zkr* twice with *šwb* (*Hiph.*) . . . *lb.* The common element is the combination of *zkr* twice with the *Hiphil* of *šwb ʾl* (*ʿl*) *lb.*

Some scholars read v. 8 as the end of v. 7 and begin a new stanza with v. 9. I read 8–9a as a line-trio, seeing it as a unit. The pattern of the parallel lines may be diagrammed as follows:

a b a′
a′ c
a b′

Each begins with a plural imperative, the verbs are synonymous, and in the case of *zkr* there is repetitive parallelism. Each occurrence of *zkr* is followed by an object: *zʾt* and *rʾšnwt mʿwlm.* The subject of these plural imperatives, *pwšʿym,* is in the middle line and serves quadruple duty for all of the verbs. Some scholars[101] consider vv. 5–8 to be editorial additions to the section and fail to see the relationship between vv. 8 and 9. Whybray is led to the extreme observation that 9a "lacks a parallel and it is possible that some words have fallen out." Since he ignores the obvious parallels with 8a and b, he has to create an extra line to maintain the structure of parallelism.

46:9a. *rʾšnwt* "first things"

The word *this* in 8a is parallel with "the first things of old" in 9a. It is not necessary to hold that because *zʾt* is singular and *rʾšnwt* is plural, they cannot be parallel, or that they must be referring to totally unrelated things. There have been extensive studies done on the subject of the "first

101. Köhler, Elliger, Westermann, Melugin, and Whybray.

things" (and the "last things") in DI.[102] Before making comparisons with the rest of the book on the various suggestions of scholars about these matters, a close examination of the verses at hand should be undertaken to see what meaning the terms have in their immediate context.

Lines 8ab and 9a call the audience to remember not just one thing, but several. They are to keep in mind what has previously been stated: that Yahweh carried them, made them, and delivered them (lines 3c–4d); they are reminded of the folly of idol-makers whose gods do no such things (lines 5a–7e). The following verses also describe things that Israel ought to keep in mind: that Yahweh is El, that he knows things that are going to happen, that he turns history to his plans, and so on. Like the people in Deut 4:39ff., who are to remember that Yahweh alone is God (*hʾlhym*) in the heavens and on the earth, the audience in Isa 46:9 is urged to remember "that [he is] El and there is no other." In the immediate context, the things of old are cited to support the belief that Yahweh is El, and there is no other.[103]

North considers the first things to be limited to the exodus, as in 43:18. Clifford believes they refer to the creation-exodus-conquest cycle. Muilenburg, Whybray, and Westermann see the first things as a reference to Israel's history in general. Gileadi translates, 'prophecies of the events of old'. There is no reason to limit the first things to the exodus (with North) or the creation-exodus-conquest cycle (with Clifford). Habel[104] interprets the references to the first things in DI as the "fulfilled words" of God the creator and includes among these fulfilled words creation events or normative events in Israel's distant past, rather than recent acts of Yahweh. I have referred above to Gunn's thesis of multiple allusions in DI. He demonstrates that the passages in DI referring to the drying up of waters are allusions to the creation, the exodus, and the flood. Here, the first (or "former") things of old could be understood as alluding to the creation or the exodus or the conquest or any momentous event of Israel's past. With Gunn, I agree that "one particular allusion . . . need not necessarily exhaust the allusive content of a line."[105]

102. For a bibliography on the numerous studies that have been written on the subject of the "first things" and the "last things" in DI, see Stuhlmueller, *Creative Redemption*, 136.

103. N. Habel ("Appeal to Ancient Tradition as a Literary Form," *ZAW* 88 [1975] 265) says of the allusions to ancient traditions in DI that "the prophet is not so much emphasizing the greatness of the events of antiquity as he is asserting the priority of the divine word that initiated those events."

104. Ibid., 265; see also 265 n. 27.

105. Gunn, "Deutero-Isaiah and the Flood," 495.

46:9b. *ky ʾnky ʾl* "that I am El"

Most translations read "*for* I am God (El)," taking the conjunction *ky* as causal. Others (JB) read it as an emphatic. However, *ky* also has a nominalizing force, especially introducing noun clauses.[106] This is not a demand on Yahweh's part that people remember the past *because* he is God, as though God were using his authority to see that they followed the imperatives. The audience is asked to look to their past in order to be reminded that Yahweh is their God and there is no other.[107]

46:9bc. *ky ʾnky ʾl wʾyn ʿwd* "that I am El and there is no other,
***ʾlhym wʾps kmwny* Elohim, and there is none like me."**

This is like the previous statement in v. 4. Similar assertions on Yahweh's part that there is none like him appear throughout the first part of DI. Isa 45:5 and 6 contain parallel assertions:

v. 5	*ʾny yhwh wʾyn ʿwd*	*zwlty ʾyn ʾlhym*
	I am Yahweh and there is no other	Except me there is no god
v. 6	*ky ʾps blʿdy*	*ʾny yhwh wʾyn ʿwd*[108]
	That there is none besides me	I am Yahweh and there is no other

45:21 and 22 make similar assertions with some variations:

v. 21	*hlwʾ ʾny yhwh*	*wʾyn ʿwd ʾlhym mblʿdy*
	Am I not Yahweh?	And there is no other god besides me
	ʾl ṣdyq wmwšyʿ	*ʾyn zwlty*
	El the Righteous and Savior	There is none except me
v. 22	*ky ʾny ʾl wʾyn ʿwd*	
	For I am El and there is no other	

These are all claims that Yahweh is the one and only deity, claims that are supported and proven by various activities. These activities include the foretelling of events in the past and events in times yet to come, the sending of Cyrus, the creation of the world from chaos, as well as the saving events of the Exodus.

106. R. J. Williams, *Hebrew Syntax: An Outline* (2d ed.; Toronto: University of Toronto Press, 1976) 73.

107. See Delitzsch: "*zikhru* is connected with the accusative of the object of remembrance, and *ky* points to its result." See Levy, Von Orelli, Slotki, and Whybray for the nominalizing of *ky* in 46:9b.

108. Verse 18 has this assertion following three participles describing Yahweh's creative powers (*bwrʾ*, *yṣr*, and *ʿśh*) and two affirmations that he is god (*hwʾ ʾlhym*) and creator (*hwʾ kwnnh*).

In chaps. 45 and 46, Yahweh identifies himself by his names Yahweh, El, and Elohim. Muilenburg points to the covenant connotations of the words "I am Yahweh" (cf. commentary on 43:11). Westermann emphasizes that this is a "formula of revelation."[109] Clifford sees 46:9–11 as describing an encounter with Yahweh's very self, the divine "I." But it is to be noted that the name Yahweh does not appear in this poem. The two names Yahweh claims for himself here are El and Elohim. Zimmerli considers this to be an example "of the free variation of the formula of self-introduction."[110]

The word *ʾl* occurs 15 times in DI, all between chaps. 40 and 46 (it appears a total of 21 times in the whole book of Isaiah; all other occurrences are in chaps. 9–31). In DI *ʾl* refers both to the God of Israel and, as a generic, to the images made by the idol-makers. In the poem against idol-makers 44:9–20, *ʾl* is one of the words used to describe the idol that is fashioned (vv. 10 and 15 and twice in 17). Those who worship idols are called ignorant because they pray to *ʾl*, who does not save, in 45:20. Immediately following (in v. 21) is Yahweh's assertion that there is no other *ʾlhym*, that he is *ʾl ṣdyq*, and in v. 22, *ʾny ʾl*. In chap. 46, *ʾl* is also used to refer both to an idol (line 6c) and to Yahweh (line 9b). Clearly, a contrast is intended between the *ʾl* of the idol-maker, and *ʾl* as a reference to Yahweh. The question posed in 5ab—"to whom will you compare me . . . ?"—is answered in lines 9bc: "there is no other . . . there is none like me." Yahweh is not to be compared to the *ʾl* of the idol-makers. The reference to *ʾl* here and in chap. 44 is satirical. In fact, there is no *ʾl* except for Yahweh.

46:10a. *mgyd mrʾšyt* "one who declares from the beginning . . . "

Connected to the "I" of *kmwny* (Delitzsch points to the connection between vv. 9c and 10) is a series of three participles that are used to demonstrate Yahweh's claims to divinity. This is the third in a series of participles used in the poem (see 3cd, 6a) to clarify or define certain assertions. What is being demonstrated in the poem is Yahweh's power in several areas: his word is powerful; he can make and support his people through all times; he can affect the course of history. This third series of participles emphasizes the power of Yahweh's declarations using synonyms for *ngd*, *ʾmr* and *qrʾ*. Here Yahweh's power to announce things before they occur is affirmed.

109. See W. Zimmerli, *I Am Yahweh* (trans D. W. Stott; Atlanta: John Knox, 1982) 1–28; cf. S. H. Blank, "Studies in Deutero-Isaiah," *HUCA* 15 (1940) 14ff.

110. Zimmerli, *I Am Yahweh*, 19.

mrʾšyt ʾḥryt **"from the beginning the end time"**

His power goes back to the days of creation, *rʾšyt* ('the beginning'), to times of old (*mqdm*). In those ancient days he foretold things that were to come, 'the end' (*ʾḥryt*), things not yet done. The parallelism with the second half of the line extends and clarifies this notion: *mrʾšyt* ('from the beginning') is parallel with *mqdm* ('from ancient days'). *Qdm* can be an indication of temporal or geographical place. Here it indicates temporality.[111] The parallel of *rʾšyt* with *qdm* occurs also in Prov 8:22, where Yahweh's work at the beginning of creation is discussed; *ʾḥryt* ('the end') is further defined (in 10b) by its semantic parallel *ʾšr lʾ nʿśw* ('things not yet made/done').

46:10b. ***ʾšr lʾ nʿśw*** **"things not yet done"**

There is an element of ambiguity here. Does *lʾ nʿśh* refer to things yet to be created or to events which have yet to occur? The verb *ʿśh* appears five times in this poem: in lines 4c, 6c, 10b, 10d, and 11d. In 6c it clearly refers to the "making" of a god by an idol-maker. In 11d it is parallel with *yṣr* 'plan, devise', *dbr* 'speak', and *bwʾ* (*Hiphil*) 'bring'. In the other verses the emphasis appears to be on the accomplishment of a deed or deeds.[112] Thus this line could refer either to Yahweh's power to foresee events, to create or bring something into being (by speaking), or to do both.

46:10c. ***ʾmr ʿṣty tqwm*** **"one who says, 'my plan will stand'"**

The next line begins with another participle, a synonym for *ngd* (10a) and *qrʾ* (11a). While the first participle emphasizes Yahweh's ability to describe in the very beginning of time things yet to occur, the second, *ʾmr*, seems to be aimed more at the present and future. This line also offers a direct quote from Yahweh, so that 10cd is a quotation within a quotation (the direct speech of Yahweh began in line 3a and continues through to the end of the poem). Yahweh asserts that his plan will stand; all that he intends will be done.

ʿṣty **"my plan"**

Duhm, Köhler, and JPSV translate 'plan'. Others translate 'purpose' (NEB, JB, Herbert); 'Ratschluss' ('resolution, decree'—Fischer, König); 'projet' or 'plan' (Lack). The RSV reads 'counsel'. Levy understands the passage to mean "my forecast will be fulfilled."

111. Dahood, in *Psalms III* (287), considers the combination *ʾḥryt wqdm* in Ps 139:5 to be a case of merismus. According to him, this association of words "secondarily suggests 'east and west.'"

112. Stuhlmueller (*Creative Redemption*, 138) points out the difficulty of making a fine distinction between 'making' and 'doing' in Second Isaiah. As will be seen below, in the discussion of chap. 48, *ʿśh* especially means 'doing' in the sense of 'speaking'.

The meaning and possible translations of *ʿṣh* and *yʿṣ* have been discussed by many.[113] Fichtner connects the two meanings of 'advise/counsel' and 'plan' in that a counselor advises a plan of action and calls for a resolution. McKane emphasizes the relationship between *ʿṣh* and the power to execute the policy or plan. The terminology as used in the book of Isaiah has to do with Yahweh's action in history, not just the history of Yahweh's people, but in the wider context of world history,[114] even universal history.[115] Jensen states that in Isaiah of Jerusalem, *ʿṣh* is used to refer only to the negative aspect of Yahweh's activity.[116] There is some ambiguity about whether or not God's plan will always be accomplished. Jensen, in his summary, says that scholars are totally agreed on this point.[117] However, he goes on to say that Wildberger is concerned to avoid any determinism and emphasizes the "conditional aspect that Isaiah's demand for faith introduces." This is why Wildberger believes that history can take different courses—it is dependent upon people's responses to Yahweh.

However, here in 46:10c the notion of *ʿṣh* leaves no room for ambiguity. It is clear that Yahweh's plan will be accomplished. This direct quote in v. 10 has a familiar ring. Scholars have pointed to a similar claim in 44:26, 28, which connects Yahweh's creative powers with his plan or counsel, his purpose, which will be fulfilled through Cyrus.[118] In fact, 44:24–28 is an extremely long series of participles ending with the threefold repetition of *hʾmr* and the infinitive form *lʾmr*, all claims that Yahweh makes regarding his plans for the future.

Duhm points out the connection between 46:10 and 44:26 but also draws attention to similar vocabulary in Isa 14:24.[119] In 14:24ff., Yahweh declares his plan and promises that it will stand (*tqwm*). Clifford develops

113. P. A. H. DeBoer, "The Counsellor," *Wisdom in Israel and the Ancient Near East* (Harold Henry Rowley *Festschrift*) (VTSup 3; Leiden: Brill, 1955) 42–71; von Rad, *OT Theology*, 1:154–55, 161–62, 164, 191, 375–76, 380; W. McKane, *Prophets and Wise Men* (SBT 44; London: SCM, 1965); J. W. Whedbee, *Isaiah and Wisdom* (Nashville: Abingdon, 1971). Also see articles by J. Fichtner, "Jahves Plan in der Botschaft des Jesaja," *ZAW* 64 (1951) 16–33; H. Wildberger, "Jesajas Verständnis des Geschichte" (VTSup 9; Leiden: Brill, 1962) 83–117; Joseph Jensen, "Yahweh's Plan in Isaiah and in the Rest of the Old Testament," *CBQ* 48 (1986) 443–55. Jensen's article is more of a review of recent studies on *ʿṣh/yʿṣ* than it is an in-depth treatment of the use of the words in Isaiah.

114. See Fichtner, "Jahves Plan"; Wildberger, "Jesajas Verständnis des Geschichte."

115. Von Rad, *Theology*, 2:162.

116. Jensen, "Yahweh's Plan," 488.

117. Ibid., 455.

118. See Whybray, Westermann, Muilenburg, North, etc.

119. Duhm, *Das Buch Jesaia*, 268.

this notion of the connection between DI and First Isaiah.[120] It is his thesis that DI borrowed from the portrait of the Assyrian king in First Isaiah (and in Jeremiah) and even further, that "the ideas and even the outline of the great First Isaian poem on the Assyrian king show their influence on all parts of 44:24–45:13."[121] He goes on to lament the fact that the relationship and influence of First Isaiah on Second Isaiah has not been sufficiently developed, especially in the correspondence between the Assyrian king and Cyrus.[122]

The inevitability of God's plan in 14:24ff. is underscored by the repetition of *yʿṣ* and *ʿṣh* in connection with Yahweh's oath that "what I have devised will be, and what I plan will stand" (*kʾšr yʿṣty hyʾ tqwm*), and the rhetorical questions in v. 27: "Yahweh . . . has planned (*yʿṣ*), who can prevent it?" The same sense of inevitability and certainty is found in 46:10 in Yahweh's assertion that "my plan will stand" (*ʿṣty tqwm*).

46:10d. *ḥpṣ* "purpose"

46:10c and d make up a parallel line, with *ʿṣty* parallel to *kl ḥpṣy.* The word *ḥpṣ* is translated by BDB in Isa 44:28, 46:10, and 48:14 as 'good pleasure, will, purpose' of Yahweh. Lack draws attention to the connection between these three chapters based on the repetition of *ḥpṣ*, *ʿṣh*, and *qwm.* He translates *ḥpṣ* 'dessein' or 'vouloir'.[123] The connection with 44:24ff. has already been discussed above. Lack points ahead to ties with 48:14. The plan or design of Yahweh is connected to the person of Cyrus, who is called "man of my plan" (46:11).

For *ʾʿśh* 'I will accomplish', 1QIsa[a] reads *yʿśh.* Clifford adopts this reading and translates 10cd:

> who states my plan that will take effect,
> my good will that will be done.

He does not read the line as direct speech of Yahweh but as another of the assertions that Yahweh is making about what he has said, as in lines 10ab and 11ab. If 1QIsa[a] is correct, a more even parallel between *tqwm* and *yʿśh* would be achieved with the two 3 s. impf. verbs, instead of a 3 s. and 1 s., as the MT reads. My translation reflects the MT and understands this to be a quotation of Yahweh.

120. Clifford (*Fair Spoken and Persuading,* 37) holds that DI was a self-conscious disciple of Isaiah of Jerusalem, entrusted with his writings. See also J. Jensen, *The Use of tôrâ by Isaiah: His Debate with the Wisdom Tradition* (CBQMS 1; Washington, D.C.: Catholic Biblical Association, 1973), who sees a close relation between DI and Isaiah. Certain passages in DI came "from circles that consciously carried on Isaiah's teachings" (p. 132).

121. Clifford, *Fair Spoken and Persuading,* 118.

122. Unfortunately, he himself drops the matter without further discussion.

123. Lack, *Symbolique,* 100.

The expression *ʿśh ḥpṣ* appears in 46:10 and 48:14.[124] (It also occurs in 58:13 but there refers to a person "doing his [own] will on the sabbath," not to Yahweh's will or pleasure being done.) This is the fourth occurrence of the verb *ʿśh* in the poem; it is parallel with *tqwm* and continues the emphasis on the irresistible power of Yahweh's actions.

46:11a. *qrʾ mmzrḥ ʿyṭ* "One who calls from the east a bird of prey"

The third participle in the series concludes with the most specific statement in the series of participles: Yahweh's intervention in history by calling upon Cyrus to accomplish the plan. The series of participles began in 10ab with Yahweh's declaration of his involvement from the very beginning, from times of old (*mrʾšyt, mqdm*). The preposition *mn* had a temporal function in 10ab; its function in 11ab is spatial—he calls one from the east, from a land afar (*mmzrḥ*; 46:11b *mʾrṣ mrḥq*).

Elsewhere in DI, references are made to *mzrḥ*. In 41:2 Yahweh stirs up someone (Cyrus) "from the east"; in 41:25 the expression *mmzrḥ šmš* is used in reference to the call of Cyrus. In 43:5 the east is not the place from which Cyrus is summoned; it is one of the places from which Yahweh will summon his people. And in 45:6 it is used in connection with *mʿrb* ('the west') to indicate the universal scope of those who will know Yahweh. The latter two references are examples of merismus, in which the author wishes to point to the totality of Yahweh's powers. From east to west (i.e., from everywhere), Yahweh will call back his people. From east to west (everywhere), it will be known that Yahweh is God and there is no other.

DI uses a number of terms for directions, and frequently they are used to communicate a sense of all-inclusiveness, especially the terms for east and west, north and south, as in 43:5–6 (see also references to the "ends of the earth" and the "far corners," as in 41:9). In 11a *mzrḥ* is parallel with *ʾrṣ mrḥq* ('a distant land'). Delitzsch identifies the east as Persia (connecting "the east" with Isa 41:2) and the distant land as Media (based on Isa 13:5). These suggestions are highly speculative; there is no indication that DI had such specific distinctions in mind here. Isa 13:5 is not a clear reference to Media. The noun *mrḥq* is meant to emphasize distance rather than geographical locale and hence the immensity of Yahweh's dominion.

***ʿyṭ* "bird of prey"**

This is a general term for a bird of prey.[125] Most scholars draw comparisons between the image of Cyrus as a bird of prey and Nebuchadnezzar

124. See Avi Hurvitz, "The History of a Legal Formula, *kōl ʾăšer ḥāpēṣ ʿāśā*" (*VT* 32 [1982] 265–67); for legal usage, see also Judges 9 and 2 Sam 10:5.

125. BDB 743. Recall *hʿyṭ* that descended upon Abraham's offering in Genesis 15. Elsewhere in the Bible, the term refers to the enemies of Israel, as in Ezek 39:4 or Isa 18:6. In Jer 12:9 it may be Judah itself that is referred to as *ʿyṭ*.

as an eagle (*nšr*) in Jer 49:22 and Ezek 17:3. Attention has also been drawn to references in Xenophon to the eagle as the ensign of Cyrus and his successors. In Isa 46:11, Cyrus is a bird of prey with the object of his attack being Babylon.

Torrey has a different interpretation of the passage. His thesis about DI is that the material is very late, and references to Cyrus should be eliminated. He identifies the one "from the east" as Abraham, not Cyrus, and gives the following as his reasons. The parallel of *ʿyṭ* with *ʾyš ʿṣtw* is unusual. The word *ʿyṭ* is therefore emended to *ʿbdy* 'my servant' to achieve an improvement in "the sense and the meter." He cites a more usual parallel between "man of counsel" and "servant" in Isa 44:26 in support of the emendation. However, the parallel in Isa 44:26 is between *dbr ʾbdw* ('word of his servant') and *ʿṣt mlʾkyw* ('counsel/plan of his messengers'). Torrey fails to make his case here. While the pairing of "bird of prey" with "man of his counsel" is unusual, the portrayal of Cyrus carrying out God's plan against Babylon is consistent with Isa 44:26–28.

ʾyš ʿṣtw **"the man of his plan"**

The *Qere* reads "the man of my plan," and many scholars adopt this reading. Torrey sees the *waw* as a late copyist's blunder and calls on "the whole Jewish tradition, including the LXX, the Syriac, and even the Latin and the Targum" in defense of the reading *ʿṣty*.[126] Duhm and Marti point out that while the *Qere* is clearer, it is unnecessary, citing the identical phrase in 40:13, where in a long series of rhetorical questions, Yahweh refers to *ʾyš ʿṣtw*. However, in 40:12–31, there are numerous references to Yahweh in the third person, while in chap. 46 the overwhelming number of references are in the first person. Also supporting this view is the fact that in several key locations in this poem, as well as in chap. 48, the poet uses combinations of five or ten 1 s. verbs, suffixes, and pronouns in a given section.[127] Reading with the *Qere*, section IV would also have ten such occurrences. The man of Yahweh's plan is Cyrus, who like Assyria in Isa 10:5, will be used by Yahweh as his instrument.[128]

46:11cd. *ʾp . . . ʾp . . . ʾp* "Indeed . . . !"

The threefold repetition of the emphatic adverb *ʾp*,[129] along with the four parallel verbs in 11cd summarize in a forceful fashion the thrust of this section (vv. 8–11). Volz sees the repetition of *ʾp* here standing "in feinem

126. 1QIsa[a] reads with the MT.

127. See above, p. 40 on section II.

128. See Clifford ("Function of the Idol Passages," 456 n. 21), who considers 46:11ab to be the equivalent of Isa 10:5—"Ho, Assyria is the rod of my anger, a staff is he in my hand of wrath."

129. See Williams, *Hebrew Syntax*, 64.

Kontrast" to 40:24. In 40:24 the princes of the earth are portrayed in the image of plants that have been sown and have taken root in the earth; these plants are easily withered and blown away by the force of Yahweh's breath upon them. The threefold repetition of this adverb should also be seen in contrast with the two other occurrences of *ʾp* within the poem. In vv. 6 and 7, the empty actions of the idol-worshipers are emphasized—"they bow down to it," "they cry to it." The repetitions here heighten the sense of Yahweh's power to speak and bring into being, to form and to act. According to BDB,[130] *ʾp* is used emphatically to introduce a new thought, and is used in the "impassioned rhetoric" of Second Isaiah, between 40:24 and 48:15 (the following are cited: 40:24; 41:10, 26; 42:13; 43:7, 19; 46:11; 48:15). According to North, DI uses *ʾp* 25 times.

dbrty . . . ʾbyʾnh, yṣrty . . . ʾʿśnh

"I spoke, . . . I will bring it forth. I formed, . . . I will do it"

The four verbs are grammatically parallel in an ab/ab pattern: pf. V + impf. V. The purpose of the previous lines was to underscore Yahweh's influence from the beginning into the future (temporally), and throughout the world to lands far away (spatially). The four verbs in 11cd summarize the two directions by the variation of pf. (past) and impf. (future) verbs. Duhm and Marti suggest reading *yʿśty* instead of *yṣrty* to achieve a certain parallelism (based on 10cd). But, the root *yṣr* is not alien to DI.[131] Though the root *yṣr* itself does not appear elsewhere in chap. 46, the idea of Yahweh's creative power is one of the elements of this section, and his power to accomplish things from the beginning and into the future is one of his key assertions in this poem and elsewhere in the book.

Furthermore, of the four verbs used in 11cd, only one is used elsewhere in the poem, and that one is used frequently—*ʿśh* occurs five times in chap. 46. Four times it describes Yahweh's activity, once the activity of an idol-maker. The generic word 'to make, do, speak' sums up the activity of the other verbs and participles used to describe Yahweh's actions.

46:12. ***šmʿw ʾly ʾbyry lb*** **"listen to me, O mighty of heart!"**

The final section begins with another imperative, repeating the injunction to listen from line 3a. The audience in v. 3 was "the house of Jacob / remnant of the house of Israel." In v. 12 the addressees are "the mighty of heart / ones far from justice." Some translators (see JB, NAB, Duhm) have

130. BDB 64.

131. In Isa 43:7, 44:22, and 45:18, *yṣr* and *ʿśh* are paired. In 45:7, there are four participles used of Yahweh: *yṣr* + *brʾ* are parallel with *ʿśh* + *brʾ*, and both lines are summed up by the phrase *ʾny yhwh ʿśh kl ʾlh*. See also 44:24 and 45:9 for the combination of these two words. Delitzsch points to a similar use of *yṣr* in Isa 22:1 and 37:26.

difficulty with the reference to "mighty ones" and follow the LXX, which reads *ʾbdy lb* 'faint of heart', instead of *ʾbyry lb*. These commentators cite passages such as 40:27ff., which describe a downcast and dispirited Israel, to support their view of this audience as fainthearted. However, as Muilenburg and others point out, the Hebrew makes sense, since it is supported by the reference to *pwšʿym* in v. 8, who were ordered to remember and "bring to mind (heart)" the deeds of Yahweh. This same notion of the recalcitrant Israel is more fully developed in 48:1–11. Delitzsch and others see DI's use of *ʾbyry lb* here to be synonymous with Ezek 2:4 (*ḥzqy lb*) and Ezek 3:7 (*qšy lb*), all of which refer to people who resist God's "work and grace."

The only other passage in the Bible that refers to *ʾbyry lb* is Ps 76:6. There reference is made to "mighty men" who are broken and lie stunned and stripped of their spoil in the presence of Yahweh. In the psalm the terms do not emphasize the stubbornness of people but instead draw a contrast between human and divine might. If this were the sense intended by DI, the use of the term here would be ironic, emphasizing not their might or their stubbornness, but their own inabilities before Yahweh.[132]

Another direction is taken by G. A. F. Knight, who sees a "double pun" in the use of *ʾbyr*. He compares Yahweh's title in 49:26, "Mighty One of Jacob," with the title by which Jacob/Israel is called here. The sin that "Jacob is committing at this point" is to think he himself is the mighty one, instead of believing in the providence of God.[133] The second pun is a play on the word *ʾbr* 'pinions'. Knight sees the remnant "now soaring on its own pinions (40:31)" and ignoring the pinions of Cyrus, the vulture.

Knight's theologizing of the text is unconvincing, but he does point to some recognized features of DI's style, the use of homonyms, and the device of paronomasia. If *ʾbyr* is the correct reading, we might expect to see it used in other ways in DI and in the book of Isaiah as a whole. See, for example, the king of Assyria in Isa 10:13, who boasts of being *kʾbyr* (usually translated 'like a bull') in plundering the kings of the earth. Isa 34:7 refers to the slaughtered Edomites as *ʾbyrym* ('bulls'). None of these examples is identical to that in 46:12, but in each of them, as in Psalm 76, the fate of the *ʾbyrym* is in the hands of Yahweh, and in each case, their might is nothing compared to Yahweh's.

132. See also Lam 1:15 for a similar use of the term *ʾbyr*: Yahweh crushes, piles up, all the mighty, the young warriors, of Jerusalem. Job 34:20 and Jer 46:12 also describe the *ʾbyr* taken away, thrust down by Yahweh.

133. As discussed above, the sin of Israel is idolatry and apostasy, not refusal to believe in the providence of God.

As a title for Yahweh, *ᵓbyr* occurs three times in the book of Isaiah, always as part of a longer title. In 1:24 the title is *hᵓdwn yhwh ṣbᵓwt ᵓbyr yśrᵓl.* In 49:26 and 60:16 it is *yhwh mwšyᶜk wgᵓlk ᵓbyr yᶜqb.* In each of these passages, the portrayal is of Yahweh against his foes: a god seeking to avenge himself on his enemies (1:24), causing Israel's oppressors to eat their own flesh and drink their own blood (49:26) and causing kings to become nursing mothers for the previously despised Zion (60:16) (the only other occurrences of the title "mighty one of Jacob" are in Gen 49:24, where it is parallel with "shepherd, rock of Israel," and two occurrences in Ps 132:2, 5).

hrḥwqym mṣdqh **"ones far from justice"**

This is the second occurrence in the poem of a word formed from the root *rḥq*. The first was the noun *mrḥq*, which referred to the land afar, from which the bird of prey, Cyrus, was to come. Here the adjective *rḥwq* is used with *ṣdqh* to describe the state of the community. The phrase is parallel with *ᵓbyry lb* ('mighty of heart'). The phrase *far from justice* is considered by Clifford to be more than a metaphor. He sees it as a description of the actual physical state of the remnant Israel of v. 3. "Far from justice" is another way of saying "in Babylon, far from Zion."

The translation of *ṣdq/ṣdqh* in DI has been the subject of much discussion in recent years.[134] Scholars have moved in one of two directions in translating 14:12b and 13a. Most translate 'deliverance' and translate the parallel term *tšwᶜh* 'salvation'.[135] The JPSV, JB, and NEB use the term *victory* and achieve a similar meaning.[136] A different sense is achieved in the translations of Clifford, Bonnard, Skinner, Gileadi, Delitzsch, and Torrey, who translate 'righteousness' or 'justice' for *ṣdqh.* Some emphasize the notion that the audience is hopeless and discouraged and does not see or anticipate that God is near to deliver them. Others see this as a harsh address to Israel that describes either their actual physical state (they are in Babylon, not Zion) or their ethical-religious standing before God. The last assessment of the meaning is in line with the opprobrious title "rebels" of line 8b.

The translation and interpretation of line 12b are influenced by the translation of 12a and the way in which the address to Israel (either "mighty of heart" or "faint of heart") is understood. Whybray acknowledges the parallel between lines 12a and 12b and the difficulty of deciding upon an accurate rendering of the two terms. His solution is to appeal to 13a, where *ṣdqh* is repeated. There, he says, the word "can only mean something like 'deliverance', (and) that is likely to be the meaning here also."

134. John Scullion, *Isaiah 40–66*, has two excursuses on the terms (138–40, 211–12).
135. Duhm, North, Whybray, and Muilenburg, for example.
136. See also Clifford, "Function of the Idol Passages," 456.

There are several weaknesses in this argument. First of all, it is not necessarily true that a repeated word has the same meaning each time it occurs in a given piece of literature. As Torrey pointed out many years ago, a favorite literary device of DI was the repetition of a word in a second, distinct use. Torrey illustrates this device in his translation and, instead of trying to recapture the aa/bb pattern of lines 12b–13c, renders each word differently:

12b Ye who are far from *righteousness*,
13a I bring near my *triumph*, it is not far off,
13b And my *rescue* will not delay.
13c I will put *salvation* in Zion . . . [137]

A second flaw in Whybray's argument is that he begs the question when he says that 13a must mean something like 'deliverance'. See the comment below for ways other commentators have translated 13a.

46:13a. ***qrbty ṣdqty*** **"I brought near my justice"**

The Piel form of the verb *qrb* is unusual (1QIsa[a] reads *qrwbh* '[my justice] is near'). It occurs seven times in the Old Testament (though in Hos 7:6 it is suspect), twice in DI. In Isa 41:21 it is parallel with *ngš* in the *Hiphil* and occurs in a forensic setting, "bring forth your case . . . your proofs." Job 31:37 also has a legal setting. Job is described as coming before his adversary with an indictment and defending himself. The word in Ezekiel is found in the context of the return and reunion of exiles. In Ezek 36:8 the exiles will return home (*qrbw lbwʾ*); in 37:17 the two sticks Judah and Joseph are to be brought together (*qrb*, imperative) and made into one. Ps 65:5[4] proclaims blessed the one who is "chosen and brought near" to dwell in Yahweh's courts.[138] The sense of Isa 46:13a is closest to the usage in Isa 41:21. In both cases the object of the verb is identified: the "case" or "proofs" in chap. 41 and Yahweh's "justice" in chap. 46.[139]

Clifford's translation and interpretation of the phrase are strained. "I have made my justice present" is explained as "a Hebrew idiom meaning 'I have brought it in the sanctuary.' " No explanation is offered for the source of this idiom.[140] It may be that Clifford based his interpretation on the use

137. Torrey, *Second Isaiah*, 367.

138. Dahood (*Psalms II*, 110) compares the Piel of *qrb* here with *UT* 77:27, "I will bring near to you her father Baal," meaning, "I will introduce you."

139. See Y. Hoffman, "The Root QRB as a Legal Term," *Journal of Northwest Semitic Languages* 10 (1982) 72–73.

140. Essential to Clifford's thesis in *Fair Spoken and Persuading* is the notion that Zion is the antithesis to Babylon and that Babylon will be destroyed, while Zion must be built up. He goes so far as to say that the contrast between Zion and Babylon "makes clear that Zion is the only place where Yahweh can be worshiped" (p. 46). This is because

of *qrb* in Psalm 65, which alludes to Yahweh's chosen dwelling in the courts (of the temple). Clifford also relates 46:13a to Isa 45:19a, which he paraphrases, "I revealed myself . . . openly . . . in the shrine." He understands the command in 45:19, "seek me!" to mean "come and worship at my temple!" The interpretations are forced, and Clifford's cursory treatment of the issues is not convincing.

***lʾ trḥq* "it is not far off"**

Within this line, the poet has included two verbs that define one another by way of contrast (*qrbty . . . trḥq*). This is the third time the root *rḥq* has been used in this stanza, and the form used is yet another form, a 3 f. s. impf. verb. First, *rḥq* was used (line 11b in a noun form) to describe the distance from which Cyrus was to come. In 12b the adjective *rḥwqym* described the state of the mighty of heart: they were far from justice. Here the verb is negated and describes not the distance of Yahweh's justice, but its nearness. As such it is one of the several occurrences of litotes in the chapters under study.[141] The use of one root, *rḥq*, connects the lines of the poem, but the various forms enable the poet to achieve multiple meanings.

46:13b. *wtšwʿty lʾ tʾḥr* "And my salvation which will not tarry"

Line 13b is parallel with 13a: *ṣdqty* parallels *tšwʿty*; *lʾ trḥq* parallels *lʾ tʾḥr*.[142] The verb *qrbty* serves double duty for the antecedents of both of these relative clauses.

Babylon is full of false gods. He also interprets Isa 48:2 to mean that "God is so intimately bound to his city that he is not 'validly or fittingly' worshiped outside of it" (p. 143).

141. A "litotes" is a figure that uses deliberate understatement for intensification or makes an affirmative statement by way of a negative, usually for emphasis or irony (Alex Preminger, ed., *Princeton Encyclopedia of Poetry and Poetics* [Princeton: Princeton University Press, 1974] 459; see also F. B. Huey and B. Corley, *A Student's Dictionary for Biblical and Theological Studies* [Grand Rapids: Academie Books, 1983] 119). Watson (*Classical Hebrew Poetry*, 317) defines *litotes* simply as the "antithesis of hyperbole" or as understatement and claims that it is "not much used in Hebrew poetry." He cites only two possible cases, in Gen 18:4 and Isa 10:7. My examination of DI shows that Watson underestimates the use of litotes.

North identifies two examples in DI: in 48:8, where "not opened" is an understatement for "firmly closed," and in 42:3 in a description of the work of the servant. Further investigation uncovers instances in the Bible other than the two possibilities cited by Watson. For example, in Psalm 40, the psalmist makes several negative statements meant to affirm: v. 10, "I did not restrain my lips" = "I told the good news"; v. 11, "I did not hide your righteousness in my heart" and "I did not conceal your lovingkindness" = "I spoke of it"; v. 21, "Do not tarry!" = "Be speedy!" Huey and Corley cite Ps 51:17, where a negative statement is used to make a positive one (p. 119).

142. This, like its parallel in v. 13a, may be considered an understatement, another example of litotes, with the affirmative meaning "my salvation will come speedily."

The noun *tšwʿh*, from the root *yšʿ*, in most translations is rendered 'salvation', but some read 'victory' or 'triumph' to communicate the notion of national deliverance. It is parallel with *ṣdqh* in Ps 71:15, where the wondrous deeds and mighty acts of the past are recounted and celebrated.[143]

The root *yšʿ* appeared in v. 7e. There it was negated; the emphasis was on the lack of saving abilities of the idol that had been constructed. Again the author draws attention to a contrast between the idol and Yahweh by the repeated use of a root word.

46:13d. *lyśrʾl tpʾrty* "to Israel my glory"

Translators do not agree on the meaning of the phrase and consider it ambiguous. *Tpʾrty* can either be read in apposition to Israel, "to Israel, (who is) my glory," or as an object of the verb in 13c, *ntty*, "I give . . . my glory to Israel." Whybray considers these to be "alternative" translations. Clifford, in his 1984 commentary, has made subtle adjustments to the translation in his 1980 article:

1980: I have put in Zion my victory,
for Israel in whom I glory.
1984: I have put victory in Zion,
to Israel I have given my glory.

By 1984 Clifford had committed himself to reading the phrase as an object of the verb, as do the JB, NEB, and JPSV. Skinner prefers "for Israel my glory" and refers to 49:3, "Israel in whom I will be glorified." In addition to 49:3, Marti cites 44:23 and 54:11–17 in support of the idea that Israel is Yahweh's glory.

In order to understand v. 13cd, it is necessary to look at the meaning of *tpʾrh*, and the function of the verb *ntn* in connection with the two prepositions *b-* and *l-*. The f. noun *tpʾrh* does not have the same meaning as *kbd.* In Isaiah it is used of physical beauty: the beauty of a crown (28:1, 4, 5; 62:3),[144] of garments (52:1), of Yahweh's dwelling place (60:7, 63:15, 64:10), and of human form (44:13). In 63:12, 14 it is in construct with *šm*

143. Polan discusses the word-pair *yšwʿh/ṣdqh* in Isaiah 40–66. It occurs six times in 40–55 and six times in 56–66, though sometimes in reverse order. The occurrences are: 45:8, 26; 46:13; 51:5 ,6 ,8; 56:1; 59:16, 17; 61:10; 62:1; and 63:1. He suggests that there may be some way in which this word-pair, along with the word-pair *mšpṭ/ṣdqh*, functions as a structuring device throughout the book of Isaiah (*Ways of Justice*, 58–61).

144. In Isa 28:1–6 the proud crown will be trodden under foot, the glorious beauty of Ephraim will fade, and Yahweh will be a crown of glory, a diadem of beauty, a spirit of justice and strength to his people. In 62:3 it is the people who become the crown of glory in God's hand.

'name' and *zrʿ* 'arm' and is associated with Yahweh's power and might. In 60:19 *tpʾrh* is parallel with *ʾwr ʿwlm* 'everlasting light'. The theme of 60:19ff. is Yahweh as the light of his people, whose days of mourning are at an end. These people will all be righteous (*ṣdyqym*) and will possess the land forever.[145] Nowhere in Isaiah is *tpʾrh* used as a title of Israel. In 46:13 it refers to the victory, or power and might, that Yahweh will give to Israel.

The verb *ntn* serves double duty in line 13cd, as did the verb *qrb* in 13ab. However, the different prepositions prefixed to *ṣywn* and *yśrʾl* give the verb different shades of meaning: "I *set in* Zion my salvation"; "I *give to* Israel my glory." The suffix *yod* also serves double duty for *tpʾrh* and the previous *tšwʿh*.

The last six lines of the poem are closely tied to one another by patterns of repetition of nouns, pronoun suffixes, and syntax. The two vocatives in lines 12a and b are parallel: mighty of heart // ones far from justice. Line 12b is joined to 13a by the repetition of *ṣdqh*, though there is a variation with the addition of the 1 s. suffix, "my justice," in 13a. 13a and 13b are parallel with the double-duty verb *qrbty* in 13a:

I brought near my justice which is not far off,
and my salvation which will not tarry.

In addition to the double-duty verb, the grammatical pattern is: object with 1 s. suffix + neg. + 3 f. s. impf. verb.

The same grammatical structure is repeated in 13c and d. Again there is a double-duty verb in the first part of the line, *ntty*, followed by the pattern in 13c and d of prepositional phrase + object:

I put in Zion my salvation,
(gave) to Israel my glory.

There is a further parallel between 13ab and 13cd. In each line the pattern is a 1 s. pf. verb serving double duty to two objects:

I brought near my justice . . . my salvation
I gave . . . my salvation . . . my glory.

While the parallels between these lines are clear, the development is more complicated and must be described in a number of ways from a number of angles. For instance, the use of the double-duty verb *ntn* does not allow a simple repetition of meaning but calls for a nuanced understanding. The word *tšwʿh* is not simply repeated in 13c; the suffix is omitted. This omission may also accomplish another purpose of the poet—the

145. In First Isaiah, the noun refers to the boastful kings or nations who claim to have power over Israel, as in 10:12, 13:19, 20:5, but this is not the meaning intended in 46:13.

fivefold repetition of first-person forms in v. 13. This is similar to the fivefold repetitions of first-person verb forms and first-person independent pronouns in v. 4 (see p. 40).[146] The poet uses and stretches the device of parallelism here and elsewhere to achieve subtle and artful effects.

Structure

Introductory Notes

Chapter 46 begins with a vivid portrayal of a procession of the Babylonian gods Bel and Nebo being carried into exile. It ends with God's promise of imminent salvation to Zion/Israel. The body of the poem deals with the idolatry of the exiles living in Babylon and calls them to remember that for them there is only one God. It contrasts the gods of the Babylonians with Israel's God: the gods of the Babylonians can promise only a march into exile, but Israel's God promises a return to Zion.

Commentators who emphasize the literary aspects of the work stress the unity of the poem. Muilenburg describes it as a "splendid example of the combination of old and new elements." He sees the themes of the collapse of the Babylonian Empire and the liberation of captive Israel as uniting features. Clifford sees chap. 46 as a continuation of chap. 45 with the overriding theme of Zion. The unity of chap. 46 is accomplished by the pairing of certain polarities: Zion and Babylon, Yahweh and the Babylonian gods, the exiled Israelites and the Babylonians. The use of key words and the repeated use of imperatives, in addition to the thematic considerations, are clear indications to Clifford of the unity of the passage.

Certain form critics, such as Gressmann and Westermann, who point to the multiplicity of forms within the chapter, still regard it as a unit. Gressmann[147] correctly observes that chap. 46 is a unit composed of several genres, the hymn and the mocking-song.[148]

Westermann, like Clifford, sees a relationship between chaps. 45 and 46. Chapter 46 is "the second part of the longish poem introduced by 45:18–19." Unity is achieved by correspondences between the address to the survivors of nations in 45:18 and the address to the remnant of the house of Israel in 46:3. Both are survivors of the "downfall of a state." Within the "longish poem," 46:1–13 "forms a unity" (with the exception

146. D. N. Freedman points out that the same phenomenon occurs in v. 11 if the *Qere* is read instead of the *Kethiv* (personal correspondence).

147. Gressmann, "Die literarische Analyse Deuterojesajas," *ZAW* 34 (1914) 264.

148. Ibid., 283.

of vv. 5–8), in that it "present[s] the positive message of salvation." Westermann also points to the stylistic device of the use of imperatives in vv. 3, 9, and 12. His criteria for unity here are based on thematic and grammatic considerations.

Other commentators who study the text from a form-critical perspective (for example, Köhler, Mowinckel, Elliger, Begrich, and more recently, Melugin, Schoors, and Whybray) do not see chap. 46 as a single composition but rather break the chapter down into short genre units. (Whybray does not always directly discuss genre as a distinguishing factor; he prefers short units in general, whether or not they may be identified with a specific genre.) Since a great majority of commentators on DI treat it as if it were a collection of short, originally unrelated genre units, it is important to examine the methodology these scholars use when commenting on the text and especially the presuppositions that underlie their approach.

Melugin divides chap. 46 as follows: vv. 1–4 = a speech of salvation;[149] vv. 5–11 = a disputation speech; vv. 12–13 = a "free creation of DI, shaped to some extent by the form of the salvation-assurance oracle."[150] Köhler and Begrich differ from Melugin in that they divide vv. 1–4 into two units: vv. 1–2 and vv. 3–4. Mowinckel sees vv. 1–2 as separate from the longer unit vv. 3–13. Begrich, Elliger and Schoors, in contrast to Mowinckel, agree with Melugin about the division of vv. 12–13 into a separate unit. Köhler, Elliger, Westermann, and Whybray regard vv. 5–8 as a nonauthentic passage, *not typical* of DI. For example, Westermann considers the polemic against idols in vv. 5–8 to have been "taken into the text here," since he finds it to be unlike DI's own polemic in vv. 1–4.

Whybray, like Westermann and Elliger, questions the continuity (and in part, the authenticity) of vv. 5–8. However, his reasoning is not the same as Westermann's; he considers some of the verses to be like DI, perhaps genuine DI. He entertains a number of possibilities for these verses. For instance, they are not a continuation of vv. 1–4 because vv. 1–4 are "complete in themselves and not improved by the addition of the themes of Yahweh's incomparability . . . and of the folly of idolatry." He dismisses

149. It should be noted that though Melugin believes that vv. 1–4 were "juxtaposed by a collector," he states that "the repetition of the image of the gods who must be carried is a significant connecting feature. The answer to the question, 'To whom will you compare me?' (v. 5), becomes even more obvious when read in the light of the images in 46, 1–4. How can a deity who carries be compared with a god who must be carried into exile?" (*Formation,* 135). I agree that this is a significant connecting feature. Along with other evidence, this fact either disproves Melugin's contention about the juxtaposing of originally disparate pieces by a later editor, or points to the consummate artistry of that final editor.

150. Ibid., 132.

the repetition of key words such as *lift* and *carry* as proof of original continuity. Instead, they are examples of "an editorial use of keywords as an artificial means of providing continuity," or they may indicate that some verses were "deliberately composed by a later author as an extension of vv. 1–4." Another possibility for vv. 5–8 is that they may not be a literary unit in themselves. Verse 5, according to Whybray, may or may not be a "genuine Deutero-Isaianic verse." Although it is "in the style of Deutero-Isaiah," it may be "a later imitation." Verses 6–8 may be "an interpolation"; vv. 6–7 have vocabulary similar to 44:9–20, which is not the work of DI. Unfortunately, he does not demonstrate how to determine when key words are a sign of authenticity and when they are editorial additions that are merely "in the style of Deutero-Isaiah." In the face of such assumptions, it is preferable to work from the existing final form rather than to deal with artificial constructs.

Schoors expresses an opposing view. In his opinion, "the authenticity of vv. 5–8 is beyond any doubt."[151] He bases his opinion on a comparison of 46:5–8 with 40:18–20 and 41:6–7. All of these units "must belong to the same genre," that of disputation. As to the length of the disputation genre in this passage, Schoors extends vv. 5–8 to include 9–11. Schoors finds "no proof that vv. 5–7 (8) and 9–11 were originally one unit," but he thinks that it is "highly probable" that they were. His reasons are the following. There is no clear conclusion in vv. 5–7 to the statement that Yahweh cannot be compared to any idol. While v. 8 ("remember this and stand firm! bring it to mind, you rebels") could be a conclusion, it "also seems to be an introduction to the following verses,"[152] because of the repetition of *zkrw*. He acknowledges that it links two sections together but cautions against "overstress[ing] the importance of this repetition." The clear conclusion follows in v. 9: Yahweh alone is God; the end of the disputation is v. 11: God rules history. In other words, Schoors sees a connection between what others consider to be separate units, based on his perception of the progression and development of a theme and the repetition of a key word. Strictly form-critical considerations are not used to demonstrate unity.

Von Waldow divides Isaiah 46 differently.[153] For him, vv. 8–11 are an example of a typical DI genre, the prophetic disputation. He also considers them to be a "hymn of praise," in the "special form . . . [of] self praise of God."[154]

151. Schoors, *I Am God Your Savior: A Form Critical Study of the Main Genres of Is XL–LV* (VTSup 24; Leiden: Brill, 1973) 274.

152. Ibid., 277.

153. H. Eberhard von Waldow, "The Message of Deutero-Isaiah," *Int* 22 (1968) 268–69.

154. Ibid., 273.

The above summary presents examples of methods form-critical scholars of DI have used in determining the units within chap. 46. Most of these studies take for granted Gunkel's notion that we are dealing with short units; there seems to be little inclination to prove this assumption. Rather, subjective opinions are offered as to why a given short unit has certain parameters. One of the considerations often used by Whybray is whether or not a given passage is "complete in itself." Melugin uses a similar criterion when dividing verses into units. Of vv. 1–4 and 5–11 he says, they "did not originally belong together" because "each is capable of being understood without the help of the other."[155]

But what does it mean to say that a given unit is "complete in itself," or is "capable of being understood without the help of another"? Any sentence or independent clause with a subject and predicate can be considered grammatically complete in itself and is capable of being understood without the help of another sentence. For instance, the sentence *kr*^{c} *bl* ("Bel bowed down") is complete in itself and can be understood without the help of another sentence. If one can identify Bel and knows the meaning of the past tense "bowed down," one can understand this sentence. Completeness in itself and capability of being understood without the help of another are not adequate criteria for making judgments about the limits of a unit.

Another extremely subjective consideration in the limitation of units is whether a passage is improved by the addition of themes. Whybray identifies additional the themes in vv. 5–8 as "Yahweh's incomparability" (v. 5) and "the folly of idolatry" (vv. 6–7), and says that these themes do not improve vv. 1–4. Melugin also deals with this issue in chap. 46. He sees vv. 5–11 as a unit and believes that vv. 1–4 and 5–11 have in common the carrying of idols. However, he also sees a change of theme in vv. 5–11, that of "the deity's ability to declare the future." Melugin sees another change in that vv. 1–4 emphasize the "promise to Israel as remnant-in-exile," while vv. 5–11 emphasize the "sinful Israel." Because of these changes in emphasis, Melugin believes that the two sections "did not originally belong together."[156] What is assumed is that in a given unit or poem the theme must remain exactly the same. We might expect just the opposite in a creative poet. A theme may be changed or developed within a given poem so that the poet can move the audience to a new level of awareness. Melugin is a champion of the creativity of DI's uses of genres, and yet he would restrict evidences of this creativity in order to fit the notion that genres usually are indicators of different units.

155. Melugin, *Formation*, 133.
156. Ibid., 133.

The subjectivity of the application of the criteria should also be noted. Melugin[157] and Whybray are willing to accept both the fusion of two genres and the change of theme from the picture in vv. 1–2 of Bel and Nebo going down into exile, to the picture in vv. 3–4 of Yahweh commanding his people to remember how he carried them. Elsewhere in his treatment of chap. 46, Melugin argues in the opposite direction for division based on difference in genre or theme. Melugin admits that vv. 1–4 and 5–11 have one common theme,[158] but because of another change in theme, he opts for division between the two sections. By this criterion, vv. 1–2 ought to be separated from vv. 3–4. While there is a common theme, there is also a radical change in theme between the picture of Bel and Nebo and that of Yahweh commanding his people to be aware of his actions on their behalf. Change or development of theme is not an adequate criterion on which to base a judgment concerning the limitation of a unit.

Whybray's opinion that vv. 1–4 are "not improved" by the additional verses is a matter of taste and reflects a lack of appreciation of literary development. If vv. 1–2 and 3–4 belong together because they "draw a devastating contrast" between Yahweh and the Babylonian gods, then why not include vv. 5–7 and 8–13 in the same unit? The whole chapter may be seen as a devastating contrast between Yahweh and the impotent Babylonian deities.

The repetition of key words is downplayed by Whybray and Schoors as a factor affecting the limits of a unit.[159] In his judgment of vv. 5–8, Whybray believes the repetition of key words to be no indication of original continuity. He admits that certain repetitions do provide continuity, but he attributes these repetitions to a later editor.

However, in Whybray's decision about the unity of vv. 1–4, one of the factors that makes it "one of the best constructed and most effective passages" in DI is the use of "a number of keywords." Schoors also warns against using repetition of words as a factor in determining the length of a unit, but he himself does it in his assessment of the relationship between vv. 8 and 9, where he finds the repetition of *zkr* to be a uniting factor.[160] These scholars are not clear about when one might interpret repetition as a sign of unity and when one interprets it as a device used by an editor as

157. Ibid., 23–24.

158. Ibid., 133.

159. Mowinckel's interpretation of the repetition of words is that small units were joined together by the mechanical process of catchwords and that these were therefore signs of the originally independent existence of smaller units ("Cult and Prophecy [1922]," *Prophecy in Israel: Search for an Identity* [ed. D. L. Petersen; Philadelphia: Fortress, 1987] 74–98).

160. Schoors, *I Am God*, 277.

"an artificial means of providing continuity." It is clear that repetition and the use of key words *are* sometimes interpreted as signs of literary unity.

Melugin, in a more discriminating vein, alludes to "verbal repetition" as "an important factor in the arrangement of the units."[161] He asks the question: "Is this repetition the result of a collector's arrangement of originally separate units, or have we an author of a lengthy poem?" His answer is: since the chapter can be broken down into genre units, "it is best to begin by analyzing the relationship of genre units rather than starting with the assumption of a lengthy composition." This is not an answer to the question posed. Difference in genre becomes equated with separate poem or unit. Though Melugin is more critical than Whybray about the functions of repetition, his conclusions do not follow from any evidence. The fact that certain verses *can* be identified with certain genres is no proof that those verses *must* therefore be independent literary units.

Another factor affecting the credibility of the form-critical approach to chap. 46 is the variety of genre units that scholars identify there and the speculative nature of their suggestions about genre. Melugin believes that breaking chap. 46 into genre units is the best way to begin because it is possible to do so. However, the genre units are far from being clearly defined. Notice the different units that various scholars identify (vv. 1–2 or vv. 1–4; 2–4 or 3–13; 5–8, 5–11, 9–11, 9–13, 12–13) and the different forms or genres that they assign to the units (disputation, trial speech, hymn, proclamation of salvation, oracle of salvation, psalm of lamentation, song of victory, salvation speech).

Melugin is correct in his statement that one ought not to analyze a text based on assumption.[162] One of the main weaknesses in his approach (and in the approach of most form critics) is the basic assumption that lengthy poems were originally short units. Melugin thinks that it is an assumption to regard Isaiah 46 as a lengthy composition. In view of the fact that there are other poems of extended length from the same period (the acrostic poems in Lamentations, for example), this can hardly be termed an assumption.[163] Acrostic poems may be said to suffer from many of the same

161. Melugin, *Formation*, 132–33.

162. Ibid., 133.

163. Melugin takes into account the facts that strophes can occur in acrostic poems and that some strophes are "clearly marked off by refrains," but he does not reason further on these points (ibid., 8). He dismisses strophic analysis because "most poems are not acrostics," because clear marking by refrains is a "rare phenomenon," and because regular division of lines is an exception and cannot be used to determine strophes. Strophic analysis may be difficult, but this is not a sufficient reason for substituting arbitrary criteria, such as the assumption of short form-critical units, in analyzing a text. A better approach is to accept obvious phenomena existing in the biblical text, such as divisions

problems form critics find in chap. 46, yet it is not assumed that an editor arranged lines in alphabetical order so that originally independent lines would appear to be a single composition.

Since there are other poems of similar length[164] or structure from the same period, it seems appropriate to begin an analysis of the structure of chap. 46 from this perspective. Then, if clear indications of disunity or disruption within a unit are observed, questions can be asked about whether or not a given verse or section is part of the poem.

What is the evidence for viewing chap. 46 as a unit, a poetic whole? How can one determine the boundaries of the poem? Muilenburg and Clifford (and with some reservations, Westermann) do consider the poem to be a literary whole. Muilenburg sees the whole poem as a development of the vivid scene of the opening lines. He describes the progression of the writer's thought from the picture of the exodus of the Babylonian gods through to the announcement of salvation in the final verses. According to Muilenburg there are two dominant themes binding this poem together: the collapse of the Babylonian Empire and the consequent liberation of captive Israel. The use of contrasting themes—the gods being borne versus Israel's God bearing his people, the worshiping of idols instead of the God of Israel, the fate of Israel versus the fate of its captors—is carried throughout the poem and is another factor in determining unity of composition. The repetition of imperatives is still another.

Clifford defines the original boundaries of the unit using several methods. He, like Muilenburg, sees these compositions as unified by more than one technique or device. Important to Clifford's analysis is what he calls "strophic patterning."[165] This is a structuring device by which the author patterns one strophe after another. This can be done by: (1) developing the same themes in two sections of the same composition (as in Isa 41:1–

---

that Melugin himself admits, and to look for evidence of the same phenomena elsewhere in the text.

164. Lamentations 5 is a 22-unit, 44-line poem. Isaiah 46 also has 22 units, with 46 lines. As discussed in chapter 1, the term *line* is equivalent to what is often called a *colon*. Instead of *bicolon* and *tricolon*, the terms *line-pair* and *line-trio* are used in this book. D. N. Freedman, in "Acrostic Poems in the Hebrew Bible: Alphabetic and Otherwise" (*CBQ* 48 [1986] 416), describes the standard unit (or line) in Hebrew poetry as the bicolon, with the familiar 3:3 stress pattern and 8:8 syllable count. The difference in the terminology used by Freedman and that used in this book is shown below:

Freedman	*Franke*
line or *unit* is composed of	*unit* is composed of
bicolon or *tricolon*	*line-pair* or *line-trio*
with 2 or 3 *cola*	with 2 or 3 *lines*

165. Clifford, *Fair Spoken and Persuading*, 39ff.

42:9,[166] where there are two summons to trial, two legal questionings of nations, two verdicts); (2) presenting similar themes in two sections of the composition (as in chap. 49, where the disbelief of Zion is patterned after the disbelief of the servant); (3) using proportional strophes (as in 40:12–31 and chap. 55, where both have three strophes of proportional length; chap. 40 has three strophes of 18, 22, and 26 cola, and chap. 55 has 18, 21, and 9 cola); (4) composing strophes in which the number of cola are equal (as in 44:24–45:13 and 54:1–27, each of which has three strophes of approximately equal length: 44:24ff. has 20, 28, and 20; 54:1ff. has 21, 20, and 22).

Related to strophic patterning is a technique that Clifford refers to as parallelism of scenes and actors.[167] One of the ways in which longer units are composed is that the author compares, or more often contrasts, scenes and characters. For instance, the old exodus from Israel's ancient past is contrasted to the new exodus, which is or will be part of Israel's present situation. In chap. 46 Clifford points to parallelisms of actors Zion and Babylon (in the person of Bel and Nebo), Yahweh and the Babylonian gods, the exiled Israelites and the exiled Babylonians.[168] These parallelisms attest to the integrity of this chapter as a single composition.

Clifford also considers rhetorical devices in his analysis of the unity of a given composition. These include wordplay, repetition of sounds and rhymes, chiasm, and various other parallelisms. Most important in chap. 46 are the repetition of the imperatives "hear" and "remember," as well as the use of key words "carry," "bear," and "escape."

Another factor important in Clifford's determination of the original length of a composition is his assessment of DI as an orator rather than a lyric poet.[169] The element of persuasion is important in Clifford's analysis of the units (speeches). Unity of composition can be demonstrated if there is a compelling and coherent argument. In his analysis of chap. 46, coherence of thought is the most important factor in determining the unity of the passage. He sees a logical development from the impotence of the Babylonian gods in vv. 1–2 to the saving power of Yahweh in Zion in the

166. See also Jerome T. Walsh, "The Case for the Prosecution: Isaiah 41.21–42.17," *Directions in Biblical Hebrew Poetry* (ed. E. Follis; JSOTSup 40; Sheffield: JSOT Press, 1987) 101–18, who does a stylistic analysis of this unit. *Contra* Clifford, he sees only one court-room scene.

167. Ibid., 41–43.

168. However, Clifford does not show specifically where these Babylonian exiles are referred to in the poem. He refers to the worshipers of Bel and Nebo and the worshipers who have made statues for themselves but does not go further to identify these individuals.

169. Clifford, *Fair Spoken and Persuading*, 4–5, 36.

closing verses. This entire chapter, according to Clifford, is a speech intended to compel the Israelites to return to Zion, where Yahweh's saving power dwells.

Westermann also sees chap. 46 as a unit, with some qualifications. According to him, vv. 5–8 are from another hand, though "their place of insertion into the text has been deliberately chosen." Westermann sees 46:1–13 as the second part of a "longish poem" that began in 45:18. Criteria for unity of composition, for Westermann, include the following. The address to Israel in 46:3 corresponds to the address to the nations in 45:20. The nations are addressed as "you survivors of the nations"; similarly, Israel is addressed as "the remnant of the house of Israel." Another criterion is the positive message of salvation in 46:1–13, which addresses Israel's "despondency" of the earlier section. Westermann also cites the recurrence of imperatives in 46:3, 9, and 12 as forming the passage into a unity.

There are some problems with Westermann's assessments regarding unity of composition. He seems to vacillate between considering 45:18–46:13 a unit and calling chap. 46 a unit in itself. The language he uses in describing the units lacks precision. For instance, after calling 46:1–13 "the second part of a longish poem," he then refers to 46:1–13 as a "relatively self-contained unit." In describing 46:1–2, he calls these verses "this short poem" and later "this brief oracle." He does not commit himself to identifying the limits of the poem he is analyzing. The unit at times appears to be as short as two verses (46:1–2) and at other times as long as 21 verses (45:18–46:13).

Each of the three commentators makes divisions within Isaiah 46, though their reasons for these divisions and the divisions themselves differ. Muilenburg is the only one who specifies division into strophes. Clifford alludes to separate stanzas, but he does not specify stanzas or discuss reasons for the divisions. Interestingly, both Clifford and Westermann betray confusion in their division of the chapter into separate lines and sections. In their translations of the text, each offers an arrangement of verses different from the arrangement of the same verses in the commentary.

Clifford divides the text into three sections in his translation and into (apparently) five in his commentary:

translation division	commentary division
1–4	1–2
5–7	3–4
	4–7 [sic]
8–13	8–11
	12–13

He speaks of division into stanzas in a general way but does not explain how he arrives at these stanzaic divisions.

Westermann's divisions are as follows:

translation division	commentary division
1	1–4
2	(5–8)
3–4	9–13
5–8	
9–10	
11	
12–13	

He, like Clifford, does not always specify why he arranges the text as he does. His delineation in the translation is interesting, especially since he considers three verses (1, 2, and 11) to be separate units. None of the form critics examined have made such divisions. Verse 11 is always seen as part of a larger unit, either 8–11, 9–11, or 11–13; vv. 1–2 are always joined, and sometimes are part of 1–4. Westermann himself does not separate the verses on form-critical grounds. His criteria for the arrangement remain a mystery.

Muilenburg is the only one with a specific interest in dividing the chapter into strophes and discussing reasons for the divisions. He sees five strophes, arranged as follows:

1–2	8–11
3–4	12–13
5–7	

His method of dividing the text into strophes includes observations on theme, balance of lines within a strophe, repetition of words for emphasis and climax, beginning strophes with imperatives, contrast, and comparison. Verses 1–2 are seen as a dramatic scene, the removal of the idols, which sets the stage for the rest of the poem. Verses 3–4 open with an imperative and make up a strophe balanced by two four-line units. Muilenburg refers to this as "a strophic arrangement not uncommon to our poet." Verses 5–7, while at first appearing intrusive, make up a complete strophe in that they echo several verbs of the previous two strophes and end with an accent on salvation, as the previous strophe does. Verses 8–11 also begin with an imperative. The conclusion in 11cd reinforces the previous lines by repetition, thus making a powerful conclusion. Verses 12–13 are the culmination of the motifs of salvation and deliverance and form a "superb finale" by contrasting the fate of Israel with that of her oppressor.

It is my position, along with Muilenburg, Clifford, and Gressmann, that chap. 46 is a single literary unit. I am not convinced that Clifford's assessment of the chapter as a speech rather than a lyric poem is compelling. I deal with this text as a literary artifact and do not venture opinions about its origins. My arrangement of the sections of the poem is in agreement with the strophic arrangement of Muilenburg. I discuss additional reasons to support this arrangement as well as other thoughts about the relationship of the sections of the poem to one another.

An important factor in support of this division is evidence from the MT and 1QIsa[a]. The MT indicates exactly the same divisions as suggested by Muilenburg. 1QIsa[a] shows major divisions after vv. 2, 11, and 13 (the scribe begins a new line after these verses) and also shows large divisions after vv. 4, 7, and 8.[170]

Structure of Individual Sections: Microstructure

Section I (vv. 1–2)

This vivid scene of the procession of the Babylonian idols into exile serves as an introduction to vv. 3–13. It is a section of 8 lines arranged in an intricate pattern of 4 line-pairs. The section is united by the repetition of certain key words in significant locations, the repetition of the perfect form of the verb, and the skillful arrangement of the lines.

The key words that illustrate the theme of the section are the combination *krʿ/qrs* and the forms of the verb *nśʾ*. The combination *krʿ/qrś* occurs twice. In line 1a the verbs are singular and have Bel and Nebo as subjects. In line 2a the verbs are repeated but in reverse order, forming a chiasm with 1a, and are plural rather than singular. In 2a the plural subjects are the animals as well as the burden they carry, the gods. The view now is not only of Bel and Nebo, but of the procession, in which all are stumbling and kneeling.

The other key word in the section is *nśʾ*, which occurs once as a passive participle and twice as the related noun *mśʾ*. *Nśʾtykm* and *mśʾ* form a parallel in the pattern ab // a′c in lines 1d and 1e. *Mśʾ* is repeated in 2b, this time at the end of the line, forming a chiasm with 1e. These repetitions, like that of *krʿ* and *qrs*, link the two verses and draw attention to the theme, the downfall of the Babylonian gods.

The two groups of key words—the combinations of *krʿ/qrs* and *nśʾ/mśʾ*—form a brilliant contrast to one another, thus drawing greater attention to the theme of downfall. One combination has the basic meaning "to kneel or stoop down"; the other originates from a root that means "to

170. Muilenburg did not mention the divisions in MT and 1QIsa[a] in his commentary in support of his strophic divisions.

lift up." This combination of words not only links vv. 1–2 to each other, but also to the rest of chap. 46. The theme of going down and rising up is an important motif in all of Isaiah 40–55 and perhaps in the entire book of Isaiah.[171]

Another technique to be discussed in the structuring of vv. 1–2 is the sixfold repetition of the perfect verb form.[172] The use of the perfect and the absence of the imperfect single out this section from the rest of the poem. Such a striking and consistent usage cannot be unintentional. The exclusive use of this verb form (with the participle for variation) helps to draw attention to this section as setting the scene for the remaining lines. The events this line describes are used as points of reference throughout the rest of the poem. The verbs are probably examples of the prophetic perfect, since there is no indication that Cyrus's takeover of Babylon involved his humiliation of the Babylonians.

The arrangement of the lines is important to the discussion of the unity of this section. The 8 lines in the section are all line-pairs. However, the order of the lines is more complicated than a simple pattern of 4 line-pairs in sequence. The first and last lines (vv. 1a and 2c) form an envelope around the other 3 line-pairs: 1bc, 1de, 2ab. This pattern becomes clear when close attention is paid to the syntax, the MT's use of pronouns and other parts of speech, and when the results of syllable and stress counting are carefully analyzed.

Verses 1 and 2 have perplexed commentators for years, and they have been rearranged and emended to the point of no return. Westermann's treatment can serve as an example. His suggestion is to divide the first verse into 3 line-pairs as follows:

Bel bows down; Nebo stoops.[173]
Their idols have become burdens for cattle,
burdens for cattle, burdens for the weary.

This rendering is achieved by his rearrangement of the order of the MT to:

hyw ʿṣbyhm mśʾ lḥyh
nśʾtykm lbhmh ʿmwswt lʿyph[174]

171. See, for example, Isa 2:9–19, 14:4ff., 22:1ff., 27:19, and 31:1ff.

172. The participle *qrs*, occurring as the second word in the list of seven, is an exception in this list of perfect verbs. Freedman pointed out a similar case in Jer 51:20–23, where, in a long list of identical forms (*wnpṣty* is repeated nine times) the word in the second position is different. Instead of *wnpṣty*, a different verb, *whšḥty*, is used. The meaning is similar, but the poet has varied the list (D. N. Freedman, personal correspondence).

173. Westermann reads v. 1a as two lines, whereas I see it as one line.

174. It should be noted that while he does incorporate the unusual 2 m. pl. suffix in his transcription of the Hebrew, he ignores it in his translation. He also makes no

He correctly sees a "strong 2.2 rhythm" here but rearranges the words into an artificial pattern. Clifford and Whitley[175] rearrange the lines to come up with a pattern of 3+3 stresses. Not only are their arrangements forced, but their analysis of the stresses also is surely incorrect.[176]

One of the difficulties with this section is how to delineate and count the first four words, *krʿ bl qrs nbw.* Are they to be considered one line or two? How are the syllables and stresses to be analyzed? In my schema, mentioned above, 1a (*krʿ bl qrs nbw*) is read as one line,[177] which forms an envelope with 2c. The 3 m. pl. suffix of *npšm* refers to the 3 m. s. verbs in line 1a.[178] The *npš* of 2c refers to the image of the god(s) Bel and Nebo in 1a, which stumble and kneel and go into captivity. These lines together make up a unit or line-pair of 7+9=16 syllables and 7 stresses. The standard or common meter of Hebrew poetry is 16 syllables and 6 stresses.[179] That there are 7 stresses rather than 6 can be explained by the fact that these are opening and closing lines of a section.

In between this envelope are other units that go together grammatically and syntactically. Lines 1b and c form a unit of 6+8=14 syllables with 2+2=4 stresses. This is matched in chiastic order by 1d and e, a unit of 8+6=14 syllables and 2+2=4 stresses, making a symmetrical pattern. In addition, 2a and b are different from the preceding four lines in that they form a unit of 8+8=16 syllables and 3+3=6 stresses, another example of the standard meter. This matches the unit formed by 1a+2c, which has 16 syllables and 7 stresses.

The section is thus made up of 4 line-pairs: 1a and 2c matching 2ab; 1bc matching 1de.[180] The MT system of indicating line division supports

---

distinction in his translation between *ḥyh* and *bhmh,* translating 'cattle' for both; nor does he differentiate between *mśʾ*, *nśʾykm* or *ʿmwswt.* Such a translation captures none of the subtlety and variety present in the text. The artistry of the poet is completely lost by such a rendering.

175. Clifford, *Fair Spoken and Persuading*; Whitley, "Textual Notes on DI."

176. See above, in Notes on Translation and Text (p. 30) on 1bc for the specifics of their delineations.

177. According to M. O'Connor, the phrase in question could be read as one line or two. The combination of verb/subject fits his definition of the dominant line form. "Most lines of Hebrew verse contain one clause and either two or three constituents." The combination of verb/subj., verb/subj., as in my reading of 1a, also fits O'Connor's definition of the constraints of a line, although it is not the preferred or dominant form (*Hebrew Verse Structure* [Winona Lake, Ind.: Eisenbrauns, 1980] 87).

178. Lines 1a and 2c have the only specifically masculine subjects in this first section. The other verb forms are 3 common pl. and 3 f. s.

179. This is the pattern of the standard or common meter of Hebrew poetry, according to Freedman ("Acrostic Poems," 409–10, 416, 430).

180. This is a variation of the 4+4 line arrangement that Muilenburg found to be common in DI.

	line	line-pair
16, 7 (envelope)	1a	
	1b	14, 4
	1c	
	1d	14, 4
	1e	
	2a	16, 6
	2b	
	2c	

this arrangement: the *ʾatnaḥ* in v. 1 follows 1c; in v. 2 it follows 2b. This division is superior to others in that it requires no emendations, omissions, or rearrangements of words or lines; it is supported by *ʾatnaḥ* dividers in the MT; it matches the syntax and the usage of parts of speech in the individual lines; and, especially, because it reveals the intricate and balanced structure of the section. The poet has used the line-pair skillfully, working within the limits of the structure, but with variety and creativity.

Section II (vv. 3–4)

The plural imperative *šmʿw* and the vocatives signal the beginning of a new section. The vocatives also specifically identify the audience of the poem, which was alluded to in line 1d by the use of the 2 m. pl. suffix. The scene of the procession of the Babylonian gods is over. The body of the poem begins with God ordering his audience to listen and reminding them of his dynamic activity on their behalf. This section, like the previous one, has 8 lines, composed of 4 line-pairs. I will show, however, that this division is not as clear-cut as Muilenburg indicates in his commentary.

The stress counts and syllable counts for the lines are as follows:

line	stress		syllable	
3a	4	=8	7	=16
3b	4		9	
3c	3	=6	7	=14
3d	3		7	
4a	4	=8	7	=15
4b	4		8	
4c	4	=7	10	=19
4d	3		9	

The most outstanding feature that unites this section is the use of the first-person singular suffix, independent pronoun, and verb forms. Another uniting feature is the interrelationship between various line-pairs in the poem. The lines are woven together so that each set of line-pairs is related to what follows and/or precedes. The poem is an artful construction of interwoven line-pairs and groups of line-pairs, the combination of which makes a tightly blended section.

The first line-pair is made up of an imperative (*šmʿw*) and two vocatives that parallel one another (*byt yʿqb, byt yśrʾl*). The single imperative and vocative in line 3a are balanced in 3b by an extended vocative (*wkl-šʾryt byt yśrʾl*). The addressees are identified as the house of Jacob and all the remnant of the house of Israel. The phrase *kl šʾryt* in the second line of the line-pair serves a double-duty function for the phrases "the house of Jacob" and "the house of Israel," just as the imperative "listen to me" in the first line serves a double-duty function.

This simple line-pair is an excellent example of both forward-gapping and backward-gapping.[181] The first is an accepted phenomenon in Hebrew poetry. The second is questioned by some, namely J. Kugel and R. Alter,[182] who oversimplify the relationship between the A and B line in poetry. They mass the whole phenomenon of parallelism under the rubric of "A and what's more, B," in which the second (B) line is seen to go beyond or to intensify or add something more to the A line. Their systems do not seem to allow that at times, the A line means the same thing as the B line.[183] Here, for example, because of the double-duty function of *kl šʾryt*, the object of the address is understood to be "all the remnant of the house of Jacob" and "all the remnant of the house of Israel." The same group is meant in both lines.

The next line-pair, 3c and d, is an evenly constructed series of participles (*hʿmsym, hnśʾym*) that expand on the identification of the audience in 3a and b. The grammatical parallelism is quite regular:

181. Watson (*Classical Hebrew Poetry*, 48, 257, 306) alludes to the phenomenon of gapping. For a more comprehensive treatment, see M. O'Connor, *Hebrew Verse Structure*, 122–29 and 401–7, on gapping. He refers to "rightward" and "leftward" gapping. James L. Kugel disputes O'Connor's treatment and finds it "oversimplified" (*The Idea of Biblical Poetry* [New Haven: Yale University Press, 1981] 322).

182. Kugel, *Idea*, and Alter, *Art of Biblical Poetry*. See also R. Alter, "The Characteristics of Ancient Hebrew Poetry," in *The Literary Guide to the Bible* ([ed. R. Alter and F. Kermode; Cambridge: Belknap Press of Harvard University, 1987] 615): "The ancient Hebrew poets are constantly advancing their meanings . . . the dominant pattern is a focusing, heightening, or specification of ideas."

183. It is not disputed that in my example, an important detail is added in the second line; what is in dispute is whether the B line means something different from the A line. Berlin (*Dynamics of Biblical Parallelism*, 90) is also critical of Kugel: his system "seems to exclude equivalence by definition." See also pp. 98–99 in Berlin's discussion of "disambiguation," "ambiguity," and "polysemy," where she states that both facets of parallelism, redundancy and ambiguity, can coexist and that it is not necessary to choose between something that is "synonymous" and something that "goes beyond."

art. + m. pl. pass. part. / prep. / f. n.
art. + m. pl. pass. part. / prep. / m. n.

Lexically, the parallelism is diagrammed a b c / a′ b c′. The stress pattern and syllable count of both lines are identical: 3+3 and 7/7. This is a further characterization of the house of Jacob and Israel as ones borne from the womb, carried from birth. This line-pair represents a change from the first pair in that it is a series of participles, but it is linked to the first pair in that it continues to identify and describe the addressees. The use of the passive participle here serves both to identify the object of the action and to hold in suspense the identity of the agent.

The next line-pair (4a, 4b) is joined to the previous pair in several ways. It repeats part of the grammatical pattern of the pair in 3c and d, the combination of preposition /noun. The grammatical parallels between the lines can be outlined in this manner:

3c	ones carried **from the womb**	A	B
3d	ones borne **from birth**	A	B
4a	and **unto old age** I am he	B	C
4b	and **unto gray hair** I, I bear	B	C′

It is also joined by the double merismus, the combination of from womb/ birth to old age / gray hair. Also functioning to unite the lines are the poetic devices of parallel word-pairs and the break-up of stereotype word-pairs.[184] The two word-pairs, *bṭn/rḥm* and *zqnh/śybh*, are divided among the lines.[185] It could be said that all six lines (vv. 3a–4b) are woven together as an extended imperative addressed to the house of Jacob, the ones carried from birth to gray hair. At the same time, however, this line-pair introduces a new element to the section, a description in the first person of the one who does the carrying.

The parallelism between 4a and b is also tightly woven. Grammatically, the following parallelism is achieved:

conj. + prep. / f. s. n. / 1 s. pron. / 3 m. s. pron.
conj. + prep. / f. s. n. / 1 s. pron. / 1 s. impf. V

The pattern of this grammatical parallelism can be compared to that of lines 3c and d. The lines are also an example of lexical parallelism and may be

184. Watson (*Classical Hebrew Poetry*, 329) refers to the interrelationship between word-pairs and merismus.

185. Watson (ibid., 331) offers 46:4ab as an example of the breakup of pairs, but oddly, does not notice the example of word-pairs in 3cd. His omission is all the more striking since he cites Job 3:11 (p. 330), which contains the very word-pair in question. There the word order is reversed, *rḥm/bṭn*.

diagrammed as follows: a b c c′ // a b′ c d. Of the eight words in these lines, two are repetitions, two are word-pairs, and only one—*ʾsbl*, the last word in the line-pair—is not grammatically or lexically paired. This last word, by its uniqueness, functions both to close off the description of Jacob/Israel and to move into the new development, that of the self-description of Yahweh, which was begun by the phrase *ʾny hwʾ* in line 4a.

The final line-pair of the section is joined to the previous line-pair by the repetition of two key words: *ʾny* and *ʾsbl*. The fivefold repetition of both *ʾny* and of 1 s. verbs is striking in this section. The motif here is obviously Yahweh's self-description and, possibly, self-defense. Muilenburg observes that in this section, the first 4 lines (3abcd) are introductory to the 4 lines of v. 4. The key words of the first 4 lines, which serve to introduce Yahweh in the last 4, are the passive participles *ʿms* and *nśʾ*, synonyms for 'carry' or 'lift'. The root *nśʾ* is repeated in 4c, and another synonym is added: *sbl*, which is repeated in order to emphasize the bearing abilities of Yahweh.

There are four 1 s. impf. verbs here, and one 1 s. pf. verb. Not only does *ʿśyty* stand out from the pattern in this way, it is also a more all-purpose word to characterize Yahweh's activity. It summarizes everything that Yahweh has done or accomplished in the past, which serves as a pledge and sign of what Yahweh will do in the future, described by the imperfect verbs: he will bear a load (*sbl*), he will lift (*nśʾ*), he will deliver (*mlṭ*).

The fivefold repetition of the first-person pronoun *ʾny* along with the fivefold repetition of the 1 s. verb form emphasize God's description of himself. However, the pattern of these repetitions is not one of exact repetition. While the pattern is balanced, it is a more complex and intricate symmetry. Each personal pronoun is not tied to each verb. Line 4a, which begins the self-description of Yahweh, contains the verbless clause *ʾny hwʾ*. In 4d, which ends the self-description, the verb appears without the emphatic pronoun. The complex interlocking of verb and pronoun can be diagrammed as follows:

pronoun:	1st	2d	3d	4th	5th	
	ʾny(hwʾ)	*ʾny*	*ʾny*	*ʾny*	*ʾny*	
verb:		1st	2d	3d	4th	5th
		ʾsbl	*ʿśyty*	*ʾśʾ*	*ʾsbl*	*(w)ʾmlt*

This fivefold clustering of first-person forms in reference to God appears several times in the poems under study.[186] Here, with ten instances in one verse, the emphasis is striking.

186. See 46:13 and 48:9, 11, and 15.

These variations and divergencies from the pattern serve to mark transitions within the unit. The stress pattern, which in the previous 3 lines (4abc) was 4+4+4, now drops to 3 (4d), another variation marking a transition and the end of the unit. These verses (3–4), like those in section I, make up an 8-line, 4-line-pair pattern.

Section III (vv. 5–7)

Like section I, this is another scene that has the Babylonian idol as a key figure. It portrays the construction of an idol, from the hiring of an idol-maker through to the stationing of the idol in its place, to the assertion of its ineffectuality. As in section I, the idol is carried in a procession, but here it is human beings instead of animals who do the work of carrying. The continuation of the first-person pronoun indicates that Yahweh is still speaking. The addressees are his own people, as above, who need to be reminded that there is no one like Yahweh.

The rhetorical questions of lines 5a and b serve several purposes. These questions introduce this section of the poem in much the same way as the imperatives of sections II, IV, and V. They also set the stage for the following scene by implying that there is no one to whom God can be compared. The entire section is united by the fact that the answer to the questions is provided in v. 7: idols cannot be compared to the God of Israel, because they cannot move, answer, or save.

Another feature that unites this section is the development of the scene in chronological order. It begins, after the rhetorical questions, with the extravagant people digging in their purses for money, which is then weighed out on a scale. Next they hire a smith, who makes an idol that they proceed to worship. After this they lift the idol on their shoulders, bear it away, and then set it down in the place where it is to stand. There someone prays to it for deliverance but to no avail. The people who are making and worshiping idols have been identified above as the Israelites living in exile.

The structure of this section is different from the preceding 2 sections, which were composed of 8 lines each. Section III has 11 lines, varying in stresses from 2 to 4 per line, and in syllables from 7 to 11 per line. There are 3 long lines with respect to syllables (6c=10, 7a=11, 7b=10), and 2 lines stand out from the dominant 2- or 3-stress pattern because they have 4 stresses (lines 6c and 7d).

There are 2 obvious line-pairs in the section, lines 5ab and 6ab, but the relationships among the remaining lines are not as obvious. Lines 6c through 7b are linked by a profusion of m. pl. impf. verbs that describe the actions of the idol-worshipers. Lines 7cde are linked by the recurrence of the negative particle *lʾ* in each line and the emphasis on the inactivity of the idol. However, the MT indicates by the *ʾatnaḥ* after 7c that 7abc is a unit. A further uncertainty about the arrangement of the lines from 6c through 7c is reflected in BHK and BHS.[187] Several possibilities for arrangement of the lines exist.

The actual scene begins with the line-pair of 6a–b, the structure of which was described above.[188] The scene is set for those who lavish huge sums of money to have an idol made. This line-pair is related to the following lines not only in theme—verb form (3 m. pl. impf.) and chronological ordering (they must first weigh out the money before they can hire a smith)—but also by a sound pattern—the repetition of *k*/*q* and *s*/*ś*/*š* sounds. Note the following alliterations: *mkys*, *wksp*, *bqnh*, *yšqlw*, *yśkrw*, *wyʿśhw*, *ysgdw*, *yšthwu*, *yśʾhw*, *ktp*, *ysblhw*.[189] Assonance is also present in the repetitions of the 3 m. pl. *waw*, and the 3 m. s. suffix *hw*.

Continuing the chronological development are 4 lines, vv. 6c–7b. There is a total of eight 3 m. verbs in these 4 lines. Six pl. verbs massed in 4 lines describe the frenetic activity of the idol-worshipers, one singular verb describes the action of the idol-maker, and the last s. verb refers to the idol itself. The difficulty with determining the delineation of these verses (as in v. 4) is due to the interweaving of the verbs and adverbs or prepositions with one another.

Line 6c in my translation is one line composed of two clauses with 4 stresses.[190] It is possible to divide 6c into 2 lines:

yśkrw ṣwrp	They hire a smith,
wyʿśhw ʾl	And he makes it a god

This arrangement fits the preferred lineation according to M. O'Connor's scheme. However, I read them as one line, since a syllable count of 5 per line occurs nowhere else in the poem and therefore seems out of place here.[191]

187. BHK divides the sections of the first half of v. 7 as follows: *yśʾhw ʿl-ktp ysblhw*/ *wynyḥhw tḥtyw wyʿmd* / *mmqwmw lʾ ymyš*. BHS divides differently and reflects indecisiveness on the part of the modern-day editor about the relationship of the words to one another: *yśʾhw* / *ʿl-ktp* / *ysblhw* // *wynyḥhw* / *tḥtyw* / *wyʿmd* / *mmqwmw lʾ ymyš*.

188. See Notes on Translation and Text, above p. 45.

189. See above, n. 38, on alliteration and assonance.

190. And four constituents, according to O'Connor's definition. See *Hebrew Verse Structure*, 87, and examples of this configuration on p. 355. It should be noted that his examples include almost all vocatives with verbs. Only in one case is there a combination of two verbs with different subjects, as is the case here.

191. 1a is a line of similar construction, having four units (according to O'Connor's terminology), a combination of two verbs with two different subjects. The same reasoning holds true for 7d, which, if divided into these two lines:

Lines 7abc are a unit in the MT by virtue of the placement of the *ʾatnaḥ*. Line 7c has the same general pattern as 7ab, a verb and prepositional phrase (*mmqwmw lʾ ymyš*); in addition, 7c is a parallel expression for *wyʿmd*.[192] However, 7c also serves as a bridge between 7b and 7de. The structure of line 7c is echoed in the closing line, 7e, and the overall theme of lines 7b–e is the inactivity of the idol (it stands, it does not move, it does not answer, it does not save). As a result of these complicated interconnections, it is difficult to decide how to describe the 5 lines. There are four options: (1) 7abc is a line-trio, and 7de a line-pair; (2) 7ab is a line-pair, 7cde is a line-trio; (3) 7ab and 7de are 2 line-pairs, with 7c acting as a bridge between the 2; (4) the entire verse is a 5-line construction (a pentacolon), representing two units. The last option is uncommon, though, as will be seen in the discussion of section IV, not unique. In any case, this unusual construction indicates the end of the third section.

Section IV (vv. 8–11)

This section begins, as did section II, with imperatives, "Remember," Stand firm," "Bring to mind," and a vocative, "O rebels." The audience's attention is drawn away from the previous scene to God, who again describes himself in terms of his activities. There are 13 lines in this section. The pattern of stresses is very regular, all lines except 2 having 3 stresses. The syllable pattern is within the expected range, between 6–9. The section is united by the theme of Yahweh's self-description. After the introductory imperatives and address, the whole section is composed of first-person singular verbs and a regular pattern of participles, all describing God. It is also united by certain repetitions: imperatives are used four times for emphasis in the beginning, the first-person pron. suffix or verb form occurs ten times,[193] and three emphatic particles are used to stress the idea of Yahweh's sovereign power.

Some scholars disagree about the relationship of line 8a to 8b–9a. They see 8a as the conclusion to the previous section, in that the audience is being called to remember "this," that is, the impotence of the idol. Others (e.g., Muilenburg) understand the imperatives to refer only to what follows in vv. 9–11. The verbs of line 8a are imperatives and are different from those of the preceding lines. Habel[194] considers 46:8–11 to be an example

---

ʾp yṣʿq ʾlyw	even if he cries to it
wlʾ yʿnh	still it will not answer

would yield a syllable count of 5 and 4, again, uncharacteristic of the rest of the poem

192. "It stands (there); // from its place it does not move."

193. Reading *ʿṣty*, with the *Qere*. See notes on v. 11 above, p. 64.

194. Habel, "Appeal to Ancient Tradition," 266.

of the literary form of an appeal to ancient tradition. Since a description of a scene has been replaced by a pattern of repeated imperatives, I see 8a as the beginning of a new unit. However, I do not disagree with those who see a relationship between these two sections. All of the imperatives can refer both to what has preceded as well as to what is to follow. There is no need to limit the point of reference of these imperatives to either one or the other section.[195]

Lines 8a–9c begin in the same way as the previous section ended, with a complex arrangement of 5 lines. Again, because of the complicated connections among the lines, there are several possible ways to describe their relationship. The threefold call to "remember" or "bring to mind," as well as the repetition of the imperative *zkrw* in vv. 8a and 9a, could make up a line-trio. Line 9a could also be interpreted as relating more closely to 9bc, thus forming a line-trio with these lines. The key is 9a, much like 7c, which is an integral part, both of what precedes and what follows. Lines 7c and 9a function as a hinge between the line-pairs to which they are adjacent, forming a pattern AA′BCC′. This pattern is discussed by Watson;[196] he calls it a pentacolon with a chiastic sequence and gives an example from Hos 14:10.

The placement of the vocative is unusual. Normally the vocative follows an opening imperative.[197] Here, however, the vocative appears in the second line, and furthermore, it breaks up the combination *hšybw ᶜl-lb.* This inversion and disruption of the expected order may be a way the poet has of highlighting the disturbing and condemnatory characterization of Jacob/Israel.

The particle *ky* (9b) introduces the object(s) of the commands to remember. Muilenburg states, "The twofold call to remember is connected

195. H. Van Dyke Parunak has discussed the various ways in which one strophe develops into another ("Oral Typesetting: Some Uses of Biblical Structure," *Bib* 62 [1981] 153–68; and "Transitional Techniques in the Bible," *JBL* 102 [1983] 525–48). However, he has not to my knowledge discussed the double-duty function of one line as a bridge or hinge between 2 sections. "Remember this, and stand firm," 46:8a, can be seen to be a line with just such a function. It calls the people to remember the negative results of worshiping impotent idols and also to remember that their God is powerful.

196. Watson, *Classical Hebrew Poetry,* 187–88.

197. For examples in DI see 40:9; 41:1, 14; 44:1, 2, 21, 23; 45:8, 22; 46:3, 12; 47:1, 5 (two imvs.), 8; 48:1, 12, 14; 49:1, 13; 51:1, 4, 7, 21; 52:2 (2 imvs.), 9; 54:1. Isa 45:20; 51:9, 17; and 52:1 have three imperatives followed by a vocative. 52:11 has six. But see 42:18 and 55:1, where the vocatives precede the imperatives. See Watson, ibid. (358), for other examples of the normal pattern—opening imperative / vocative—and the inversion of the pattern.

by the particle *ky* 'for', to the twofold declaration of monotheism, 'I am God.' " However, this only explains in part the function of the particle and does not deal with the fact that there are four imperatives, two of them synonyms of *zkr.* The particle *ky* not only governs the claims of God to divinity, it also governs the whole long sentence that begins with these claims in 9b and is carried through in the series of participles to 11b. The rebels are charged to remember not only that Yahweh is God, but also that his divinity manifests itself in activity.

Regarding the fourfold call to remember, the four imperatives are balanced by four declarations on Yahweh's part regarding his identity. Two are positive statements: "I am El" and "I am God." Two are negatives that eliminate other possible claimants to divinity: "there is no other" and "there is none like me."

This four-part declaration of God's divinity following upon the fourfold call to remember has another function within the larger unit of chap. 46. Section III began with a rhetorical question, which was stated in four 2 m. pl. verbs, all synonyms for 'compare'. The "you" of those 2 m. pl. verbs was not specifically identified in section III. But the subjects of the 2 m. pl. verbs are identified in section II, 3a and following (the house of Jacob / the remnant of the house of Israel) and in 8b (rebels). There is no reason to believe that those to whom the rhetorical questions were addressed are any different from those to whom the imperatives were addressed. Verses 8–9 can be read as a response to the questions posed in section III. The answer to the four-part question in v. 5, "To whom will you compare me and liken me, and equate me, that we are alike?" is found in the response, "Remember this, stand firm, bring it to mind, remember . . . I am El and there is no other. God, and there is none like me."

A similar pattern is present in Isa 40:12ff., esp. vv. 18ff. and 25ff. In v. 18 two rhetorical questions are posed: "To whom will you compare God? What comparison will you set up to him?" The questions are not directly answered. Instead, a description of the making of idols follows in vv. 19–20, just as it did in 46:5 and 6ff. In 40:25, two more rhetorical questions are posed: "To whom will you compare me and liken me?" (both chapters use the verb *dmh* twice and *šwh* once). These are followed by imperatives charging Israel to "look and see" that Yahweh, the everlasting God, the creator, is the one who acts on their behalf. In 40:12ff., as in chap. 46, Yahweh's actions are described in a series of participles that emphasize his creative and saving powers.

The participles in vv. 10a–11b describing Yahweh's activities are part of a series of three line-pairs, each of which is arranged in the pattern abc // b′c′. The line-pairs are connected by the repetition of a masculine singular participle synonymous with 'speak, declare' at the beginning of each line-pair. In each second line, there is ellipsis of the participle.[198]

Verses 10a and 11a are grammatically parallel: each line has the pattern m. s. part. / prep. + s. n. / s. n.:

10a	*mgyd*	*mrʾšyt*	*ʾḥryt*
11a	*qrʾ*	*mmzrḥ*	*ʿyṭ*

The only difference in these lines is the use of two feminine nouns in 10a, two masculine nouns in 11a.[199]

Verses 10b and 11b both begin with the preposition *mn*. In both the first and third line-pair in this series, there are words that indicate direction either primarily or secondarily: *ʾḥr, qdm, mzrḥ, ʾrṣ mrḥq*. The middle line-pair in the series (10c and 10d) stands out from the others in that it quotes Yahweh: "My plan will stand, and all I intend I will do." Within the 6 lines of vv. 10a–11b, the 2 matching lines (10a and 11a) form an envelope around the middle line-pair.

The section concludes with the threefold occurrence of the particle *ʾp* and the fourfold use of the verb in the first person. The assertion of lines 9a and b, "I am God"—is affirmed in the concluding lines, "I speak, bring, form, act."

Section IV, like section III, has a complex arrangement of 5 lines, a combination of a line-pair and a line-trio. In this case, however, the 5-line pattern begins rather than ends the section. In all, there are 13 lines composed of 5 line-pairs and one line-trio.

Section V (vv. 12–13)

The final lines of the poem begin with the familiar pattern of imperative and vocatives, which marked the start of sections II and IV. God again demands the attention of his listeners, and tells them he has already done for them things of which they are apparently unaware. Even though this is the shortest section of the poem, it incorporates many of the elements of the poem by repetition of key words, especially the imperative *šmʿw*, the name Israel, and variations of the root *yšʿ*. In this respect it functions as the coda, to sum up the previous lines. Another uniting feature is the appearance in every line but one of the 1st s. suffix or verb indicator. Muilen-

198. According to Watson (ibid., 176), the abc // b′c′ couplet tends to occur in clusters. In this case there is a cluster of three such couplets (or line-pairs).

199. Watson (ibid., 43 and 123ff.) sees patterning at work in gender-matched parallelism, in which the genders of the nouns in each line match. The most straightforward pattern is m. + m. // f. + f. I am not convinced that this is a basic component to the patterning of this or most other lines in poetry. Since there are only two genders from which to choose, the probability of this occurring unintentionally is high.

burg observes that it also brings to full realization the motif of salvation and deliverance that ran throughout the poem.

The first 2 lines introduce the final message with the imperative and two vocatives, which characterize Jacob/Israel as mighty of heart and far from justice. As in section II, the imperative and vocative in 12a are balanced by a lengthier vocative in 12b, reflected in the syllable count 8+8=16 and stress pattern 4+2=6. Here is an example of the standard meter described by Freedman.[200] While the dominant pattern of the standard meter is 8+8 and 3+3, this line-pair furnishes an example of the skill of the poet in varying the pattern of line length so that the pause is not in the middle, while maintaining an overall balance.[201]

In the next 2 line-pairs (13ab, 13cd), each begins with a 1 s. pf. verb that governs both lines. The stress pattern is 3+2, 3+2, and the lines are syntactically parallel, yielding the following pattern:

13a:	a b c	*qrbty ṣdqty lʾ trḥq*
13b:	b′ c′	*wtšwʿty lʾ tʾḥr*
13c:	a′ d b″	*wntty bṣywn tšwʿh*
13d:	d′ b‴	*lyśrʾl tpʾrty*

The line-pairs are joined together by the objects of each of the verbs. In the case of lines 13b and c, the f. noun *tšwʿh* is repeated and forms a chiasm. The close of the section (also the close of the poem) is indicated by the final line, which is shorter in stress and syllable count than the previous line (3+2 stress count, 10+7 syllable count for the two last lines).

Structure of the Poem: Macrostructure

After examining the individual words and lines of the poem, then the relationships among the lines and their division into larger sections, we can proceed to examine the structure of the poem as a whole. Michael O'Connor, when beginning his analysis of the macrostructure of selected poems, was skeptical about the process: there is nothing "that is clear about the gross structure of Hebrew verse."[202] What is clear is that there are poems of some length. My approach is to analyze individual poems and make observations about their patterns and structures. Then more general observations can be made about relationships between the structures of poems within the Bible,

200. Freedman, "Acrostic Poems," 430.

201. Syllables can also be varied in like manner, so that the total count is 16, while the individual lines are not divided in the middle. For example, see Lam 5:2, 9, 11, and 12, using Freedman's counting in "Acrostic Poems" (417–18).

202. O'Connor, *Hebrew Verse Structure*, 424.

with the end in mind to make clear some things about the gross structure of Hebrew verse.

The following observations are offered about the overall structure of chap. 46 and the features that demonstrate that it is one poem rather than a collection of originally disparate short pieces.

1. The poem has 46 lines, divided into 20 line-pairs and 2 line-trios, making 22 units. This fits the typical pattern of the acrostic (alphabetic or nonalphabetic) discussed by D. N. Freedman.[203] He shows that chap. 5 of Lamentations, as well as a number of other poems (Psalms 33 and 94) that do not use the alphabetic sequence as a structuring device, nonetheless are made up of 22 or 23 units.

2. The total number of syllables for this 22-unit poem is 368. Other acrostic (or nonalphabetic acrostic) poems of 22 units studied by Freedman[204] have remarkably similar syllable counts: Lamentations 5, 362 syllables; Proverbs 31, 360 syllables; Psalm 25, 362 syllables; Psalm 34 (21 units), 351 syllables. Psalm 37, which has twice the units (44), has twice the syllables (719 = 359.5 × 2). The overall length of this poem is extremely regular when compared to poems of similar structure. This is true, in spite of the fact that individual lines vary considerably in length.

3. The average number of syllables per line[205] in this poem is 8 (total syllables 368, divided by total lines 46 = 8); the average number of stresses is 2.9 (total stresses 135/6, divided by 46 lines = 2.93/2.96). This matches almost exactly the standard pattern of alphabetic acrostic poems, which average 16 syllables per line-pair (8 per line), 6 stresses per line-pair (3 per line).[206]

4. The poem is divided into 5 sections.

I	8 lines
II	8 lines
III	11 lines
IV	13 lines
V	6 lines

The first section of 8 lines functions as an introduction to the body of the poem. Section I stands out from the rest of the poem, while at the same

203. Freedman, "Acrostic Poems," 415ff.

204. D. N. Freedman, "Acrostics and Metrics in Hebrew Poetry," in *Pottery, Poetry, and Prophecy: Collected Essays on Hebrew Poetry* (Winona Lake, Ind.: Eisenbrauns, 1980) 76.

205. The syllables vary considerably from line to line, from 6 to 11 syllables per line.

206. Freedman, "Acrostic Poems," 429.

time it forms an excellent introduction to the development in sections II–V. It is the only section of the poem that does not begin with an address in the second person. It is also the only section of the poem in which God does not speak in the first person. It introduces the themes of idolatry and of the impotence of idols, which serve as counterpoints to the incomparability of Yahweh and the importance of Israel's acknowledgement of Yahweh rather than any other deities.

5. The remaining sections are united by the verbs that begin each section. The first line of each has at least one m. pl. verb (II, *šmᶜw*; III, *tdmywny*; IV, *zkrw*; V, *šmᶜw*). The imperatives *šmᶜw* and *zkrw* control the structure by their placement:

vv. 3 and 8	*šmᶜw . . . zkrw*
vv. 9 and 12	*zkrw . . . šmᶜw*

The body of the poem is also structured by the two adjoining 5-line combinations in the middle of the poem, at the conclusion of section III and the beginning of section IV. Both the placement of the imperatives and the contiguity of the two 5-line sections are evidence of the chiastic structure of the body of the poem.[207] The sections are also quite symmetrical by virtue of the equal distribution of lines: 19 lines in sections II–III, 19 in IV–V. The chiasm at the center highlights the theme of the dangers of idolatry.

6. Furthermore, sections II, IV, and V are identical in their larger structures in that each begins with an imperative and vocative(s), and each ends with first-person verbs in which Yahweh describes his activities. Section III, which deals with the idol-makers, ends with a declaration of the inactivity of the idol, which stands in direct contrast to Yahweh's activity.

7. The poem is developed by alternating dramatic scenes that emphasize Babylonian gods and idol-makers (sections I and III) with Yahweh's declarations of his supremacy (sections II and IV and the conclusion in V).

8. Sections II and V form an inclusio, or envelope, around sections III and IV by the repetition of the imperative *šmᶜw*, as well as the address to Jacob/Israel in the beginning of section II and the promise to Zion/Israel in the end of section V.

9. The entire poem is built upon a complicated interweaving of contrasts and comparisons on several levels:

207. Jack Lundbom (*Jeremiah: A Study in Ancient Hebrew Rhetoric* [SBLDS 18; Missoula: Scholars Press, 1975] chap. 3) discusses chiasmus as a structuring device for entire poems in the book of Jeremiah. See also Ceresko, "The Function of Chiasmus in Hebrew Poetry" (*CBQ* 40 [1978] 2–6), on the structuring function of chiasmus. In his discussion, he shows that the AB/BA pattern stands almost at the center of the poems.

Bel and Nebo // Yahweh: The Babylonian gods must be carried, but Yahweh carries (the point of comparison centers on the word *nśʾ*). While Yahweh carries a burden, by contrast, the Babylonian gods are a burden.

Bel and Nebo // Jacob/Israel: These two are compared in that both are carried, borne up. The contrast is in the agents who carry. In the case of Bel and Nebo, it is the animals in vv. 1–2 or the people in vv. 6–7 who must carry them. The people of Israel by contrast are carried by their God.

Bel and Nebo // idol-worshipers: Both are comparable in their actions of bowing down, going down. The gods in the procession can be seen to bow down as heavy burdens on the animals and to go down into exile. The worshipers fall down in fruitless worship to impotent idols. A further implication may be drawn that those who worship idols will also go down into exile with them.

Yahweh // idols: Yahweh is in no way like idols. Their existence depends upon a contract made with a smith and a process of manufacturing. The idol must be lifted up and carried through the streets to its resting place, where it stands, immobile. The idol is stolid, unhearing, unheeding, and does not answer cries for help. By contrast, Yahweh's existence does not depend on a process of manufacturing, nor does his ability to move depend on a parade of workers. He is not in any way immobile, and he can and does respond to the pleas of his people. Yahweh is contrasted to the idols or gods in that he is able to describe events that have not yet happened, to make and execute plans, to control the processes of history. In fact, Yahweh is incomparable.

Another aspect of the comparison between Yahweh and the idols is found in vv. 7 and 13 in the repetition of the root of *yšʿ*. The focus of comparison between Yahweh and the Babylonian gods is whether or not each is powerful. This was no doubt a question for the exiles, who felt abandoned by Yahweh, and as the years went by, wondered whether or not he was in fact powerful enough to answer their pleas. The people in the wilderness at Sinai had a similar concern when Moses disappeared. After a while they felt they needed a god they could worship who would go before them to lead them. Their solution was to make a god. Here in Babylon they have encountered similar difficulties and have taken similar steps, that is, the making of an idol. They need to be told what will come of such action. Verse 7 sums up the consequences of calling on an idol: it does not move, does not answer, does not save (*lʾ ywšyʿnw*). Verse 13 describes the consequences of fidelity to Yahweh by the repetition of the root of *yšʿ*, *tšwʿh*: it is the God of Israel who brings near, gives salvation.

Yahweh // idol-maker: The idol-maker makes (*ʿśh*) a useless and ineffectual idol; Yahweh makes and forms (*ʿśh, yṣr*) plans and activities that are effective and valuable.

Through the interplay of a variety of comparisons and contrasts, the poem develops the notion of Yahweh's incomparable power. The poem moves from the downward spiral of Bel/Nebo // and their worshipers, to the upward direction of Yahweh // and Jacob/Israel/Zion, who acknowledge that Yahweh is God and there is no other.

Isaiah 47

Text

		Syllable Count	*Total*	*Stresses*
Section I				
1a	rdy wšby ʿl-ʿpr	2+3+1+2	8	3
b	btwlt bt-bbl	3+1+2	6	3
c	šby-lʾrṣ ʾyn-ksʾ	2+2+1+2	7	3
d	bt-kśdym	1+2	3	2
e	ky lʾ twsypy yqrʾw-lk	1+1+3+3+1	9	3
f	rkh wʿngh	2+3	5	2
2a	qḥy rḥym	2+2	4	2
b	wṭḥny qmḥ	4+1	5	2
c	gly ṣmtk	2+3	5	2
d	ḥśpy-šbl	2+1	3	2
e	gly-šwq	2+1	3	2
f	ʿbry nhrwt	2+3	5	2
3a	tgl ʿrwtk	2+3	5	2
b	gm trʾh ḥrptk	1+3+3	7	3
c	nqm ʾqḥ	2+2	4	2
d	wlʾ ʾpgʿ ʾdm	2+2+2	6	3
4a	gʾlnw yhwh ṣbʾwt šmw	4+2+3+2	11	4
b	qdwš yśrʾl	2+3	5	2
	18 lines		101	44
Section II				
5a	šby dwmm wbʾy bḥšk	2+2+3+2	9	4
b	bt-kśdym	1+2	3	2
c	ky lʾ twsypy yqrʾw-lk	1+1+3+3+1	9	3
d	gbrt mmlkwt	2+3	5	2
6a	qṣpty ʿl-ʿmy	3+1+2	6	2
b	ḥllty nḥlty	3+3	6	2
c	wʾtnm bydk	4+3	7	2
d	lʾ-śmt lhm rḥmym	1+1+2+3	7	3
e	ʿl-zqn hkbdt ʿlk mʾd	1+2+2+2+2	9	4

Translation

Section I

1a Go down and sit down in the dust,
b O virgin daughter Babylon.
c Sit down on the earth—unthroned—
d O daughter Chaldea.
e You shall not continue to be called
f "tender and delicate."
2a Take millstones,
b and grind meal.
c Uncover your hair,
d strip off (your) skirt,
e uncover (your) leg,
f cross over rivers.
3a Your nakedness will be uncovered;
b what is more, your shame will be seen.
c Vindication I will take,
d and I will not deal kindly with anyone.
4a Our redeemer—Yahweh of Hosts is his name—
b is the Holy One of Israel.

Section II

5a Sit down silently and go into darkness,
b O daughter Chaldea.
c You shall not continue to be called
d "mistress of kingdoms."
6a I was angry at my people;
b I profaned my inheritance,
c so I gave them into your hand.
d You did not show them compassion;
e upon the old you made your yoke exceedingly heavy.

7a	wtʾmry lʿwlm	4+3	7	2
b	ʾhyh gbrt ʿd	2+2+1	5	2/3
c	lʾ-śmt ʾlh ʿl-lbk	1+1+2+1+2	7	3
d	lʾ zkrt ʾḥryth	1+2+3	6	2
	13 lines		86	33/34

Section III

8a	wʿth šmʿy-zʾt ʿdynh	3+2+1+3	9	4
b	hywšbt lbṭḥ	3+2	5	2
c	hʾmrh blbbh	4+3	7	2
d	ʾny wʾpsy ʿwd	2+3+1	6	3
e	lʾ ʾšb ʾlmnh	1+2+3	6	2
f	wlʾ ʾdʿ škwl	2+2+2	6	3
9a	wtbʾnh lk šty-ʾlh	4+1+1+2	8	3/4
b	rgʿ bywm ʾḥd	1+2+2	5	3
c	škwl wʾlmn ktmm	2+3+3	8	3
d	bʾw ʿlyk	2+3	5	2
e	brb kšpyk	2+4	6	2
f	bʿṣmt ḥbryk mʾd	3+4+2	9	3
10a	wtbṭḥy brʿtk	4+4	8	2
b	ʾmrt ʾyn rʾny	2+1+3	6	2/3
c	ḥkmtk wdʿtk	3+3	6	2
d	hyʾ šwbbtk	1+4	5	2
e	wtʾmry blbk	4+3	7	2
f	ʾny wʾpsy ʿwd	2+3+1	6	3
11a	wbʾ ʿlyk rʿh	2+2+2	6	3
b	lʾ tdʿy šḥrh	1+3+2	6	2
c	wtpl ʿlyk hwh	3+2+2	7	3
d	lʾ twkly kprh	1+3+3	7	2
e	wtbʾ ʿlyk ptʾm	3+2+2	7	3
f	šwʾh lʾ tdʿy	2+1+3	6	2
	24 lines		157	60/62

Section IV

12a	ʿmdy-nʾ bḥbryk	2+1+4	7	2/3
b	wbrb kšpyk	3+3	6	2
c	bʾšr ygʿt mnʿwryk	3+2+4	9	3
d	ʾwly twkly hwʿyl	2+3+2	7	3
e	ʾwly tʿrwṣy	2+3	5	2
13a	nlʾyt brb ʿṣtyk	2+2+3	7	3
b	yʿmdw-nʾ wywšyʿk	3+1+4	8	2/3

7a And you said, "Forever I will be
b mistress forever."
c You did not lay these upon your heart;
d you did not remember its end.

Section III

8a And now, hear this, luxury-lover,
b who sits securely,
c who says in her heart,
d "I am, and there is no other.
e I will not sit as a widow,
f and I will not know bereavement."
9a Yes, these two will come to you,
b suddenly, in one day.
c Bereavement and widowhood in their full measure
d come upon you.
e Oh, the abundance of your sorceries;
f Oh, the great might of your spells!
10a But you were secure in your evil;
b you said, "No one sees me."
c Your wisdom and your knowledge—
d this is what leads you astray.
e And you said in your heart,
f "I am, and there is no other."
11a And evil will come upon you;
b you will not know its dawn.
c And ruin will fall upon you;
d you will not be able to appease it.
e And it will come upon you suddenly,
f devastation you did not know.

Section IV

12a Stand up, now, with your spells,
b and with the abundance of your sorceries
c for which you toiled from your youth.
d Perhaps you will be able to profit;
e perhaps you will inspire awe.
13a You are wearied by the abundance of your counsels.
b Let them stand up, now, and save you,

c	hbrw šmym	2+2	4	2
d	hḥzym bkwkbym	3+4	7	2
e	mwdyʿm lḥdšym	3+3/4	6/7	2
f	mʾšr ybʾw ʿlyk	3+3+2	8	3
	11 lines		74/75	26/28
Section V				
14a	hnh hyw kqš	2+2+2	6	3
b	ʾš śrptm	1+4	5	2
c	lʾ-yṣylw ʾt-npšm	1+3+1+2	7	3
d	myd lhbh	2+3	5	2
e	ʾyn-gḥlt lḥmm	1+2+2	5	2/3
f	ʾwr lšbt ngdw	1+2+2	5	3
15a	kn hyw-lk ʾšr ygʿt	1+2+1+2+2	8	4
b	sḥryk mnʿwryk	3+4	7	2
c	ʾyš lʿbrw tʿw	1+3+2	6	3
d	ʾyn mwšyʿk	1+3	4	2
	10 lines		58	26/27
Totals				
	76 lines		476 syllables	189/195 stresses

Average syllables and stresses per line:
2.49/2.57 stresses/line; 37 units (35 line-pairs, 2 line-trios);
12.9 syllables/unit; 5.1/5.27 stresses/unit

Notes on Translation and Text

47:1a, c. *rdy wšby ʿl-ʿpr* "Go down and sit down on the dust"
***šby-lʾrṣ ʾyn-ksʾ* "Sit down on the earth—unthroned"**

Like chap. 46, this chapter begins abruptly. This time it is with a series of feminine singular imperatives addressed to Babylon. The initial verb, *yrd*, occurs only once in the poem, but the next verb, *yšb*, appears as an imperative three times (twice in v. 1, once more in v. 5) and three times more in other forms (v. 8 as feminine singular participle and first singular impf., and v. 14 as an infinitive). Each time it is used, it takes on a different shade of meaning.

In the first usage, it is parallel with *yrd*. Babylon is to go down, descend to the dust, in a posture of humiliation and perhaps a gesture of

c those who divide the heavens,
d those who gaze at the stars,
e those who make known through the new moon
f what will come upon you.

Section V
14a Behold, they are like chaff.
b Fire burns them.
c They will not deliver themselves
d from the hand of the flame.
e This is not coal to warm oneself,
f a blaze to sit before.
15a So they are to you, those with whom you toiled,
b your traders, from your youth.
c Each wanders in his own direction;
d There is no one saving you.

---

mourning. Then the imperative is repeated: Babylon is to "sit down on the earth" (*lʾrṣ*), another expression used for mourning.[1] For similar expressions of mourning, see Isa 3:26, "Her gates shall lament and mourn; ravaged she shall sit upon the ground (*lʾrṣ tšb*)"; and Lam 2:10, "The elders of the daughter of Zion sit on the ground in silence (*yšbw lʾrṣ ydmw*); they have cast dust (*ʿpr*) on their heads and put on sackcloth; the maidens of Jerusalem have bowed their heads to the ground (*hwrydw lʾrṣ rʾšn*)." For the humiliation of a vanquished city, see Isa 25:12, where the destruction of the fortifications of Moab includes bringing her down, laying her low, casting her to "the ground, even to the dust (*lʾrṣ ʿd ʿpr*)." Isa 26:5 has similar expressions for laying low a lofty city to the ground, casting it to

1. 1QIsa[a] reads *šby ʿl hʾrṣ*, adding the definite article as well as *ʿl* instead of *l-*.

the dust.[2] In these examples, the mourners willingly take their places on the ground as part of the ritual, while by contrast the vanquished nation or city must be forcibly laid low by God. Here in Isaiah 47 God orders Babylon to go down to the dust.

The second time *yšb* occurs in this poem is in conjunction with the expression *ʾyn ksʾ* 'unthroned'. The expression *yšb l-* is used elsewhere in connection with Yahweh's sitting in judgment or sitting as king: Ps 9:5, 8; 29:10; and others.[3] It is ironic that here the sitting is in reference to the loss of a throne. The second imperative *šby* is more than command to sit down in mourning. It is a command for Babylon to climb down from her throne, no more to rule.

There is a parallel to Babylon's descent in the Ugaritic text Baal and Anath,[4] where *Lṭpn* (i.e., El) goes down from the throne, sits on the footstool, and from the footstool sits on the earth.

ʿpr . . . ʾrṣ **"dust . . . earth"**

Gevirtz[5] and Dahood[6] discuss *ʾrṣ* and *ʿpr* as a fixed word-pair in Ugaritic and Hebrew. In Ugaritic it occurs 10 times; in Hebrew 13.[7] Watson also points out that the standard sequence is earth //dust.[8] The sequence is inverted at times to portray an "abnormal event," or to achieve emphasis.

'Dust' and 'earth' also appear in construct state, as in Gen 13:16; Exod 8:12, 13; Isa 40:12; Amos 2:7; and Job 14:1. Tromp refers to the spontaneous association of the pair "earth-dust" with the thought of the dead and

2. See Isa 10:13, in which the king of Assyria boasts of bringing down (*yrd*) those who are enthroned (*yšbym*).

3. See F. M. Cross, *Canaanite Myth and Hebrew Epic: Essays in the History of the Religion of Israel* (Cambridge: Harvard University Press, 1973) 97 n. 24. According to Cross, the normal idiom is *yšb ʿl*. The idiom *yšb l-*, referring to enthronement, is frequent only in early Hebrew poetry, such as Ps 132:12, Judg 5:17, Ps 29:10, or in archaizing contexts such as Ps 9:5 and Isaiah 47. For the expression *ʿl ʿpr*, L. Boadt suggests that the preposition was chosen for reasons of alliteration. Since the verb *yšb* can take either *l-* or *ʿl*, the poet chose *ʿl* in order to achieve alliteration with the *ʿayin* of *ʿpr*. He also suggests that the author "may have seen an advantage in balancing the syllable count," though he is not specific on this point ("Intentional Alliteration in Second Isaiah," *CBQ* 45 [1983] 359).

4. C. H. Gordon, *Ugaritic Literature* (Scripta Pontificii Istituti Biblici 98; Rome: Pontifical Biblical Institute, 1949) 42.

5. S. Gevirtz, *Patterns in the Early Poetry of Israel* (Chicago: University of Chicago Press, 1963) 38.

6. M. Dahood, *Psalms III: 101–150* (AB 17A; Garden City, N.Y.: Doubleday, 1970) 446.

7. Gevirtz, *Patterns*, 38.

8. Wilfred G. W. Watson, *Classical Hebrew Poetry: A Guide to Its Techniques* (JSOTSup 26; Sheffield: JSOT Press, 1984) 357.

cites Isa 29:4 as an example of this connection. He further cites several occurrences of *yrd ᶜpr* and concludes that the expression "means 'to go down to the grave / the netherworld.' " Furthermore, dust is part of the milieu of the underworld.[9] The mourning gesture of covering the head with dust could be a way of bringing to mind "the earth whence the human has been taken and whither he must return."[10]

It may be that in Isaiah 47, *ʾrṣ* also has connotations of the underworld. This is reminiscent of Jonah 2:7, where Jonah went down (*yrd*) to the underworld (*ʾrṣ*) to Sheol; or Isa 14:11–12, 15, where the king of Babylon was brought down (*yrd*) to Sheol, cut down to earth (*ʾrṣ*).[11] Ps 30:10[9] associates 'the pit' (*šḥt)* with 'dust' (*ᶜpr*), another connection with the underworld: "If I go down to the pit, will the dust praise you?" Other nuances of meaning are attached to the root *yšb* in 47:8 and 14, which will be discussed below.

47:1b . . . d. *btwlt bt-bbl . . . bt-kśdym*
"O virgin daughter Babylon . . . O daughter Chaldea"

The entire poem is addressed to the city Babylon, here personified as "virgin daughter Babylon" and "daughter Chaldea." The MT reads *btwlt* and *bt* in construct with *bbl* and *bt* with *ksdym.* Most translations read "Virgin daughter *of* Babylon" and "daughter *of* Chaldea."[12] BDB and GKC[13] discuss the "double construct state," the connection of *btwlt* with *bt-*, as in Isa 37:22, *btwlt bt-ṣywn* 'virgin daughter of Zion'. GKC reads *btwlt* as connected to the following word in apposition. This is what most translations reflect. However, it makes more sense to read both nouns in apposition to Babylon.[14] Clifford renders the lines 'Fair Maiden Babylon'

9. N. J. Tromp, *Primitive Conceptions of Death and the Netherworld in the Old Testament* (BibOr 21; Rome: Pontifical Biblical Institute, 1969) 29.

10. Martin-Achard, *From Death to Life: A Study of the Development of the Resurrection in the Old Testament* (trans. John Penny Smith; Edinburgh: Oliver and Boyd, 1960) 27.

11. See Tromp, *Primitive Conceptions*, 23ff., and also Dahood, *Psalms I*, for a listing of texts where *ʾrṣ* means 'underworld'.

12. I.e., RSV, Westermann, McKenzie.

13. BDB 144; GKC §130e/p. 422.

14. See Elaine R. Follis ("The Holy City as Daughter," in *Directions in Biblical Hebrew Poetry* [ed. E. Follis; JSOTSup 40; Sheffield: JSOT Press, 1987] 173ff.), who translates the related expression *bt-ṣywn* as 'daughter Zion' rather than 'daughter *of* Zion' in its 26 occurrences in the OT; and W. F. Stinespring ("No Daughter of Zion," *Encounter* 26 [1965] 133–41). His contention is that the expression, a personification, represents an occurrence of the appositional genitive and should be translated 'the daughter, Zion'. This is also the opinion of A. Fitzgerald, in "BTWLT and BT as Titles for Capital Cities" (*CBQ* 37 [1975] 167–83, esp. 181), where he also suggests that "the apparent construct *btwlt* may be an archaic absolute state preserved because it has overtones *btwlh*

and 'Fair Chaldea'. Fitzgerald interprets these phrases and others like it (namely, *bt ṣywn*) as designations of a capital city. Thus he translates 47:1 'virgin daughter Babylon', and, because of the parallelism with *bt ksdym* 'daughter (or capital) Chaldea'.[15] The alliterative effects of the repetition of *b* (*bet*) and *t* (*taw*) are striking.

The proper noun *kśdym* usually refers to the Chaldeans, those living in Chaldea,[16] but it also refers to the land itself. In Jer 50:10 *kśdym* is the subject with a 3 f. s. verb and is related to a 3 f. s. suffix (*šllyh*)—"Chaldea will be plundered, and her plunderers will be satisfied." The expression *yšby kśdym* 'dwellers of Chaldea' in Jer 51:24, 35 and the phrase in Ezek 23:15, "Babylonians, whose native land was Chaldea," as well as the locative *he* with *kśdym* in Ezek 11:24, 16:29, and 23:16, are further illustrations of this usage. In Isa 47:1d and 5b either translation is possible. The focus of the poem is on the city, virgin daughter Babylon; the city is a synecdoche for the nation that will be destroyed.

Babylon is given several other names or titles in this poem, most of which continue this image of Babylon as a woman. Whenever a city is referred to in the OT as "virgin," it almost always refers to a city that has been involved in a disaster or is about to be so involved.[17] The title here sounds an ominous note for proud Babylon, who is about to be overpowered at the hands of Yahweh's servant, Cyrus.

A similar note is sounded in the lament in Isaiah 14.[18] There the king of Babylon, who boasts of setting his throne on high in the mount of the assembly in the recesses of the north, is brought low by Yahweh. The motif in Isaiah 14, as here, is one of ascending and descending. There the king saw himself ascending above the heavens, but he was to descend into the depths of the pit, into Sheol. The same theme sounds through chap. 47. Babylon must descend to earth, to the dust, in the same manner as the humiliating descent of the king of Babylon in chap. 14.

ʾyn-ksʾ **"unthroned"**

This expression describes the state of daughter Chaldea. A relative clause is implied. As mentioned above, Babylon will lose her throne, just as

---

would not have." Boadt ("Intentional Alliteration," 360) also reads *btwlt* as an archaic feminine absolute. *Bt* is also read by Boadt as an absolute form. For other examples of the expression, he cites Jer 14:17; Isa 23:12, and 37:22.

15. Fitzgerald, "BTWLT and BT," 171.

16. BDB (505), gives illustrations of both usages. BDB interprets the phrase in 47:1a to be referring to Chaldeans.

17. See A. Fitzgerald, "The Mythological Background for the Presentation of Jerusalem as Queen and False Worship as Adultery in the OT," *CBQ* 34 (1972) 416. However, he misses Isa 37:22, the boast of a city that has escaped disaster.

18. Or parody of a lament; see Gale Yee, "The Anatomy of a Biblical Parody: The Dirge Form in 2 Samuel 1 and Isaiah 14," *CBQ* 50 (1988) 565–86.

the king of Babylon in chap. 14 was deprived of his; he, like other kings in Sheol, was weakened and humbled when he was brought to Sheol, never more to possess the earth (14:14). Negatives, such as *ʾyn, lʾ,* and *ʾpsy,* are used to good effect throughout this poem, and they serve to set the stage for Babylon's future condition.[19] She will be bereft of all her strengths and left with nothing. *ʾyn* occurs four times in the poem, vv. 1, 10, 14, and 15: no throne, no one seeing, no warmth, and no one saving. In vv. 1 and 14 it is used in conjunction with a noun: no "throne" and no "coal."

Both of these verses also use the verb *yšb* and develop the theme of sitting. In v. 1 Babylon has no throne on which to sit but must sit upon the ground. In v. 14 Babylon (or her cohorts, advisors) cannot sit in front of this particular coal, blaze, to warm themselves. The other occurrences of *ʾyn* appear with participial forms and will be treated below.

The two line-pairs (lines 1ab and cd) are parallel, but the parallelism is uneven. Two imperatives in 1a are balanced by one imperative and the negative *ʾyn ksʾ* (omitted in *Codex Vaticanus*):

1a	*rdy wšby ʿl-ʿpr*	imv/imv/prep. phrase	8 syls.	3 stresses
1c	*šby-lʾrṣ ʾyn-ksʾ*	imv/prep. phrase/neg.	7 syls.	3 stresses

The title in line 1b, "virgin daughter Babylon," is paralleled by "daughter Chaldea" in 1d. The syllable count in 1d is shorter than in 1b and reflects this unevenness.

1b	*btwlt bt-bbl*	6 syls.	3 stresses
1d	*bt-kśdym*	3 syls.	2 stresses

There are several areas of ambiguity in counting the syllables and stresses of these lines. The first has to do with whether to consider *bt* as stressed or unstressed. According to the system presented above, if it is considered a content word, it receives one stress. It is joined by the *maqqep* to the following word and could be considered unstressed. However in 1d, which is a short line of three syllables,[20] it must receive a stress, since no lines are made up of fewer than two stresses.[21]

19. Tromp (*Primitive Conceptions*, 187ff.) considers the piling up of negations to be one of the conditions associated with death and the netherworld. Some of these negations include no memory, no possessions, no knowledge, no joy.

20. While this is an exceptionally short line, with only 3 syllables, there are others in the poem—22ed—so it should not be eliminated from consideration as a single line solely for this reason.

21. Freedman (personal correspondence) suggests rearranging the lines as follows:

šby lʾrṣ	4 syls.	2 stresses
ʾyn ksʾ bt kśdym	6 syls.	3 stresses

The advantage of this arrangement is that *bt kśdym* does not stand by itself with the questionable stress count of 2, and it reflects a pattern seen elsewhere in the poem, where

Another question related to stress is whether to consider the one-syllable *ʾyn* as stressed or not. The word appears throughout the poem (vv. 10b, 14e, and 15d), and the problem of whether to consider it stressed will be discussed at each occurrence. Here, because it is joined by a *maqqep* to the following word, and because there are very few lines of 4 stresses in the rest of the poem, I tentatively consider it unstressed.[22]

Based on the syllable count, the lines are good examples of the Qinah meter with the following pattern:

1a	8 syls.	3 stresses
1b	6 syls.	3 stresses[23]
1c	7 syls.	3 stresses
1d	3 syls.	2 stresses

The meter was discussed extensively by K. Budde.[24] The Qinah meter, according to Budde, was a 3+2 beat; the two lines must be of unequal length, the first longer than the second.[25] Lines 1a–d clearly exhibit this pattern when syllables, not just stresses, are considered.

Freedman's studies of Lamentations, especially chaps. 2–3, have confirmed Budde's hypothesis about Qinah meter, or falling rhythm.[26] The great majority of the lines are in a 3+2 pattern of stresses and 7+6 or 8+5 pattern of syllables, showing a distinctive pausal arrangement: the first line is regularly (but not always) longer than the second.[27] Not only can this be shown with regard to stress, but it can also be demonstrated with more precision by syllable count.

---

the so-called Qinah meter, with the falling rhythm in the second line, has been reversed, and the shorter line occurs in the first line.

22. Even if it were counted, the pattern of falling rhythm would still be maintained, with a 4+2 count.

23. If *bt* is given no stress, then the pattern is 3+2, 3+2, which would reflect even more clearly the falling rhythm of the so-called Qinah meter, along with a syllable count of 8+6 and 7+3.

24. K. Budde, "Das hebräische Klagelied," *ZAW* 2 (1882) 1–52; "Ein altehebräisches Klagelied," *ZAW* 3 (1883) 299–306; "Die hebräische Leichenklage," *ZDPV* 6 (1883) 180–94; "Zum hebräischen Klagelied," *ZAW* 12 (1892) 31–37, 261–75.

25. See W. R. Garr's recent study of the syntax of the Qinah in "The Qinah: A Study of Poetic Meter, Syntax and Style," *ZAW* 95 (1983) 54–75.

26. D. N. Freedman, "Another Look at Biblical Hebrew Poetry," in *Directions in Biblical Hebrew Poetry* (ed. Elaine R. Follis; JSOTSup 40; Sheffield: JSOT Press, 1987) 18–23, esp. 22. See also idem, "Acrostic Poems in the Hebrew Bible: Alphabetic and Otherwise," *CBQ* 48 (1986) 410.

27. It is important to note that there is a wide variation in individual lines and sections. Freedman points to this deviation from the pattern as an example of the versatility and virtuosity of the poet and as an effort to avoid monotony ("Another Look," 21).

47:1e. *ky l*ʾ *twsypy yqr*ʾ*w-lk rkh w*ʿ*ngh* **"You shall not continue to be called 'tender and delicate'"**

This is the first in a long list of qualities or titles of Babylon that will be taken away. She will be stripped of the designation "tender and delicate (one)." These adjectives, *rkh* and ʿ*ngh*, occur in Deuteronomy 28, where the spoiled, delicate men and women who are living under siege have had to give up their luxuries. The man who was tender and delicate begrudges his children food; the pampered woman who would not set the sole of her foot upon the ground now eats her own afterbirth and the flesh of her own children. In like manner, Babylon will no longer dwell in luxury but will suffer like people under the effects of a siege, as did those whom she subjected to siege earlier.

The first line-pairs of the poem were parallel to one another, but this is a long line-pair that stands by itself. Here is the first example of the type of parallelism used several times in the poem and elsewhere within the book of DI. Line 1e is repeated later on in the poem, in 5c. Line 1f is parallel to 5d; both are titles that Babylon will lose. This is an example of a discontinuous bicolon, identified by F. I. Andersen and D. N. Freedman[28] (see discussion below, p. 160).

The strange construction in both verses with the repetition of *ky l*ʾ *twsypy yqr*ʾ*w-lk* is to be noted.[29] It is possible to consider Isa 47:1e as two

28. F. I. Andersen and D. N. Freedman, *Hosea: A New Translation with Introduction and Commentary* (AB 24; Garden City, N.Y.: Doubleday, 1980) 321.

29. GKC (§120c / p. 385) explains this phenomenon: when a relative verb (incomplete in itself) receives its necessary complement in the form of a verbal idea, the latter is subordinated in the infinitive construct or infinitive absolute, in the form of a participle (in a few instances), or the imperfect without the copula. In such combinations the principal idea is represented by the subordinate member; the governing verb contains a mere definition of the manner of the action. GKC goes on to provide examples of subordination in the impf. with both verbs in the same person (Isa 42:21 after the pf.; Ps 88:11, 102:14, etc., after impf.; Isa 5:11a after a part.), or with a difference in person (Lev 9:6 after pf.; a neg. impf. following *ṣwh* in Lam 1:10, "which you commanded they will not come"; after the impf., Isa 47:1, 5. (But notice that the Hebrew GKC quotes from Isaiah is as follows: *ky l*ʾ *twsypy* ʿ*wd yqr*ʾ*w lk*; ʿ*wd* has been added. I can find no textual evidence for this reading.) Then GKC goes on to give an example from Hos 1:6: *l*ʾ ʾ*wsyp* ʿ*wd* ʾ*rḥm* 'I will no longer continue (and) have mercy'. Here there is agreement in person. In Isa 52:1 there is agreement in person, and the verb *ysp* is also used. Prov 23:35, "I will continue; I will seek still." Again there is agreement in person. All of these examples use *ysp*. Num 22:6, "perhaps I will prevail (that) we smite them, etc." GKC also notes in a footnote that this kind of subordination (the complementary verbal idea in the impf.) is frequent in Arabic and Syriac; as a rule, a conjunction corresponding to English "that" is inserted. GKC does not mention Isa 51:22, which has *ysp* with an infinitive. For similar constructions, see Isa 51:21 and 52:1.

lines instead of one, dividing after *twsypy.* However, this would yield a 2+2+2 pattern of stresses and a low syllable count for each line. Lines with 2+2 stresses in this poem do not follow this pattern,[30] and I do not adopt this delineation. However, it should be noted that throughout the poem a wide variety of line arrangements exists, more so than in the other poems studied. This is one of several features that distinguish this poem from chaps. 46 and 48.

The phrase "tender and delicate" is amplified in line 5b by the phrase "mistress of kingdoms." The losses to Babylon grow in magnitude as the poem progresses. The title or phrase that Babylon loses in 1f is one that pertains to her personal stature or well-being, "You shall not continue to be called 'tender and delicate.'" In 5b it is her international acclaim that is attacked. The poem is made up of several interlocking devices such as this, which bind it together into a tightly knit whole.

47:2ab. *qḥy rḥym* "take millstones
***wṭḥny qmḥ* and grind meal"**

The dual *rḥym* (probably meaning two millstones) refers to the hand mills that were common household utensils.[31] The verb *ṭḥn* 'grind' is used of a variety of activities: grinding of grain with hand mills (Num 11:8), grinding of the material for the golden calf (Deut 9:21), grinding of the teeth (Qoh 12:3), and the grinding of the face of the poor (Isa 3:15).[32]

The pattern of imperatives begun in v. 1 continues in 2ab with two more imperatives directing Babylon to take millstones and grind meal. This is the chore of a maidservant (Exod 11:4), a prisoner (see Judg 16:21, where it is used in the humiliation of Samson, who grinds grain at the mill in the prison at Gaza after his eyes are put out by the Philistines),[33] or, in

30. See the parallel lines in v. 2, for example.

31. "Ṭḥn," BDB 932; *IDB* 3.380.

32. The related noun *ṭḥwn* is used in Lam 5:13, where it causes translators some problems. D. Hillers objects to the expression "the young men had to carry the mill" because "a mill was not usually carried from place to place" (*Lamentations* [AB 7A; Garden City, N.Y.: Doubleday, 1972] 99). However, the difficult picture of the young men bearing the mill can be cleared up if the mill referred to is not a small hand mill, but a large community mill in which a heavy wheel-shaped stone was rolled around on a large lower stone by an animal. *IDB* (3.380) suggests that *ṭḥwn* may be the term used for this type of mill, though BDB (377) interprets this *hapax legomenon* to be a hand mill. This would also explain the notion in Lam 5:3 that the young men had to "bear the yoke." They were performing the task of pushing the large mill, a task usually done by beasts of burden.

33. Freedman suggests that the blinding of Samson was comparable to the blinding of the beasts of burden, who were consigned to the boredom of walking in endless circles in the process of turning the millstone (personal correspondence).

difficult times, the obligation of young men (Lam 5:13). Tender and delicate Babylon is charged with the duties of a maidservant. Muilenburg points to the onomatopoeia of the verbs, suggesting grinding of the mill.

47:2cde. ***gly ṣmtk*** **"uncover your hair,**
ḥśpy-šbl **strip off your skirt,**
gly-šwq **uncover your leg"**

Three more imperatives introduce another development. Now virgin daughter Babylon is ordered to disrobe. Some scholars feel that the commands to Babylon to remove her clothing are part of the preparation for the task of grinding grain; others believe that they are for the purpose of preparing Babylon to cross over streams for the performance of hard labor or are preparation for deportation to a distant land.[34] If they were meant to indicate that Babylon was to dress herself appropriately for the job of grinding grain, we might in that case expect them to appear before the command to take up the millstones (the chronological order would call for preparing to do the job of grinding). In addition, there is more at work in this poem than a superficial description of a woman reduced to the status of a servant. The woman is really vanquished Babylon, who suffers all the consequences of defeat, humiliation, and debasement in many forms.

gly ṣmtk **"uncover your hair"**

The feminine noun *ṣmh* is translated in BDB and many commentaries as 'veil'.[35] It is a rare word, occurring only here and three times in Cant (4:1, 3; 6:7). The problem with translating the word as 'veil' in 2c is that Babylon is asked to "uncover (*Piel* of *glh*) her *ṣmh*." The object of the *Piel* of *glh* is something uncovered, not something removed. North indicates that *ṣmh* can mean either 'plaited hair' or 'veil', and the NEB translates "uncover your tresses," which is preferable.[36] Another possibility is to repoint the MT and read *gly* as a *Qal* imv., translating 'remove your veil'.[37] In either case, Babylon is to begin the process of disrobing by removing her veil to uncover her head.

ḥśpy-šbl **"strip off (your) skirt"**

The word for 'skirt' is a hapax legomenon; 1QIsa[a] reads the more familiar *šwlyk* 'your skirts' instead, also adding the f. s. pronoun missing in the MT. The 2 f. s. suffix of *ṣmtk* performs a triple-duty function, also

34. Whybray, Muilenburg.

35. "ṣmh," BDB 855.

36. See also G. R. Driver for the two possible translations of *ṣmh* ("Isaiah 6:1: 'His Train Filled the Temple,'" in *Near Eastern Studies in Honor of William Foxwell Albright* [ed. Hans Goedicke; Baltimore: Johns Hopkins University Press, 1971] 92).

37. However, BDB considers *Qal glh*, meaning 'remove', to be intransitive.

modifying *šbl* and *šwk*. According to Driver[38] *šwl* has the meaning 'buttocks, fringe, hem', that is, what is lax or loosely pendent; *šbl* means 'long hair, or skirt', that is, what is flowing or hanging down. He agrees that evidence is insufficient to decide the meaning of *šbl* and that it eludes definition. The cognates *šblt* 'flowing stream or ear or spike of grain' and *šblh* 'path' also have meanings related to flowing and thus would support the translation of 'flowing hair' or 'skirt'. Another suggestion is to read *šbl* as 'well', relating it to 'flowing stream' or 'watercourse', as above.[39] This in combination with the verb *ḥsp*, translated 'draw (water)', as in Isa 30:14 and Hag 2:16, yields the imperative 'draw water at the well' and suggests, according to Beeston, a more fitting parallel with line 2f, 'cross over rivers'.

Similar ideas of humiliation and lifting the skirt occur in Jer 13:18ff. The king and queen must take a lowly seat, the crown has been removed from the head, Judah is taken into exile, her skirts are lifted up because of her great iniquity (v. 22), and God will lift her skirts over her face and expose her shame (v. 26). In Lam 1:9, the uncleanness of Jerusalem was in her skirts.

The noun *ḥśp* is used in Jer 13:22 and elsewhere to describe the stripping bare of captives for humiliation. In Isaiah 20, the prophet removes his clothes and walks naked as a sign of the exile of Egyptians and Ethiopians at the hands of the Assyrians. Young and old are led away naked, barefoot with buttocks stripped bare, to their shame.[40] The verb *ḥśp* occurs only one other time in DI, in 52:10, where it refers to the baring of the arm of Yahweh. The contrasts here are instructive. Babylon's being stripped bare results in humiliation and loss of status. Her nakedness and shame are uncovered. But when Yahweh strips his arm, bares his arm, it is in a show of strength and victory.

The verb *glh* is repeated in line 2e; first Babylon was to uncover her hair, but now she must reveal even more by uncovering the leg. Babylon is to be stripped completely naked. The results are shown in the third occurrence of *glh* in 3a.

47:2f. *ᶜbry nhrwt* "cross over rivers"

The final imperative directed to Babylon in this verse is the least specific of all of the commands. Scholars suggest that this continues a picture of deportation of exiles, where the prisoners wade through streams, but there is no specific text clearly indicating such activity. Elsewhere DI

38. Driver, "Isaiah 6:1," 92.

39. A. F. L. Beeston, "Hebrew *šibbolet* and *šobel* (Is 47,2)," *JSS* 24 (1979) 175–77.

40. North and Muilenburg cite an archeological illustration from the bronze doors of Balawat, where women taken captive by Shalmanezer III raise their skirts to their knees. See A. Jeremias, *Das AT im Lichte des alten Orients* (4th ed.; Leipzig: Hinrichs, 1930) 689.

speaks of passing over waters. In Isa 43:2, Jacob/Israel is encouraged to "fear not" when it passes over (*ᶜbr*) waters and rivers. Isa 51:10 refers to a way for the redeemed to pass over. Israel's tormentors in 51:23, who forced God's people to lie down and make their backs like a street for them to pass over, will be punished for this. Israel's oppressors pass over in chains and bow to Israel in 45:14. All of these instances of the verb *ᶜbr* occur in passages in which Israel is oppressed by her enemies (51:23) or redeemed by Yahweh (43:2, 16; 51:10); in passages in which Israel's enemies triumph (51:23) or are defeated (47:2, 45:14). The idea that "passing over" indicates "going into exile" is seen in Mic 1:11, where the inhabitants of Shaphir pass over "in nakedness and shame" as they go into exile (1:16). Babylon's crossing over rivers is more than a trip across a body of water. It is another indication of her defeat.

47:3ab. *tgl ᶜrwtk* **"Your nakedness will be uncovered,**
gm trʾh ḥrptk **what's more, your shame will be seen."**

The third occurrence of the verb *glh* in the impf. and its parallel *trʾh* announce the results of the commands directed to Babylon. Because she has been reduced to the status of a servant, because she has been stripped of her garb, because she has gone into exile, her shame and nakedness are revealed. Duhm and others eliminate 3ab for metrical reasons, but it is premature to assign a metrical pattern based on a hypothetical construct. The question to be asked first is whether we can identify the meter of the text that we have before us.

The particle *gm* in the second line of the line-pair is unusual. It would ordinarily appear in the first line also, as it does in Isa 48:8. It is also unusual in that, had the poet not included it, the two lines would be evenly balanced (*tgl ᶜrwtk // trʾh ḥrptk*) and would also follow the pattern of the previous three line-pairs. Its presence here lends imbalance to the line, and thus further emphasis is achieved. This is the reason for the attribution of a stress to this one-syllable particle.

Some commentaries read 3ab as a reference to sexual intercourse or abuse,[41] based on the expression *glh ᶜrwh* in Leviticus 6. Others, citing Jer 13:26, Hos 2:12, and Ezek 16:37, interpret this as the public humiliation of an adulteress. While *ᶜrwh* often refers to physical nakedness or pudenda,[42] *ḥrph* 'reproach', its parallel, has a more extended meaning, especially elsewhere in DI. In 51:7 it refers to the taunt or reproach by enemies or men.[43] The shame or reproach of Israel's widowhood is the

41. North, Whybray, and McKenzie.
42. "ᶜRwh," BDB 788–89.
43. See also Lam 3:61.

topic of 54:4. Elsewhere *ḥrph* refers to the shame of rape (2 Sam 13:13). There are many levels of meaning here in 47:3. The figure of Babylon, personified as a woman, is shamed in several ways. Babylon's reproach would include physical mistreatment, exposure, or rape, as well as the humiliation of her widowhood and bereavement.[44] There is irony in the fact that though Babylon's shameful condition will be exposed, later (v. 10) she claims that no one sees her evil deeds. Lines 3ab are a brief hint at what will be more fully developed in the rest of the poem.

47:3c. *nqm ʾqḥ* "Vindication I will take"

There is an abrupt change in this line. The previous verbs were imperatives, or second-person imperfects, all addressed to virgin daughter Babylon. The entire focus of interest was Babylon. In lines 3cd the speaker refers to himself. Previously the speaker was never mentioned or identified. Bonnard suggests that the speaker is Israel, who rejoices in the fall of Babylon. He renders the passage as follows:

La vengeance, je la prendrai,
et je n'aurai pas recours à un homme:
notre rédempteur? Son nom est: Yahweh des armées,
le Saint d'Israël.

This attempts to deal with the problem of the translation of *pgʿ*. According to Bonnard's translation, it is not God who is the subject, but Israel who refuses to "have recourse to" or "entreat" a man. Instead of entreating a man, Israel calls upon God the redeemer for vengeance. Bonnard points to the connection between Yahweh the redeemer (*gôʾēl*) and Yahweh the avenger (*nāqam*), as stated in Isa 63:4.

However, this brief but frightening threat is delivered by Yahweh, not by Israel. Other passages in which Yahweh takes or brings vindication or vengeance (*nqm*) are Deut 32:35ff., Ezek 24:8, Isa 35:4, and Mic 5:14. The feminine noun *nqmh* is also used in reference to God's vengeance, usually in combination with the verbs *nqm*, *ʿśh*, or *ntn*, or in construct with *ywm*. It occurs once with *lqḥ* (Jer 20:10), but there it is the enemies of Jeremiah who take vengeance, not God. The only other address in the first person in this poem is in v. 6, and there it is clear that the speaker is Yahweh.

The noun *nqm* is found nowhere else in Isaiah 40–55. In Isaiah it occurs in 34:8, 35:4, 59:17, 61:2, and 63:4. In 35:4, Yahweh comes with *nqm* and "recompense" (*gmwl*). In 34:8 the phrase "a day of *nqm* for Yah-

44. Isa 54:4 refers to the status of widowhood as shameful, *ḥrpt ʾlmnwtyk* 'the shame of your widowhood', in reference to the city of Zion.

weh" is paralleled with "year of retribution for the cause of Zion." Isaiah 61:2 and 63:4 also parallel "day" and "year" in similar fashion. Isa 61:2, "year of the Lord's favor," and 63:4, "year of my redeemed," are both parallel with "day of vengeance." A contrast in the above two passages is drawn between the year of favor and the day of vengeance. In 59:17 another contrast is drawn where *nqm* appears. The image now includes garments of battle. A breastplate of righteousness and helmet of salvation are paralleled with garments of *nqm* and a mantle of fury. These garments are donned because in v. 16 Yahweh saw that there was "no man" (*ᵓyn ᵓyš*), no one to intervene (*mpgyᶜ*). The lack of justice displeases Yahweh, so He himself then seeks victory, righteousness, salvation and *nqm*. These notions of Yahweh's vengeance, especially in 59:17, may be instructive in understanding the second part of 47:3cd, which has caused problems for commentators, both ancient and modern.

While *nqm* is translated 'vengeance' in BDB,[45] Mendenhall's nuancing of the term deserves close attention.[46] He cautions against interpreting the root in any way that suggests lawless blood vengeance.[47] Rather, it is used in situations where the normal legal channels are not sufficient, and the exercise of force is on an executive rather than a judicial level.[48] In the Bible it designates "the use of force by legitimate sovereign authority" for defensive or punitive purposes. In chaps. 34–35 and 40–66 of Isaiah, the root takes on new meaning. In addition to having the sense of punitive action against an enemy, it is also seen as an action that "gives redress, comfort and restoration after a long period of suffering."[49]

Mendenhall underscores the fact that in all of the occurrences of the root from Jeremiah to DI, all political sovereignty is condemned for competing with God. In Isaiah 47 Babylon must suffer the consequences for attempting to usurp God's rule over his people. The rights of his people must be upheld, or "vindicated."

45. BDB 668. *Nqm* (masculine noun) is taken by God, by Samson against the Philistines, and by enemies against Judah. The feminine noun *nqmh* is also translated 'vengeance'. Again God, Israel, and the enemies of Israel take vengeance.

46. G. E. Mendenhall, *The Tenth Generation: The Origins of the Biblical Tradition* (Baltimore: Johns Hopkins University Press, 1973), in the chapter entitled "The 'Vengeance' of Yahweh" (69–104).

47. Ibid., 69: "There is not a single classical instance of blood vengeance in the Hebrew Bible."

48. Ibid., 76, 90. A synonym for *nqm* is the root *špṭ* (p. 77).

49. Ibid., 84, 99.

47:3d. *wlʾ ʾpgʿ ʾdm* "and I will not deal kindly with anyone."

The interpretation of *pgʿ* is difficult. BDB[50] lists *Qal* meanings 'meet, encounter, reach'; *Hiphil* 'cause to entreat, make entreaty, make attack'. Isa 64:4 is interpreted to mean "meet (with kindness)," and this is how North and BDB understand the use of the same verb in chap. 47.

A further difficulty is that the reading and/or placement of *ʾdm* has been questioned. Ancient manuscripts offer a variety of readings: LXX, "I will no longer deliver you to men," though some MSS begin v. 4 with *eipen* or *legei*, as though reading *ʾmr* for *ʾdm*. The Vulgate and Symmachus read *et non resistet mihi homo* ("and no one will resist me"). 1QIsa[a] is virtually identical with the MT.

Contemporary emendations of the texts are variations on these difficult readings. A sample of the suggestions include repointing *pgʿ* and reading as a *Niphal* ("I will not be entreated") or *Hiphil* ("I will not intervene or make entreaty"); reading *ypgʿ* for *ʾpgʿ*; substituting *ʾmr* for *ʾdm* and reading it as the beginning of v. 4 ("Our redeemer says . . . "); emending *pgʿ* to *prʿ* ("I will let no one go"). These proposals do nothing to solve problems with the text and only substitute one problem for another.

Similar difficulties with the verb *pgʿ* are found in Jer 15:11. It is uncertain who is speaking, Yahweh or Jeremiah. The NAB reads, "Have I not interceded with you in the time of misfortune?" The RSV translates, "Let it be, O Lord, if I have not entreated thee for their good, if I have not pleaded with you."[51] Here it is difficult to understand the relationship between the verb and the object. Verse 15, which the NAB transposes to follow directly after v. 12, has the request that Yahweh take vengeance, *hnqm*, on Jeremiah's persecutors. As in Isa 47:3cd, vindication (vengeance) and the difficult *pgʿ* are connected.

The clue to the translation of *pgʿ*, as indicated by North and BDB, lies in the comparison of Isa 47:3 with 64:4. The sense in 64:3–4 is that no one has seen a God like Yahweh, who "works" (*ʿśh*) for those who wait for him, who "treats kindly, meets" (*pgʿ*) one who rejoices, acts righteously, and brings to mind (*zkr*) God's ways. The sense is that God will welcome, accept, treat with kindness, and act on behalf of those whose behavior reflects a proper response to God. In 47:3 the verb is negated: God will not act on behalf of anyone who does not respond appropriately. In vv. 6–7 Babylon is characterized as one who mistreats the elderly, does not act with compassion, elevates herself to a position of supreme authority, and does not bring to mind (*zkr*) the outcome of such actions. The sense of the verb

50. BDB 803.

51. The beginning of chap. 15 seems to indicate that God will no longer be convinced by mediators, as he was in the past. Even if Moses and Samuel pleaded for Jerusalem, God would not be convinced by their pleas, as he was in the past. He is weary of relenting (v. 6). No one, not Moses, Samuel, or Jeremiah, can entreat him to be merciful.

pg^{c} is that God will not deal kindly with such a one. The translation "deal kindly" may be too mild to convey the severity of the threat. It is possible that this is another example of understatement, or litotes, a device used elsewhere by the author.[52]

Regardless of how 47:3d is translated, the monitory tone of 3c is clear. Yahweh promises to take action against Babylon, there is to be no benevolent encounter, and as will be seen in the end of the poem, there is no one to rescue her. The chiastic pattern ab / b′a′ is to be noted in 3cd, with the pattern of noun / 1 s. impf. / 1 s. impf. / noun, as well as the chiasm formed by the pattern of the vowels. The negative used here (*lᵓ*) is typical of usage throughout the poem. This and other negatives appear eighteen times. They effectively underscore the hopelessness of Babylon's situation. No one will intervene to help Babylon.

47:4ab. ***gᵓlnw yhwh ṣbᵓwt šmw*** **"Our redeemer—Yahweh of Hosts is his name—**
qdwš yśrᵓl **is the Holy One of Israel."**

Another abrupt shift occurs here. This is the only first pl. possessive suffix of the poem. It is also the only reference to Yahweh in the third person. This line-pair stands apart from the preceding and following lines in several ways. The other lines in the poem abound in verbs in the imperative and imperfect. This line-pair consists solely of names that identify Israel's God: Redeemer, Yahweh of Hosts, Holy One of Israel. No speakers are identified, and several scholars consider the passage to be a liturgical gloss.[53] Others, such as Westermann, consider it to be a deliberate addition, related to the astrological interests in v. 13.

An extensive study of the formula *yhwh ṣbᵓwt šmw* was done by J. L. Crenshaw.[54] Usually the formula or refrain "the Lord of Hosts is his name" appears in connection with four motifs: judgment, creation, idolatry, and oath. According to Crenshaw, the expression is a doxological formula that appeared in the exilic community, when the notion of Yahweh as creator

52. See above, note on 46:13b (p. 69 n. 141). Understatement may be expected in a satirical or ironic work such as this poem.

53. Whybray. See also R. Martin-Achard, "Esaïe 47 et la tradition prophetique sur Babylone," in *Prophecy: Essays Presented to Georg Fohrer on his Sixty-Fifth Birthday, 6 September 1980* (ed. J. A. Emerton; BZAW 150; Berlin: de Gruyter, 1980) 83–105.

54. J. L. Crenshaw, "*YHWH Ṣᵉbaᵓôt Šᵉmô*: A Form-Critical Analysis," *ZAW* 81 (1969) 156–76. The article is extensively documented; however, there are some glaring errors. Some of the work appears to be carelessly documented. For example, Crenshaw indicates that Isa 47:3 "asserts that no man will be spared," but two sentences later he emends the text from *ᵓdm* to *ᵓmr* (157). His citations of passages are frequently incorrect—he often confuses chap. 46 with 47; these errors may be typographical, but the reader is misled. He states on p. 165 that the vivid picture of waters of judgment occurs in Isa 48:8. It does not. He identifies an appeal to return in Isa 48:4. There is no such appeal.

and redeemer became prominent. It functioned as a confession to be used on special days of penitence and was an expression of faith in Yahweh as the only sovereign creator and judge, by whose name all oaths must be sworn. He also sees a polemical aspect to these expressions: "the oneness of God is emphasized by the attack against idolatry."[55]

The polemic nature of this poem is clear. It is a denial of the claims Babylon has made for herself. It emphasizes the powerlessness of Babylon (and indirectly, the power of Yahweh). That Babylon comes under judgment is clear from the very beginning. There should be no doubt about Yahweh's names in this poem: his titles are categorically stated.

As for the suggestions of commentators on the placement of v. 4 of chap. 47, it is impossible to prove that the verse has been inserted by a later editor. To call it a "deliberate addition" is curious (see Westermann). Certain form critics, especially Westermann and Melugin, are fond of referring to "deliberate" additions or "intentional" placement of pericopes. Is one to imagine that there are other passages that have been placed willy-nilly, without intention or deliberation? Such adjectives are not helpful in discussing the relationship of a given verse or section to a larger unit. Crenshaw's work shows that the formula, while at first blush appearing to be out of place and intrusive, does relate to some of the key motifs of the poem, especially the judgment against Babylon and the polemic against the claims Babylon makes for herself.[56]

This line-pair is unique in relation to the meter of the rest of the poem in that it is an example of the standard unit, having sixteen syllables and six stresses. This pattern is found nowhere in the rest of chap. 47; the prevailing pattern is 3+2 (or 2+3). 1QIsa[a] also indicates that the verse is unusual by separating it from the rest of the poem.

47:5ab. ***šby dwmm wbʾy bḥšk*** **"Sit down silently and go into darkness,**
bt-kśdym **O daughter Chaldea"**

Verse 5 is a shortened version of the beginning of this poem (lines 1bd). Instead of having two line-pairs, it has only one. It repeats the key elements of v. 1 with certain modifications. The command to sit down is repeated but with a modifying adverb, *dwmm*: the descent is to be in silence. This is reminiscent of the one who "sits alone in silence" and "puts his mouth in the dust" in Lam 3:26, 28–29.

The problem with reading *bt-kśdym* as a single line rise again.[57] As indicated in the commentary on chap. 46,[58] the dominant pattern of the line

55. Ibid., 156, 175–77.

56. Crenshaw, "YHWH *Ṣᵉbaʾôt Šᵉmô*."

57. See comments on 1d above, p. 109.

58. See p. 84 n. 177, in Microstructure of chapter 2 for comments by O'Connor.

is the combination of verb and subject. The lines could be rearranged to fit this definition.[59] However, this combination, verb/subj., verb/subj., also fits O'Connor's definition of the constraints of a line, although it is not the preferred or dominant form.[60]

The verb *bwʾ* is introduced. It appears five more times in the poem. This new command adds more specifications to Babylon's destination. She is to go into darkness. This is another intimation of her descent to the underworld (see p. 107 on the meaning of *ʾrṣ*). The combination *ʾrṣ ḥšk* occurs in Job 10:21, and the terms are parallel in Ps 88:13, where they clearly refer to the underworld. DI specifically refers to darkness as a place where prisoners dwell (42:7, 49:9). The device of repetition, and the specifying of the imperatives with modifications, such as the adverb *dwmm* and the preposition *bḥšk*, recall one of the key ideas of the poem, the descent of Babylon, and leave no mistake about her destination.

47:5d. *gbrt mmlkwt* "mistress of kingdoms"

This is one of the many titles that Babylon has taken for herself. The LXX reads "the strength of a kingdom"; North seems to read the feminine noun *gbyrh* 'lady, queen' for the MT *gbrt.* The LXX translation misses the personification that is the basis for the poem. North's reading (or emendation?) is unnecessary. The feminine noun *gbrt* is used for one who is mistress of servants,[61] which is an apt figure for Babylon, since it further extends the contrast between Babylon's claimed status and her real status.

47:6abc. *qṣpty ʿl-ʿmy* "I was angry at my people;
***ḥllty nḥlty* I profaned my inheritance,**
***wʾtnm bydk* so I gave them into your hand."**

For the second and last time in this poem, Yahweh speaks in the first person. The only other uses in this poem of the first person, either verbs (all impfs.), suffixes, or pronouns, are in statements that Babylon makes about herself. They are all in section III, the longest section of the poem. In 3cd, Yahweh promised to vindicate (*nqm ʾqḥ* in the imperfect). Here in

59. Freedman's arrangement (Freedman, personal correspondence) is as follows:

šby dwmm	syls. 4, stress 2
wbʾy bḥšk bt-kśdym	syls. 8, stress 3

The pattern of 2+3, that occurs with some frequency in the rest of the poem is present in this arrangement. If the grammar were ignored, a third division would be possible to achieve the 3+2 meter, by dividing after *wbʾy.* This illustrates that there are a number of different ways to describe the phenomena and that this poem especially does not lend itself to clear-cut line divisions on every hand.

60. Michael O'Connor, *Hebrew Verse Structure* (Winona Lake, Ind.: Eisenbrauns, 1980) 87.

61. BDB 150.

6a Yahweh explains how it was that his people, his inheritance, came to be under the domination of Babylon. The verbs used of Yahweh's action in v. 6 are two perfects (*qṣpty* and *ḥllty*), followed by an imperfect *waw*-consecutive (*wʾtnm*). Within these three lines, one of two line-trios in the poem, are five uses of the first singular verb or suffix. This same phenomenon, the repetition of five first-person forms, with Yahweh as subject, is also noted in chaps. 46 and 48.[62]

The first time the perfect form is used in the chapter is in v. 6. Along with the *waw*-consecutive with impf., it is clearly a description of something that happened in the past. Yahweh was angry, he profaned his people, he gave them into Babylon's hand.

The wrath of Yahweh against his people in past times explains how they came to be in such dire straits. Isa 43:27–28 contains an example of Yahweh's anger against his people. There, because of their transgressions, Yahweh "killed (*ḥll*)[63] the princes of the sanctuary" and delivered his people to destruction.[64] In 54:8–9 Yahweh's overflowing wrath (*šṣp qṣp*) momentarily overtook his people, and he hid his face from them. The emphasis in chap. 47, however, is not so much on Yahweh's past anger against his own people, as it is on his anger at Babylon because of the excesses of her treatment of the very people whom he turned over to her.

The verb *ḥll* usually refers to sexual or ritual defilement or the profaning of the name of God, the last a familiar motif in Leviticus and Ezekiel. Yahweh as the subject of the *Piel* of *ḥll* is rare. In DI, Yahweh pierces, or profanes, the princes of the sanctuary (43:27–28) and here, his inheritance. In Ps 89:40ff., Yahweh profanes the crown of his anointed servant by casting his throne to earth (89:45[44], *ksʾw lʾrṣ*). Yahweh profanes, brings down to earth, the kings and princes of Judah in Lam 2:2. In each case, except for Isaiah 47, the objects of Yahweh's wrath and profanation are rulers.

The *nḥlh* is the object of God's profanation in 47:6b. This term can refer either to the land or to the people.[65] In 47:6b it is parallel with

62. An investigation of this phenomenon in the whole of DI may uncover other such examples.

63. BDB 320, the RSV, and other translations read 'profane' here instead of 'pierce, bore' (see BDB 319). BDB indicates that piercing in the sense of killing or wounding occurs in the *Poel* or *Poal*, as in Isa 51:9 and 53:5. The sanctuary would be profaned by the piercing of the princes, so perhaps this is an example of paronomasia.

64. See also Isa 42:25, where the heat of Yahweh's anger set on fire and burned his people.

65. See Michael Fishbane, *Biblical Interpretation in Ancient Israel* (Oxford: Clarendon, 1985) 301, on the oscillation between land and people as God's inheritance, especially in Jeremiah and in deuteronomic circles.

people, "my people" / "my inheritance," and it was "them" (3 m. pl. suffix, *wʾtnm*) whom he gave into the hand of Babylon.

Similarities exist between Yahweh's handing over his people to Babylon in chap. 47 and handing over his people to Assyria in Isa 10:5ff. In each case the foreign powers exceeded their mandates and did not put the right things to heart regarding Yahweh's intent for his people. Both First and Second Isaiah emphasize that God's punishment was not to exceed certain limits (10:6–7, 40:2, 54:7–8). Assyria and Babylon exceeded these limits, and for this the wrath of Yahweh was turned in their direction.

This line-trio, an extremely unusual formation in the poem, explains the reason that Yahweh's inheritance was under the sway of Babylon. There is a chronological development in the line-trio: God was angry at his people, so he profaned his inheritance by giving them into the hand of Babylon. The pattern of parallelism is ab/a′b′/cd or A/A′/B.[66] The reason for the people's oppression by Babylon is clear and logical. It had nothing to do with Babylon's power; it was God's decision to allow them to be oppressed.

47:6de. ***lʾ śmt . . . hkbdt . . .***

These two 2 f. s. impf. verbs accuse Babylon of her crimes of cruelty against God's inheritance. First is a general accusation of lack of compassion; next, the more specific charge of mistreatment of the aged. The suffering of the elderly during the time of the exile is a repeated theme in Lamentations (1:21; 2:21; 5:12, 14). Babylon laid a heavy yoke on the elderly, a load that surpassed all bounds of expected oppression and mistreatment by conquering peoples. Making the elderly do forced labor was considered a crime even outside Israel.[67] The yoke is exceedingly (*mʾd*) heavy. The length of the line itself (nine syllables, four stresses) serves to emphasize that heaviness. The line-pair of 6de is also heavy in syllables (16) and stresses (7). No line-pair in the poem has more syllables; none has as many stresses.

Scholars generally assert that the Babylonian rule was not particularly tyrannical or cruel,[68] but this is not the impression one derives from passages such as this in Second Isaiah.[69] Lamentations makes it clear that the treatment of the people in Jerusalem was brutal. The forced march to Babylon could not have been easy, especially on the elderly. The exodus

66. Watson (*Classical Hebrew Poetry*, 180–81) cites an example of a tricolon with an A/A′/B pattern from Cant 4:11; he also cites Job 24:12, 31:34.

67. Whybray, 121.

68. Westermann and Muilenburg.

69. See also Isa 42:22ff.; 51:13, 17, 22–23. The entire poem dedicated to the servant who is oppressed and mistreated should also not be overlooked.

motif is an essential part of DI, and that motif is associated with liberation from cruel oppression.[70] This passage thus presents a different view of the exiles' life under the Babylonians.

The elderly bear a heavy burden imposed by Babylon. The motif of bearing a load, carrying a burden, occurs throughout DI. See for example, chap. 46, where Babylonian worshipers bear the burden of their gods' images, but Yahweh bears the burden of his people from birth to old age. The same motif occurs in the fourth servant song, where the servant lifts up, bears the ills of God's people. The figure of yoke-bearing is usually related to notions of servitude. It is ironic that Babylon, who made servants of God's people, is herself made a servant.

47:7ab. ***wtᵓmry lᶜwlm ᵓhyh gbrt ᶜd*** **"And you said, 'Forever I will be mistress forever.' "**

Following upon the charge of cruelty toward the aged is an arrogant claim made by Babylon that she will be mistress forever and ever. The reader has already seen that this is not to be the case, because her title "mistress of kingdoms" is to be taken away (5b). The claim Babylon makes here in the first person is somewhat different from the statement in v. 5, where it was announced that Babylon would no longer be the number one world power. This is more than a declaration of political primacy. Babylon is making claims to divinity. Echoes of Exod 3:14, *ᵓhyh ᵓšr ᵓhyh*, can be heard, especially in view of similar assertions in lines 8d and 10f.

Lines a (*lᵓwlm*) and b (*ᶜd*) are an example of the breakup of the stereotyped phrase *lᶜwlm wᶜd*.[71] This phrase also echoes part of the stock Ugaritic blessing formula, "May the gods protect you . . . forever and always (*ᶜd ᶜlm*)."[72] Based on the MT, which puts the pause before *ᶜd*, some translations add *ᶜd* to the following line, reading, "*so that* you did not. . . . " How-

70. K. Baltzer ("Liberation from Debt Slavery after the Exile in Second Isaiah and Nehemia," in *Ancient Israelite Religion: Essays in Honor of Frank Moore Cross* [ed. P. D. Miller, P. D. Hanson, and S. D. McBride; Philadelphia: Fortress, 1987] 477–84) points to texts in DI that produce "a relatively consistent picture of desperation." He concludes that DI was anticipating a specific type of liberation, that is, release from debt slavery, a common practice in times of general impoverishment (481).

71. For a discussion of this line and the masoretic punctuation of *gbrt ᶜd*, see D. N. Freedman, " 'Mistress Forever': A Note on Isaiah 47,7," *Bib* 51 (1970) 538. Freedman, in personal correspondence, suggested another possibility for translation, that is, to read *ᶜd* as 'booty', as in Gen 49:27. See similar usage in Isa 33:23 (BDB also points to Zeph 3:8, Isa 9:5). Thus line 7b would be parallel with v. 5: "mistress of kingdoms" // "mistress of booty." The main problem is how to read *ᶜd*. Is it a preposition, an adverb, or a noun?

72. See Watson, *Classical Hebrew Poetry*, 331.

ever, the symmetry of *lʾ śmt* and *lʾ zkrt* would be disturbed by adding *ʿd* to the beginning of the next line. Also affected would be the symmetry with the line-pair in 6de. *lʾ śmt*, "You did not put . . . ," occurs twice, in lines 6d and 7c. The two line-pairs (6de and 7cd) are parallel with one another in structure, each having two 2 f. s. pf. verbs, each beginning with the same verb (*lʾ śmt*):

> 6de: You did not show (*lʾ śmt*) them compassion;
> upon the old you made your yoke exceedingly heavy.
> 7cd: You did not lay (*lʾ śmt*) these upon your heart;
> you did not remember its end.

The meaning of the verb *śym* is different in each line. In the first case, it means showing compassion; in the second, it has the sense of remembering, or reflecting on something. Another reason for reading *ʿd* as part of 7b is the similarity or parallel of this phrase with other assertions Babylon makes in 8c and 10f, where the lines end with the word *ʿwd*. While there is a difference in meaning, there is similarity in sound. The lines are similar in that each is an arrogant claim made by Babylon. The line-pair 7ab has no internal parallelism, and division into two lines is not done on the basis of grammar. The line could be divided anywhere, since it is really a long sentence. There are similar lines elsewhere in the poem (e.g., 9ab) in which the decision about where to place the caesura is not clear-cut.

47:7cd. *lʾ-śmt ʾlh ʿl-lbk* "You did not lay these upon your heart;
***lʾ zkrt ʾḥryth* you did not remember its end."**

Following upon Babylon's foolish assertion of her queenship is another indictment of Babylon. In fact lines 6de and 7cd form an envelope around this assertion, showing its absurdity even more.

The antecedent of the pl. *ʾlh* 'these' could be *zqn* 'the old' of 6e, reading it as parallel with the following *ʾḥryth* 'its end'. Clifford translates 'final end', interpreting it as a "biblical idiom meaning the final term in a series of actions which provides a perspective for right judgment of those actions." It could also refer to the consequences of these oppressive deeds, thus functioning as a hinge,[73] identifying what precedes and what follows in the poem. Lines 6d–7d function both as a reminder of Babylon's cruel

73. See A. Ceresko, "A Poetic Analysis of Psalm 105 with Attention to Its Use of Irony," *Bib* 64 (1983) 36, on the "hinge." H. Van Dyke Parunak ("Transitional Techniques in the Bible," *JBL* 102 [1983] 525–48) describes a similar phenomenon. G. Polan (*In the Ways of Justice toward Salvation: A Rhetorical Analysis of Isaiah 56–59* [New York: Peter Lang, 1986] 133, 205–6, 291) discusses this technique as it is used in Isaiah 56–59.

treatment, her failure to be compassionate, and as an indication of what is to come as a consequence of this cruel treatment.

Jerusalem was accused of similar behavior in Lam 1:9: *lʾ zkrh ʾḥryth* (the RSV translates, "She took no thought of her doom"). Other similarities between Jerusalem in Lam 1:8–9 and Babylon in Isaiah 47 include the exposure of nakedness, the spectacular fall, and the lack of anyone to comfort.[74]

Lines 7c and d are parallel: both begin with the negative *lʾ*, followed by the 2 f. s. pf. verbs and the objects of each verb. The same combination, *lʾ zkrt* (2 f. s.) and *lʾ śmt ʿl lbk*, is found in Isa 57:11. The order of verbs is reversed but the thought is similar. The addressee (not identified directly in chap. 57, though the form is 2 f. s.) is accused of not remembering or giving a thought to Yahweh. There are other striking similarities of language and thought in chap. 57.[75] Among them are the idea of the addressee's being wearied (*ygʿt*, cf. chap. 47:12c, 15; 47:13a) and her foolish dependence on things that cannot help *yʿl* (57:12, 13; cf. 47:12d, *yʿl* with 15d, *mwšyʿk*).

47:8a. ***wʿth šmʿy-zʾt ʿdynh hywšbt lbṭḥ*** **"And now, hear this, luxury-lover, who sits securely"**

Accusations against Babylon have been made, and now comes the announcement of the punishment to be meted out. The proclamation of doom begins with an extended form of address to Babylon. At the beginning of the poem, the speaker addressed Babylon as "virgin daughter." Now Babylon is called by another title, *ʿdynh*, variously translated as 'lover of pleasures',[76] 'pampered jade',[77] 'pampered one',[78] 'pleasure seeker',[79] 'indulgent one',[80] 'jouisseuse' or 'voluptueuse',[81] and 'living blissfully in Eden'.[82] In Gen 18:12 *ʿdnh* refers to sexual pleasure, from which some translate 'voluptuous one' in Isaiah 47. But the root *ʿdn* is usually used in the Bible in connection with luxurious foods ('dainties, delicacies') and

74. See also Jer 12:4, where wicked men said, *lʾ yrʾh ʾt-ʾḥrytnw* 'He will not see our end'.

75. In fact, Torrey sees many similarities between 56:9–57:21 and chaps. 47 and 48. He lists sarcasm, the condemnation of idol worship, the use of irony, the feminine form of address as some of these similarities (pp. 429ff.).

76. The RSV; Köhler, Westermann.

77. C. R. North.

78. JPSV.

79. J. McKenzie.

80. R. Clifford.

81. Martin-Achard, "Esaïe 47."

82. Duhm.

often in association with the losses of a plundered people. This is the sense of the word *ᶜdynh* as it is used in Isaiah 47. For instance, in Jer 51:34, "Nebu-chadnezzar . . . filled his belly with my delicacies."[83] The lack of food, especially for those who originally lived as royalty, is described in Lam 4:4–5: "the children beg for food . . . those who feasted on dainties (*mᶜdnym*) perished . . . "; and in v. 10: "women boiled their own children" for food. The references in Jeremiah and Lamentations are to losses suffered by plundered Jerusalem.

Lines 8a and b are parallel to one another: *ᶜdynh* 'luxury-lover' and *hywšbt lbṭḥ* 'one sitting in security'. The expression *hywšbt lbṭḥ* calls to mind the idyllic existence of Benjamin and Joseph in the blessing of Moses in Deut 33:12–16, where Benjamin dwells securely (*lbṭḥ*) and Joseph enjoys all the produce of the land.[84]

The title *ᶜdynh* 'luxury-lover' also recalls the earlier title, which Babylon lost, "tender and delicate" (line 1f; see p. 111). There too the association was with well-fed people who were reduced to refusing food to their own children or even to devouring them in the desperate times of siege. Having enough food and dwelling in safety are paired in line 8a and elsewhere.[85] Babylon's attitude is one of complacency. She believes herself to be secure, well-fed, above any concern for the future.

47:8cd. *hᵓmrh blbbh* "who says in her heart,
***ᵓny wᵓpsy ᶜwd* 'I am, and there is no other.' "**

Babylon asserts in her heart that there is no other besides her.[86] This assertion is repeated in v. 10, just before another announcement of evil that is to come upon Babylon. It is similar to Babylon's claim that she would be mistress forever (v. 7). But it is more than an affirmation of imperial superiority; it is a claim to divinity. (Earlier, in 7a, Babylon made a similar, though perhaps more indirect, claim to divinity.) DI puts similar (though not identical) words in the mouth of Yahweh.[87] It is clear that a contrast is intended between Babylon's arrogant and misguided claims to divine status and Yahweh's assertions. The effect achieved by placing words so similar to

83. See also Ps 36:9, Neh 9:25.

84. See Gevirtz, *Patterns*, for a general discussion of "dwelling in security" (pp. 60–61).

85. Lev 15:18, 19; 26:5, 1 Kgs 5:5; Ezek 34:28.

86. See Zeph 2:15 for the identical phrase, where Nineveh is the subject: *hywšbt lbṭḥ hᵓmrh blbbh ᵓny wᵓpsy ᶜwd.*

87. Isa 45:5, 18, 21, *ᵓny yhwh wᵓyn ᶜwd* 'I am Yahweh, and there is no other'; or 45:22, *ᵓny ᵓl* 'I am El'; and 46:9, which adds *ᵓlhym wᵓps kmwny* 'God, and there is none like me'.

the words of Yahweh in the mouth of Babylon heightens the sense of irony pervading the poem.

This line-pair, like 7ab, is one continuous sentence rather than two parallel phrases and like 7ab, could easily be divided differently. In my division it yields a pattern of 7+6, 2+3. However, the independent pronoun *ʾny* could be placed in the first half, yielding 9+4, 3+2, which would reflect the more typical falling rhythm that scholars find characteristic of this poem. The poem has a number of sentences with no intralinear parallelism. What is certain, regardless of how the divisions are made, is that this is a 13-syllable line-pair with 5 stresses.[88]

47:8e. *ʾlmnh* "widow"

The city as widow occurs in four chapters of the Hebrew Bible. In addition to chap. 47, it is found in Isa 54:4, Jer 51:5, and Lam 1:1.[89] In Lam 1:1 there is a parallel between the city as a widow (*hyth kʾlmnh*)[90] and the city subjected to forced labor (*hyth lms*). In Jer 51:5, Judah and Israel are "not widowed" (*lʾ ʾlmn*), that is, not forsaken by God.

Of special help in understanding the figure of the widow in chap. 47 is the figure of widow applied to the woman in Isaiah 54. Beuken correctly notes that the woman is never named and has several different "manifestations": ancestress (mother), wife, and city.[91] They allow the reader to see this figure as representing both the "miserable city and the oppressed exiles who long for return."[92] In 54:4 the parallel with *ḥrpt ʾlmnwtyk* 'the shame of your widowhood' is *bšt ʿlwmyk* 'the shame of your youth'. The latter expression has been the subject of numerous suggestions, some more infelicitous than others.[93] While the exact meaning of the parallel between the

88. 10ef has the same pattern of syllables, stresses, and structure as 8cd. Again, the question of where to divide the line cannot be answered with certainty. The standard line-pair for this kind of poetry is in evidence: 13 syllables and 5 accents.

89. Chayim Cohen, "The 'Widowed City,'" *JANESCU* 5 (The Gaster Festschrift; 1973) 75. Cohen sees a relationship between the *ʾlmnh* in Hebrew, and the *almattu* in Mesopotamian legal terminology. An *almattu* is a widow who has no relatives to support her and needs special protection from the court (p. 76). The word *widow,* when applied to a city, means a "once independent city which has become the vassal of another state" (p. 79), and this is the reason for the use of the term in Isa 47:8.

90. The presence of the preposition *k-* in Lam 1:1 is to be noted. While a similar comparison is made in Isa 47:8, the preposition is not used. This is a clear example of the fact that poets do leave out prepositions, even when the meaning calls for one.

91. W. A. M. Beuken, "Isaiah LIV: The Multiple Identity of the Person Addressed," *OTS* 19 (1974) 28–70.

92. Ibid., 63.

93. For example, Muilenburg, Whybray, and others propose that the period of Egyptian bondage, or the period before the exile when Israel was unfaithful, is meant.

terms *ᵓlmnwt* and *ᶜlwmym* is uncertain, the larger parallel, between chap. 47, Babylon as widow, and chap. 54, Jerusalem/Zion as once but no longer a widow, is clear.

47:8f. *škwl* "bereavement"

The verb *škl* usually refers to loss of children or barrenness.[94] The m. noun occurs only here and in Ps 35:12, *škwl lnpšy* 'bereavement for my soul'.[95] The psalm, in v. 14, speaks of one who mourns the death of his mother. Bereavement is a theme in chaps. 49 and 54 of Isaiah, where the bereaved Zion will once again have numerous children.[96] Fitzgerald[97] and Clifford perhaps push the image of Babylon as widow too far, in trying to identify the implied figures of husband and children.[98] Sometimes the god is considered to be the husband of the city, which is what makes the city holy. The children are the worshipers. According to Clifford, Babylon is widowed because she has lost her "husband(s)," the gods Bel and Nebo, who have departed in chap. 46. The image can be understood without recourse to this interpretation, which stretches the symbolism too far. While Babylon believes herself to be living in security, she will suffer the loss of that security, the husband who supports her, and the children upon whom she should be able to depend in the future.

The word-pair *ṯkl* and *ulmn* occurs in Ugaritic (*CTA* 23L:8–9).[99]

47:9b. *rgᶜ* "suddenly"

This is a masculine noun for "moment," a category of time that usually has negative connotations and is often used in the context of words denoting disaster or calamity. The devastation of Jerusalem at the hand of Babylon is compared to the punishment of Sodom, which happened in a "moment." Isa 54:7–8 uses the word twice in describing God's momentary abandonment of his people.

Schoors, in "Two Notes on Isaiah xl–lv" (*VT* 21 [1971] 503–5), basing his idea on a Ugaritic cognate *ǵlm* 'servant', translates "the shame of your bondage." But Beuken thinks that her shame is that "while being an adult girl she is living without husband" ("Isaiah LIV," 35, n. 1).

94. BDB 1013.

95. See M. Dahood, however, who reads *škll* 'ravaging' instead (*Psalms I*, 213).

96. See also Isa 66:7ff., which develops a similar theme.

97. Fitzgerald, "Mythological Background," 403–16.

98. Whybray says, "It would be pedantic to enquire who was Babylon's husband."

99. See Mitchell Dahood and Tedeusz Penar, "Ugaritic-Hebrew Parallel Pairs," *Ras Shamra Parallels* (AnOr 49; ed Loren R. Fisher; Rome: Pontifical Biblical Institute, 1972) 1.#599 / p. 378 (*ṯkl // ulmn*: אלפנה // שכול).

In a little moment (*rgᶜ*) I abandoned you,
but in great compassion I gathered you.
With overflowing wrath I hid my face from you for a moment (*rgᶜ*),
but with everlasting love I had compassion on you.

Here Babylon's demise comes suddenly, like that of Sodom and Jerusalem. She who did not show compassion to God's people will not have compassion shown to her, but her devastation will be complete and sudden.[100] Babylon denies that she will ever see widowhood or loss of children, the typical consequences of people in conquered cities, or figuratively, of conquered cities themselves (Lam 1:1, 20; 5:3). But no sooner does Babylon assert this than it is announced that these very things will come upon her, and suddenly, in full measure. All of the assertions made by Babylon, all the grand names and titles that she claims, are negated "suddenly, in a moment," almost as soon as they are made.

47:9c. *škwl wᵓlmn* "bereavement and widowhood"

The word-pair forms a chiasm with lines 8ef above and may be another way of demonstrating the reversal of Babylon's fortunes and the finality of her downfall. Instead of the f. noun *ᵓlmnh*, as in 8e, the MT in 9c has the masculine noun *ᵓlmn*; 1QIsa[a], however, has *ᵓlmnh* in both places. Torrey believes that the *ᵓatnaḥ* has been misplaced and belongs under *ᵓḥd*. However, these lines, like others previously discussed, are not composed of obvious parallels, and it is not clear where the divisions are to be placed throughout v. 9. See below for the comments on the function of *ktmm*.

***ktmm* "in their full measure"**

With the verb *tmm* or the m. noun *tm*, a sense of wholeness or integrity is expected. Most often in the psalms the noun is used with the meaning 'integrity of mind' or 'walking in integrity', as in Proverbs.[101] Lam 4:22 reads *tm-ᶜwnk bt-ṣywn* 'Your punishment is complete, O daughter Zion'.[102] The verb *tmm* in Lamentations 4 is used to indicate that Jerusalem's punishment is completed, finished. The threat to Babylon in 47:9 indicates that the time of her widowhood and bereavement is about to begin. Some important versions[103] read *ptᵓm* 'suddenly', apparently in anticipation of v. 11, where the same word occurs. Some emend to *tᵓmym* 'like twins', referring to "these two" in 9a. Whybray and North suggest a connection with 2 Sam 15:11 and 1 Kgs 22:34, where *tm* indicates a "sense of

100. Tromp, *Primitive Conceptions*, 81ff.; and D. Daube, *The Sudden in Scripture* (Leiden: Brill, 1964) 9ff.

101. BDB 1070.

102. Hillers (*Lamentations*, 93) compares this with Isa 40:2.

103. LXX, Syriac, and modern commentators, including Duhm.

guilelessness or lack of suspicion" or "all unawares."[104] In these two passages, there is more of a sense of innocence and unawareness than the perverse naïveté that is part of Babylon's style in chap. 47. However, in 2 Sam 15:11 their going in innocence is paralleled by the statement that "they did not know a thing" (*wlʾ ydʿw kl-dbr*). Babylon's lack of knowledge is emphasized in 47:11, so it may be that this is another example of irony, in which Babylon's claim to knowledge and supremacy is shown to be false and misleading.

The phrase "in their full measure" was read by the Masoretes with the following line 9b, "in their full measure they come upon you." I interpret it as having a dual function and see it as relating to both the preceding and following phrases.

47:9d. *bʾw* "they come"

The majority of translations render "they will come," without commenting on the perfect form of the verb. Duhm and Marti suggest *ybʾw* would be better. Delitzsch is more careful, reading "they come upon you." Volz considers the perfect verb used here to be an excellent expression of certain fulfillment and, like Delitzsch, translates in the present, "kommen sie."

47:9ef. *brb kšpyk* "Oh, the abundance of your sorceries;
***bʿṣmt ḥbryk mʾd* Oh, the great might of your spells!"**

The poet uses irony to good effect when discussing the effects of the Babylonians' religious practices.[105] The exclamation is emphasized by the use of *mʾd* in 9f. Not only are the sorceries abundant, but the magic by means of spells is exceedingly powerful. The word *mʾd* is used twice in the poem. In v. 6 the literal meaning is intended: Babylon laid an extremely heavy load on the old. In v. 9 it is used ironically to highlight Babylon's imagined claims to greatness with regard to the power of her incantations.

The denominative noun *kšp* only occurs in the plural in the biblical text,[106] in Mic 5:11, Nah 3:4, 2 Kgs 9:22, and here in Isaiah 47 (vv. 9 and 12). In Micah, God is full of anger and wrath toward his people because of the sorceries, soothsayers, images, pillars, and the asherim. In Nahum, it is

104. Whybray and North.

105. For a discussion of Babylonian divination, magical-practices, and astrology, see A. Leo Oppenheim, "The Arts of the Diviner," *Ancient Mesopotamia: Portrait of a Dead Civilization* (rev. Erica Reiner; Chicago: University of Chicago Press, 1977) 206–27. The large number of texts from the time of the late Old Babylonian period to the time of the Seleucid kings testify to the importance of magic in Mesopotamian civilizations. Divination was considered "a major intellectual achievement in Mesopotamia and surrounding countries" (p. 206).

106. BDB 506.

the "bloody city" Nineveh that is called *bᶜlt kšpym* 'mistress of sorceries', who lures peoples and nations with her sorceries. There are parallels in Nahum and in 2 Kings between sorceries and harlotry (*znh*). Jehu refers to the "harlotries and sorceries" of Jezebel in 2 Kgs 9:22. In the biblical texts there are connections between *kšp* 'sorcery', *ḥbr* 'magic' (or 'enchantment' or 'spell'), and harlotry.[107]

Of particular interest in this chapter, which condemns Babylon to childlessness, is the connection between the root *kšp* and the casting of spells to render a man impotent.

> In spite of Babylon's numerous spells and powerful enchantments, she will suffer both childlessness and widowhood; the implication is that the unavailing magic was intended to secure a healthy husband and abundant offspring.[108]

If a connection is made between magic spells and charms that make one potent or impotent, then the sense of irony is even more sharply defined. The proud Babylon who could imagine no loss of children cannot be helped, even by her powerful magical spells, to overcome her childlessness.

The meaning of the root *ḥbr* is 'to unite, be joined, tie a magic knot or spell, charm'.[109] Andersen and Freedman discuss this root as it appears in Hos 4:17. One of the meanings refers to the binding of people "by the weaving of spells, or the tying of magic knots."[110] Andersen and Freedman also point to the connection between harlotry, magic, and idolatry in 47:9f and elsewhere in the Bible. It is clear that the lure of magic attracted not only the Babylonians, but was also considered important and powerful by the Israelites themselves. Prophets from earliest times condemned its use. It must be remembered that while Isaiah 47 was ostensibly addressed to virgin daughter Babylon, it was meant for the exiles who themselves were no doubt attracted to such practices and needed to be warned against them.

47:10a. *wtbṭḥy brᶜtk* "But you were secure in your evil;
***ᵓmrt ᵓyn rᵓny* you said, 'No one sees me.' "**

The pattern in v. 8 of *bṭḥ* and *ᵓmr* is repeated here but with significant variations. In v. 8 Babylon dwelt in security; here Babylon's security is attributed to an element of evil. It is her wickedness that makes her secure. Babylon said in her heart (v. 8) that she dwelled alone or was supreme. Here

107. Nah 3:4; 2 Kgs 9:22; Mal 3:5; cf. Isa 1:21–23.

108. See Andersen and Freedman, *Hosea*, 158, and the citation of a text from CAD K 284. The authors refer specifically to Isa 47:9 in their discussion of the connection between sex and sorcery.

109. BDB 287–88.

110. Andersen and Freedman, *Hosea*, 378.

Babylon does not assert her supremacy but assures herself that no one can see her evil deeds. Security is the focus of both v. 8 and v. 10. The word *bṭḥ* is associated with two different ideas: dwelling with (*yšb*) and evil with (*rʿh*). Taken together, the full idea is that Babylon feels she can sit on her throne securely because of her wicked deeds. The observer, however, knows that it is because of her evil that she will *not* be secure on her throne. 1QIsa[a] reads 'knowledge' (*dʿt*) for 'evil'. There is no reason to adopt this reading; the MT makes good sense. Babylon does not want her evil to be seen. There would be less reason for Babylon to be concerned about her knowledge being seen. Furthermore, Whybray points to a play on meanings between *rʿh* here and in v. 11. Because of her evil, evil will come upon her. Psalm 94 contains a similar message, that the arrogant evildoers who crush Yahweh's people (Yahweh's "heritage") in the belief that God does not see, will be wiped out by him for their wickedness. See also Ps 59:8, where the treacherous nations who plot against Israel ask as they come back to the city, "Who will hear us?" For their presumption they are "brought down" by God.

***rʾny* "sees me"**

This form of the participle of *rʾh* with the suffix is irregular according to GKC, and thus the text ought to be repointed.[111] But Delitzsch provides examples in which *ṣere* becomes either *pataḥ* (Isa 42:22) or *qameṣ* (Job 22:20) in pause. There is no need to repoint the text.

The division of 10ab into lines seems clear. Each line begins with a 2 f. s. verb. The totals for the syllable and stress count are 14 and 4/5, which are quite regular and close to the counts in a standard line-pair of 13/13.5 and 5 in Lamentations 1–4.[112] However, while the syllable count of 8+6 reflects the falling rhythm, the stress count of 2+2/3 does not. In fact, if we take the higher figure, it reflects the opposite. Such a phenomenon occurs several times in Isaiah 47.[113]

47:10c. *ḥkmtk wdʿtk* "Your wisdom and your knowledge—
***hyʾ šwbbtk* this is what leads you astray."**

Line 10c contains a scornful designation of Babylon's magic and divination.[114] The wisdom is that of Babylon's sorcerers and magicians.[115] In Isa 44:25 the word-pair *ḥkmh/dʿt* appears in connection with terms associated with Babylonian diviners. Yahweh the creator in Isa 44:24ff. performs several important acts for his people: he stretches out the heavens and the

111. GKC §61h / p. 164; §75v / p. 212.

112. Freedman, "Acrostic Poems," 429.

113. See, for instance, vv. 8cd, 10ef, and possibly 7ab and 13ab.

114. McKenzie.

115. The wise men in Dan 2:2ff. were magicians, enchanters, sorcerers, Chaldeans.

earth, he confirms the word of his servants, he declares that Jerusalem will be built, frustrates the work of diviners (and Babylonian bārû priests?), turns back (*mšyb . . . ʾḥwr*) the wise (*ḥkmym*), and makes their knowledge (*dʿtm*) foolish. The diviners and the wise are put together in one group. God foils their plans, and turns them back.

In Isaiah 47 the same verb that was used in chap. 44, *šwb*, is used in the *Polel* form to describe the effect that Babylon's wisdom has on her. Clifford interprets the word with the meaning 'refresh, restore' and translates, "Your wisdom and your lore, these provided sufficient guidance." He reasons that the whole of v. 10 is spoken by the arrogant queen and that this queen would hardly admit that she had been led astray. However, unlike other quotes in this chapter, which are all in the first person, 10cd is 2 f. s. North understands *šbb* in the sense meant in Ezek 38:4, "to be turned back."[116] There, however, and in 39:2, it is not the foolish knowledge of magicians, but God who leads Israel's enemies astray or turns them back. This line also reads well as a corrective to Babylon's mistaken notions of her self-sufficiency. The passage could be read with Clifford as an ironic statement about Babylon's powerful magic or with North and others as a literal corrective to her mistaken notions. The rarely used word is ambiguous here, perhaps purposely so.

The pronoun *hyʾ* (translated 'this is what') is used for emphasis;[117] it may refer to Babylon's wisdom and knowledge or may also include her evil, from 10a above. The pattern of assonance and alliteration binds all three feminine singular nouns together. Babylon sought security in all of these, and all led her astray.

47:11a–f.	***wbʾ ʿlyk rʿh***	**"And evil will come upon you;**
	lʾ tdʿy šḥrh	**you will not know its dawn.**
	wtpl ʿlyk hwh	**And ruin will fall upon you;**
	lʾ twkly kprh	**you will not be able to appease it.**
	wtbʾ ʿlyk ptʾm	**And it will come upon you suddenly,**
	šwʾh lʾ tdʿy	**devastation you did not know."**

In this verse the verb *bwʾ* appears twice (*wbʾ* and *tbʾ*) along with the verb *npl* to describe three evils (*rʾh, hwh, šwʾh*) that come to Babylon. 1QIsa[a] has *wbʾh*, so that all verbs of v. 11 agree in gender as well as person and number.[118] It is not necessary to emend here. However, it is to be

116. North, *Second Isaiah*, 172.

117. See Ronald J. Williams, *Hebrew Syntax: An Outline* (2d ed.; Toronto: University of Toronto Press, 1976) §118 / p. 24, on the use of a pronoun for emphasis.

118. However, see Williams: "When the verb precedes, the third masculine singular of the verb is often used regardless of the gender or number of the subject, especially when the latter is inanimate" (ibid., §227/p. 41).

noted that if the reading of 1QIsa[a] were adopted, the syllable count of the three line-pairs would be identical: each would have a count of 8+6 syllables. This would be consistent with the very regular grammatical and lexical parallelism of the verse.

BDB[119] lists *šḥr* as a m. noun with the meaning 'dawn'. Levy translates 'its dawning' (which seems to be the way the LXX and the Vg have interpreted the word), even though he says that "the simile is farfetched." The simile of the dawn or sunrise is used in Hos 6:3, where it is compared to Yahweh's going forth (or "utterance").[120] In Hosea, the coming forth of the dawn is used as a figure of a "sure thing"; it is certain to happen. Andersen and Freedman ask whether the coming forth of (the utterance of) Yahweh in Hos 6:3 is beneficial or destructive and agree that it is not easy to decide. In chap. 47, which is filled with irony, it would not be surprising to find a similar idea. There is a play on words between *rᶜh* of v. 10 and *rᶜh* of v. 11: Babylon trusted in her evil; now evil comes upon her. Babylon boasted that her misdeeds, her *rᶜh*, would not be seen, yet here in v. 11, *rᶜh* begins to dawn, is brought into the light. And while darkness is usually a figure of judgment, here it is the dawn of Babylon's evil that brings disaster.

The word *šḥr* (line 11b) is also problematic in Isa 8:16–22. There too the use of magic is an issue. People apparently were consulting "wizards and mediums" instead of consulting God. The word *šḥr* itself has mysterious or magical connotations. The enigmatic *ltwrh wltᶜwdh* 'to the teaching and to the testimony' in 8:20 seems to be some sort of formula or injunction directed to Isaiah's followers. The passage that follows seems to be another formula, its opposite.[121] Dahood cites a Ugaritic text in which the gods 'Dawn' and 'Sunset' are mentioned.[122] He associates it with Isa 14:12, where *bn šḥr* refers to the Assyrian/Babylonian king. The passage in Isa 8:20 is difficult to translate, but the context, the folly of workers of magic, is the same as 47:11.

Others[123] who are not satisfied with interpreting *šḥr*[124] as a noun suggest repointing to the form of a *Piel* infinitive and propose a Hebrew word cognate with the Arabic word meaning 'to charm, enchant, cast a spell'.

119. BDB 1007.

120. See Andersen and Freedman, *Hosea*, 423–24.

121. *ʾm-lʾ yʾmrw kdbr hzh ʾšr ʾyn-lw šḥr.*

122. Dahood, *Psalms II*, 55.

123. Delitzsch, Orelli.

124. See also Mark Smith, " 'Seeing God' in the Psalms," *CBQ* 50 (1988) 175, for a discussion of the root *šḥr*. Smith cites L. D. Merendino, "Il vocabolario relativo alla 'ricerca di Dio' nell' Antico Testamento: La radice *šḥr*," *Bibbia e Oriente* 25 (1983) 35–38, and suggests that two originally different roots may be involved.

The majority of commentators prefer this suggestion,[125] especially because of the emphasis on the sorceries and spells in v. 9, and translate, "You will not know how to charm away."

Torrey and Clifford emend the text to *šḥd* 'to offer a bribe'; Clifford's translation is, "You will not know how to avert it by a bribe." In support of this rendering is the parallel in Prov 6:35 between *šḥd* and *kpr*. However, ancient versions do not support this emendation, and since there are several proposals that accept the MT, it is unnecessary to emend.

Parallel with *šḥrh* is *kprh* 'to appease it, to atone for it'. The parallelism is not grammatical; *šḥrh* is a noun with 3 f. s. suffix, while *kprh* is an infinitive with suffix (this is additional reason for those who propose to emend "its dawn" to an infinitive form). The meaning is not "atonement" in the sense of atonement for sins. A similar usage appears in Prov 16:14: "A king's wrath is a messenger of death, and a wise man will appease (*kpr*) it." Many translations of v. 11 read, "You will not be able to avert it" or "buy it off (with a ransom)." The sense is that Babylon will not be able to avoid these disasters by any maneuvers, be they sorceries, spells, shows of power (see 12e), or other types of appeasement.[126]

The disasters mentioned here are all of a generic nature. *Rʿh* can refer to any variety of evil or calamity; *hwh* occurs here and in Ezek 7:26 (2 times) and is related to the verb meaning 'become, gape, yawn', and to the noun *hwh* 'chasm, destruction'. The final calamity, *šwʾh*, may refer to devastation as something that comes upon a person, to the effects of a storm (Zeph 1:15, Ezek 38:9), or the ruins or waste of the desert. The generic quality of these nouns is in contrast to the very specific threats of widowhood and bereavement above, though all are symbolic of the fall of Babylon.

The word *suddenly* (*ptʾm*), with one or two questionable exceptions, always occurs in connection with disaster.[127] The same negative association is present in the word *rgʿ* in 9b.

The pattern of v. 11 is quite regular, though there are some variations in word order and form. It is composed of three line-pairs, the first half of each line consisting of a 3 s. verb + prep. phrase (plus an additional element), the second half consisting of a 2 f. s. impf. verb with the negative *lʾ* (plus an additional element). The first parts of each line-pair can be compared as follows:

125. E.g., Duhm, Muilenburg.

126. Oppenheim states that it was believed that supernatural forces, if contacted through appropriate means, could avert predicted or threatened evil (*Ancient Mesopotamia*, 207).

127. D. Daube, *The Sudden in Scripture* (Leiden: Brill, 1964) 1–8. See below on Isa 48:3 (p. 180).

a and-will-come upon-you evil — 3 pf. V / prep. phr. / f. subj.
c and-will-fall upon-you ruin — 3 impf. V / prep. phr. / f. subj.
e and-will-come upon-you suddenly — 3 impf. V / prep. phr. / adv.

The second parts of the line-pairs are compared here:

b not you-will-know its-dawn — neg. / 2 f. s. impf. V / DO
d not you-will-be-able to-atone — neg. / 2 f. s. impf. V / inf.
f devastation not you-will-know — subj. / neg. 2 f. s. impf.

There is a variation in each line of this section, but each variation is balanced. For instance, in line e the pattern varies in that, instead of the subject following the prepositional phrase, there is an adverb. This is balanced by the appearance of the subject in line f and the omission of the object, present in lines b and d. In addition, the syllable count is remarkably regular: 6+6, 7+7, 7+6. If the 1QIsa[a] reading were adopted, the pattern would be 8+6 throughout.

Many scholars believe that something has fallen out of the last line. Whybray, who substituted an infinitive in 11b for the noun in the MT, now sees the need for a third infinitive to achieve parallelism in 11f. But this would disrupt the carefully constructed and balanced variations in the existing text. Again Whybray misses the creativity of the poet. The variation in the last line, with the addition of the adverb and the placement of the subject *šwʾh* at the beginning of the second half-line instead of the end of the first, serves to emphasize the suddenness and unexpected nature of these disasters. Thus *ptʾm* acts as a triple-duty word, modifying the verbs in lines 11a, c, and e. The last negated verb, *tdʿy* (line f), needs no additional infinitive. The previous infinitive of 11d (*kprh* 'to atone') and/or object of 11b (*šḥrh*) perform similar double duty.

The elements that are common in each line and give the sense of regular patterning are the prepositional phrase *ʿlyk* and the negative *lʾ*, each of which occurs three times. The threefold repetition of *lʾ* and *ʿlyk* emphasize the powerlessness of Babylon and the inevitability of the disasters.

The uncertainty about line divisions has been mentioned above. In line 11f I have divided the line-pair so that the subject, *šwʾh*, is placed in the second line and is divided from the verb, *wtbʾ*, in the first line. While grammatical considerations are important, in this case another factor was considered more important, that is, the stress and syllable pattern. All three line-pairs that belong together (11a–f) have the pattern 3+2. The syllable count is 6+6, 7+7, 7+6. If the subject had been placed in the first line the syllable count would have been 6+6, 7+7, 9+5, and the stress pattern would be 3+2, 3+2, 4+1. According to my system, a line must have at least two stresses. Since a single-syllable noncontent word receives no stress, the latter arrangement would be unacceptable.

47:12a–c. ***ʿmdy-nʾ bḥbryk*** **"Stand up, now, with your spells,**
wbrb kšpyk **and with the abundance of your sorceries**
bʾšr ygʿt mnʿwryk **for which you toiled from your youth."**

The imperative mood is resumed with *ʿmdy* and begins a new section of the poem. Previous imperatives ordered Babylon to go down, descend, sit down. Now, another direction is indicated. She is to take her stand in defense of her position.

Duhm offers a different interpretation, comparing this text with 2 Kgs 5:11, in which Naaman the leper voiced his expectation that the prophet Elisha would stand, call on the name of the Lord, wave his hand, and cure. According to Duhm, this is an example of a magician doing an exorcism. Babylon is called to stand with her spells and sorceries and defend herself. Another suggestion is to translate "persist in your spells" (as in the NAB or NEB). All of these translations connote irony, as many commentators have noted. The challenge to Babylon is compared with the taunting challenge made by Elijah to the Baal prophets in 1 Kgs 18:27. There is no real expectation that Babylon will be able to defend or protect herself. The repetition of *ḥbryk/kšpyk* from v. 9 is to be noted, as well as the reversing of word order to form a chiasm.

Line 12c, "for which you toiled from your youth," is eliminated by some commentators, following Duhm and Köhler, who omit it because of its similarity to 15ab. 1QIsa[a] adds the phrase *wʿd hywm* 'and unto this day' immediately following 12c and omits the rest of v. 12, as well as the first word of v. 13. Muilenburg suggests the possibility that the lines omitted in 1QIsa[a] are a satirical gloss. Others omit line 12c because it disrupts the rhythm, but Torrey observes that "the extra three-beat line in the middle of this verse illustrates a common feature of the poems written in the 3/2 meter." It is united to the previous lines by the repetition of the preposition *b-*, which occurs in each line. The alliteration of the 2 f. s. suffix at the end of each line is also striking and unites the line-trio.

ygʿ **"toil"**

Of the 26 occurrences of this verb in the Bible, almost half are in Isaiah, all in chaps. 40–66. *Ygʿ* has the meaning 'toil, grow or be weary'.[128] The expression *ygʿ b-* 'toil for' is found in Josh 24:13 and Isa 62:8, where the people toil for the land. It is not necessary to delete the *bet,* as suggested in BHS.

Throughout DI, the subject of the verb, in addition to Babylon in chap. 47, is both Yahweh and Yahweh's people. In Isa 40:28–30, Yahweh

128. BDB 388.

asserts that he does not grow weary and that he makes the weary strong. The servant in 49:4 is weary but strengthened by Yahweh. In 43:22–24, the root appears three times, where Yahweh accuses the people of having made him weary with their sins. He also defends himself for not having wearied them with offerings. In Isa 57:10, similarities with chap. 47 have already been noted above. The addressee there has been "wearied by the length of (her) way," and the context here is that of a woman who has sent far and wide in her pursuit of idolatrous worship. Here the toiling of Babylon can be compared to the toil described in 43:22–24 and 57:10. She spent her energies on magical practices and incantations.

47:12d. *ᵓwly* "perhaps"

The adverb *ᵓwly* 'perhaps, peradventure' can express either a hope or a fear for the future.[129] Here the word is, on the surface, expressing a hope for Babylon, but the meaning is ironical, as in Jer 51:8 ("Take balm for [Babylon's] pain. Perhaps she may be healed"). The repetition of the adverb emphasizes the sense of irony.

The poet suggests that Babylon "may be able to profit, to inspire awe." The verbs used are *yᶜl* 'gain profit, benefit' and *ᶜrṣ* 'cause to tremble, strike with awe'. *Yᶜl* is used especially in reference to idols as unprofitable (Isa 44:9, 10; 57:12; see also Jer 2:8 and Hab 2:8). According to BDB[130] the verb always occurs with a negative, or in questions implying a negative. The negative implication is surely here in 47:12. The verb *ᶜrṣ* is used several times with Yahweh as the subject (see Isa 2:19, 21, and Ps 89:8, where people are struck with awe by Yahweh). In Deut 1:29, Josh 1:9, and Isa 8:12, Israel's enemies cause them to tremble. But in Isa 8:13, the prophet is told not to be awestruck by these enemies. Rather, Yahweh is to be the one who inspires awe (*Hiphil* participle of *ᶜrṣ*). In Job 13:25, Job asks God in a sarcastic vein (similar to that found in Isaiah 47) whether he, Yahweh, will terrify a leaf. According to M. Pope[131] the verb *ᶜrṣ* carries a connotation of ruthless violence.

The ironic suggestions of lines 12de communicate the idea that Babylon, like the idols, is of no substance and cannot gain benefit for herself or others. And unlike Israel's God, to whom none can be compared, Babylon will strike fear into no one. Neither is Babylon to be feared, as were Israel's early enemies. The once ruthless or awe-inspiring Babylon (see Isa 13:11, 49:25) is now taunted. The boastful claims Babylon made in the early sections of the poem, "I am and there is no other . . . I will be mistress forever," are shown to be a sham.

129. BDB 19.

130. BDB 418.

131. Marvin H. Pope, *Job* (3d ed.; AB 15; Garden City, N.Y.: Doubleday, 1983) 102.

47:13ab. ***nlʾyt brb ʿṣtyk*** **"You are wearied by the abundance of your counsels.**
yʿmdw-nʾ wywšyʿk **Let them stand, now, and save you."**

These lines repeat a similar notion from lines 12bc above, that Babylon toiled for (or was wearied by) the abundance of her sorceries. *Brb kšpyk . . . ygʿt* is parallel to *nlʾyt brb ʿṣtyk.*[132] (For a similar use of the verb *lʾh*, see Isa 16:12. There Moab presents and wearies itself on the high place and at its sanctuary, but its prayers do not prevail: *lʾ ywkl.*) The powers of Babylon do not strengthen her; rather, they weaken her, as is obvious from the use of the verbs *ygʿ* and *lʾh.* This is one of the main contrasts in DI: it shows what Yahweh can do for his people and what the idols cannot do for theirs.

ʿṣtyk **"counsels"**

The use of a singular noun with a plural suffix in the MT has led commentators to emend to "counselors." 1QIsa[a] reads the singular *ʿṣtk.* The anomalous form *ʿṣtyk* may have been used to achieve a better phonological parallel with *kšpyk* in line 12b. This is not the only place in DI where ambiguity exists because of the use of *ʿṣtyk* (see 46:11b). Rather than emend the consonants to 'counselors', I read 'counsel(s)'. The reference is to the advice or wisdom (and by extension, to those who dispense such wisdom) that Babylon has received (mentioned in vv. 9 and 12) from the astrologers. They are now ordered (*yʿmdw-nʾ wywšyʿk* has jussive force here) to take their stand in defense of Babylon.

47:13c–f. ***hbr[y] šmym*** **"those who divide the heavens,**
hḥzym bkwkbym **those who gave at the stars,**
mwdyʿm lḥdšym **who make known through the new moon**
mʾšr ybʾw ʿlyk **what will come upon you."**

For 'dividers of (the heavens)' *hbr[y]*, MT *Kethiv* has the perfect *hbrw*, but the *Qere* has the m. pl. construct participle, as does 1QIsa[a], and this is reflected in my translation. Now the astrologers, those who divide the heavens[133] and gaze at the stars, are named as the ones to save (*ywšyʿ*) Babylon (see 13b). Part of their function is to tell the future by the seasons, the movements in the heavens. They are to declare the direction from which danger is coming. The prophet has emphasized the fact that Cyrus

132. It may be that the two lines form a distant parallel with one another, and that instead of having a line-trio in 12abc, 12abc and 13a form two line-pairs (12a//12b and 12c//13a).

133. J. Blau ("*Hōbərē šāmājim* [Jes xlvii 13] = Himmelsanbeter?" *VT* 7 [1957] 183–84) and E. Ullendorff ("Ugaritica Marginalia II," *JSS* [1962] 339–51) read "worshippers of the heavens," from a Ugaritic root.

comes swiftly from the distant parts of the world, and his advance may be what is meant by the unusual expression *mʾšr* 'what' or 'whence'.

Scholars have problems with the plural of *bwʾ* and the relative *mʾšr*. Duhm emends *bwʾ* to a singular form, which 1QIsa[a] also has. Torrey sees evidence of a conflated text. He rejects *mʾšr* as "mere nonsense." He thinks that one way to interpret "the new" is "new enemies" that will come against Babylon; another is to substitute *mh* for *mʾšr*, translating "making known by the new moons *what* will come. . . . " This is not one of Torrey's more convincing textual manipulations. Others propose, in order to clear up the text, that the *mem* on *mʾšr* is an example of dittography. North finds the subject of *ybʾw* "vague and indefinite."

There is no need to emend *ybʾw*. Whether *mʾšr* is read with the MT ("the ones who make known from where they will come upon you") or the *mem* is taken as an example of dittography (translating "the ones who make known what will come upon you"), the subject of the plural verb is all the calamities that were previously mentioned.

The passage is profoundly ironic. There is no point in calling upon the stargazers to save Babylon. Even if they were able to do what they claimed (i.e., correctly predict the future), all they could do in this case would be to tell Babylon about the unhappy fate in store for her. More likely, the text is meant to show that the astrologers are unable to tell the future.

Throughout DI the ability to make known things to come is a function of Yahweh, and he asserts that he and he alone is able to do this. In vv. 9 and 11, the calamities that were to come upon (*bʾw ʿlyk*) Babylon would come swiftly, without warning. It would be consistent with the rest of DI to conclude that the challenge in vv. 12–13 is a rhetorical device meant to illustrate that the astrologers cannot really tell the future and thus to warn Babylon about what is to come upon her (*ybʾw ʿlyk* in v. 13f).

47:14a. *kqš* "like chaff"

The word 'chaff' in the biblical text is almost always used in a simile. It refers to destruction because of Yahweh's anger. In Exod 15:7 Yahweh's anger consumed the Egyptians "like chaff"; in Isa 5:24 Yahweh's anger burned against those who rejected his Torah, and they were "burned up like chaff." Elsewhere in DI Israel's enemies are compared to chaff. They are blown away (40:24), trod upon by Cyrus (41:2), and in 47:14, burned in fire. Gitay sees the simile to be descriptive of the impotence of the astrologers, who cannot save Babylon.[134]

134. Y. Gitay, *Prophecy and Persuasion: A Study of Isaiah 40–48* (FTL 14; Bonn: Linguistica Biblica, 1981).

47:14b–f. *ʾš śrptm . . .* "fire burns them . . . "

Westermann sees in these verses the ring of doom so familiar in the preexilic prophets, where fire is a metaphor for God's chastisement and doom. Torrey sees the image of fire as "the standing feature of Second Isaiah's eschatology" and cites 34:9–10; 50:11; and 66:16, 24 as examples. Several words are used in chap. 47 to describe the fire: *ʾš*, *yd lhbh*, *gḥlt*, *ʾwr*. The feminine noun *gḥlt* 'coal' can refer to coals used in the ritual on the Day of Atonement (Leviticus 16); in 2 Sam 14:7 the quenching of coals refers to the loss of a woman's children and husband, her posterity; in Ezek 1:13 and Ps 18:9, 13 it is used in descriptions of theophanies; Ezek 24:11 describes a city that will be set upon hot coals and burned as a punishment; in Isa 44:19 there is a long description of the making of an idol from wood, and part of the description includes burning half of the wood on the coals.

The feminine noun *lhbh* is frequently used in theophanic descriptions (see Ps 29:7, Isa 5:24, and Lam 2:3). A rare word, *ʾwr* 'flame', also occurs in 44:17, 50:11, and 31:9 (where it is parallel with *tnwr* 'stove, firepot, furnace'; in Gen 15:17 *tnwr* symbolizes God's presence). These two words are often used in spectacular descriptions of Yahweh's awesome presence. In chap. 47 they are underplayed. The picture drawn is not one of the awesome presence of Yahweh, accompanied by smoke and flame. It is almost a domestic one, especially in view of the related picture of the idol-maker in Isaiah 44, who performs domestic chores, such as cooking his food over the coals and warming himself while he hews out an idol. Duhm has also noted the similarity between 44:16 and 47:14ef, but he concludes that 14ef is the prosaic addition from a later hand.

The tone of v. 14 is negative. The simile in line a describes Babylon's advisors as chaff; line b asserts that they will be burned. The rest of the verse continues with what will not happen: they will not deliver themselves from the flame, the coals are not coals to be used for warming, the fire is not to sit before. Wade is correct in pointing to lines b–f as "ironical litotes, suggestive of the real magnitude of the fire which will be kindled for Babylon." Far from being a prosaic addition, it is a fitting device to use in a poem replete with ironic expressions.[135]

This theophanic vocabulary may bring to mind the spectacular flashes of lightning in Psalm 29, the pyrotechnic displays of Ezekiel's vision, and the smoke, fire, and coals flaming forth from the sky in Psalm 18. But the main thrust seems to be that the astrologers (and Babylon) will not have the comforts of home. The threat of destruction is unmistakable, but it is

135. See p. 69 n. 141 on 46:13a and the device of litotes, and p. 119 on 47:3d.

understated in the extreme. That Babylon was not destroyed by fire but willingly gave herself into the hands of Cyrus is further proof that the prophecy originated in a time before the collapse of the empire.

47:15ab. ***kn hyw-lk ʾšr ygʿt*** **"So they are to you, those with whom you toiled,**
sḥryk mnʿwryk **your traders, from your youth."**

BHS suggests reading *bʾšr* for *ʾšr*, based on the Syriac, the targum, the Vulgate, and the combination of *bʾšr ygʿt* in 12c. However, 1QIsa[a] reads with the MT, and one might expect ellipsis in this long line. Throughout the poem the relative *ʾšr* has been employed in unusual ways.[136]

The m. pl. part. of *sḥr* 'trader, trafficker'[137] with 2 f. s. suffix, *sḥryk*, has provoked much discussion on the part of commentators, some of whom emend to *šḥr* and read 'your conjurers'.[138] A similar suggestion was made about the root *šḥr* in v. 11, though there it was not necessary to emend the text. Rather, a Hebrew root meaning 'to conjure', based on Akkadian and Arabic, was proposed. Those who opt for the emendation find the abrupt change from native astrologers to foreign traders to be unlikely.

In support of the translation 'traders' are those who point to the fame of Babylon as a great trading city (Ezek 17:4, "a land of trade . . . a city of merchants"). Torrey finds it to be a general term that is more suitable than the specific designation of one class of people. Slotki straddles the issue by translating 'trafficked with thee' and noting that this means "sold thee omens." The term *sḥr*, referring to "traders," is found in several poems that lament the fall of great cities. Isaiah 23 uses the root several times in the oracle on Tyre, in which the virgin daughter Sidon, who was proud of her international power and her trade, will have no more reason to exult. The satirical lament against Nineveh in Nahum 3, which has many similarities with Isaiah 47, speaks of her numerous merchants,[139] who in the end fly away like locusts, and no one knows where they are. They, like the merchants in chap. 47, are of no use to her when she needs them.

136. In spite of the occurrences of such prose particles (the sign of the def. dir. obj. is also used in 14c), the prose particle count is low, and there is no question that this is poetry. See F. I. Andersen and A. Dean Forbes, " 'Prose Particle' Counts of the Hebrew Bible," in *The Word of the Lord Shall Go Forth: Essays in Honor of David Noel Freedman in Celebration of His Sixtieth Birthday* (ed. Carol L. Meyers and M. O'Connor; Winona Lake, Ind.: Eisenbrauns, 1983) 174.

137. BDB 695.

138. Duhm, McKenzie, Whybray.

139. The word used here is from the root *rkl* 'to go about for trade'.

In the end, it should be admitted that both interpretations are possible. As Sasson[140] and Watson[141] have observed, wordplay is found in a variety of forms in the Hebrew Bible. According to Sasson, the use of paronomasia "promoted a certain aura of ambiguity, which was intended to excite curiosity and to invite a search for meanings that were not readily apparent." Both authors cite numerous examples from Second Isaiah; it is clear that this author is adept at such a technique.

There is a good deal of ambiguity about the meaning of the roots *šḥr* and *sḥr* in chap. 47. Convincing arguments have been marshaled for various translations of the roots. Both of the words, by their grammatical forms, give rise to suggestions of ways to manipulate or emend the text, but no one meaning or interpretation is convincing over others. In one case, *šḥr* is a homonym that can mean 'dawn' or 'conjure'. In the other, there is a similarity in spelling, *šin* and *samek*, which Sasson calls "equivocal word play," that is, similarity of sounds among varying words. Slotki, in his ambiguous rendering of the word, is perhaps closest to the correct reading of the passage. The author may have intended to bring both ideas (of foreign traders and of sorcerers) to mind by the unusual placement, grammar, and usage of the root *sḥr*. Alliteration and assonance between *sḥryk* and *mnᶜwryk* are also emphasized by placing the two words together.

47:15cd. ***ʾyš lᶜbrw tᶜw*** **"Each wanders in his own direction;**
ʾyn mwšyᶜk **there is no one saving you."**

The root *tᶜh* 'to err' is used to indicate wandering about, either physically or ethically (Isa 53:6, "All of us like sheep wander, turn to our own way"). It also has connotations of drunkenness (Isa 28:7, 19:14). In either sense, Babylon's former partners are unable to help her because they have no sense of direction themselves. They wander or stagger aimlessly, each in his or her own direction. This is variously interpreted as a panic-stricken flight out of the city, a drunken staggering about in doddering helplessness, a disregard for the troubles of Babylon, and an erroneous forecast of the coming series of events.[142] Again one is left with a variety of possible images. The key to understanding 15c is in 15d: there is no one to save Babylon. As in the previous verse, this verse is understated. It does not describe the spectacular punishments seen in similar oracles against the nations, such as Jeremiah 50–51, or Isaiah 13–14. Babylon's demise is described in

140. J. M. Sasson, "Wordplay in the OT," *IDBSup* (ed. Keith Crim et al.; Nashville: Abingdon, 1976) 968–70.

141. Watson, *Classical Hebrew Poetry*, 237ff.

142. Herbert, Levy, Delitzsch, and Kissane, respectively.

what she will not be, rather than in vivid depictions of calamities to come. Babylon's world ends, "not with a bang, but a whimper."

Structure

Introductory Notes

Isaiah 47 is different from the other two chapters under consideration for several reasons. Unlike chaps. 46 and 48, which have suffered greatly under the surgery of form critics, chap. 47 is considered a literary whole by the vast majority of critics. This also distinguishes it from the rest of Isaiah 40–66, at least in the history of recent scholarship. Furthermore, most scholars do not question its authenticity, despite the fact that there are some distinctive features in the chapter. Included among these features are the unusual vocabulary (40 words appear here but nowhere else in DI), the extended length of the poem, and the fact that nowhere else in DI is so much attention totally dedicated to a foreign power.

Various suggestions have been put forth regarding the background and genre of the poem. It has been variously called a taunt song (Clifford) or mocking song (Muilenburg), triumph song (Duhm), oracle against foreign nations (Westermann, McKenzie), and a funeral song or dirge over the dead (Whybray). As a funeral song or lament, one might expect evidence of the Qinah meter, and indeed many following Köhler point to the poem as a classic example of the Qinah, with its 3+2 stress pattern.

Comparisons have been drawn between this lament over Babylon and other sections of Isaiah and Jeremiah: Isa 13:1–22, 14:3–23, 21:1–10, and Jeremiah 50 and 51.[143] Isaiah 13 is in the form of an oracle against nations and declares the downfall of Babylon. Chapter 14 is a taunt song, depicting the downfall of the wicked king (of Babylon). Isa 21:9 declares, "fallen, fallen is Babylon, and the images of her gods." Jeremiah 50–51 is a lengthy collection including oracles against Babylon. D. Christensen has noted that the material in Jeremiah is "close to the thought world of Second Isaiah, and probably stems from the literary circle of that great prophetic figure of the Exilic period."[144] Dating these chapters is very difficult, and conclusions will not be drawn here about influences among Isaiah 47 and the

143. Martin-Achard has a brief discussion of these chapters in "Esaïe 47" (pp. 96–104).

144. Duane Christensen, *Transformations of the War Oracle in Old Testament Prophecy: Studies in the Oracles against the Nations* (HDR 3; Missoula: Scholars Press, 1975) 263.

other anti-Babylon passages. There are similarities between Isaiah 47 and the lamentation over Tyre in Ezekiel 27–28, another example of an oracle against the nations.

Another striking feature of the studies on Isaiah 47 is the way it is handled by scholars who are interested in the larger units of chapters 40–48 or 40–55. M. Haran's statement in the beginning of his article on the structure and framework of chaps. 40–48 is telling and typical: "[I]gnore, for the moment, the ironic lament over Babylon." Haran says of chap. 47 and its relationship to 40–48 that the "ironic lament over the fall of Babylon has found its way into our division." He believes that it was composed after Babylon fell and that there is no reason to doubt that it is the work of DI.[145] Gitay, who understands chaps. 40–48 as a long chain of well-developed arguments, wants to fit chap. 47 into his schema, even while admitting that it does not have the essential features he considers important to unite the larger unit.[146] Many others simply ignore the chapter in their discussions of the structure of the whole and make no decisions one way or the other about it.[147] Regarding the date of composition, most point to the fact that Babylon was not subjected to a humiliating defeat by Cyrus and conclude that chap. 47, like other oracles against nations, was written before the event it described (i.e., Cyrus's successful march on Babylon in 539).

There is general agreement that the passage is a great literary work. However, no one has gone into any great detail about the techniques and devices that make the chapter a well-crafted literary work.[148] In the minority on this question are Elliger and Smart,[149] who are bothered by the legalistic and vindictive nature of the poem and do not find it to be typical of the high style of DI. They question Deutero-Isaianic authorship on this ground.

Several elements serve to unite this poem. The most obvious is the theme, the announcement to Babylon of her humiliation and downfall. Throughout the poem Babylon is addressed in the second person, either in the form of imperatives telling Babylon what she must do, or in perfect or imperfect verbs describing what Babylon did in the past to deserve this

145. M. Haran, "The Literary Structure and Chronological Framework of the Prophecies in Is xl–xlviii," *Congress Volume: Bonn, 1962* (VTSup 9; Leiden: Brill, 1963) 127, 140.

146. Gitay, *Prophecy and Persuasion*, 206.

147. See, for instance, H. E. von Waldow, "The Message of Deutero-Isaiah," *Int* 22 (1968) 259–87.

148. Martin-Achard comes closest to this in his article "Esaïe 47."

149. K. Elliger, *Deuterojesaja in seinem Verhältnis zu Tritojesaja* (BWANT 4/11; Stuttgart: Kohlhammer, 1933); James D. Smart, *History and Theology in Second Isaiah: A Commentary on Isaiah 35, 40–66* (Philadelphia: Westminster, 1965) 139.

humiliation and what happened or will happen as a result of her past deeds. Second-feminine suffixes are used throughout the poem. The only other subjects of discussion in the poem are Babylon's sorcery (sorcerers), astrologers, and, in vv. 4 and 6, God and his people, his inheritance.

An important unifying element is the repetition and placement of several key words. Forms of the word *yšb* occur six times.[150] It appears at the beginning of the poem and two more times as an imperative, directing Babylon to "sit down." Occurring at the beginning, this imperative sets the tone for the entire poem. In v. 8 it describes an entirely different situation for Babylon, her false sense of security, her notion that she is secure and will never know the loss of husband or children. A feature of this poem (and of Second Isaiah in general) is the use of contrasts to develop a theme. The last occurrence of the root *yšb* is in v. 14, where it is used with a negative or foreboding sense. Babylon will not be sitting before a warm fire in security and comfort.

Another verb repeated throughout the poem is *bwʾ*.[151] It first occurs in v. 5, where it is parallel with *yšb*, in the imperative form. It is an important unifying element of the poem in that it picks up and continues the theme of Babylon's humiliating descent that began with *yrd* and *yšb* in the first line. It is part of the motif of descending and rising that holds together the verses. *Bwʾ* in v. 5 is in the imperative; Babylon is to descend into darkness. However, in the other five occurrences,[152] it is in the perfect or imperfect and describes, not Babylon's descent, but the coming down on Babylon of all the evils with which she is to be punished. The theme of the descent of Babylon in the beginning of the poem moves into the theme of the descent of disasters upon Babylon, with which the poem ends.

Related to the verbs for "sitting" or "going down" are other words that also indicate direction. Babylon is not only to go down (in mourning, to the netherworld, to darkness), she is to "pass over" rivers, perhaps indicating her path into exile. Babylon and her cohorts are directed later on in the poem to "stand up," to arise, which is the opposite direction to the earlier

150. Lines 1a, 1c, 5a, 8b, 8e, and 14f.

151. R. Lack sees this as a key word and a theme word in Isaiah 40–55. It appears in the prologue, 40:10, applied to the coming of Yahweh. It refers to the coming of Cyrus: 41:3, 25, 46:11, 48:15; the coming of the nations: 45:20, 24, 49:22; of evil—47:9, 11; and the coming of future events: 41:2, 42:9, 44:7, 47:13, 48:3, 5. It is used of the return of Israel: 43:5, 6, 49:12, 18, 51:11. Lack considers all of these comings to presuppose an irresistible force. They demonstrate the transcendence of Yahweh bursting into the horizontal plane of history (*La symbolique du livre d'Isaïe: Essai sur l'image littéraire comme élément de structuration* [AnBib 59; Rome: Pontifical Biblical Institute, 1973] 85–86).

152. Lines 9a, 9d, 11a, 11e, and 13f.

imperatives to go down. In the end, Babylon's aides wander aimlessly, without direction.

Negatives also serve to unify this poem by their frequent occurrences and placement. The negative particle *ʾyn* occurs four times: in vv. 1, 10, 14, and 15. Twice, at the beginning and end, it describes the situation as it is or will be for Babylon. "Unthroned" is the assertion at the beginning (v. 1); "no coal to warm you" (v. 14) and "no one to save you" (v. 15) conclude the poem and, in an understated way, sum up the poem. In v. 10 Babylon's mistaken sense of her own security is betrayed by her assertion that "no one sees" her. Babylon's shame will indeed be seen—*rʾh* is used twice in chapter 47. In v. 10 Babylon mistakenly believes that her evil deeds will not be seen, but in v. 3 *rʾh* is used without the negative and correctly states the situation. Just as the verb *yšb* was used to describe both the real situation of Babylon and her imagined and misguided self-assessment, here too the negative particle is used: Babylon thinks she can hide her evil deeds but she cannot. Her humiliating fate will be seen by all.

Other negatives are used to set the tone of this poem. The word *lʾ* is repeated twelve times[153] from beginning to end. It mainly is used to detail the various losses that Babylon will suffer (her privileged status, her title and role) and her inability to change the unfortunate direction that has been taken. She does not know what to do, nor is anyone able to help her. Another word, *ʾpsy*, is used twice, in vv. 8 and 10. This negative is used in a statement made by Babylon. Here is another misguided self-assessment: Babylon describes herself as having no equal. The word *ʾpsy* is found in a similar but not identical form elsewhere and is predicated of God. Again the contrast between Babylon's imagined state and the actual situation is heightened by the use of a negative word. Babylon is not without equal; Babylon is not beyond compare.

In addition to the key words that are repeated throughout the entire poem, there are numerous examples of repetition on a smaller scale, words in close proximity to one another. As a general rule, Mowinckel drew upon such repetitions to develop his theory of a rather mechanical process of composition, the combination of separate units by means of catchwords. He concluded that repeated words were yet another way to prove the existence of originally independent short units. Watson[154] defines "catchword" as a key word within a poem but does not interpret its function in the same way as Mowinckel. For Watson, the catchword, rather than signaling the existence of originally separate units, functions to link separate verses or stanzas within a single literary unit.

153. Isa 47:1, 3, 5, 6, 7, 8e, 11b, 11d, 11f, and 14.

154. Watson, *Classical Hebrew Poetry*, 288.

Examples of the repetitions of words in close proximity with one another in chap. 47 include: *bt* 'daughter': 1b, 1d; *lqḥ* 'take': 2, 3; *glh* 'uncover': 2c, 2e, 3; *gbrt* 'mistress': 5, 7; *śym* 'put': 6, 7; *ʾmr* 'say': 7, 8, 10; *lbb*, *lb* 'heart': 7, 8, 10; *ydʿ* 'know': 8, 10, 11b, 11f; *škl* 'bereavement': 8, 9; *ʾlmnh*, *ʾlmn* 'widow(hood)': 8, 9; *bʾw* 'come': v. 9 (2x), v. 11 (2x), etc.; *ykl* 'be able': 11, 12; *ʿlyk* 'upon you': 11a, 11c, 11, 11e; *ʾwly* 'perhaps': 12e, 12f; *ʿmd* 'stand': 12, 13. Some of these words are repeated in identical form and/or syntax for emphasis (*ʾwly* in v. 12, for instance, is an example of initial repetition). Others, such as *glh* in vv. 2 and 3, are used with different forms, thus developing and transforming the theme of the poem. Watson[155] discusses the use of the key word as a poetic device, as well as a structuring feature. He distinguishes among three types of key words, and two of the three are amply attested in chap. 47. The *dominant word* is a lexical item that provides a basis for understanding a stanza or poem, such as *cauldron* in Ezek 24:3–13. The *repeated word* is a word that occurs with "insistent frequency" within a poem, though he states that it is a matter of judgment and not "statistical computation" whether or not a word is significant. *Thematic words* are synonyms on a dominant theme; for instance, words concerning time or speaking. The repeated word, as defined by Watson, is used on large and small scales in Isaiah 47. Thematic words are used in synonyms and antonyms for ascending and descending within the poem, as well as on a larger scale in DI in general.

Lack specifically treats repetitions within Isaiah in his investigation of the structural unity of the book as a whole. He makes a distinction between *theme words* (*mots-themes*) and *key words* (*mots-clefs*)[156] and uses the word *bwʾ* as an example. The first type, *theme words*, relates to content. For instance, a text that treats the coming of Yahweh may be expected to use the common word *bwʾ*. The second, *key words*, relates to the structure of a given unit.

Michael Fishbane also discusses the use of the *key word* (or *theme word*). The two terms (*key word* and *theme word*) are interchangeable for Fishbane. Not only does the *key word* highlight matters of content, it also "gives the text a certain texture," that is, it relates to structure as well as

155. Ibid. (287ff.). Andersen and Freedman, in *Hosea* (133), discuss the way key words are used in Hosea. They unify the whole section, and they enable a given theme to be enumerated more than once. The same idea can be expressed by the recurrence of a word or by the use of different words. "Such variation is part of the art of repetition." They add that matching words and ideas do not necessarily occur at symmetrical points in the poem, and one ought not look for a geometrical system. What is important is the final effect of the repetitions, "an intricate extended network of correspondences."

156. Lack, *Symbolique*, 85, n. 20.

content.[157] In my use of the term *key word*, I refer to the repetition of a word, or synonym of a word, that is important to the content and /or structure of a poem.

There are numerous suggestions as to strophic divisions within this chapter. Martin-Achard's comment, "La division d'Esaie 47 en strophes n'offre pas de difficultes majeures," is puzzling, since divisions by scholars range from no individual strophes to seven.[158] The table on p. 151 outlines the various opinions. There is obviously no consensus among scholars regarding patterns or formulas used to divide the poem into sections. Most seem to depend on a change of theme or motif, observations of characteristic formulas (such as *hnh* or *w*ᶜ*th*), and the use of imperatives to make strophic divisions. The only element the divisions have in common (except for the NEB, in which the divisions and stichometric outline of the chapter are eccentric) is that there is a major break after v. 7.

Some find regular or even divisions within the poem: Fohrer has six strophes of six lines each; Köhler, five strophes with seven lines apiece.[159] Others, such as Muilenburg and Martin-Achard, consider the divisions to be uneven in length. However, Martin-Achard's divisions do have a definite pattern. They are arranged in a "decrescendo":

strophe 1	vv. 1–3	7 lines
strophe 2	vv. 5–7	7 lines
strophe 3	vv. 8–9	6 lines
strophe 4	vv. 10–11	6 lines
strophe 5	vv. 12–13	5 lines
strophe 6	vv. 14–15	5 lines[160]

This strophic arrangement could serve to emphasize further the theme of Babylon's descent. However, in order to achieve this attractive pattern, Martin-Achard too must make some line arrangements that are not entirely convincing. The complex verbal and thematic interweavings, the distant parallels or repetitions of words and phrases, make precise strophic division difficult.

Arguing against strophic divisions, Remi Lack points to the disagreements of several scholars on the strophic structure of the poem. His criteria for strophic divisions are repetition and refrain, usually occurring at regular

157. M. Fishbane, *Text and Texture: Close Readings of Selected Biblical Texts* (New York: Schocken, 1979) xii, 35, 50–52, etc.

158. Martin-Achard, "Esaïe 47," 88.

159. It must be noted, however, that Köhler's even structuring is achieved by extensive emendation, artificial rearrangement of lines, and reversal in word order from the MT.

160. Martin-Achard, "Esaïe 47," 89.

Table of Strophic Divisions by Scholars and Versions					
Three Divisions	NEB	JPSV			
	1. 1–4	1. 1–5			
	2. 5–11	2. 6–7			
	3. 12–15	3. 8–15			
Four or Five Divisions	Delitzsch	Duhm	Kissane	Elliger	North
	Skinner		Marti		Westermann
	Pieper		Köhler		
			NAB		
	1. 1–4	1. 1–4	1. 1–4	1. 1–4	1. 1–(4)
	2. 5–7	2. 5–7	2. 5–7	2. 5–7	2. 5–7
	3. 8–11	3. 8–10	3. 8–10b	3. 8–9	3. 8–9
		4. 11–12	4. 10c–12	4. 10–11	4. 10–12
	4. 12–15	5. 3–15	5. 3–15	5. 12–15	5. 13–15
Six or Seven Divisions	Herbert	Martin-Achard	Clifford	JB	
	Muilenburg				
	Volz				
	RSV				
	Whybray				
	Fohrer				
	1. 1–4	1. 1–3	1. 1–5	1. 1–3	
	2. 5–7	2. 5–7	2. 6–7	2. 4–5	
				3. 5–7	
	3. 8–9	3. 8–9	3. 8–9	4. 8–9	
	4. 10–11	4. 10–11	4. 10–11	5. 10–11	
	5. 12–13	5. 12–13	5. 12–13a	6. 12–13	
	6. 14–15	6. 14–15	6. 13b–15	7. 14–15	

intervals. He therefore concludes about chap. 47: "Pour notre part, nous pensons qu'il est inopportun de chercher à compter des strophes dans notre poème sur Babylone."[161] The many possible divisions point to a complexity of structure of this poem and to its concentric development by the use of overlapping themes, motifs, and repeated words.

Since repetitions do not occur regularly, Lack looks for another principle of composition for the chap. 47 poem, especially in its stylistic details. The element that Lack finds pervasive is the "binary" character of chap. 47. Individual words and whole phrases occur twice in the poem (e.g., lines 1e and 5c both state, "for no longer shall you be called . . . "). Furthermore, several words are frequently repeated throughout the poem, as has been observed above.

Lack demonstrates that the poem is developed by using words and themes in such a way that they contrast with one another. (Clifford's treatment is similar in this regard, though he looks at larger units.) Babylon believes she will not "sit" as a widow, but she will. Further, she "sits" in the dust in mourning. The binary character of the poem is what gives the poem its structure: what Babylon believes to be a nightmare is reality, and what she believes to be reality is only a dream. Lack emphasizes that his method investigates the literature from the point of view of esthetics. He contrasts his approach to that of Westermann and other form critics, who, he says, are not interested in the artistry of the individual poem and the literary effects that the individual stylistic details create but in forms in general.

The strophic patterning of 1QIsa[a] is also important. Every chapter in Isaiah 40–55 in 1QIsa[a] shows some evidence of paragraphing, that is, there are spaces between some verses in each of the chapters. Chapter 47 is no exception. There are spaces dividing v. 4, both from what precedes and follows, as well as a division between vv. 7–8.[162] This does not support Lack's thesis about a lack of strophic patterning in chap. 47. Lack's thesis that refrain and repetition ought to come at regular intervals in order to signal strophic division is too much of a generalization. He does not demonstrate this thesis elsewhere. Others have shown that there are additional techniques and devices that can be used to indicate divisions within a poem. For example, Watson lists these: use of the refrain, key words, certain particles, gender patterns, chiastic or concentric pattern, introductory formulas,

161. Lack, *Symbolique*, 103.

162. The spaces are not large, but there is no question that they are larger than the spaces between words. The MT also breaks after v. 3 (but not after v. 4) and between vv. 7–8, with 1QIsa[a]. The LXX is an exception. While it signals larger divisions in chaps. 46 and 48 (in chap. 46 after v. 2 and in chap. 48 after vv. 11 and 19), it makes no indications of any divisions within chap. 47.

change of speaker, and other patterns, such as tricolon and pivot patterns.[163] All of these factors are important in my discussion of the divisions and interlocking features of Isaiah 47.

Structure of Individual Sections: Microstructure

Section I (vv. 1–4). The poem begins with a dramatic portrayal of Babylon as a woman. The series of imperatives directing her to "go down" are important to the development of the entire poem, which stresses in a variety of ways the descent of Babylon. The poem is composed of 18 lines (9 line-pairs, not 7 as Martin-Achard and Köhler believe), the last of which is a doxological formula that contains one of two references made to Yahweh in the poem.

The poem is often pointed to as an example of Qinah (3+2) meter, and several lines in this section are good examples of this. The stress count for v. 1 has the pattern 3+3, 3+2, 3+2. Some scholars are rather rigid in the matter of stress counting. Here, for instance, Köhler, who finds 3+2 stress count throughout the poem, has a problem with line 1b. The combination *btwlt bt* has too many stresses, especially in view of 1d, so Köhler emends (excising *bt* in line 1b) to maintain the strict 3+2 pattern. The only thing that this approach to the text reveals is that the commentator wants to make the text conform absolutely to his theoretical pattern.

It must be admitted that the counting of stresses has always been somewhat ambiguous. And, against Köhler, surely nothing is gained by changing the text to fit an external pattern. Stress counting, however, can be helpful in seeing an overall pattern. The most important principle with regard to identifying Qinah meter has to do with the relationship between the first line of the bicolon and the second; the first line is longer than the second.[164] In this regard, syllable counting, which has more precision, is a helpful tool. The syllable count for the first verse is 8+6, 7+3, 9+5; this reflects the Qinah meter, in that the first line in each case is longer than the second.

This pattern of v. 1 is not maintained in the succeeding lines (vv. 2–3), which I outline as a series of 5 line-pairs, with a prevailing stress pattern of 2+2.[165] Again, in his concern to find a 3+2 stress count everywhere, Köhler misses the extremely regular pattern of lines 2a–f. Each line is

163. Watson, *Classical Hebrew Poetry*, 163ff.

164. Garr, "The Qinah," 61.

165. These lines could also be viewed as an extended line-trio, with syllable count of 9+8+8 = 25, and stress 4+4+4. However the lines are arranged, they are unusual. The flexibility of line arrangement in this poem has elsewhere been discussed. This is another example of this feature.

grammatically parallel, being composed of f. s. impf. + DO. Semantic parallelism is also present, especially between 2a and 2b ("take millstones, grind grain"), 2c and 2d ("uncover your hair, strip off your skirt"). Furthermore, the threefold repetition of the root *glh* in the first line of each line-pair—2cd, 2ef, and 3ab—is another factor in my arrangement. This is clearly a 2+2 stress pattern.[166] The syllable count of each line is rather low, as might be expected in a short, 2-stress line.

Verses 2–3b are united by the theme of the humiliation of Babylon. While v. 2 is composed entirely of imperatives, and lines 3ab have the imperfect, the same pattern of V/obj. is maintained throughout. These verses are also remarkable for the high concentration of verbs. There are seventeen words in the section, eight of which are verbs. Alliteration is achieved with the frequent repetition of *qop* and *ḥet*. The device of asyndeton is apparent, in that no conjunctions are used to unite the lines, except for the final *gm*, which draws them to a grim conclusion, "your shame will be seen."

Verse 4, as discussed above, stands outside the pattern of the poem, and this is apparent in the unusual number of syllables and stresses. The syllables and stresses show the verse to be a lop-sided standard line of 16 (11+5) syllables and 6 (4+2) stresses, the only one of its kind in this poem.

The section is united by the portrayal of the descent of Babylon and the progressively worse humiliations that she is to suffer. Verse 3 is a clear statement explaining why these things will happen to Babylon: God will take vindication. This is balanced by the doxological assertion of v. 4, which makes a connection between God's action against Babylon, the bitter enemy of his people, and his role as Israel's redeemer. If v. 4 is eliminated, as Martin-Achard, North, and others suggest, the connection between Babylon's fall and the redemption of God's people is lost. Verse 4 marks the end of the section by the change in meter and the formulaic nature of the verse itself.

Section II (vv. 5–7). The resumption of 2 f. s. imperatives marks the beginning of a new section, which consists of 13 lines (5 line-pairs and one of 2 line-trios in the entire poem). The imv. *šby* is repeated from line 1a, and a new imperative, *bʾy*, is added to replace *rdy*. The theme of Babylon's descent continues, but the adverb *dwmm* 'silently' and the prep. phr. *bḥšk* add specification to the descent.

Between vv. 1a–f and 5a–d, there is an excellent example of discontinuous or distant parallelism. Not only are 1a and 1b parallel with 1c and 1d, they also parallel 5a and 5b. The pattern of interlinear parallelism is diagrammed as follows:

166. Martin-Achard ("Esaïe 47") ignores these factors when he counts 7 bicola.

1a	Go down and sit down in the dust,	A
1b	O virgin daughter Babylon.	B
1c	Sit down on the earth—unthroned—	A′
1d	O daughter Chaldea.	B′
5a	Sit down silently and go into darkness,	A″
5b	O daughter Chaldea.	B′

Another example of distant parallelism appears in vv. 1e and 5a. The repetition of 1e and 5c is similar to a refrain. The pattern continued is as follows:

1e	You shall not continue to be called	C
1f	"tender and delicate."	D
5c	You shall not continue to be called	C
5d	"mistress of kingdoms."	D′

The distant parallelism and repetition function to unite sections I and II.

Looking at these lines (1a, 1c, and 5a), it can be seen that there is a development from line A to line A′ to line A″. The second line increases or heightens the sense of doom by adding to the command "go down to the dust" the idea of the loss of the throne. The third line further intensifies the idea by the ominous note of prison or worse, the netherworld, with the word *darkness*. Likewise, a comparison of the D and D′ lines shows that line D′ amplifies the losses to Babylon. The title or identity that Babylon loses in line D ("tender and delicate") is one that pertains to her personal stature or well-being. But in the loss of the title "mistress of kingdoms" in D′, her international status and acclaim are attacked.

Section II is also more specific about the reasons for Babylon's descent. Where section I spoke in general terms of Yahweh's vindication, section II explains that Babylon treated his people without compassion and had more regard for her titles than for the consequences of her actions. The negative *lʾ*, occurring three times in vv. 6 and 7, stresses this lack of compassion and also, in 7d, serves as a bridge to the following section.

In section II the Qinah meter prevails. Line-pairs 5ab, 5cd, 7ab, and 7cd, by syllable count, have longer first lines than second; the stress pattern supports this in all of those pairs except 7ab. There is one example of rising, rather than falling meter, in the line-pair 6de (7+9, 3+4).

5ab	9+3 syllables	4+2 stresses
5cd	9+5	3+2
7ab	7+5	2+2/3
7cd	7+6	3+2

The line-trio does not follow the Qinah pattern, nor does the pair 6de, though Martin-Achard sees 6e as a line-pair, in which case the two lines *ʿl-zqn hkbdt* (2+3 stresses? 5 syllables) and *ʿlk mʾd* (2 stresses, 4 syllables) would fall into the Qinah meter.

Section III (vv. 8–11). The ominous "now hear this" is the beginning of the formal announcement of doom, which has already been hinted at in the preceding verses. This section, the longest in the poem, announces, through a series of contrasts, the devastation that will come upon Babylon. Babylon's mistaken notions of her position are set in sharp contrast to the announcement of what her position really will be.

The words *bwʾ*, *ydʿ*, *lʾ*, and *ʿlyk* are used in a variety of ways to emphasize Babylon's fate and the worthlessness of her knowledge. The repetition of *yšb, bṭḥ*, the root *ʾmr* in various forms, and the phrase *ʾny wʾpsy ʿwd* are also uniting features. The fivefold use of the first-person singular form[167] throughout the entire section is striking. The use of the first-person forms in connection with Yahweh has been noted above. Here, where the emphasis is on Babylon and her fate, the phenomenon has been used in a different fashion.

This is the longest section in the poem, consisting of 12 line-pairs (24 lines). Many see vv. 8–11 as two sections, with a division made at v. 10. Such an arrangement has merit, since several key words and phrases from vv. 8–9 are repeated in the same order in vv. 10–11. Muilenburg points out that vv. 8–9 and 10–11 are both divided into two parts, with the same contrasts. The relationship between vv. 8–9 and 10–11 are illustrated by the following diagram:

Verses 8–9	*Verses 10–11*
And now hear this, luxury lover	
who sits *securely*,	. . . you were *secure* in your evil;
who *says in her heart*,	you *said*, "No one sees me."
	Your wisdom and knowledge—
	leads you astray.
	You *said in your heart*,
"*I am, and there is no other.*	"*I am, and there is no other.*"
I will not sit as a widow,	And evil will come upon you;
I will not *know* bereavement."	you will not *know* its dawn.
Yes, these two will come to you,	Ruin will fall upon you;

167. The repetition of the independent pronoun *ʾny* in lines 8d and 10f forms an envelope around the other three first-person forms, two impf. verbs in 8ef and a suffix in 10b.

	you will not appease it.
suddenly, in one day.	It will come upon you suddenly,
Bereavement and widowhood	devastation you did not know.
in full measure—	
they come upon you.	

Each section describes, in similar language, Babylon's arrogance and her mistaken notions about her future. Each clarifies, in different terms, what Babylon's future will really be like. In both sections the disasters mentioned are to "come upon" her, and this will happen "suddenly." The verb *yd*^{c} is used to contrast Babylon's "knowledge" in vv. 8–9 with what she does not "know" in 10–11. In this poem, whenever the verb *yd*^{c} occurs, it is in connection with the verb *bw*$^{\supset}$. In v. 8, Babylon says she will not know bereavement; in line 9a, it is announced that bereavement and widowhood will come upon her. In v. 11 there is a twofold repetition of the combination *bw*$^{\supset}$*/yd*^{c}, which emphasizes her ignorance of her fate. In both sections Babylon "says" ($^{\supset}$*mr*) certain things. In each case, what she says is incorrect. While there is not much intralinear parallelism or symmetry, especially in v. 9,[168] it is clear that there is an overall pattern.

While there are good arguments for the view that vv. 8–11 make up two short sections rather than one, the more convincing view is that there is one long section, based on the following: the single theme occurring throughout the section, the repetition of several key words, the fivefold repetition of the first person, the fact that the only obvious divider is at v. 12, and the imperative challenge to Babylon and her advisors to defend themselves.

Section IV (vv. 12–13). The challenge in the form of the imperative ^{c}*mdy-n*$^{\supset}$ begins a new section of the poem. The major theme that unites these verses is the ironic invitation to Babylon's astrologers and magicians to save her or at least to foretell the evils that will come upon her. The

168. The verse can be divided a number of different ways. Freedman, in personal correspondence, suggested the following:

And there will come upon you	5	2
These two things at once	4	3
In one day	4	2
Bereavement and widowhood, according to their completeness.	8	3
Let them come upon you	5	2
In the midst of your spells,	5	2
In the great number of your sorceries.	8	3

It is possible to divide at a number of different points in this verse because of the lack of parallelism. Freedman's division departs from mine and from that of BHS, and all of the modern commentators are at odds with the MT, which has a division before *ktmm*.

section is composed of 11 lines (the beginning line-trio and 4 line-pairs); the Qinah meter is not much in evidence here. Only in 12de is the first part of the line-pair longer than the second, with a stress of 3+2 and a syllable count of 7+5. The final line-pair, 13ef, ends with the longer line (stress count 2+3, syllable count 7+8); the beginning line-trio also ends with a long line (2+2+3, 7+6+9).

Key words that unite this section are two words derived from the root *ᶜmd*, the emphatic *n*ᵓ, the repeated *ᵓwly*, the synonyms *ygᶜ* and *lᵓh* ('weary'), the ironic *rb* in 12b and 13a, and the list of Babylon's reputed saviors: spells, sorceries, counsels, dividers of the heavens, stargazers, and foretellers. Alliteration unites individual lines, as well as the larger section, the repetition of the 2 f. s. possessive suffix at the end of 12a, b, c, 13a, and 13f. The sound combination *b/r* is repeated in lines 12a–c, as well as in 13a and c; in 12de *w/l* are repeated; in 13c–e the 3 m. pl. ending occurs five times. The overall ironic tone of the entire section is also a uniting element.

Section V (vv. 14–15). The final section begins with *hnh*, which frequently introduces a pronouncement of doom or judgment. The emphatic *kn* confirms the judgment in line 15a. *Hyw* marks a division within the section and points to the two ideas that dominate these verses: first, the imagery of fire, portraying the punishment for Babylon and her cohorts by the use of words for fire, flame, and burning; second, the inability of Babylon and her helpers to deliver themselves, described in 14c (*lᵓ-ysylw*) and 15d (*ᵓyn mwšyᶜk*). The uselessness of Babylon's advisors is underscored by the repetition of *hyw*: "behold, *they are* like chaff" (14a) and "so *they are* to you" (15a).

In the closing section, Qinah meter predominates, as can be seen by the pattern of both syllable and stress counts: 3+2, 6+5; 3+2, 7+5; 2/3+3, 5+5; 4+2, 8+7; 3+2, 6+4. Only the line-pair in the middle departs from the pattern of falling rhythm.

Structure of the Poem: Macrostructure

Scholars are in general agreement that chap. 47 stands as a literary unit by virtue of the single theme that runs throughout. There are also other features and literary devices the poet has used to develop and emphasize the theme of the downfall of proud Babylon. I have discussed the use of key words in uniting small sections of the poem. However, there are also numerous key words and phrases that appear throughout the entire poem and are not limited to one or another section. These key words are woven throughout to connect sections, to move the theme to another level, or to develop the thought of the poem through contrast and comparison. Some of these key words have been treated in detail by R. Lack in his structural analysis of DI and of the book of Isaiah as a whole. The three key words in chap. 47 that Lack points to are: *yšb* 'sit, sit down' (occurring five times between vv. 1 and 8), *yd*ᶜ 'know' (occurring five times between vv. 8 and 13), and *bw*ᵓ 'come' (occurring five times between vv. 9 and 13; he does not include line 5a in his count).[169]

Each of these words is emphasized by synonyms or antonyms that appear throughout the poem. Commands to "sit down" are paralleled by commands to "descend" (*yrd*) or "go" (*bw*ᵓ). A contrast to the order to sit down is the command to "stand up" (ᶜ*md*). The motif of *knowing*, or more accurately, *not knowing*, is amplified in various ways: in lines 7cd Babylon does not remember or bring to mind; in 10c the wisdom (*ḥkm*) and knowledge of Babylon's advisors are mentioned, and these "knowledgeable ones" are referred to ironically throughout the poem. The poem begins with Babylon's going down to the dust, to earth (the netherworld); her destination is specific. The poem ends with her advisors wandering in confusion in no specific direction whatsoever.

Other key words and /or phrases are used only twice, usually in different sections. They can be used to emphasize a certain idea, as in the repetition of ᵓ*šr yg*ᶜ*t mn*ᶜ*wryk* from section IV, where the emphasis is on Babylon's toiling from the time of her youth for her ineffectual advisors. Or they can be used to strike a contrast. In III and IV the verb *twkly* is so used: Babylon is unable to prevent the coming of evil, compared to the possibility that she may be able to succeed. Another example is in IV and V: "let them save you" versus "no one saving you." In the latter two examples, the contrast is a superficial one, since the suggestion that Babylon may be able to succeed and the jussive "let them save you" are ironic.

Another feature unifying the poem is what I have referred to above as discontinuous or distant parallelism. I noted the difficulties critics have in coming to any agreement about the strophic divisions of Isaiah 47. Some scholars interpret the repetition of a phrase as the beginning of a new unit; others take it as an example of an envelope construction and read repetition as the close of the unit. Clifford, for instance, reads v. 5 as the end of the first unit, because of the parallels between lines 1a and 5a and the repetition in 1e and 5c. However, v. 5 marks the beginning of a new unit rather than the close of a unit.

A similar ambiguity with regard to strophic patterning can be seen in vv. 8–12. I previously discussed the parallel developments in vv. 8–9 and why I considered vv. 8–11 to be one section. However, not mentioned in that discussion was the continuation of the pattern into v. 12. This is a

169. Lack, *Symbolique*, 104.

phenomenon similar to that in vv. 1–5, an example of an envelope, in which lines 9ef, "the abundance of your sorceries . . . the great might of your spells," are repeated in a chiastic arrangement in lines 12ab, "your spells . . . the abundance of your sorceries." The imperative that begins v. 8 is echoed in a similar imperative in v. 12: "now, hear this" and "stand up, now."

The question to ask is this: Do these lines (5ab and 12ab) have uniting or dividing functions in this poem? I suggest that they serve both to relate to the previous section of the poem, as well as to look ahead to what is to come. A similar example is found in Isa 54:14.[170] In response to the question of whether 14a belongs to the first or second section of the poem, Beuken states, "I think it can conveniently be considered as the 'hinge-verse': on the one hand it continues the topic of the new city to be founded (11–13), on the other hand the word *ṣdqh* encloses the second element of this section (14–17)."

Parunak[171] makes comparable observations about passages that function as hinges between strophes, which he refers to as "panels." Parunak sees the hinge as a transitional unit of text, independent of either of two big panels, that does not add significant information to the information presented by its neighbors. In Isaiah 47 the matter is more complicated, because the passage in question is repeated and is not independent of the neighboring sections. Nonetheless, when a phrase is repeated (as in 5c or 12ab), it can be seen to operate as a hinge, since it marks a transition and relates to both strophes or panels that it adjoins.

The progressive humiliation of Babylon is described in a number of ways: in her descent to the earth, to the netherworld, and then the descent of evils upon her; in the stripping away of her titles of respect, one by one; in the exposure of her advisors as impotent and inept, and in their destruction and confusion. Until the very end, the tone of irony prevails. Even at the end, the understatement with regard to the fate of Babylon and her cohorts is consistent with the ironic tone, in which what is said on the surface level is incongruous with what is understood on another level.

That Babylon is the subject of this poem is clear in every line. Of special note in this regard is the middle section, the longest in the poem. The fivefold repetition of the first-person singular forms referring to Babylon emphasizes the centrality of this section to the entire poem. Elsewhere, Yahweh makes claims about himself, and this is often done with the same five- or tenfold repetition of first singular forms. That Babylon's similar as-

170. Discussed by Beuken in "Isaiah LIV," 56.
171. Parunak, "Transitional Techniques," 529.

sertions are totally without force and not at all like those of Yahweh's is an underlying motif of section III.

The meter of this poem is mixed, but the so-called Qinah meter, in which the second line is shorter than the first, predominates. The poem can be compared to chaps. 1–4 of Lamentations, which were written in Qinah meter. The poems have been analyzed in detail by Freedman.[172] He points to the great freedom with which the poets composed individual lines and stanzas, as well as certain constraints that strictly regulated the length of the entire poem. He finds that in chaps. 1–4 of Lamentations, the lines are divided unevenly, with the average syllable pattern of 7/6 or 8/5 (that is, 13 syllables per bicolon) and the 3+2 meter, which fits Budde's hypothesis. Freedman also demonstrates that these poems are absolutely regular in length.

How does chap. 47 compare with Freedman's assessment of Lamentations 1–4? With regard to the number of lines or line-pairs, chap. 47 does not have the acrostic pattern of multiples of 11, or 22 units. There are 37 units (35 line-pairs and 2 line-trios) in the poem. With regard to meter, the comparison is instructive. If stress is used as the only indicator of meter, then less than half of the poem (16 of 37 units) shows evidence of falling rhythm. If syllables alone are indicators of meter, more than half of the poem (22 of 37 units) is in Qinah meter, with the first line longer than the second. There are 14 units within the poem in which both syllables and stresses show the first line to be longer than the second—lines 1cd, 1ef, 4ab, 5ab, 5dc, 7cd, 8ab, 9cd, 11ef, 12de, 14ab, 14cd, 15ab, and 15cd. Of these, only 3 show the basic pattern that Freedman found in Lamentations 1–4: 13 syllables, 5 stresses.[173]

The units of Isaiah 47 are complex, in that some lines that indicate falling rhythm by syllables show the reverse by stress pattern. There are two such units in the poem. Unit 8cd has a total of 13 syllables and 5 stresses, which fits the dominant pattern. However, while the syllable pattern is 7+6 with the longer line first, the stresses are 2+3 with the longer line second. See also lines 10ef, with a pattern of 7+6 = 13 and 2+3 = 5, another example of the same phenomenon. In 5 units, the stress and syllable pattern is not a falling, but a rising rhythm: 3ab, 3cd, 6de, 9ef, and 13ef. Four additional units show a rise in syllables but not in stresses: 2ab, 2ef, 13ab,

172. D. N. Freedman, "Acrostics and Metrics in Hebrew Poetry," *Pottery, Poetry, and Prophecy: Collected Essays on Hebrew Poetry* (Winona Lake, Ind.: Eisenbrauns, 1980) 51–76.

173. Freedman, "Acrostic Poems," 429. See also "Acrostics and Metrics," pp. 60–61, in which the syllable count of Lamentations 1–3 is shown to be 12.7–13.0 per unit; Lamentations 4 has a slightly larger count, 13.0–13.75.

and 13cd. There are also a number of line-pairs in which the stresses are even, with a 2+2 or 3+3 pattern. Four lines are even with respect to syllables. As has been observed throughout this analysis, the determination of the caesura within each line-pair is difficult, if not impossible, in a number of cases, because of the lack of intralinear parallelism. This makes the assessment of falling (or rising) rhythm within the line-pairs somewhat speculative.

However, in spite of the wide variety in arrangement of lines and combinations of syllable and stress patterns, the overall pattern of the poem is quite regular. The dominant unit of the poem is a line-pair of 5 stresses (23 units out of 37). The syllable count of each unit (line-pair) varies between 8 and 16. Including the 2 line-trios, the average for the entire poem is 12.9 syllables per unit and 5.1–5.27 stresses per unit. This is comparable to the pattern of Lamentations 1–4, which is 12.7–13.0 syllables per unit. The lines that vary from the Qinah pattern vary in such a way that the long lines balance out the short lines; the overall syllable and stress pattern show that this is done with a great deal of precision.

All of these techniques—the rhetorical devices, the strophic patterning, the overall development of theme, and the metric or quantitative structure of the poem—are helpful in understanding how this particular poet worked and the way in which the poet used the conventions of the day to construct this lament over Babylon.

Isaiah 48

Text

		Syllable	*Total Count*	*Stresses*
Section I				
1a	šmʿw-zʾt byt-yʿqb	2 + 1 + 1 + 2	6	4
b	hnqrʾym bšm yśrʾl	4 + 2 + 3	9	3
c	wmmy yhwdh yṣʾw	3 + 3 + 3	9	3
d	hnšbʿym bšm yhwh	4 + 2 + 2	8	3
e	wbʾlhy yśrʾl yzkyrw	4 + 3 + 3	10	3
f	lʾ bʾmt wlʾ bṣdqh	1 + 2 + 2 + 3	8	3
2a	ky-mʿyr hqdš nqrʾw	1 + 2 + 2 + 3	8	3
b	wʿl-ʾlhy yśrʾl nsmkw	2 + 3 + 3 + 3	11	4
c	yhwh ṣbʾwt šmw	2 + 3 + 2	7	3
	9 lines		76	29
Section II				
3a	hrʾšnwt mʾz hgdty	4 + 2 + 3	9	3
b	wmpy yṣʾw wʾšmyʿm	3 + 3 + 4	10	3
c	ptʾm ʿśyty wtbʾnh	2 + 3 + 4	9	3
4a	mdʿty ky qšh ʾth	3 + 1 + 2 + 2	8	3
b	wgyd brzl ʿrpk	2 + 2 + 2 / 3	6/7	3
c	wmṣḥk nḥwšh	3 / 4 + 3	6/7	2
5a	wʾgyd lk mʾz	3 + 1 / 2 + 2	6/7	3
b	bṭrm tbwʾ hšmʿtyk	2 + 2 + 3 / 4	7/8	3
c	pn-tʾmr ʿṣby ʿśm	1 + 2 + 2 + 2	7	3
d	wpsly wnsky ṣwm	3 + 3 + 2	8	3
	10 lines		76–80	29
Section III				
6a	šmʿt ḥzh klh	2 / 3 + 2 + 2	6/7	3
b	wʾtm hlwʾ tgydw	3 + 2 + 3	8	3
c	hšmʿtyk ḥdšwt mʿth	3 / 4 + 3 + 3	9/10	3
d	wnṣrwt wlʾ ydʿtm	4 + 2 + 3	9	3

Translation

Section I

1a Hear this, O house of Jacob,
b the ones who call themselves by the name Israel,
c and from Judah they came forth;
d the ones swearing by the name of Yahweh,
e and the God of Israel they invoke—
f not in true righteousness—
2a but they call themselves ones from the holy city,
b and upon the god of Israel they lean.
c Yahweh Sabaoth is his name.

Section II

3a The first things from time past I declared,
b and from my mouth they went forth and I announced them.
c Suddenly I acted and they came forth.
4a Because I know that you are stubborn,
b and an iron sinew is your neck,
c and your forehead is bronze.
5a And I declared it to you from time past;
b before it came I announced it to you,
c lest you say, "My image made them,
d and my idol commanded them."

Section III

6a You heard; see it all!
b And you, won't you declare?
c I announced to you new things only now,
d and secret things, and you did not know them.

7a	ʿth nbrʾw wlʾ mʾz	2 + 3 + 2 + 2	9	4
b	wlpny-ywm wlʾ šmʿtm	3 + 1 + 2 + 3	9	4
c	pn-tʾmr hnh ydʿtyn	1 + 2 + 2 + 3	8	3
8a	gm lʾ-šmʿt gm lʾ ydʿt	1 + 1 + 1 + 2 / 3 + 2 / 3 + 1	8/10	4
b	gm mʾz lʾ-ptḥh ʾznk	1 + 2 + 1 + 3 + 2 / 3	9/10	3/4
c	ky ydʿty bgwd tbgwd	1 + 3 + 2 + 2	8	3
d	wpšʿ mbṭn qrʾ lk	3 + 2 + 2 + 1	8	3
	11 lines		91–96	36–37

Section IV

9a	lmʿn šmy ʾʾryk ʾpy	2 + 2 + 2 + 2	8	4
b	wthlty ʾḥṭm-lk	5 + 2 + 1	8	2
c	lblty hkrytk	3 + 3 / 4	6/7	2
10a	hnh ṣrptyk wlʾ bksp	2 + 3 / 4 + 2 + 2	9/10	4
b	bḥ[n]tyk bkwr ʿny	3 / 4 + 2 + 2	7/8	3
a	lmʿny lmʿny ʾʿśh	3 + 3 + 2	8	3
b	ky ʾyk yḥl	1 + 1 + 2	4	2
c	wkbwdy lʾḥr lʾ-ʾtn	4 + 3 + 1 + 2	10	3
	8 lines		60–63	23

Section V

12a	šmʿ ʾly yʿqb	2 + 2 + 2	6	3
b	wyśrʾl mqrʾy	4 + 4	8	2
c	ʾny-hwʾ ʾny rʾšwn	2 + 1 + 2 + 2	7	4
d	ʾp ʾny ʾḥrwn	1 + 2 + 2	5	2
13a	ʾp-ydy ysdh ʾrṣ	1 + 2 + 3 + 1	7	3
b	wymyny ṭpḥh šmym	3 + 3 + 2	8	3
c	qrʾ ʾny ʾlyhm	2 + 2 + 3	7	3
d	yʿmdw yḥdw	3 + 2	5	2
	8 lines		53	22

Section VI

14a	hqbṣw klkm wšmʿw	4 + 3 + 4	11	3
b	my bhm hgyd ʾt-ʾlh	1 + 2 + 2 + 1 + 2	8	3/4
c	yhwh ʾhbw yʿśh ḥpṣw	2 + 3 + 2 + 2	9	4
d	bbbl wzrʿw kśdym	3 + 4 + 2	9	3
15a	ʾny ʾny dbrty	2 + 2 + 3	7	3
b	ʾp-qrʾtyw	1 + 3	4	2
c	hbyʾtyw whṣlyḥ drkw	4 + 3 + 2	9	3
16a	qrbw ʾly šmʿw-zʾt	2 + 2 + 2 + 1	7	4
b	lʾ mrʾš bstr dbrty	1 + 2 + 2 + 3	8	3

7a Now they are created and not in time past;
b not before today, and you did not hear them,
c lest you say, "Behold, I knew them."
8a No, you did not hear; no, you did not know;
b no, in time past your ear did not open.
c Yes, I knew you acted very treacherously,
d and a rebel from birth you were called.

Section IV

9a For the sake of my name I am slow to anger,
b and for the sake of my praise I will restrain for you
c in order not to cut you off.
10a Behold, I refined you, but not like silver;
b I tested you in a furnace of affliction.
11a For my sake, for my sake I act
b (for how will it be profaned . . . !),
c and my glory to another I will not give.

Section V

12a Listen to me, Jacob,
b and Israel, whom I named:
c I am he, I am first.
d Indeed, I am last.
13a Indeed, my hand founded earth,
b and my right hand produced the heavens.
c When I call to them
d they stand together.

Section VI

14a Gather, all of you, and hear!
b Who among them declared these?
c "Yahweh-loves-him," will accomplish his purpose;
d against Babylon and Chaldea is his arm.
15a I, I spoke;
b indeed, I called him.
c I brought him and his way prospered greatly.
16a Draw near to me, hear this:
b not from the very first did I speak in secret;

c	mᶜt hywth šm ᵓny	2 + 3 + 1 + 2	8	3/4
d	wᶜth ᵓdny yhwh	3 + 3 + 2	8	3
e	šlḥny wrwḥw	4 + 3	7	2
	12 lines		95	36–38
Section VII				
17a	kh-ᵓmr yhwh gᵓlk	1 + 2 + 2 + 3 / 4	8/9	3
b	qdwš yśrᵓl	2 + 3	5	2
c	ᵓny yhwh ᵓlhyk	2 + 2 + 3 / 4	7/8	3
d	mlmdk lhwᶜyl	4 + 3	7	2
e	mdrykk bdrk tlk	3 / 4 + 2 + 2	7/8	3
18a	lwᵓ hqšbt lmṣwty	1 + 2 / 3 + 4	7/8	2/3
b	wyhy knhr šlwmk	3 + 3 + 3 / 4	9/10	3
c	wṣdqtk kgly hym	4 / 5 + 3 + 2	9/10	3
19a	wyhy kḥwl zrᶜk	3 + 2 + 2 / 3	7/8	3
b	wṣᵓṣᵓy mᶜyk kmᶜtyw	4 + 2 / 3 + 3	9/10	3
c	lᵓ-ykrt wlᵓ-yšmd	1 + 3 + 2 + 3	9	3
d	šmw mlpny	2 + 4	6	2
	12 lines		90–98	32–33
Section VIII				
20a	ṣᵓw mbbl	2 + 3	5	2
b	brḥw mkśdym	2 + 3	5	2
c	bqwl rnh hgydw	2 + 2 + 3	7	3
d	hšmyᶜw zᵓt	3 + 1	4	2
e	hwṣyᵓwh ᶜd-qṣh hᵓrṣ	3 / 4 + 1 + 2 + 2	8/9	3
f	ᵓmrw gᵓl yhwh	2 + 2 + 2	6	3
g	ᶜbdw yᶜqb	2 + 2	4	2
21a	wlᵓ ṣmᵓw	2 + 3	5	2
b	bḥrbwt hwlykm	3 + 3	6	2
c	mym mṣwr hzyl lmw	1 + 2 + 2 + 2	7	4
d	wybqᶜ-ṣwr	3 + 1	4	2
e	wyzbw mym	4 + 1	5	2
22*	ᵓyn šlwm ᵓmr yhwh lršᶜym	1 + 2 + 2 + 2 + 3	10	4
	12 lines		66–67	29
Totals	82 lines		608–29 syllables	236–40 stresses

* Verse 22, as an editorial insertion, is not part of the poem proper, and therefore not part of the total count.

c from the time it happened, there I was.
d And now Lord Yahweh
e sent me and his spirit.

Section VII

17a Thus says Yahweh, your redeemer,
b the holy one of Israel.
c I, Yahweh, am your god,
d who teaches you for your profit,
e who leads you in the way you should walk.
18a If only you had hearkened to my commands,
b then like a river would have been your peace,
c and your justice like the waves of the sea.
19a Then like the sand would have been your seed
b and the issue of your loins like its grains.
c His name will not be cut off and not be destroyed
d from before me.

Section VIII

20a Go forth from Babylon!
b Flee from Chaldea!
c In a ringing voice declare—
d announce this—
e send it forth to the end of the earth—
f say: "Yahweh redeems
g his servant Jacob."
21a And they did not thirst
b when in the waste places he led them;
c waters from the rock he made flow for them,
d and he cleft the rock,
e and waters gushed.
22 There is no peace, says Yahweh, for the wicked.

Summary is on p. 170.

	lines	*syllables*	*stresses*		*lines*	*syllables*	*stresses*
Section I	9	77	29	Section V	8	53	22
Section II	10	76–80	29	Section VI	12	95	36–38
Section III	11	91–96	36–37	Section VII	12	90–98	32–33
Section IV	8	60–63	23	Section VIII	12	66–67	29
Totals	38	304–16	117–18		44	304–13	119–22

Average syllables and stresses per line:
7.4–7.67 syllables/line;
2.87–2.9 stresses/line.

Notes on Translation and Text

48:1b. *hnqrʾym bšm yśrʾl*
"the ones who call themselves by the name Israel"

In the beginning of the poem (vv. 1–2) there are six verb forms, four of them in the *Niphal*. The *Niphal* participle of *qrʾ* can have reflexive or passive force, and translations reflect both of these possibilities.[1] All of the verbs are active rather than passive (in line 2a *nqrʾw* again can be read reflexively or passively). The emphasis is on what Israel does to its discredit rather than what has been done to Israel, so I translate with the reflexive rather than passive. See also Isa 44:5, which describes a situation in which people call themselves and name themselves Jacob/Israel, though in 44:5 it is to their credit.

48:1c. *wmmy yhwdh* "and from Judah"

Scholars are divided on whether or not to emend this text to read *mmʿy* ('from the loins'). Those who emend refer to v. 19, *wṣʾṣʾy mʿyk* 'and the issue of your loins', and Gen 15:4, which has the expression *yṣʾ mmʿyk*. Some find the MT "meaningless" (Whybray), or the comparison with similar passages in the Bible "remote" (North). Skinner finds the passage inexplicable, though he cites Ps 68:26, which has a metaphor comparing the ancestor of the nation to a fountain. While he seems to prefer the emendation *mmʿy*, he finds this difficult also, in that Judah is nowhere named the ancestor of the people. The LXX reads simply "from Judah," which is the translation I have adopted.

1. E.g., RSV, "who are called by the name of Israel," and Clifford, "who call yourselves Israel."

Those who prefer the MT cite (in addition to Ps 68:26) Deut 33:28, where "the fountain (*ᶜyn)* of Jacob" is a synonym for "Israel."[2] Prov 5:15, 9:17, and Num 24:7 are examples of expressions in which waters or fountains are used as metaphors for family or fruit of the loins. Muilenburg seems to allow for either possibility, quoting the RSV emendation, but also citing the Hebrew text. Bonnard's translation reflects a similar approach to the text: he translates "des sources de Juda," which reflects a metaphoric reading of both 'waters' and 'loins'.[3]

Another possibility is that *mmy* is simply the compound form of the preposition *mn.* This is the form normally used with pronominal suffixes (e.g., *mmnw*), derived from *mnmn.*[4] A similar usage is found in Isa 39:7, where *yṣᵓ* occurs with *mn* plus a suffix. (1QIsa[a] has *mmᶜykh* in 39:7, just as it does in 48:1.) An expanded form of the preposition *mn* also occurs in Isa 46:3, and this may be another alternative in 48:1.

The flexible translations of Bonnard and the LXX correctly reflect the ambivalence of the expression in the MT. The motifs of waters and descendants are an important part of this poem. The potency or fruitfulness of waters appears in vv. 18 and 21. The metaphor of surging waters of the sea in v. 18 is parallel with the figure of the seed/descendants that are as numerous as the grains of sand. The poet seems to be playing on the similarities between *mmy* and *mmᶜy* to call up both ideas. That this play on words was somewhat effective is evident in ancient and modern translations and commentaries, most of which entertain all possibilities and decide hesitatingly on one or the other.

yhwdh **"Judah"**

The word is used infrequently in DI, here, and in 40:9 and 44:26, where it refers to "cities of Judah."[5] Scholars interpret this word partitively or as an all-inclusive term. For example, Torrey reads it in support of his thesis of the lateness of composition of DI, seeing it as written at a "time when the term *yhwdym,* 'Jews', was used (and had for some considerable time been used) to include all the children of Israel." Bonnard reads Judah as a prestigious title and also as a name that designated all of the Palestinian population according to the Persian name for their province, which would place the time of composition sometime after Cyrus's takeover of

2. F. M. Cross and D. N. Freedman, "A Note on Deuteronomy 33:26," *BASOR* 108 (1947) 6–7. The root here is *ᶜwn,* with the sense of settling, or the like, not *ᶜyn.*

3. Bonnard also refers to Gen 19:37 and the name Moab, which he understands to mean 'water of the father'. He interprets this as an instance in which "waters" designates sperm. This does not appear to be the interpretation in the MT or the LXX, which reads the name Moab to mean 'from the father'.

4. GKC §103m / p. 303.

5. See also 65:9, "descendants from Jacob and heirs from Judah."

Babylon. In the opposite direction, Kissane believes that the exiles in Babylon were mostly members of the tribe of Judah; this is his explanation for the use of the name Judah here. Whybray interprets the mention of the three names, Jacob, Israel, and Judah, as a wish on the part of the prophet to make clear that the whole nation, not only the Judeans, are involved in his message. Coggins says that the term *Israel* in DI frequently denotes the community exiled from Judah to Babylon. He interprets the expression "who came forth from the loins of Judah" to be evidence in support of his thesis that there is apparently no reference at all to northern Israelites throughout chaps. 40–55. He believes that DI envisioned restoration only for the community exiled in Babylon and that the status of northerners and those remaining in Judah was lowered.[6]

According to Clifford, one of DI's main intentions was to make the people realize the importance of returning to their own land, the only place where they can legitimately worship Yahweh. Since DI used the name *Judah* elsewhere in reference to the uninhabited cities, both times in combination with Jerusalem, it may be that in 48:1 the word *Judah* is also used to draw attention to that place (line 2a also functions to highlight "the holy city," Jerusalem).

48:1d, e, 2b. *nšbᶜym . . . yzkyrw . . . nsmkw* "swear by . . . invoke . . . lean on"

These verbs are drawn from the language of the cult. Muilenburg cites other passages as examples: Exod 23:13; Deut 6:13, 10:20; Ps 20:7; and Jer 12:16. Whybray sees the three verbs as references to "liturgical professions of faith." In 1 Sam 20:42, the swearing of an oath between people is a sign of allegiance. Amos 8:14 reads, "they swear by the Ashmat of Samaria" (*hnšbᶜym bᵓšmt šmrwn*), where the people are invoking a deity (probably Asherah, under another title, or a derogatory play on the name). They are binding themselves by oaths in business and/or cultic transactions.[7] In DI the people make false oaths in the name of Yahweh, a violation of the third commandment.

For the expression *invoke the name*, Beuken cites Exod 23:13, Josh 23:17, Isa 26:13, Amos 6:10, and Ps 20:8. Westermann points out that the only aspect of worship mentioned by the prophet is its "spoken element." He describes swearing by the name of Yahweh as a "confirmation of something by appeal to God as judge," invoking Yahweh as remembering his acts in praise, and leaning upon Yahweh (v. 2a) as a way of "describing the

6. R. J. Coggins, *Samaritans and Jews* (Atlanta: Knox, 1975) 36–37.

7. Suggestion of D. N. Freedman.

'confession of trust,' the central part of supplication." Sacrificial worship is not a concern here.

Form critics discuss at length whether or not DI's message is taken from the cult or is an imitation of cultic language and make decisions that go far beyond the available evidence.[8] For instance, North reads chap. 48 as supportive of the suggestion that DI spoke at some assembly for worship. Bonnard does not attempt to make a decision about this but, more conservatively, suggests that while it is possible, but not necessary, that DI may have addressed a group brought together for worship, at least the passage makes allusions to activities of the cult.

The transition from participle to finite verb is not unusual in DI; it twice happens in these verses (*hnqrʾym* to *yṣʾw*, *hnšbʿym* to *yzkyrw*). See also 40:26 (*hmwṣyʾ* to *yqrʾ*).

48:1f. *lʾ bʾmt wlʾ bṣdqh* "not in true righteousness"

This phrase is an example of a hendiadys, "a single concept expressed by two words linked by the conjunction *w-*."[9] See also Gen 1:14, where the phrase "for signs and for seasons" means "as signs to mark seasons" and prepositions function as part of the connection. There are other occurrences of this combination *bʾmt* and *bṣdqh*: 1 Kgs 3:6, "he walked in true righteousness . . ."; Jer 4:2, "and you swore (*nšbʿt*) . . . in faith . . . and in righteousness"; and Zech 8:8, "I will be their god in true righteousness." See also Ps 85:12, where *ʾmt* and *ṣdq* are a word-pair: "truth from the land will spring up, and righteousness from the heavens." A related example commonly translated as a hendiadys is the expression *ḥsd wʾmt*, translated as 'loving kindness'.

Line 1f is the first of several in the chapter that are considered by scholars to be nongenuine additions or interpolations. The main problem some scholars have with this line, and others like it, is the harshness of tone, or the negative nature of the ideas expressed. Westermann finds this negative tone to be "completely out of harmony" with the purpose of the rest of the material.[10] Other verses eliminated by Westermann because of harshness of tone are 4, 5cd, 7c, 8c–10, and perhaps 11b.

8. For the classical discussion of the relationship between prophet and cult, see S. Mowinckel, "Cult and Prophecy (1922)," in *Prophecy in Israel: Search for an Identity* (ed. with introduction by D. L. Petersen; IRT 10; Philadelphia: Fortress, 1987) 74–98.

9. Ronald J. Williams, *Hebrew Syntax: An Outline* (2d ed.; Toronto: University of Toronto Press, 1976) §72/p. 16.

10. See Westermann's commentary, as well as his "Jesaja 48 und die 'Bezeugung gegen Israel,'" in *Studia Biblica et Semitica: Theodoro Christiano Vriezen Dedicata* (ed. W. C. van Unnik and A. S. van der Woude; Wageningen: H. Veenman en Zonen, 1966) 356–66 for a fuller treatment of the chapter.

Duhm is also concerned about the harsh tone. To eliminate it, he does not excise the line but reads line 1f as a question with an affirmative sense and relates it to the beginning of v. 2: "Is it not in truth and righteousness that they name themselves after the holy city?"

Torrey does not find the harsh tone disruptive. In fact, he considers rebuke to be the most prominent feature of the poem. He sees no need to dissect the book. However, his arrangement differs from mine in that he divides between 1a and 1e and between 1f and 2a, agreeing with Cheyne on this point. According to Torrey, line 1f is not the ending, but the beginning of a new stanza, and he translates, "It is not in truth, not by right, that (*ky*) they name themselves." Kissane makes the same division, noting that the conjunction *ky* at the beginning of v. 2 favors such a view. In his opinion, line 1f qualifies lines 2a–c, because the accusation against the people has to do with their rejection of Yahweh. He observes that 2a could not qualify 1a–c: the people could not be accused of falsely claiming to descend from Judah, since in truth they did. He also sees no relationship between 2a and 1de, since that would be "equivalent to an accusation of false swearing."

Kissane is correct in reading 2a as a continuation of 1f. However, it does not necessarily follow that 1f is not connected to the preceding lines. Kissane does not think that Israel can be accused of both false swearing or insincerity and rejection of Yahweh. Line 1f should be read as qualifying both what precedes and what follows it. Judgments are made against Israel based on her insincere worship (she does not swear by the name of Yahweh and invoke him in true righteousness), and she does not sincerely depend upon Yahweh and identify herself with Jerusalem ("not in true righteousness do they call themselves after the holy city, [nor do they] lean upon their god"). Line 1f can be read as a double-duty phrase, modifying both 1d and e and 2a and b. Muilenburg comes closest to this in an alternative rendering: "It was not by truth nor by right, even though they call themselves after the holy city."

John Miller[11] discusses 48:1–2 as an example of conflict between the prophet and his audience.[12] Such conflict is not unheard of; earlier prophets published accounts of their calls when there was tension between them and their audiences. For Miller, this harshness against his audience is transformed in chaps. 49–55 into conflict between the prophet and his audience, on the one hand, and the oppressor, that is, the Babylonian authorities, on

11. John Miller, "Prophetic Conflict in Second Isaiah: The Servant Songs in the Light of Their Context," in *Wort, Gebet, Glaube, Walter Eichrodt zum 80. Geburtstag* (ed. J. J. Stamm; Abhandlungen zur Theologie des Alten und Neuen Testaments 59; Zürich: Theologischer Verlag, 1970) 78–79.

12. Other examples in Isaiah 40–48 include 40:27; 42:18ff.; 45:9ff.; and 46:8, 12.

the other hand. With Torrey, Miller does not find the harsh tone disruptive, but sees it as fitting to the role of prophet.

Lack[13] looks at the whole of 48:1–49:13 in a discussion of the conflict of the prophet with his audience. The reason for the harsh tone is the fact that the prophet sees the audience as the only remaining obstacle to the new exodus. In 44:24–46:13, one obstacle to Israel's return, the idols, was eliminated. In chap. 47, another obstacle, Babylon's political power, was broken. In chap. 48, Israel alone blocks the new exodus and thus is the subject of the prophet's harsh tone.

Not only are there many examples within Isaiah 40–55 of this negative attitude toward the people (the harsh criticism of the people was demonstrated in chap. 46 above), but also in the books of Jeremiah and Ezekiel. Such evidence militates against attributing these harsh words to another source simply because they are harsh. One can well imagine the prophet addressing a community about whom he had mixed feelings. They themselves were a complicated community, characterized by internal conflict. It cannot be doubted that the people living in exile in Babylon had faults and weaknesses for which they could rightly be called to task. Succumbing to the worship of Babylonian deities was one of their major failings. To imagine DI as a happy, happy man who could see or speak of no wrong is to portray him as a one-dimensional figure with little depth.

The passage is confusing because of the poet's employment of irony, which is sometimes difficult to detect. The poem begins with what appears to be a positive assessment of Israel's status. But the context makes it clear that Israel's attitude toward God is not worthy of praise; it is just the opposite. Gitay explains the switch in meaning caused by the presence of line 1f and other verses characterized as "harsh." He says that the seemingly positive tone in the beginning was set to "avoid a head-on collision with his audience," and also to attract the audience's attention.[14] The switch in tone served to strengthen the impact of the irony.

48:2a. *mᶜyr hqdš* "from the holy city"

Most translations render *mn* 'after', but this is not a common rendering of the preposition. Bonnard reads the phrase as though it were a name or title—"*ils s'appellent pourtant: 'De la Ville Sainte!'*" This is consistent with the various names and namings in this section of the poem, and it also is parallel with 1b, where the same verb, *qrʾ*, in the *Niphal* is used in reference

13. R. Lack, *La Symbolique du livre d'Isaïe: Essai sur l'image littéraire comme élément de structuration* (AnBib 59; Rome: Pontifical Biblical Institute Press, 1973) 106.

14. Y. Gitay, *Prophecy and Persuasion: A Study of Isaiah 40–48* (FTL 14; Bonn: Linguistica Biblica, 1981) 221.

to the name of Yahweh. *Ky* is translated 'but' or 'nevertheless', an adversative, following *lʾ* of line 1f.[15] The idea is that the people take pride in identifying themselves with Yahweh's city,[16] even though they don't deserve to make this claim, since they do not adhere in true righteousness to Yahweh.

The title *ʿyr hqdš* also appears in 52:1 and in late literature: Dan 9:24 and Neh 11:1, 18. Whybray suggests that the phrase, which occurs frequently in later literature, would have "come more naturally to Jews after the exile" and the restoration and repopulation of Jerusalem. Wade observes that this would be a more appropriate description of the actual residents of Jerusalem than of the Jewish exiles in a foreign land. Kissane sees the title "the holy city" as an allusion to 1:21ff., where the once faithful Zion became faithless. Clifford's interpretation is that the phrase "seems to be a condensed way of saying that the people are to be known by the city of their origin." It is his contention that the prophet's goal was to make the people realize the importance of their return to Jerusalem. The possibility of their return with the advent of Cyrus meant that in the future, worship of Yahweh that was done anywhere else but Jerusalem would be invalid.

The city, and identification with it, is certainly important here in chap. 48 and in the rest of DI. The prophet's message begins with the idea that Jerusalem is to be comforted (40:2), and throughout the chapters the city Jerusalem is assured that she will be inhabited and rebuilt (44:26), her suffering will be alleviated (51:17ff.),[17] she will no longer be a captive city (52:1–2), and her waste places will see the return of Yahweh (52:9). This makes it all the more possible that at least some of those addressed by the prophet in chap. 48 are Jerusalemites. It is difficult to say whether the prophet is addressing them in Jerusalem or in Babylon.

48:2b. *nsmkw* "they lean"

This is not the usual verb used to express trust in God. Elsewhere it is used to describe misplaced trust, as in Isa 36:6 (2 Kgs 18:21), where the foolhardiness of Israel's dependence on Egypt is meant. In Psalm 71, which

15. See Williams, *Hebrew Syntax*, on this usage (§447 / p. 72).

16. Are they claiming to be citizens of Jerusalem, claiming rights to that citizenship? D. N. Freedman (private communication) suggests the possibility that there is a distinction between these people, described in third-person clauses, and those addressed in 1a in the imperative. The puzzling presence of alternation between second- and third-person address throughout the poem may perhaps be explained by the existence of two separate groups. Some suggestions concerning their identities are that one is the group who went into exile in 597, and the other is the group who went into exile in 587, who were discredited by Ezekiel. The criticisms of DI could also be levelled at a group still in the land, making claims against those of the exile.

17. This passage is reminiscent of the descriptions in Lamentations of the people who remained in and around Jerusalem after the exile.

has several similarities to the chapters under discussion, the psalmist describes his dependence on Yahweh from the time he was taken from his mother's womb and asks that Yahweh will continue to support him in his days of old age and grey hair (vv. 6, 18).[18] Given the ironic nature of the passage, it is difficult to say whether Israel is being criticized for having false confidence in Yahweh or merely for claiming to rely on Yahweh, while in reality pursuing other gods (lines 5cd).[19]

48:3a. *hrʾšnwt mʾz* "the first things from time past"

The "first things" (or "former things," as in the RSV) are mentioned in 46:9.[20] There the expression appeared without the article and with the prepositional phrase *mʿwlm.* Here it has the article and is modified by the prepositional phrase *mʾz* 'from time past'.

The expression *mʾz* in DI is an indicator of a "remoter past."[21] But E. Vogt cautions against reading *mʾz* (and other similar terms in DI, such as *mqdm, mʿlm, mʿth, mrʾš, mrʾšt, mlpnym*) as references to earliest or ancient days. He cites 2 Sam 15:34, where *mʾz* is used for close proximity in time.[22] C. R. North cites this and other texts where the expression may refer to relatively recent events.[23] My translation reflects this uncertainty of reference, rendering 'in time past' instead of RSV 'of old' or 'long ago', as in the JB, JPSV, and the NEB.

18. It also is used of Samson's actions in Judg 16:29, where he leans against the pillars of the house in which the Philistines had gathered to offer sacrifice to Dagon. There are other similarities between the chapters in DI and the story of Samson, e.g., the humiliating act of being forced to grind grain is the plight of both Samson in Judg 16:21 and virgin daughter Babylon in Isa 47:2.

19. K. Elliger, who is interested in showing the Trito-Isaianic authorship of this as well as of other passages in DI, discusses the usage of the verb *smk* in Isaiah. He says that the only other place in Isaiah 40–66 that the word occurs is in TI, in 59:16 and 63:5. This is another reason that the passage should be attributed to TI instead of DI. However, he does not point out that the usage is quite different in chaps. 59 and 63. There they appear in the *Qal* and are words attributed to Yahweh, who has no one to "uphold" and whose own wrath and righteousness uphold him. The only other occurrence of *smk* (*Qal*) is in Isa 26:3, where it describes the faithful one who relies on Yahweh. Elliger appears to be grasping at straws here in his attempt to show Trito-Isaianic authorship of the passage based on the appearance of the root of *smk* (*Deuterojesaja in seinem Verhältnis zu Tritojesaja* [BWANT 4/11; Stuttgart: Kohlhammer, 1933] 191).

20. See above, pp. 56–57, for a brief discussion of this theme.

21. BDB 23.

22. E. Vogt, "Eine hebräische Wortbedeutungen, I: 'Voraussagen' in Is 40–48," *Bib* 48 (1967) 57–63.

23. In addition to C. R. North's commentary, see "The 'Former Things' and the 'New Things' in Deutero-Isaiah," *Studies in Old Testament Prophecy* (ed. H. H. Rowley; Edinburgh: T. & T. Clark, 1950) 111–26.

In addition to the occurrences in this chapter (vv. 3a, 5a, 7a, 8b), *mʾz* also occurs in 44:8 and 45:21, both times in connection with the verb *ngd*, as here in lines 3a and 5a. The emphasis is on Yahweh's ability to announce things before they happen (in 42:9 Yahweh demonstrates his divine ability to make things come to pass by declaration). In 41:22ff. a challenge is made to the nations that their gods declare the first things or the things to come as proof of their divinity. A similar challenge to the nations occurs in 43:9.

An exact identification of the things that were foretold is not possible here. A sampling from commentators gives an indication of the wide variety of speculation on what the "first things" are in this chapter. Kissane says the phrase refers to the "chastisement of Israel for its apostasy." Pieper says it "never refers to things that have been announced beforehand," rather it means things that were done earlier. Delitzsch says just the opposite, that the reference is to earlier occurrences foretold by Yahweh. Skinner identifies the former things with "the events that have now taken place, especially the appearance of Cyrus." Beauchamp[24] sees the "former things" as prophecies fulfilled in the destruction of Jerusalem.[25] Knight translates *rʾšnwt* 'my primal actions' and interprets them as the redemption from Egypt, which was suddenly proclaimed and suddenly came to pass. Slotki considers the reference to be to all that God had foretold and fulfilled. Whybray also sees it as a reference to Yahweh's past deeds in general, not the previous career of Cyrus. Haran considers *rʾšnwt* to be "former prophecies" as opposed to "new prophecies" (*ḥdšwt*).[26] The emphasis here, as in 41:22, is not so much on the exact identification of the thing or things that Yahweh declared, as it is on the fact that Yahweh did declare things before they happened (the verb *ngd* occurs three times in vv. 3a, 5a, and 6b; the *Hiphil* of *šmᶜ* twice in vv. 3b and 5b). Isa 46:9ff. also emphasizes the relationship between Yahweh's ability to announce things before they happened and his claims to divinity.

48:3b. *wmpy yṣʾw* "and from my mouth they went forth"

The image of the word of Yahweh issuing forth from his mouth occurs in several significant locations in DI: 40:5, 45:23, 55:11, as well as in

24. Beauchamp, *Le Deutero-Isaïe*, 1970, p. 33, cited by P.-E. Bonnard in *Le Second Isaïe, son disciple et leut éditeurs, Isäie 40–66* (Paris: Gabalda, 1972) 203.

25. See above, p. 136, and below, p. 180, on 48:3c and the connotations of the adverb *ptʾm*, which may support Beauchamp's interpretation.

26. M. Haran, *Between Riʾshonot (Former Prophecies) and Ḥadashot (New Prophecies): A Literary Historical Study in the Group of Prophecies Isaiah XL–XLVIII* (Jerusalem: n.p., 1963) Heb.; idem, "The Literary Structure and Chronological Framework of the Prophecies in Is. xl–xlviii," *Congress Volume: Bonn, 1962* (VTSup 9; Leiden: Brill, 1963) 127–53.

48:3.[27] Yahweh's word is also put into the mouth of Israel his servant (see 49:2) in 51:16. Freedman sees the word of Yahweh as the dominant theme of 40:1–11 and considers v. 5, which ends with "the mouth of the Lord has spoken," the finale or summation of that poem.[28] A challenge is directed to the nations in 45:20ff. to present their case (as in 41:21 and 43:8ff.) and explain who had made declarations of old. Of course the answer is Yahweh, and in 45:23 Yahweh declares *yṣʾ mpy ṣdqh dbr wlʾ yšwb*, "a righteous word went forth from my mouth and it will not return."[29] In the final chapter of DI (55:10–11), the same motif is present. Yahweh's word that goes forth from his mouth (*yṣʾ mpy*) is compared to the life-giving snow and rain that water the earth. It will not return (*lʾ yšwb*) empty but will accomplish (*ʿśh*) Yahweh's purpose, and prosper. The expression in 48:3 adds to the notion of the potency of Yahweh's declarations, especially when read in light of the entire section, chaps. 40–55.

In view of the above examples from DI regarding the typical expression *from my mouth it comes forth*, it is important to take into consideration the subject of the m. pl. verb *yṣʾ* in 48:3. One possibility is that the subject is the f. pl. 'first things' (notice that 1QIsa[a] reads f. s. *yṣʾh*), though in line 3c the verb referring to "the first things" is 3 f. pl. Another possibility is that the clause is an ellipsis implying *dbrym* as the subject of *yṣʾw mpy*. The 3 m. pl. suffix of the verb would refer to the words that went forth. The idea is that Yahweh's words came forth from his mouth, and the first things came forth.

The root *yṣʾ* appears several times in chap. 48, each time with a slightly different sense, but each time indicating fruitfulness or potency. Already mentioned was 1c, the ones coming forth from Judah. In addition, v. 19 speaks of the offspring (*ṣʾṣʾy*) of the loins, v. 20 urges Israel to go forth from Babylon, and 20c urges them to send forth (*Hiphil*) to all the earth the message that Yahweh saves his people.

***wʾšmyʿm* "and I announced them"**

The MT reads, "and I [will] announce them," but the LXX uses the past tense, reading as a *waw*-consecutive. Many ancient versions (targums, Syriac, and Vulgate) follow suit. Virtually no modern translator renders

27. C. Stuhlmueller devotes an entire chapter to "The Creative Word of Yahweh" and refers to it as "one of the most salient aspects of Dt-Is's theology" (*Creative Redemption in Deutero-Isaiah* [AnBib 43; Rome: Pontifical Biblical Institute, 1970] 169–92). Von Rad sees it as the axis on which all his preaching turned (p. 256).

28. D. N. Freedman, "The Structure of Isaiah 40:1–11," in *Perspectives on Language and Text: Essays and Poems in Honor of Francis I. Andersen's Sixtieth Birthday, July 28, 1985* (ed. E. W. Conrad and E. G. Newing; Winona Lake, Ind.: Eisenbrauns, 1987) 174.

29. The subject of both masculine verbs is 'word'; *ṣdqh* and *dbr* can be read as a hendiadys, though Freedman calls it a reverse construct chain, "a word of righteousness."

this verb according to the MT. Usually translators place the accent on what Yahweh has done (expressed by the perfect verbs in 3a, 3b, and 3c, as well as the *waw*-consecutive in 3c). However, the MT reading could be retained if the simple *waw* was read as an expression of purpose, translating 'so that I could announce them'.[30]

Another ambiguity results from the 3 m. pl. suffix. With the *Hiphil* form of the verb, there should be two objects, the person or persons who are made to hear and the thing announced. (See v. 20 for another example of the *Hiphil* of *šmᶜ* with one object stated and another understood. The object stated is *zʾt*, and object understood is the people who were made to hear.)

48:3c. *ptʾm* "suddenly"

This adverb accusative is used most often in association with the coming of a calamity.[31] In Isa 47:11 it refers to the suddenness of the disaster that will fall upon Babylon. Elsewhere it is used of disasters that come upon people as the result of war.[32] In Num 12:4 it describes Yahweh's sudden appearance during the dispute between Moses and Miriam and Aaron, when Yahweh castigated Miriam and Aaron for their challenge to Moses' authority (see also the figure in Isa 30:13). Almost invariably *ptʾm* is used in a context of a catastrophic and surprising occurrence.[33]

Used here to describe the "first things," as announced by Yahweh, and their subsequent occurrence, it seems that *ptʾm* leads to an interpretation of the *first things* as also unpleasant, even disastrous, occurrences. The reference could be to disasters that came upon Jacob/Israel or upon their enemies (as in Isa 47:11 and Jer 51:8, where the disaster came upon Babylon). In either case, there is a negative sound to the verse; the tone is harsh. Verse 3 has not been excised by form critics because of harshness. It is considered authentic, "an echo of earlier passages concerning the former things" (Whybray). Either the negative tone has been missed or the passage should be added to the already-long list of passages in chap. 48 identified by form critics as inauthentic. Or, as is more likely, the verse along with the other harsh-sounding sections should be considered an integral part of the poem.

30. Williams, *Hebrew Syntax*, §181/p. 33.

31. BDB 837.

32. Isa 29:5; Jer 6:26, 15:8, 18:22, 51:8; Ps 64:5; and Josh 10:9, 11:7.

33. For a discussion of the surprising or unexpected connotation of the word, see Stuhlmueller, *Creative Redemption*, 140. He does not make note of the aspect of calamity.

ʿśyty "I acted"

The three first-person singular verbs (*ngd*, *šmʿ*, and *ʿśh*) used in lines a, b, and c all refer to activities of Yahweh. The main issue is the power of Yahweh's word; what is demonstrated is that when Yahweh speaks, there is a result (just as in Genesis 1). When Yahweh says, "I acted," what is meant is that Yahweh *spoke*.[34] The parallel between *ʿśh* and *ṣwh* in lines 5cd, which are contrasted with *ngd* and *šmʿ* in lines 5ab, confirms this meaning. The idols don't make things happen by their actions, that is, their commands, in contrast to Yahweh who declares and announces.

48:4a. *mdʿty* "because I know"

Mn is used here with the infinitive construct of *ydʿ* in a causal sense.[35] 1QIsa[a] reads *mʾšr ydʿty*, similar to Isa 43:4, *mʾšr yqrt*.[36] Deut 9:24 shows a similar use of the inf. construct of *ydʿ* with a preposition, where Moses complains that the people have been rebellious against the Lord "from the day I knew you." Duhm also refers to Deut 7:7–8 for similar constructions.

Most translations render *dʿty* 'I knew' (JB, Kissane, Delitzsch, and Torrey), but the RSV and Muilenburg translate 'I know'. Both translations are acceptable. Yahweh knew from the beginning that Israel was stubborn and, of course, still knows this.

Some read v. 4 as a clause that modifies the preceding verse, or parts of it. Kissane, for example, says that v. 4 explains 3c and gives the reason for the disaster but not for the prediction of the disaster. The JB, RSV, JPSV, and NEB read v. 4 as an explanation of the predictions that follow in v. 5: "I knew you to be obstinate . . . and so I revealed things beforehand. . . ." Others (e.g., Duhm and Westermann) consider the verse to be an addition

34. Stuhlmueller, in his study of creation vocabulary, states that DI "uses *ʿśh* and *yṣr* more often than any other word in conjunction with *brʾ*" and also notes that *ʿśh* is used by J and P and other texts in connection with creation (ibid., 716–18).

35. See Williams, *Hebrew Syntax* (§319/pp. 55–56), for this use of *mn* and the use of a preposition with a construct infinitive for a causal clause for (§535 / pp. 89–90).

36. This is a good example of a revision in the direction of prose in 1QIsa[a]. In view of the relatively late time of composition, chaps. 40–55 are remarkably free of prose particles, as F. I. Andersen and A. Dean Forbes demonstrate, in "'Prose Particle' Counts of the Hebrew Bible," in *The Word of the Lord Shall Go Forth: Essays in Honor of David Noel Freedman in Celebration of His Sixtieth Birthday* (ed. Carol L. Meyers and M. O'Connor; Winona Lake, Ind.: Eisenbrauns, 1983). This is another similarity that is shared with Lamentations, dating from the same general period.

The 1QIsa[a] manuscript has been corrected, apparently by a later hand. Three letters, *šin*, *reš*, and *yod*, have been erased by the placement of dots above and below them. The corrector seems to have forgotten to erase the *ʾalep*. See E. Y. Kutscher, *The Language and Linguistic Background of the Isaiah Scroll (1QIsa[a])* (Leiden: Brill, 1974) 535.

by a later hand. Grammatically, the verse can modify either v. 3 or v. 5. Notice the repetition and chiasm in 3a and 5a:

mʾz hgdty	a	b
wʾgyd lk mʾz	b′	a′

This is another example of a double-duty phrase that modifies both what precedes and what follows.

***qšh* "stubborn"**

Literally 'stiff' or 'hard', the word is familiar from the stereotyped phrase in Exodus and Deuteronomy that refers to stubborn or stiff-necked people: *ʿm qšh ʿrp* (Exod 32:9; 33:3, 5; 34:9; Deut 9:6, 13) or *ʿrpk hqšh* (Deut 31:27). With *ʿrpk* in 4b, this is an example of the breakup of a stereotyped phrase, with an inventive twist. Not only is the stereotype *qšh/ʿrp* broken up, it is intertwined in a new way, so that *ʿrp* is now parallel with *mṣḥ*. This is only one of numerous examples of how the poet transformed the literary tradition to which he was heir.

Yahweh accused the people who were worshiping an idol at the foot of Mt. Sinai of being stiff-necked. He threatened to destroy them because they had made a molten idol, worshiped it, sacrificed to it, and called upon it. The phrase used in Isaiah 48 calls up the memory of those earlier days when Israel was in danger of destruction because of their offenses against the covenant. Those same offenses, making and worshiping idols, are being committed by the community to which DI is directing his message. The harshness of his language is understandable in view of the serious nature of the offenses.

***ʾth* "you"**

Several independent pronouns are used in this poem. Here and in line 6b the 2 m. pronoun is used, singular in 4a and plural in 6b. Of special interest in this poem as well as others is the first-person singular *ʾny*, which is discussed below (12cd, p. 209).

One of the many literary problems in this chapter is the combination of singular and plural verbs, independent pronouns, and suffixes. The address to the house of Jacob in line 1a takes the form of a plural imperative, 1b and 1d use plural participles, while 1c, 1e, 2a, and 2b use 3 m. pl. verbs. The use of the singular begins in 4a and continues in 4b, 4c, 5a, 5b, and following, with singular pronominal suffixes and singular verb forms beginning with 5c, 6a, and 6d. So far, no satisfactory solution to this problem has been posed, either on form-critical grounds, or on grounds of content.

The same kind of shift between singular and plural forms is noted by Dahood in Psalm 81, a psalm that has several similarities to chap. 48 of Isaiah.[37] Dahood admits that the shift is "disconcerting" and has no satis-

37. M. Dahood, *Psalms II: 51–100* (AB 17; Garden City: Doubleday, 1968) 266.

factory explanation for the phenomenon. However, he points to the fact that the shift occurs throughout the psalm and warns against assuming textual corruption. In Isaiah 48 also, because the phenomenon is so pervasive, it seems unwise to emend for the sake of assuaging the commentators' sense of unease. It is better to comment on the phenomenon and let the text stand.

The shift from plural to singular, from one grammatical person to another, is treated by J. Kugel in his chapter on the "parallelistic line."[38] His thesis is that the relationship between two lines is more than a repetition of the same idea in different words. To demonstrate his thesis that the second element in a line is an expression of something more than the first, he offers examples that he groups under the heading of "differentiation" or "alternation."[39] He shows that often the poet makes a conscious decision not to parallel, by use of a different tense (e.g., *qṭl/yqṭl*) or a different word order (especially chiasm), by differentiating between singular and plural forms, or by changing from one grammatical person to another. While in general Kugel prefers to show how this alternation affects the meaning of the lines, even he admits that "sometimes no intention can be attributed to the text other than the desire to differentiate by making B *not parallel* in every detail."[40]

Admittedly, in the lines of chap. 48, we are not dealing with the phenomenon of alternation from plural to singular within a single line. The alternation (with regard to singular and plural, for example) is rather between one section of the poem and another. Nonetheless, the phenomenon is so extensive throughout this poem that its existence cannot be emended away without doing grave damage to the MT, with little to show in the way of clarification.

48:4bc. *gyd brzl . . . nḥwšh*
"an iron sinew is your neck, and your forehead is bronze"

This same combination, *gyd*, *nḥwšh*, and *brzl*, as figures descriptive of the spectacular power of Behemoth, occurs in Job 40:17–18.[41] Job 20:24 has the combination "iron weapon // bronze arrow"; Isa 45:2 and Ps 107:16, "doors of bronze // bars of iron"; Isa 60:17 has the word-pair "bronze//iron" twice. Jer 1:18, 6:28, 15:12; Deut 33:25; and Job 41:19 have the combinations "bronze//iron." Ezek 22:17ff. portrays an image of

38. James L. Kugel, *The Idea of Biblical Poetry* (New Haven: Yale University Press, 1981) 20–21.

39. Ibid., 16ff.

40. Ibid., 21.

41. "The sinews [*gyd*] of his thighs are knit, his bones tubes of bronze [*nḥwšh*], his limbs like bars of iron [*brzl*]."

Israel as metallic elements bronze and iron (and the problematic silver), which are melted in the fiery wrath of Yahweh. The f. form *nḥwšh* used in Isa 48:4 occurs infrequently in poetic text; the m. form *nḥšt* is more common (see Ezek 22:18). The word for 'sinews', *gyd*, also occurs infrequently, two times each in Job, Ezekiel, and Genesis. BDB suggests a possible relationship to an Assyrian root meaning 'fetter, bind', but the usages in the Bible always refer to sinews of the human body. Delitzsch's translation 'clasp of iron', based on Arab. *kaid*, is probably wrong. The noun *mṣḥ* 'brow, forehead' also occurs infrequently and is used in Ezek 3:7 in the expression *ḥzqy mṣḥ* 'hard of forehead', where it is parallel with *qšy lb* 'stiff [hard] of heart'.

All of these elements are put together in v. 4 to portray a picture of the incorrigible, obdurate audience to which DI addressed his message. The prophet has combined images of the elements iron and bronze, which are extremely hard and unmalleable, with parts of the body—neck, sinews, forehead—the first two of which are more flexible, less hard. These body parts are described in an unexpected way when used in connection with the images of metal. This unusual combination of images communicates even more strongly the notion of Israel's utter rigidity and stubbornness.

There is a chiasm in 4bc, with the following pattern:

sinews of iron your-neck	a	b
your-forehead bronze	b′	a′

The entire verse makes up a line-trio, which is held together by the 2 m. s. independent pronoun in line 4a and picked up in the use of the 2 m. s. suffix in 4b and c. As mentioned above, the combination *qšh* ᶜ*rp* binds together lines 4a and b. Line 4a also functions as a general statement of introduction that is specified more concretely in the following description of 4b and c.

There is another use of the word-pair *nḥwšh/brzl* in Isaiah that may have a bearing on the larger unit, chaps. 46–48. A. Ceresko comments on the distant parallelism between *nḥwšh/brzl* and *ksp/zhb* in Psalm 105.[42] These two word-pairs are used to provide an ironic contrast between two sections of Psalm 105, vv. 18 and 37. He also observes that Isa 60:17 uses the terms to provide a contrast in the description of the materials of the new temple.[43] In chap. 48 the people of Israel in their stubbornness are compared to baser metals, while in 46:6 the materials of which the gods are constructed (or at least with which they are purchased) are the more valu-

42. A. R. Ceresko, "A Poetic Analysis of Ps 105, with Attention to Its Use of Irony," *Bib* 64 (1983) 35.

43. Ibid., n. 71.

able silver and gold. If this is another example of distant parallelism to which Ceresko refers in regard to Psalm 105, it also would communicate a sense of irony, that the inheritance of Yahweh is described using metals incomparably inferior to the precious materials of which the powerless idols of Babylon were made.

48:5a. *wʾgyd lk mʾz bṭrm tbwʾ hšmʿtyk*
"And I declared [it] to you from time past;
before it came I announced [it] to you"

There is no direct object indicated in the Hebrew. The subject is indicated by the f. s. impf. *tbwʾ* (compare with *tbwʾnh* in 3c). Most translations add "them" or "it" (Westermann: "I declared *them* to you"; Delitzsch: "I proclaimed *it* to thee").

A comparison with v. 3 helps to shed light on this verse. In 3a the first things (f. pl.) were what Yahweh declared "from time past." Here in 5a, a f. s. verb, *tbwʾ*, is used ('it came'), agreeing at least in gender with the f. pl. *rʾšnwt* of 3a and the f. pl. *tbʾnh* of 3c. In 3b there was a shift in gender and I read the m. pl. verb and suffix to refer to Yahweh's words. Verse 5 is more elliptical than v. 3. Verse 3 points to the object declared, whereas v. 5 refers to the audience of the declaration:

v. 3: *the first things* from time past I declared
v. 5: and I declared *to you* from time past

The distant parallelism between these two lines shows that the the meaning is similar: Yahweh declared his word from time past, and the first things happened.

Duhm emends *hšmʿtyk* to *hšmʿtyh* 'I announced *it*' (f. s. suffix), but the same form occurs in 6c. When there is such a bewildering profusion of suffixes, it is preferable to comment on the phenomenon rather than to smooth it over.

A chiasm is formed between lines 5a and 5b:

I-declared to-you in-time-past	a	b
before [it came] I announced-to-you	b′	a′

The parallelism is grammatical, with the combination m. s. impf. verb / prep. // prep. / m. s. pf. verb.

48:5c, d. *ʿṣby . . . psly wnsky*
"my image . . . my idol"

Three words designating idols are utilized here. *Psl* is the most common of the three and is used frequently in DI (40:19, 20; 42:17; 44:9, 10, 15, 17; 45:20; 48:5). The root *psl* means 'hew' and elsewhere refers to tablets hewn from stone (Exod 34:1, 4) or building stones (1 Kgs 5:32). The masculine singular noun is combined with the more rare *nsk*,[44] which occurs twice in DI. In 41:29 it is parallel with *mᶜśh*. North is correct in identifying the expression *psly wnsky* as a hendiadys. His translation is 'metal image'; Clifford's translation reflects a similar treatment. He renders it 'statue'. The use of the s. verbs here further supports my interpretation that only one object is meant. North refers to Judg 17:3–4, where the image that Micah makes is called *psl wnsk* and later on, in 18:31, is referred to simply as *psl*. E. Melamed interprets the combination *psl/mskh* (*mskh* is the feminine noun formed from the root *nsk*) in Isa 42:17 as a hendiadys that has been broken up and distributed between two lines of the verse and translates 'idols of molten images', similar to my rendering of 48:5d.[45]

The masculine noun *ᶜṣb* was probably vocalized to conform to *bošet* 'shame' (according to North and Torrey, the latter of whom refers to the MT pointing as "the well known mocking device of the Punctuators"). The related noun *ᶜṣbyhm* occurs in 46:1.[46]

ᶜśm . . . ṣwm **"made them . . . commanded them"**

The pronoun suffixes here are m. pl., in agreement with the suffix ending in 3b. The singular verb *ᶜśh* is used now of activity of the idol and image, in contrast with 3c, where it described Yahweh's activity. The contrast between Yahweh's activity and the incorrect attribution of this action to the idol is heightened by the repetition of the verb. As mentioned above, the action at issue is speaking—Yahweh speaks and events transpire.

Line-pair 5cd is another one of the passages considered inauthentic by most form critics because of its negative tone. However, it is considered by E. J. Bickerman to be consistent with the picture of Jews in the Diaspora.[47] Like other emigrants, the Babylonian Jews complemented their ancestral worship with that of the gods of the new country. That this was done as a matter of course is attested in Jeremiah (5:12, 16:13), Ezekiel (20:32), and Deuteronomy (4:28). Bickerman suggests that since Jews could not participate in public worship of Babylonian gods, they probably had private shrines.[48] Further, he suggests that it would have been difficult for Jews in Babylonia to resist the temptation of the gods Bel, who

44. Translated 'molten images' in BDB 651.

45. E. Melamed, "Breakup of Stereotype Phrases as an Artistic Device in Biblical Poetry," *Studies in the Bible* (ed. Chaim Rabin; ScrHier 8; Jerusalem: Magnes, 1961) 125–26.

46. See discussion above (p. 31) for this noun.

47. E. J. Bickerman, "The Babylonian Captivity," *Cambridge History of Judaism* (ed. W. D. Davies and L. Finkelstein; Cambridge: Cambridge University Press, 1984) 1.352.

48. Ibid., 352.

"grasped the hand of the fallen," and Bellit, who released captives.[49] In this passage, the fact that at least some Jews adhered to these idols, perhaps possessed them, is clear. The main reason for Yahweh's foretelling of events was to prevent a person from attributing them to an idol of which he could say "my idol."

48:6a, b. ***šmʿt . . . tgydw***

Almost no word in this line-pair has escaped the imagination of those who emend to "improve" the text. In a completely opposite direction, Muilenburg characterizes lines 6a and b as part of a "superb transition," finding its unusual form to be admirable, rather than in need of improvement.

ḥzh **"see"**

The imperative of *ḥzh* 'see, behold' follows abruptly upon the 2 m. s. pf., *šmʿt*.[50] Duhm emends the first three words to *šmʿtm wtkrh* and translates "gehört habt ihr und es erkannt." Other suggestions include reading with the Syriac (Wade and Whybray) and emending the imperative to the perfect *ḥzyth* ("you have heard") or repointing to the infinitive absolute.[51] Torrey states that the combination of a finite verb followed by an infinitive absolute is used often by DI to achieve emphasis. North would retain the imperative, because it "expresses a distinct assurance." The attempts of Wade, Whybray, and Duhm tend to render the text more prosaic, but the abrupt effect of the line is enhanced by the absence of a conjunction on *ḥzh* and should not be eliminated by emendations.

DI uses the root *ḥzh* in 47:13 in reference to those who gaze at the stars (*hḥzym bkwkbym*). The challenge is made to these stargazers to make the future known by the *ḥdšym*, the 'new moons'. In chap. 47 the inabilities of Babylon and her magicians, sorcerers, and other associates are contrasted with Yahweh's abilities. In chap. 48 the contrast is drawn between the idols and Yahweh in respect to their abilities to make the future, the 'new things' (*ḥdšwt*) known.

48:6b. ***wʾtm hlwʾ tgydw***
"And you, won't you declare?"

The shift from singular to plural is unacceptable to Torrey and Whybray. Torrey emends to the singular *wʾth hlʾ tgyd*. However, he maintains the general shape of the line. For *tgydw* Duhm suggests *tʿydw* ('you bear witness'). The LXX reads 'know' instead of 'declare'.

49. Ibid., 354.

50. Almost entirely poetic in usage according to BDB 302.

51. Torrey; see also comments of D. N. Freedman in J. McKenzie, *Second Isaiah* (AB 20; Garden City, N.Y.: Doubleday, 1967) 93 note c–c.

Whybray, on the other hand, who maintains the *waw* in the plural ending of the verb *tgydw*, by reading it as a copula attached to the verb in the next line, makes more radical changes. He says the plural *tgydw* must be changed because the "momentary change from singular to a plural form of address . . . is strange." In fact, such a shift is not strange in this poem; it seems to be a regular feature. He also suggests, along the lines of Duhm, emending *wᵓtm* to *rᵓt* 'you have seen' (Duhm emends to the plural *rᵓtm*, but Whybray disagrees with the shift to the plural here.) Whybray also justifies his manipulation of the text because he finds the emphatic *ᵓtm* to be strange: "no emphasis seems to be required."

Whybray makes the following alterations in the line-pair 6ab: he emends an imperative to a perfect verb form, changes an emphatic 2 m. pl. pronoun to a 2 m. s. pf. verb, and moves a plural ending *waw* to the next line. Only one of these decisions is supported textually—by a reading in the Syriac. His reasons for these radical changes are insufficient to justify such disruption of the text. A more conservative approach, reading the text as it exists and making note of the "strangeness," is called for.

There are several different audiences addressed by DI throughout chaps. 40–55. Two of the audiences are identified by name, God's people Jacob/Israel (40:1, 27; 41:14, etc.), and the nations / coastlands / islands (see 41:1 and 49:1; also 45:20, 21, 22; and 51:4).[52] If there were more than one audience involved, *ᵓtm* would function here to distinguish one audience from another: "you heard, now see all of it; but you [others], won't you declare it?"[53] Muilenburg interprets the shift in number as an expression of "the fluidity of individual and community to the ancient mind." This does not, however, explain why separate words were used.

The sequence of verbs in this line-pair moves from pf. (*šmᶜt*)[54] to impv. (*ḥzh*) to impf. (*tgydw*). There is chronology and a mounting sense of urgency and incredulity in the use of these different forms. The pf. verb reports what has happened, 'you have heard' and quickly moves on to the imv. 'see!' with the sense 'understand what you heard'.[55] Finally, with the emphatic *ᵓtm*, and with even more emphasis by means of the rhetorical question *hlwᵓ*, the audience is urged to a response: 'won't you declare it?'

52. On the matter of different groups addressed in DI, see Freedman, "The Structure of Isaiah 40:1–11," esp. 185ff.

53. On the use of an independent personal pronoun as a subject of a finite verb for emphasis or contrast, see Williams, *Hebrew Syntax* (§106 / p. 22).

54. *Šmᶜt* also could be read as a precative and thus be in agreement with the imperative *ḥzh*.

55. Freedman (personal communication) points out a similar progression of thought in Job 42:5: "By the hearing of the ear I heard you, and now my eye has seen you."

(JB and NAB translate 'won't you admit it?'). The demand made on the audience is fully in keeping with the picture of that audience as stubborn and intractable as described in the previous verses. The abruptness in tone is also understandable, given the nature of the audience. Line 11b has a similarly abrupt outburst (see below for discussion, pp. 206–7).

48:6c. *ḥdšwt* "new things"

The term appears three times in DI. In 42:9 it is contrasted with *rʾšnwt.* In 42:9 the new things are not specifically described. What is important is that Yahweh declares them before they happen. When they do happen, they will be swift, sudden. In 43:19 the "new thing" (singular) is again contrasted with the "first things." As in 42:9, the new thing will spring forth. It will be done by Yahweh, and when it springs forth, Yahweh asks the rhetorical question *hlwʾ tdʿwh* 'don't you know it?' The new thing is identified in 43:19ff. as the way in the wilderness and the watering of the desert. According to Muilenburg, the new things in 48:6c include the coming of Cyrus, the liberation of Israel, and the new exodus.

In his explanation of apocalyptic origins, Frank Cross refers to various ways that later prophets reformulated earlier traditions.[56] The pattern of "the doctrine of two ages, an era of 'old things' and 'new things' " is one of these reformulations. History was significant because it revealed a pattern for future events.[57] According to Cross, the "new things" were imminent, they were announced by the divine council,[58] and the "joy of salvation was present." In Isaiah 48, the new things are imminent, they are created "now," and they are used in comparison and contrast with the "first things" of 3a.

The rhetorical question posed in 43:19 ("now it springs forth; do you not perceive it?") is parallel in form to that of 48:6 ("now see all this; will you not declare it?"). The difference is that in 48:6 they are not asked if they know it, they are asked to declare it (it can be taken for granted that now they know it).

***mʿth* "only now"**

DI has used the preposition *min* in a creative fashion throughout the poem. In 1c ("from Judah") it was an indication of source. In 2a ("from

56. F. M. Cross, *Canaanite Myth and Hebrew Epic: Essays in the History of the Religion of Israel* (Cambridge: Harvard University Press, 1973) 346. Cross sees Second Isaiah as a pivotal picture in his assessment of apocalyptic origins.

57. See William R. Millar, *Isaiah 24–27 and the Origin of Apocalyptic* (Missoula: Scholars Press, 1976) 112, on the significance of history in Second Isaiah.

58. F. M. Cross, "The Council of Yahweh in Second Isaiah," *JNES* 12 (1953) 274–77.

the city") it indicates relationship. It refers to a sense of time in 3a, 5a, 6c, 7a, and 8b. In 4a ("because I knew") it has a causal meaning. Williams indicates that *min* sometimes has an emphatic force.[59] That is the way Stuhlmueller translates 48:6c: "I announce new things to you [only] now."[60] I agree with Stuhlmueller's interpretation. It continues the sense of urgency that began in 6ab. *Mʿth* is contrasted with *mʾz* of vv. 5a and 7a 'in time past'. In the same way *ḥdšwt* 'new things' are contrasted with *rʾšnwt* 'first things'.

48:6d. *wnṣrwt* "and secret things"

The word *nṣrwt* means literally 'guarded things' from the root *nṣr*, meaning 'watch, guard, keep'.[61] Bonnard translates, "mis en reserve" and compares to 42:6, where Cyrus is "kept," and 49:8, where it is the servant Israel who is "kept." In 48:6d it is parallel with *ḥdšwt* 'new things'. The unexpected, unknown element is emphasized, just as it was in the announcement of the "first things" in 3c above.

***wlʾ ydʿtm* "you did not know them"**

The *ḥdšwt* and *nṣrwt* are f. pl. nouns; *ydʿtm* has a m. pl. pron. suffix, which refers to the things that the audience did not know beforehand. The m. pl. pron. suffix is identical to that in 7b and can be contrasted with the f. pl. pron. suffix (*ydʿtyn*) in 7c. This could be another allusion to the implied *dbrym* discussed above in 3b (see p. 179). The contrast between the first things (the exodus) and the new things (the new exodus) is the long time period before the first things were fulfilled. With the new things, there will not be this distressing gap between announcement and fulfillment. As soon as God speaks and is heard, the thing happens and is seen.

The conjunction is absent from 1QIsa[a]. The two *waw*-conjunctions in this line in the MT are unusual, especially for poetry. See the same phenomenon in 7b (p. 191).

48:7ab. *ʿth . . . mʾz wlpny ywm*

The poem contains several adverbs and prepositional phrases that designate time past and present and that emphasize the contrast between events in the past and events that are just now being (or remain to be) created. The word *ʿth* 'now' in the beginning of this line emphasizes the newness of the things just created. It is repeated from line 6c. *Wlʾ mʾz* and *lpny ywm* heighten the contrast between "now" and "time past, before today."

59. Williams, *Hebrew Syntax* §325/pp. 56–57.
60. Stuhlmueller, *Creative Redemption*, 140.
61. BDB 666.

Wlpny ywm is usually translated as an adverbial phrase modifying *wlʾ šmʿtm* 'you never heard of them before today' (NEB; cf. JPSV). One problem with this reading is that the *waw*-conjunction of *wlʾ šmʿtm* is ignored. Torrey omits it, agreeing with the LXX (which reads *lpnym* 'formerly') and the Syriac. In v. 7, as in 6d above, 1QIsa^a does not have the conjunction. It is tempting to omit it, since in general, one would expect 1QIsa^a to include rather than exclude such conjunctions. If the conjunction is retained, with the MT, the passage can be translated:

> Now they are created and not in time past,
> And (not) before today; and you did not hear them.

The negative *lwʾ* of 7a can be read as a double-duty modifier for "before today," as well as for "in time past." In favor of this rendering is the fact that the pattern of lines 6cd is repeated in lines 7ab. The unusual presence of two *waw*-conjunctions was observed in 6d; the same phenomenon is present in 7b. If both *waws* are retained, in agreement with the MT in 7b, then the last two words of both 6d and 7b are grammatically and semantically parallel:

> line 6d: And you did not know them
> line 7b: And you did not hear them

Another suggestion about translating the *waws* in both lines 6d and 7b is to read them as emphatics (McKenzie). The lines would then be translated:

> line 6d: No, you did not know them
> line 7b: No, you did not hear them

More evidence in favor of the parallels between these two lines is the parallel with the same verbs in 8a, forming a chiasm:

> line 8a: *gm lwʾ šmʿt gm lwʾ ydʿt*
> No, you did not hear
> No, you did not know

The syllable count in lines 6cd–7ab is also remarkably uniform: 9(or 10)/9/9/9.

Ordinarily, we would not expect to find so many conjunctions in poetry. However, in vv. 6–7 the conjunctions function to highlight the parallel between the two line-pairs, which in turn emphasizes the point: they didn't know; they didn't hear. This emphasis is important, because the point of the lines is to ensure that the people do not say, "I knew them" (line 7c).

48:7c. *ydʿtyn* "I knew them"

The switch to the 3 f. pl. suffix is to be noted. The verb *ydʿ* occurs several times throughout the first half of the poem but never in the same form. Here, the words *I knew them* are proposed as a statement that Israel might utter regarding knowledge of "new things." However, Yahweh has taken precautions against this possibility by creating "new things" that did not occur, nor were they foretold in the past. In line 5c there was a danger of wrongly attributing things to idols. Here in 7c, the danger is that Israel might claim to have knowledge of actions or events.

While it is understandable that the prophet does not want idols to be credited with foretelling the first things, it is not as clear what the danger would be in the people saying of the new things that they knew them beforehand. One of the underlying themes of section III is that of prophecy and its fulfillment. There is a contrast between the prophecy of the first things and that of the new things. In the case of the first things, they were announced long before the events they foretold; thus, no one could attribute foretelling to another deity and no one could claim not to have known about them. With the new things, almost as soon as the events are announced, they occur. There is no possibility that people could claim prior knowledge. Somehow prophecy works differently from the way it did in previous days. In Ezek 12:26–28, people doubt the efficacy and integrity of the prophetic word. Ezekiel tells them that there will no longer be a delay between the proclamation and its accomplishment, so that they will no longer be able to make the accusation that prophecies are not fulfilled (Ezek 12:21) or that fulfillment is too far off in the future (12:26). Perhaps DI was concerned about the same problem. One can imagine people in Babylon doubting for decades that Yahweh's word had any meaning or that old prophecies would be enacted. In the time of the new things, however, people won't even be able to claim that they knew them in advance, since there will be no interval between the proclamation and the deed.

Another interpretation of the meaning of the claim "I knew them" is that it reflects the resistance of the people to the possibility of any new things happening. The audience refuses to entertain any hope for the future because they anticipate more disillusionment.[62] The lack of hope blinds people and prevents them from making plans for the future.

48:8a, b. ***gm lʾ . . .*** **"No, you did not . . ."**

The adverb *gm* is used emphatically here, along with the repetition of the key verbs *šmʿ* and *ydʿ*, to summarize the preceding lines and to repeat the idea that Israel did not know or hear either old or new things. The threefold repetition of an adverb for emphasis is a device used elsewhere by

62. Luis Alonso Schökel, "Isaiah," *The Literary Guide to the Bible* (ed. Robert Alter and Frank Kermode; Cambridge: The Belknap Press of Harvard University Press, 1987) 178–79.

DI in 40:24 and 41:26. These are prime examples of the device of anaphora.[63] In 40:24, the adverb *ʾp* is used with the negative *bl*: "scarcely are they planted, scarcely are they sown, scarcely does their stem take root. . . ." The same adverb, *ʾp*, is used three times in 41:26, this time with the negative particle *ʾyn*: "No one who declared, no one who announced, no one who heard. . . ." In each case, the threefold repetition of the adverb is used in conjunction with a negative particle, *lʾ*, *bl*, or *ʾyn*.[64]

Note the pattern in 40:24 of two plural verbs followed by a variation in the pattern, a singular *Poel*. Likewise in 41:26, there is a slight variation in the third verb form used. The first two are *Hiphil* participles; the third is a *Qal* participle. In 48:8, two *Qal* 3 m. s. verbs (*šmʿt* and *ydʿt*) are followed by a *Piel* 3 f. s. (*ptḥh*). An additional variation in 48:8 is the adverb *mʾz*, which intervenes between *gm* and the negative *lʾ*. This variation of the third element in the repetition is similar to the pattern in 40:24 and 41:26.

DI uses repetition as an emphatic or rhetorical device elsewhere. See the threefold "awake!" (*ʿwry*) in 51:9. Cross[65] sees the repetitive imperative there as reminiscent of Canaanite style.[66] In 51:17 (*htʿwrry*) and 52:1 (*ʿwry*), there is a twofold repetition of the imperative. In those examples, however, the repetition is not in consecutive lines, but is within a single line. Watson refers to this phenomenon as immediate repetition and cites Lam 4:15 and Judg 5:12 as examples.[67] See p. 205 for further discussion of this device in Isaiah 48.[68]

63. "The repetition of a word or words at the beginning of successive clauses for emphasis or effect," in *A Student's Dictionary for Biblical and Theological Studies* by F. B. Huey and B. Corley (Grand Rapids: Zondervan, 1983) 21; or "the rhetorically emphatic reiteration of a single word or brief phrase" in *The Art of Biblical Poetry* by Robert Alter (New York: Basic Books, 1985) 64. See also Wilfred G. W. Watson, *Classical Hebrew Poetry: A Guide to Its Techniques*, on initial repetition. According to Watson, the number of consecutive lines that begin with the same word or phrase is usually two or three, sometimes four or more (JSOTSup 26; Sheffield: JSOT Press, 1984) 276.

64. Watson (ibid., 278) cites an Akkadian document, Atr II ii 9–10, which also begins with the repetition of a negative particle: "*Do not* reverence your gods, *do not* pray to your goddesses." See also Prov 3:25–31, which repeats the negative *ʾl* seven times in succession.

65. Cross, *Canaanite Myth*, 107.

66. Psalm 29:1–2 is an example of this feature in Canaanite style: the imperative *hbw lyhwh* 'give to Yahweh' is repeated three times in succession. In addition, the phrase *qwl yhwh* occurs seven times throughout the psalm, exhibiting a similar use of the device of anaphora. See D. N. Freedman and C. Franke-Hyland, "Psalm 29: A Structural Analysis," *HTR* 66 (1973) 237–56, for further discussion of repetitive parallelism.

67. Watson, *Classical Hebrew Poetry*, 277.

68. Examples of triple repetition are found in Jer 7:4 and Ezek 7:1–2.

In Watson's discussion of repetition as a poetic device,[69] he lists various types of repetition and then describes the functions of repetition. Referring to the "oral aspect" of poetry, he says that repetition enables "the audience to re-hear a verse which they may have missed" and that it "reduces the need for a poet to invent new material; it helps 'fill up' a poem."[70] Repetition can be a structuring device that helps to link the components of a poem. It also has many rhetorical or nonstructuring functions, including dramatic effect, completeness, emphasis, and emphatic negation.

One problem with Watson's treatment is his discussion of the relationship of the "oral aspect" of poetry to literature of the Bible.[71] It is not exactly clear how this is related to the function of repetition in a literary piece. Since the work of Parry and Lord, there has been much discussion about whether or not poems in the Bible were composed orally and about the possible conventions used by oral poets.[72] Watson discusses these various conventions, such as the use of repetition and fixed word-pairs, and states that because of such techniques "a bard could produce quantities of verse with little effort."[73] Kugel, however, cautions against drawing conclusions about oral composition based on the use of formulaic language, since the presence of oral formulae in a line does not necessarily indicate spontaneously composed language.[74] He argues that it would stretch the limits of credibility to argue that, since formulaic language such as word-pairs make up alphabetical acrostics, the acrostics such as are found in Psalms and Lamentations were composed by poet-performers on their feet.

Alter's discussion of repetition is more finely nuanced than is Watson's. Alter especially takes issue with the idea that the poet needed to "fill up" a poem.[75] He emphasizes that the second element in a line-pair, or verse, is not "deadweight or padding brought in to fill out the metrical requirement of the line." In this respect, he would be very much at odds with Watson's

69. Watson, *Classical Hebrew Poetry*, 272–82.

70. Ibid., 278–79.

71. Y. Gitay discusses whether DI was oral or written. See "Deutero-Isaiah: Oral or Written?" *JBL* 99 (1980) 185–97.

72. M. Parry, "Studies in the Epic Technique of Oral Verse-Making II: 'The Homeric Language' as the Language of Oral Poetry," *Harvard Studies in Classical Philology* 43 (1932) 1–50; A. B. Lord, *The Singer of Tales* (Harvard Studies in Comparative Literature 24; Cambridge: Harvard University Press, 1960).

73. Watson, *Classical Hebrew Poetry*, 82.

74. Kugel, *Idea of Biblical Poetry*, 34.

75. Alter, *Art of Biblical Poetry.* See his discussion of the "ballast variant" on p. 24. The issue is not verbatim repetition, but what he refers to as "hidden repetition" (p. 23), in which a word in the first line of verse governs a clause in the second; this is otherwise known as the use of double-duty words, or gapping.

idea of the poet as someone who needs to reduce his need to invent new material. Indeed, Watson's idea of a poet[76] seems to minimize the notion of creativity and variety and emphasize the idea of the poet as a composer of something akin to greeting-card jingles.

The following functions of repetition are listed by Alter. In his treatment of Psalm 8, he sees the function of the refrain, "O Lord, our master, how majestic is Your name in all the earth," repeated at the beginning and the end, as "creating the illusion of actual simultaneity, offering . . . a single panorama with multiple elements held nicely together."[77] This is the envelope structure. By this device "a perfect circle is closed" by the verbatim repetition. But Alter emphasizes the changed meaning of the repeated words due to what has accrued in the intervening lines. The intervening lines describe more concretely what it means that God's name is majestic throughout the earth, and the audience can appreciate more fully the meaning of the refrain.

Alter also makes the same point about the use of anaphora. "[T]he repeated word or phrase in anaphora never means exactly the same thing twice. . . ."[78] The meaning of each repetition is affected by the surrounding material and its position in the series of repetitions. Another aspect of the use of anaphora is that repetitions shift the attention from the repeated element to the new material, "at once inviting us to see all the new utterances as locked into the same structure of assertion and to look for strong differences or elements of development in the new material." The repetition "How long, O Lord?" in Psalm 13 "reflects an ascent on a scale of intensity, the note of desperate urgency pitched slightly higher with each repetition."[79] Repetition achieves the effect of heightening, which Alter emphasizes throughout his book as a feature of parallelism.

Incremental repetition (or climactic or repetitive parallelism)[80] is also used to accomplish the heightening or intensifying effect,[81] which is a key feature of Hebrew poetry in Alter's schema. The effect of this kind of repetition (as seen in Judg 5:24–31, for example) is to create an overlap of meaning, again pushing the meaning of the repeated word or phrase

76. Watson, *Classical Hebrew Poetry*, 279.

77. Alter, *Art of Biblical Poetry*, 118.

78. Ibid., 64ff.

79. Ibid., 65.

80. See W. F. Albright, *Yahweh and the Gods of Canaan: A Historical Analysis of Two Contrasting Faiths* (Garden City, N.Y.: Doubleday, 1968; repr. Winona Lake, Ind.: Eisenbrauns, 1978) 4–28, who credits H. L. Ginsberg for first defining repetitive parallelism in Canaanite poetry.

81. Alter states, however, that the "rhetorical strategy of incremental repetition" is "chiefly a matter of insistence and emphasis" (*Art of Biblical Poetry*, 43ff., esp. p. 60).

further, by association with a new element. "Between her legs he kneeled, fell, lay // between her legs he kneeled and fell // where he kneeled, he fell, destroyed." The incremental repetition achieves a climax in the last line.

The examples used by Alter here are not all examples, strictly speaking, of what is usually referred to as incremental repetition, nor do they fit his definition: "something is stated, then it is restated verbatim with an added element."[82] For instance, in the line "water he asked, milk she gave, in a princely bowl she brought him curds" (Judg 5:25), there is no repetition, only increment. Alter's entire discussion of this feature of poetry is incomplete. He does not indicate that in incremental repetition, not only is there an addition of an element, but also an elimination of an element, to achieve a pattern abc/abd, or the like. In fact, in his discussion of incremental repetition in Song of Songs,[83] he seems to consider this subtraction of one element, along with the addition of the increment, a new stylistic feature.

The repetition of key words is another device discussed by Alter.[84] Sometimes key words are used for insistence and emphasis. However, sometimes key words exhibit "ironic interplay and progressive articulation of meanings." Alter uses as examples the "sayings" of the teacher in Prov 7:1 and 24 and of the seductive woman in v. 5. The key word in these verses is used with different meanings, depending on whose "sayings" are referred to. In the first case, the sayings are life-giving; in the second, they lead to Sheol.

The repetition of the particle *gm* in Isa 48:8 has emphatic force and illustrates one of Alter's (and Kugel's) main ideas about repetition. The threefold repetition of *gm lʾ* places the emphasis on the three verbs of hearing, knowing, and opening the ear. It also functions to heighten and intensify the sense of the two lines. Israel did not hear or know; what's more, Israel did not even open an ear. It is important to note, however, that this kind of heightening and intensifying is not as widespread or as universal a device as claimed by Alter and Kugel.[85] As pointed out above, in lines 6d and 7b, the same verbs appear in reverse order,[86] so there is an interaction between hearing and seeing, rather than just an intensification in one direction.

82. Ibid., 23.
83. Ibid., 188–89.
84. Ibid., 60ff.
85. See also the discussion on pp. 211–12.
86. Verse 6d, "and you did not know them" // v. 7b, "and you did not hear them."

48:8b. *ptḥh ʾznk* "your ear (did not) open"

The MT has the *Piel* 3 f. s. of *ptḥ*, but there are several variant readings. The LXX reads it as a *Qal* first-person singular, "I have not opened your ear," which has been adopted by several commentaries. 1QIsa[a] reads *ptḥt*, possibly "you did not open your ear."[87] The RSV reads the verb in a passive sense ("your ear has not been opened"), which would call for repointing or emending to a *Niphal* form. Levy reads "neither of old did they [new things] open thine ear." He does not emend the text but considers the subject to be the f. pl. "new things" with the f. s. verb, based on GKC §145k.[88]

Some feel that emendation is necessary because of the unusual form of *ptḥ*. The verb *ptḥ* in the MT is intransitive, and Cheyne and others believe that the *Niphal* is preferable. GKC agrees with Cheyne and also emends 60:11 on the same basis.[89] However, GKC admits that "with an intransitive sense *Piel* occurs as an intensive form, but only in poetic language." Others (Kissane, Skinner) emend because of the sense, preferring to read Yahweh as the subject, meaning, "he did not reveal, did not open the ear," based on a similar expression in Isa 50:5, where Yahweh opened the ear (*Qal* 3 m. s. pf.) of his servant. In this interpretation, the translators understand the text to mean that Yahweh did not give a revelation.

Torrey sees no need to emend and compares 48:8b to Isa 60:11 and Cant 7:13, where *ptḥ* is intransitive. He also draws a comparison between 48:8b and 42:19f., which have similar ideas. There, the servant sees but does not observe; his ears are open (*pqwḥ*), but he does not hear.

I read with the MT. Grammatically, the root *ptḥ* can be intransitive. The intensive *Piel* is fitting, since emphasis is what the author wishes to achieve. The previous two verbs are in the second person, and the subject is Israel. The pattern continues with Israel (or Israel's ear) as the subject. Reading with the MT, this third element serves to emphasize the fact that Israel did not see or hear by stating that the ear did not even open. North considers this to be an example of litotes, a negative statement with an affirmative meaning for the purpose of emphasis: "Your ears were firmly closed."[90] My translation would emphasize Israel's obstinacy, an idea begun above in v. 4 (see pp. 181ff.).[91]

87. However, based on 1QIsa[a] 48:6 (*šmᶜth*) or 48:8 (*ydᶜth*), one might expect *ptḥth*.

88. "Plurals of names of animals or things . . . are frequently construed with the feminine singular of the verbal predicate" (GKC §145k / p. 464).

89. GKC §52k / p. 142.

90. See comment above on 46:13a on this device (p. 69) and on 47:3d (p. 119).

91. However, the LXX rendering has merit. In emending the verb to the first singular, Yahweh is seen to be the subject ("I did not open your ears"), and the idea that Yahweh did not announce the new things until just now to prevent Israel from attributing them to an idol would be continued if one read with the LXX.

48:8c. ***ky*** **"Yes!"**

Translators are divided on whether to read *ky* as an emphatic particle, or as a causal, concessive or adversative. The JPSV and Kissane translate "although I knew . . ."; the NAB and Torrey read it as emphatic; Pieper reads it adversatively; the JB, NEB, Clifford, Westermann, and most others read it in a causal sense, "for I know (knew). . . ." Reading *ky* as an emphatic particle would continue the pattern of the negative emphatic *gm lᵓ* in the previous lines. Pieper's reading also makes the connection between lines 8ab and 8c. Israel did not hear or know, "but" Yahweh did know. Least convincing is the causal rendering. Many who translate in the causal sense show 8cd as an incomplete sentence, a dependent clause.

bgwd tbgwd **"you acted very treacherously"**

The use of the infinitive absolute with the imperfect verb highlights Israel's disloyalty and continues the notion begun in v. 1. This same pattern, the repetition of the root *bgd,* is seen elsewhere. In Isa 24:16 *bgd* occurs five times in succession (m. pl. part. + pf. verb twice, and also the m. s. noun); in Isa 21:2 the participle is repeated; in 33:1 the pattern is part. + pf. verb, and inf. + impf. verb; in Jer 12:1, part. + noun. This combination, the repetition and variation on the root *bdg,* could be considered a fixed word-pair.

In Ps 78:57 Israel's treacheries are rebellion against Yahweh, failure to observe the statutes, and the use of the high places and graven images (*psylyhm*). Here too in Isaiah 48 the treachery is associated with Israel's involvement with idols. In view of the sentiments of Yahweh in the following verse, it would not be a mistake to associate this treachery with the golden-calf incident, when Yahweh threatened to destroy his people.

qrᵓ lk **"you were called"**

This rare *Pual* perfect only appears in Ezek 10:13 and in Isa 58:12, 61:3, and 62:2 (and possibly 65:1). In the combination *qrᵓ l-,* the meaning is 'to be named, called'. The *Pual* participle also appears in 48:12. Because of the recurrence of this form in Third Isaiah and also because of the harsh tone of the passage, several form critics relegate this passage to Third Isaiah. However, the root *qrᵓ* is a key word in the poem, and the appearance of the same form in 48:12 is reason enough to refrain from relegating the passage to a different text. It can be seen to be an integral part of the poem.

48:9a. ***ᵓᵓryk ᵓpy*** **"I am slow to anger"**

Many translations render 'I will defer my anger' (RSV), which has the sense that Yahweh's rage is yet to come. BDB[92] translates the *Hiphil* of the transitive verb *ᵓrk* 'prolong, postpone'. However, based on affinities with

92. BDB 73.

Exodus 34 and on the context of the statement, my translation above is preferable. Freedman suggests the intensive function of the *Hiphil*, which would be translated, 'I am very slow to anger'.[93]

The idiom *ʾrk ʾp(ym)* 'slow to anger' is used elsewhere in reference both to human beings (Prov 14:29 and 19:11) and to God. It is part of the formula in Exod 34:6 that describes the nature of God, which is revealed to Moses after the golden calf incident.[94] B. Childs considers the frequent use in the Old Testament of the phrase to be "an eloquent testimony to the centrality of this understanding of God's person."[95]

The context of this formula in Exodus is the incident of the golden calf. God reveals his name to Moses and promises that he will forgive the people's sins (including *pšʿ*), will cut (*krt*) a covenant with the people, and will show them wonders that have never before been created (*nbrʾ*). Moses admits that this people is a stiff-necked people (*qšh ʿrp*) in need of pardon.

There are many similarities between the proclamation of God's name and nature in Exodus 34 and the promise of God in Isa 48:9 to withhold his anger for the sake of his name.[96] The people in Isaiah 48 were rebellious (*pšʿ*) from birth, stubborn, and stiff-necked (48:4). Just as God declared in Exodus 34 that he was about to create (*nbrʾ*) wonders that had never been seen before by anyone, in Isa 48:7 wonders, or new things, are created (*nbrʾ*) that have never been seen or heard of. In Exodus 34 God promises to cut a covenant. In Isa 48:9, God promises that he will be slow to anger in order to avoid cutting off (*krt*) the rebellious people.

48:9b. *thlty* "my praise"

The feminine noun occurs frequently in the psalms and in Isa 40–66. In Isa 42:8, 10, and 12 it is parallel with *kbwd* 'glory'. Here in 48:9b it is parallel with *šmy* 'my name', and the preposition *lmʿn* plays double duty for both nouns: "For the sake of my name . . . and (for the sake of) my praise. . . ."

***ʾḥṭm* "I will restrain"**

The word is a *hapax legomenon.* Cheyne suggests emending the text to *ʾḥml* 'I will spare' but without textual support. Elliger[97] suggests this same

93. See Speiser, *Genesis* (AB 1; Garden City, N.Y.: Doubleday, 1964) 90, for a discussion of this use of the *Hiphil* in Gen 12:11.

94. See also Num 14:18, Neh 9:17, Ps 86:15, Jonah 4:2, Nah 1:3 et al., for variations on the formula.

95. B. Childs, *The Book of Exodus: A Critical, Theological Commentary* (OTL; Philadelphia: Westminster, 1974) 612.

96. Among DI commentators, only North refers to the similarities. Childs, observes that "the thought and language are not far removed from Second Isaiah" (ibid., 613).

97. Elliger, *Verhältnis,* 195.

emendation based on a parallel he finds in Isa 63:9. (The reference is to Yahweh's love, *ʾhb*, and pity, *ḥml*.) Duhm observes, "Was *ʾḥṭm lk* heisst, ist unbekannt" but suggests the possibility of *ʾḥwm ʿlyk*, "I will have compassion on you." Torrey considers the MT reading and Jerome's translation to be correct. The root is an Aramaic loanword,[98] a denominative from the word for 'nose'.[99] Most translators base their renderings on this possibility and on the supposed parallel with *ʾrk* in the previous line, but the entire verse is elliptical. For this reason, appeals to possible parallels are not very helpful in coming to a clearer determination of the meaning of the *hapax legomenon.*

Elsewhere in chaps. 40–66 there are references to God's restraint or refraining from speech. In 42:14 and 57:11 God speaks of being silent for a long time (one of the verbs in 42:14 is *ḥrš*). In 42:14, 63:15, and 64:11 God restrains himself (*Hithpael* of *ʾpq*). In 42:14 it is restraint from crying out like a woman in travail; in chaps. 63 and 64 God's compassion is withheld. Yet another verb to express restraint or silence is used in 42:14, 57:11, and 64:12 [64:11], *ḥšh*, where God keeps silent or refrains from action, at least for a time, in the face of appalling events (the worship of idols or the ruination of Zion). In Isa 48:9 God restrains himself from cutting off his own people because of their treachery.

48:10ab. *ṣrptyk wlʾ bksp* "I refined you, but not like silver"

Numerous suggestions have been offered to clear up the difficulties of v. 10. Part of the problem lies in the meaning of *lʾ bksp* 'not *in*(?) silver'. Levy explains the phrase "not *like* silver" based on an interpretation of Ibn Ezra and Qimḥi, who say that this means there is still wickedness left in Israel, since all the dross was not refined out, unlike the process of refining silver where all impurities are removed. Kissane interprets it to mean that Israel is like impure silver that has been removed from the fire too early in the process, and that base metal remains. Muilenburg also interprets the passage to mean that the refining process has produced much dross.

The futility of purifying Israel is described in Jer 6:29–30, using the imagery of the processing of metal:

nḥr mpḥ	The bellows blow fiercely;
mʾštm ʿprt	the lead is consumed by the fire;
lšwʾ ṣrp ṣrwp	in vain the refining goes on,

98. See also BDB 310 for similar derivation.

99. Frederick E. Greenspahn refers also to verbal forms of this root in Akkadian, Arabic, and Mandaic that mean 'muzzle'. These verbs "confirm the likelihood of the meaning 'restrain oneself'," *Hapax Legomena in Biblical Hebrew* (Chico, Cal.: Scholars Press, 1984) 113.

*wr*ᶜ*ym l*ᵓ *ntqw* for the wicked are not removed.
*ksp nm*ᵓ*s qr*ᵓ*w lhm* Refuse silver they are called,
*ky-m*ᵓ*s yhwh bhm* for the Lord has rejected them (RSV).

Israel is not to be compared to silver that has been properly refined; instead Israel is called by the name "refuse [or reject] silver." This name reflects God's attitude toward Israel: he has rejected Israel. The Jeremiah passage clearly states what the above commentators read into the elliptical *wl*ᵓ *bksp* in Isa 48:10.

In a different vein, Slotki interprets "not *with* silver" to mean that the process of refining was not so severe that it destroyed Israel completely. Pieper also sees this as an indication of the moderation of the heat of God's anger. Orelli contrasts the smelting that was to purify Israel with the consuming fire that fell upon Babylon in 47:14 to destroy her.

Delitzsch reads the *bet* as a *bet essentiae*: "not *as* men melt silver." By this he does not understand the passage to mean that Israel was refined more severely or more thoroughly. Rather, the manner of Israel's refining was "of a superior kind, a spiritual refining and testing . . ." because it had a "salutary object."

Other suggestions include translating 'not for money', meaning 'not for any benefit'. North would prefer to read the first verb 'I bought you', based on an Akkadian root *ṣarapu* 'to buy'. Then the entire phrase could be translated 'I bought you, but not for money'. However, the root *ṣrp*, with the meaning 'to buy', is not found in the Old Testament.

Torrey emends the text, believing the MT to be "mere nonsense." According to Torrey, the "context demands" *ly kksp*, and he translates, 'I have refined thee for myself like silver'. He believes that the scribe accidentally wrote *l*ᵓ for *ly*. The corrupted verse was later possibly read, "I have purchased you . . ." because of the uses of *ṣrp* in late Hebrew and Arabic. The idea of purchase or redemption without silver is found in Isa 52:3 and is noted by those who would translate *l*ᵓ *bksp* as 'not with silver' (meaning "money"). Westermann also emends the text without explanation. Instead of *wl*ᵓ *b* . . . , he indicates in a footnote, "read *k* . . ." and translates, 'I refine you [as] silver'.

In addition to 48:10 (and the Jeremiah passage, 6:27ff.), there are several other places in the Old Testament that refer specifically to the refining (*ṣrp*) of silver. These include Ps 12:7, 66:10, and Zech 13:9. Ps 12:7 compares the promises of Yahweh to refined silver.[100] Ps 66:10 and Zech 13:9 use the figure of refining silver to describe the testing of God's people. Both

100. See especially the treatment by Dahood of the translation of this line (*Psalms I: 1–50* (AB 16; Garden City, N.Y.: Doubleday, 1965) 74.

use the *kap* + the infinitive (Zech 13:9 reads: *ṣrptym kṣrp ʾt-hksp* 'as the refining of silver'). The refining to which Psalm 66 refers is the wilderness period, when God tested Israel. Zechariah 13 refers to a time when the people will be scattered. Two-thirds will perish and one-third will be refined in the fire and tested. Dahood[101] sees the metallurgical term *baḥantanu* ('you tested us') paired with 'you refined us' as evoking "the image of the torrid desert." The fire referred to in Zechariah 13 elicits a similar picture. In both of these passages, the testing period produces a positive result. After the testing in Zechariah, people call on Yahweh's name. The result in Psalm 66 is that people are brought into a spacious place.

Another process, or aspect of the process, is described in Ezek 22:17–22. Refining is not mentioned, but instead the verb used is *ntk* 'melt'. The fierce wrath of Yahweh will blow on his people and melt them because they have all become dross. The analogy is made between the melting of silver and other metals, and the melting of the house of Israel. This process yields nothing of worth.

This evidence from Psalms, Zechariah, and Ezekiel does not help determine the meaning and result of the refining of Israel in Isaiah 48. In Jeremiah, the refining produces an imperfect product, dross. On the other hand, in Zechariah and Psalm 66, the refining does accomplish the purification, leaving a people who call upon Yahweh and receive his blessings, the spacious land.

The term *ṣrp* elsewhere in DI refers, not to the actions of God, but to those of idol-makers. In the magnificent hymn celebrating Yahweh's creative power (Isa 40:12–31), Yahweh's might is contrasted with the work of the refiners and engravers, who are making immovable idols. In 40:19 the refiner works with gold and silver.[102] In 41:7 the engraver and the refiner encourage one another in the work of securing the idol. In 46:6 a refiner is hired to make an idol; gold and silver are part of the price or the materials the refiner is to use for the construction of the idol.

Outside DI, the only other occurrence of *ṣrp* in Isaiah is in the introduction to the whole book, Isa 1:25. In Isa 1:21–26 the faithful city has become a harlot; her silver has become dross. Yahweh promises to "smelt away [*ṣrp*] . . . dross with lye." Afterwards Israel will be called "city of righteousness, the faithful city."

The image of refining silver to remove dross as a figure of Yahweh's testing of his people is not an uncommon one in the Bible. The passage in the introduction to the book of Isaiah is especially enlightening in respect to Isa 48:10, which appears in a context of people who have rebelled

101. Ibid., 122.

102. See also Prov 17:3 and 27:21 for the parallel between silver and gold.

against Yahweh, who are in need of purification and restoration. The problematic *lʾ bksp* can best be understood as a contrast to the manner of refining described in line b. Israel has been refined in the furnace of affliction, not in an ordinary refiner's fire. Herbert's translation (also adopted by the NEB) captures the sense best:

> See how I tested you, not as silver is tested, but in the furnace of affliction; there I purified you.

Another important element in the various passages in the Bible that use refining as a figure for the testing of Israel is that the people or city are named after the refining process is finished. In Zech 13:9, after the remaining one-third is refined, they will call on Yahweh, and Yahweh will declare, "They are my people." In Isa 1:26 the city will be named "city of righteousness, the faithful city." The naming of the people or the city is also an issue in Isaiah 48. Israel has claimed names for itself that are not appropriate (vv. 1–2). Israel has been called a rebel from the beginning (8c) and needs to be refined and renamed.

48:10b. *bḥ*[*n*]*tyk* "I [tested] you"

The MT reads "I chose you [*bḥrtyk*]." Virtually all translators read, "I tested you." (Levy, reading "I chose you," is an exception.) 1QIsa[a] reads *bḥntykh* 'I tested you'. But even without this textual support, numerous commentators (e.g., Delitzsch) cite the Aramaic *bḥr* 'try, melt, refine' as an equivalent of Hebrew *bḥn* and understand 10b to refer, not to Yahweh's choosing of Israel, but to his testing of Israel as one tests metal.

Other convincing evidence in favor of adopting this reading is the frequent pairing of the terms *ṣrp* and *bḥn* in the Bible. North understates the matter when he says that "sometimes" the two terms are parallel. Volz cites ten such occurrences. In view of such repeated use, the terms could be referred to as a fixed word-pair.

Dahood cites the occurrences of this word-pair in a number of psalms. In Psalms 17 and 26 he sees the use of the word-pair as an indication that both psalms are in the category of "psalms of innocence." He also points out the metallurgical aspects of the terms in Ps 66:10.[103]

Bḥr does occur twice with *ksp*, in Prov 8:19 and 10:20, in the expression *ksp nbḥr* 'choice silver'. The image is used as a superlative. Proverbs 8 uses the expression to refer to the offerings of wisdom—her fruit is better than the finest gold, better than choice silver. In Prov 10:20 the image of choice silver describes the tongue of the righteous. These connections could possibly explain why the scribe wrote *bḥr* instead of *bḥn*.

103. Dahood, *Psalms I*, 94, 161.

The parallelism between *ṣrp* and *bḥn* makes better sense than adopting the reading of the MT, "I chose you." The metallurgical imagery—the verb *ṣrp* 'to refine', the references to silver, and the reference to the furnace (*kwr*)—all support changing the MT, as does the evidence of 1QIsa[a].

Other references to God's testing of his people are found in Ps 81:8 and 95:9. It has been observed of these particular psalms that they have other similarities with chap. 48 of Isaiah.[104]

***kwr ᶜny* "furnace of affliction"**

The word *kwr* refers to a smelting pot or furnace for smelting metals (an Akkadian loanword, ultimately of Sumerian origin)[105] but in the Bible is always used as a figure of human suffering in punishment.[106] Deut 4:20, Jer 11:4, and 1 Kgs 8:51 speak of the furnace, the land of Egypt, as the place of suffering. In Ezek 22:18ff., it is used to describe Yahweh's wrath and his threat to melt the people in the middle of Jerusalem, as metals are melted in a furnace.

The phrase "furnace of affliction" is unique to this passage in Isaiah. It is an expression that recalls both an event in the distant past, the experience in Egypt (the exodus is a frequent theme in DI), and the more recent punishment at the hand of the Babylonians. Beuken[107] refers to several usages of the root *ᶜny* 'affliction' in DI. In 48:10, as well as 41:17 and 49:13, it refers to the affliction of Israel in exile. In 51:21 it refers to the affliction of Zion, the mother bereft of children. In 54:11 it is used of the forsaken wife.

Line 10b is a figure used both to compare and to contrast Israel's experience with the process of refining. The first line, 10a, states the comparison and then the contrast, "I refined you, but not like silver." The second half of the verse, 10b, explains the manner of Israel's refining. It was not in a furnace for refining metals, but in a "furnace of affliction." The lines are semantically parallel to one another:

I refined you // I tested you
not like silver // in a furnace of affliction

There is partial grammatical parallelism as well between the two first-singular pf. verbs with 2 m. s. suffixes.

104. See commentary on vv. 16 and 18ff. below, pp. 222 and 229.

105. See M. Ellenbogen, *Foreign Words in the Old Testament: Their Origin and Etymology* (London: Luzac, 1962) 83.

106. BDB 468.

107. W. A. M. Beuken, "Isaiah LIV: The Multiple Identity of the Person Addressed," *OTS* 19 (1974) 55.

48:11a. *lmᶜny lmᶜny* "for my sake, for my sake"

The repetition of the preposition *lmᶜn* has occasioned much comment. Some interpreters find the duplication redundant and emend the text. Duhm, for instance, wants to emend the second *lmᶜny* to *lmᶜn šmy* 'for the sake of my name'. This would fill in the missing subject of the following line. Others (e.g., Muilenburg, König, Torrey) consider the repetition to be an important part of the text. Levy calls the pattern a "passionate repetition" of God's assertion. Muilenburg and Torrey consider the repetition to be a fitting way to emphasize the climax of the section.

As indicated earlier, repetition is a frequently used device in DI. The threefold repetition of *gm* was noted above. In v. 9 the repeated word was found at the beginning of each line.[108] But in line 11a the pattern of repetition is somewhat different; it is an example of immediate repetition.[109] The word or phrase is used and then repeated without any intervening word.[110] Immediate repetition functions to give a sense of urgency.[111] The dramatic effect of immediate repetition is noted by Watson, as are the structuring effects.

Other examples of immediate repetition in DI include: 40:1, "comfort, comfort my people"; 48:15, "I, I have spoken"; 51:9 (also 52:2), "awake, awake, put on strength . . . awake . . ."; 51:12, "I, I am he . . ."; 51:17, "rouse yourself, rouse yourself, stand up . . ."; 52:11, "depart, depart, go out. . . ."[112] Most of these examples of immediate repetition are imperatives. This sampling shows this device to be a common one in DI. Those who would emend the text because of redundancy miss the dramatic emphasis of this verse. There is no reason to emend; there is ample reason to read the text as it stands. It is one of the many examples of immediate repetition in DI.[113]

Bonnard compares the threefold repetition in 48:9 and 11 with the threefold assertions of Yahweh's uniqueness in 42:8. There and here in

108. Anaphora.

109. König identifies this type of repetition as *epizeuxis* and refers to 40:1a for another example of it.

110. See Watson, *Classical Hebrew Poetry*, 277, for examples of this type of repetition in biblical and extrabiblical literature.

111. See Lam 4:15, "Away, away, do not touch!"; Judg 5:12, "Awake, awake, Deborah! Awake, awake, sing!"

112. The last repetition (Isa 52:11) is similar to Lam 4:15. Both verses use the m. pl. imv. *swrw* 'depart!' Both also repeat the command *ᵓl tgᶜw* 'do not touch!'

113. The device is also found in Isaiah 56–66. See 57:14, "build up, build up, prepare . . ."; 57:19, "peace, peace . . ."; 62:10, "go through, go through, prepare . . ." and "build up, build up, lift . . ."; 65:1, "behold me, behold me . . ."; 65:6, "I will repay, I will repay. . . ."

48:9 and 11, threefold repetition is a way of underlining the perfection of the one God. Also common to both passages is the emphasis on the name of Yahweh. In his dicussion of repetition in DI, Beuken refers to another example of the repetition of the preposition *lmᶜn*, in 45:3 and 4:

45:3c: So that (*lmᶜn*) you will know that it is I . . .
45:4a: For the sake of (*lmᶜn*) my servant . . .

He does not mention the third occurrence of the preposition in 45:6:

45:6: So that (*lmᶜn*) they will know . . . that I am the Lord . . .

He misses the patterning of the larger unit, 45:3–6, which, like 48:9–11, has a threefold repetition of *lmᶜn* that functions both as a rhetorical and a structuring device. It emphasizes the point that Yahweh (and Yahweh alone) acts, and it binds together the larger unit. The twofold repetition of *lmᶜny* is connected with the phrase *lmᶜn šmy* in 9a. This is an elliptical expression meaning "for the sake of my name."

***ᵓᶜśh* "I act"**

Many translations (e.g., the RSV and NEB) supply the direct object and translate 'I do (it)'. But Muilenburg, Volz, Clifford, and the JB read the verb absolutely. Such usage of *ᶜśh* is common in DI (see 41:4, 44:23, 46:4, and 48:3) and is found elsewhere in the Bible. BDB cites the absolute usage of *ᶜśh* 'to act with effect', used especially of Yahweh.[114] While it would not be incorrect to supply or understand the object *it* or *this* (referring back to the previously stated action), without a stated object the verb can be understood in a universal sense. As above, the act that produces results is Yahweh's speaking.

48:11b. *ky ᵓyk yḥl* "(for how will it be profaned . . . !)"

The MT reads *yḥl* as a *Niphal* 3 m. s. impf. of the root *ḥll* 'it will be profaned'. The LXX translates the phrase 'how should my name be profaned', supplying the subject *šmy*. Many translators adopt this reading, believing that 'my name' should be supplied from line 9a. The integrity of the entire section beginning with line 9a has been called into question. A variety of rearrangements of the lines has been suggested. Duhm, for instance, moves v. 9 to a position following v. 11. Skinner, on the other hand, sees v. 11 as a "parenthetical ejaculation" and calls it a marginal gloss related to v. 9.

1QIsa[a] presents another reading, *ᵓyḥl*, which Muilenburg seems to translate as a *Niphal* first singular, 'should I be profaned' (elsewhere in the Bible the *Niphal* first singular is written *ᵓḥl*, without the *yod*; see Ezek 22:26).

114. BDB 794.

The idea of the profanation of the name of God is a familiar motif from the book of Ezekiel. Ezek 20:9, 14, 22 repeatedly states: "I acted for the sake of my name, that it not be profaned . . ." (*ʾʿśh lmʿn šmy lblty hḥl . . .*). Other similarities with the book of Ezekiel have been identified in Isaiah 48, such as the description of the stubbornness of Israel in v. 4 and the reference to the furnace in v. 10. In fact many of the so-called "harsh" passages have been compared with similar phrases in Ezekiel. There is no no reason to read with 1QIsa[a].

The verb *ḥll* occurs two other times in DI, in 43:28 and 47:6. Both times the subject is Yahweh, and the object of the profanation is his own people. It is the princes of the sanctuary whom he profanes[115] in 43:28. In 47:6 it is his people whom he gives into the hands of Babylon. Here, with the subject as Yahweh's name, the reverse is true. It is not Yahweh's people who are profaned, but Yahweh himself who is profaned, presumably by their treacherous behavior, which has frequently been mentioned in the previous verses.

It should be noted that the form *ʾyḥl* in 1QIsa[a] could be read as the *Piel* first singular of the verb *yḥl* 'to wait, tarry'. This *Piel* verb occurs twice in DI, in 42:4 and 51:5. In these passages, the subject of the verb is not Yahweh, but the coastlands who wait for his law and his coming. The verb is used elsewhere in the Bible with human beings as subjects (see Job 6:11, 13:15; Ps 31:25; 33:18, 22, etc.). To read with 1QIsa[a] and consider Yahweh to be the one who waits or tarries would be unusual. One might possibly translate 'how should I tarry?' However, the unusual expressions of 9a and 9b are of a similar nature. There Yahweh withholds his anger for the sake of his name and restrains (a *hapax legomenon*) for the sake of his praise. We could read 11a as a passionate outburst of Yahweh similar to the ones in v. 9. His anger was barely held back in 9ab; in 11b he questions his restraint, "Should I tarry?"

However the verb is translated, either as a form of *ḥll* or less likely as a form of *yḥl*, 11b appears to be an impassioned outburst of Yahweh.[116] This line is elliptical in the extreme and does not lend itself to easy translation, but it does not appear to be out of place. Such an outburst seems appropriate following upon a declaration of the treachery and rebelliousness of the people.

115. Or 'pierces, slays'; see comment on 47:6 on the root *ḥll* (p. 122, above).

116. A similar use of *ky*, as the emphatic introduction to another emotional outburst, can be seen in 49:19, an incomplete sentence: "Surely (*ky*) your waste and desolate places, your devastated land. . . ." See also 42:14 for a passionate outburst of Yahweh, and especially the analysis of K. P. Darr, "Like Warrior, Like Woman: Destruction and Deliverance in Is 42:10–17," *CBQ* 49 (1987) 560–71.

48:11c. *wkbwdy lʾḥr lʾ-ʾtn*
"and my glory to another I will not give"

The poem returns to a familiar motif, the theme that Yahweh alone is God, and his glory and praise are to be given to no one else (see 42:8). This line sums up the previous section, lines 9a–11b. Yahweh acts for the sake of his name, his praise, and his glory. The line is parallel to 11a:

11a: *lmʿny lmʿny ʾʿśh* for my sake, for my sake, I act
11c: *wkbwdy lʾḥr lʾ-ʾtn* and my glory to another I will not give

Each line ends with a first singular pf. verb; 'my sake' is parallel with 'my glory'. Another parallel with v. 11c is 9b:

9b: *wthlty ʾḥṭm-lk* and for the sake of my praise I will restrain for you
11c: *wkbwdy lʾḥr lʾ-ʾtn* and my glory to another I will not give

There is the word-pair *thlty* and *kbwdy*, a balance between *lk* and *lʾḥr*, and concord in meaning between the verbs *ʾḥṭm* and *lʾ-ʾtn*. These lines are not contiguous, as is usually the case with parallel lines, but the connections among the lines, though complicated, can be seen.

48:12a. *šmʿ* "Listen!"

The *Qal* imperative of *šmʿ* begins this verse, and section. Unlike v. 1 (and vv. 14 and 16), the subject of the address is singular. In v. 1 it is the "house of Jacob" that is addressed; in 12a it is simply "Jacob."

48:12b. *mqrʾy* "whom I named"

The root *qrʾ* is used throughout the poem and is one of the underlying themes of the entire piece. This unusual form, a *Pual* participle with a first singular suffix, is a reminder of the same rare form in v. 8, a *Pual* impf. of the same verb. The *Pual* of this verb is infrequent, occurring in Isaiah six times (twice in chap. 48, four times in chaps. 56–66) and once in Ezekiel. Except for Isa 65:1, the word seems to be used in the sense of the giving of a new name (e.g., Isa 61:3, "you will be called 'oaks of righteousness' "; 62:2, "you will be called by a new name"). BDB translates Isa 48:12 "be called and privileged" and compares this to Isa 40:26, where God calls all the host by name.[117] We could translate literally "my called one," meaning either "one whom I called" or "one whom I named."

The KJV translates 'my called'. Those who favor this reading consider the passage to mean that Israel is a people who bear his (God's) name (Muilenburg). Levy interprets it to mean "called by my name" or "whom I called to be my people." Pieper and others refer to similar motifs, such as

117. BDB 896.

the one found in 41:8, which refers to the people whom Yahweh called. According to Pieper, the *Pual* participle in 48:12b is "equivalent" to the one chosen in 41:8. However, the *Pual* form is not identical with or equivalent to the *Qal*, and one might expect some nuance in meaning with the appearance of an unusual form. The motif of the name of God and the name or names of Israel is a key one in this poem. It appears that more is involved than the idea that God calls his people to himself. A more specific naming process, whereby the people receive a name, is involved. This verse only alludes to the process, but others (e.g., vv. 1b, 2a, and 8d) refer specifically to names and namings of Israel.

48:12cd. ***ʾny . . . ʾny . . . ʾny***

Here is another example of emphasis achieved by threefold repetition: the first line uses the pronoun *ʾny* twice; the second line repeats it a third time. The same pattern of repetition appears in lines 8ab above, where the particle *gm* appears in the same order.

> 48:12cd: *I* am he, *I* am first,
> Indeed, *I* am the last.
> 48:8ab: *No*, you did not hear; *no*, you did not know;
> *No*, in time past your ear did not open.

Another similarity in the patterning of these lines is the variation introduced into the third line by new words. The first line contains an internal parallelism, having the pattern ab/ac. The second line is semantically parallel, but elements have been added to the sentence. Line 12d adds the particle *ʾp* to reinforce the emphasis created by the repetition of *ʾny*. 8b expands 8a with *mʾz . . . ʾznk*.

The poem has switched abruptly from an identification or naming of Israel ("Israel, whom I named") to an identification of God. Muilenburg calls this threefold assertion in 48:12 "a characteristic triad, emphasizing the oneness, the uniqueness and the eternity of God."[118] More pertinent may be the fact that *ʾny* occurs a total of seven times in this section of the poem (v. 12, 13c two times, 15a two times, and 16c). Not only is the number seven frequently used in the Bible for structuring purposes, it has symbolic value as well. The sevenfold repetition of *qwl yhwh* in Psalm 29 is an obvious example of both structuring and symbolic use. There the phrase *the voice of Yahweh* binds together the body of the psalm and highlights Yahweh and his voice over against Baal's.[119] In this poem, Yahweh is identified, not

118. Isa 41:4 uses the same triad, though in a somewhat different arrangement: *ʾny yhwh rʾšwn wʾt-ʾḥrnym ʾny-hwʾ*.

119. See Freedman and Franke-Hyland, "Psalm 29," 241; W. F. Albright, *Yahweh and the Gods of Canaan*, 143.

only by what he does, but also by several names: Yahweh, God of Israel, Yahweh Sabaoth, Lord Yahweh, Redeemer, Holy One of Israel. The name Yahweh occurs seven times throughout the poem.

48:13a. *ʾp . . .*

The repetition of the particle *ʾp* serves to unite v. 13 to the previous one, in which Yahweh identified himself as the first and the last. Verse 13 continues on to explain more fully what it means that Yahweh is the first and the last.

ydy ysdh ʾrṣ	My hand founded the earth,
wymyny ṭpḥh šmym	and my right hand produced the heavens.

A common word-pair in the Bible is *šmym wʾrṣ* 'heavens and earth', which is familiar from Gen 1:1.[120] In other places where DI speaks of God in his creative activities, this traditional order is used.[121] The word-pair appears here in 48:13, but the traditional ordering is reversed to *ʾrṣ/šmym*. In either order, the terms are an example of merismus, indicating the totality of the universe.

Also common in the Bible is the pair *yd/ymyn.*[122] Dahood[123] cites several biblical[124] as well as Ugaritic texts in which *yd* specifically denotes 'left hand' and is paired with *ymyn* 'right hand'. In Isaiah 48 I have translated 'hand / right hand'. The word-pair can be understood to mean 'left hand / right hand', making it another example of merismus, like the word-pair 'earth / heavens' above. This would denote the totality of God's creative involvement. Or, it is possible to view the word-pair as an example of parallelism in which the first term, the more general "hand," is expanded or made more specific by the second, more specific, "*right* hand." This interpretation would be in line with Kugel's understanding of the way parallelism works; that is, the second term "is a going-beyond the first in its meaning."[125] Both interpretations are possible.

120. Gen 2:4 has the opposite order, but the Samaritan and Syriac reverse the terms to restore the more familiar, traditional order.

121. Isa 42:5; 44:24; 45:18; and 51:13, 16. See also 40:12, 45:8, 49:13, and 51:6.

122. Dahood, *Psalms III*, 449. The pair occurs in the Hebrew Bible, as well as in Ugaritic.

123. *Psalms I*, 163.

124. Judg 3:21, 5:26; 2 Sam 20:9–10; Ps 26:10, 138:7, and 139:10.

125. Kugel, *Idea of Biblical Poetry*, 29. In fact, for Kugel, the *essence* of parallelism is that the second part of the parallel lines goes beyond the first part (pp. 51–52). He defines his method with the formula "A, and what's more, B."

48:13b. *ṭpḥh* "produced"

The verb *ṭpḥ* is commonly translated 'spread out'. The verb is used twice in the Bible, here and in Lam 2:22.[126] Delitzsch reads the verb as the equivalent of a Syriac root meaning 'to spread out'. Skinner says the word is "Aramaic and does not occur elsewhere in the OT." Wade literally translates the word 'spanned out' from the cognate signifying a 'hand-breadth'. BDB relates it to an Arabic root meaning 'be full to overflowing, abound', and Aramaic 'extend, spread', as well as the late Hebrew word meaning 'span'. BDB translates Isa 48:13 'spread out' and Lam 2:22 'brought up, reared'.[127]

Hillers, in his treatment of Lam 2:20, discusses the *hapax legomenon ṭpḥym* and the related verb *ṭpḥty.*[128] Both are translated as having to do with child-rearing. Verse 20 is rendered 'children *they have raised*'; v. 22, 'those whom *I cherished* and brought up'. According to Hillers, his translation not only fits the context, but is also supported by an Akkadian cognate.[129] In Lamentations the verb *ṭpḥ* is parallel with the root *rbh, Piel,* 'to increase, bring up'.

In Isa 48:13ab the parallel verb is *ysd* 'to found, establish'. Bonnard discusses the term *ysd* as a metaphor that compares the fashioning of the universe to the construction of an edifice. He also states that when the word is used with Yahweh as the subject in reference to the construction of the cosmos it is only found in lyric hymns, such as Amos 9:6, Job 38:4, and so forth. Elsewhere DI speaks of "laying the foundations (*ysd*) of the earth" (51:13, 16), and there both times the parallel is "stretching out (*nṭh*) the heavens." The "stretching out" (*nṭh*) and "spreading out" (*mtḥ*, a *hapax legomenon*) of the heavens is part of the hymn to Yahweh, the incomparable creator, in 40:21.

In 48:13ab the poet moves from the notion of the laying of the foundations to the production (*ṭpḥ*) of the heavens. The verb seems to connote the idea of measuring out the heavens in the span of a hand, a motif of 40:12ff. The idea of an architectural production is extended if the verb is understood in this way.

This motif, the creation of the universe, is a common one in DI. He develops it in a number of ways, usually avoiding exact repetitions from poem to poem. Here in 48:13 (as in 40:21) for example, the poet has used

126. The related noun *ṭpḥym* occurs in Lam 2:20.

127. BDB 381.

128. D. Hillers, *Lamentations: A New Translation* (AB 7A; Garden City, N.Y.: Doubleday, 1972) 40.

129. Hillers refers to W. von Soden, "Zum akkadischen Wörterbuch, 6–14," *Or* n.s. 16 (1947) 77–78.

a more common term first, which is followed by an unusual or rare one. *Ysd* is followed by the rare *ṭpḥ*. *Nṭh*, a commonly used verb, is followed by the *hapax legomenon mtḥ* in 40:21. These are examples of what Alter refers to as the "predominant pattern of biblical poetry," moving from a common word in the first line to a "more literary or highfalutin term" in the second line.[130] Kugel's view is similar: the second word of the pair is "most often the rare and more literary term."

The examples used by Alter and Kugel are instructive and helpful in analyzing the specific texts that they use to demonstrate their ideas about parallelism.[131] The generalizations made from these specifics are less helpful. Numerous examples of the opposite phenomenon can be cited. The word-pairs "earth/heavens" and "hand/right hand" from 13ab (discussed above, p. 210) illustrate the point.

The pattern of parallelism between line 13a and line 13b is extremely regular, abc/a′b′c′, with grammatical and semantic parallelism. The use of word-pairs is a significant feature. As discussed above, the verbs are also parallel. In addition, both *yd* and *ymyn* have the first singular suffix. The only feature in 13b not repeated from 13a is the emphatic *ʾp*, which can be read as a double-duty particle, serving to emphasize both lines.

48:13d. *yʿmdw yḥdw* "they stand together"

The verb *yʿmdw* can be read as a jussive, as in the JPSV, "let them stand up!" Others translate it as a simple imperfect; the RSV reads "they stand forth together." North and the NEB translate "they sprang at once into being," but the verb *ʿmd* does not have this meaning anywhere in DI.

In Isa 44:11, another passage in which *yʿmdw* appears, there is a challenge to the idol-makers to gather together (*qbṣ*) and stand forth (*ʿmd*) and they will be put to shame. There is a challenge to anyone who would strive (*ryb*) with Yahweh's servant in 50:8. That one is to stand forth together with the servant for vindication. In 47:13, Babylon's counsels are invited to come forth and defend her; in 47:12 she is invited to stand fast (*ʿmd*) in her enchantments to protect herself. The only other use of *ʿmd* in DI is in 46:7. There the image is of the idol that stands fast (still, immobile) in its place. Scholars, especially those with form-critical interests,

130. Alter, *Art of Biblical Poetry*, 13.

131. However, see S. Geller, who disagrees with this understanding of parallelism. The binary nature of parallelism means that there is "a suspension of the final analysis of a couplet's meaning . . . until the end of the B line." He concludes: "this means that nothing could be more misleading than to view the B Line as a mere echo, simple variation or even reinforcement of its A line" ("The Dynamics of Parallel Verse: A Poetic Analysis of Deut 32:6–12," *HTR* 75 [1982] 35–56, especially p. 36).

point out the affinity of these verses with the language of the trial speech. In fact, Melugin considers 48:12–15 to be a trial speech.[132] The verb *ᶜmd*, along with *qbṣ*, is an example of legal terminology; those on trial are called to stand up and defend themselves.

The verb in 13d has as its subject the antecedent of the word *them* in 13c. This could refer to the heavens, the heavenly host (Torrey's suggestion) that Yahweh calls by name (see 40:26), or the heavens and the earth as witnesses to the proceedings.[133] Others consider the subject to be the gods to whom the challenge continues to be directed in 14b. Muilenburg sees the call as directed to heavens and earth and sees in it a typical theme in DI, the uniting of history and creation. This is another example of a line that can be read as the completion of the previous verse, or as the introduction to what follows.

48:14a–d.

This verse presents several difficulties. Numerous textual variants exist. Whybray and others see these difficulties as evidence of "textual corruption and interpolation." Some of the difficulty is due to the question of the addressees of the passage. A characteristic of the entire poem is the alternation between singular and plural and second- and third-person endings and pronouns. This feature is also seen in the *klkm* of 48:14a and *bhm* of 14b. 1QIsa[a], the LXX, and other manuscripts reflect readings that seem to attempt to address and overcome this problem.

Another difficulty is the phrase *yhwh ᵓhbw* in line 14c. Again, part of the problem is that Yahweh is in the third person, whereas in the preceding and following passages Yahweh speaks in the first person. Torrey also sees metrical difficulties here. Others point to theological problems in reading the passage with the MT.

The matter of where to divide the lines is also open to question, and again, scholars offer a number of suggestions. The regular parallelism of vv. 12 and 13 is not a feature here. A great deal of difficulty is caused by the elliptical nature of the passage. Some have commented on the absence of a preposition with *kśdym*. Others emend the MT in 14d because of what they consider to be an unusual expression or lack of parallelism.

132. R. F. Melugin, *The Formation of Isaiah 40–55* (BZAW 141; Berlin: de Gruyter, 1976) 137.

133. As in Isa 1:2. Stuhlmueller (*Creative Redemption*, 161) interprets this line as Yahweh's establishing his authority over the cosmos and invoking it as his witness. He also suggests that the creation motif was introduced to discredit the Babylonian gods, and thus he sees this as another part of the polemic against the gods. Stuhlmueller states that "the first creation is introduced and dropped very quickly, without elaboration," but see below, on v. 16 (pp. 223–24), where the motif is resumed.

Many emendations, both ancient and modern, are attempts to address and clear up difficulties with this verse. However, as Whybray indicates, the text is difficult. The proposed changes do not clarify the text, since the changes are made piecemeal and do not offer an overall view of the passage that is convincing.

48:14a. *hqbṣw klkm wšmᶜw* "Gather, all of you, and hear!"

Virtually all modern commentaries render the two verbs as imperatives, but in the MT only *hqbṣw* is in the imperative. The vocalization of the second verb is problematic. Elsewhere in the poem, the simple imperative form is used (vv. 1 and 16), but here the pointing of the verb is closer to a perfect form.[134] Commentaries (except for Beuken)[135] pass over the anomalous form. The LXX and 1QIsa[a] read both forms as 3 m. pl. impf.

1QIsa[a] also has *kwlm* for *klkm*, reading "let them gather (or they will gather), all of them, and hear." A change of the suffix to the third person does not seem to be warranted, especially since the alternation of second and third person is a characteristic feature of this poem. I tentatively render two imperatives and understand Israel to be the object of urgent commands. Along with the verb *šmᶜ*, a second verb, *qbṣ*, has been added, which emphasizes the urgency of the command and points to the serious nature of the call, since it is often used in the language of the call to trial.[136]

48:14b. *bhm* "among them"

Many manuscripts read *bkm* 'among you'. Those who adopt this reading understand that Israel is being asked, "Who of you have declared these things?" that is, "Which of you have told of the coming of Cyrus?" (see 14c ff.). Those who read with the MT see the pronoun as referring to the false gods of the nations, who are being challenged about their abilities to tell future events. In previous chapters there are frequent challenges to the

134. Freedman suggests it looks like a slightly erroneous form of a 3 m. s. *Qal* pf. with a 3 m. s. suffix, "he will hear it," though the final vowel militates against such a reading (D. N. Freedman, personal correspondence).

135. Beuken's only contribution is to mention the LXX and 1QIsa[a].

136. Y. Hoffman ("The Root QRB as a Legal Term," *Journal of Northwest Semitic Languages* 10 [1982] 67–68), on form-critical grounds, considers 48:1–16 to be a trial speech. Begrich limits the trial speech to vv. 1–11, but Hoffman points to the following characteristics of a trial speech, which are found in vv. 1–16: address to audience in second-person plural, rhetorical questions with *my*, frequent use of *šmᶜ*, use of other technical terms such as *qrb*. However, R. N. Whybray has a different idea about the genre of the trial speech and puts 48:1–11 into the category of disputation (*The Second Isaiah* [Sheffield: JSOT Press, 1983] 34–38).

nations or their gods to declare the things to come (41:21–26, 44:7, 45:21). In 48:14b, reading with the MT, it is now Israel who is being challenged to identify any others who might be able to tell of events to come. This is a rhetorical question, a familiar device of the author, and a reply must be in the negative.

***ᵓt-ᵓlh* "these"**

The sign of the definite direct object is to be noted. Duhm calls it "sonderbar." Its use in poetry is infrequent.[137] In DI, the def. article is frequently (but not solely) used in connection with participles that describe Yahweh's action.

Torrey also observes that the sign of the definite direct object is "unexpected." He emends the text here, rearranging lines and letters. Noting that in parallel passages in which DI uses the expression "who foretold this?" he always uses *zᵓt*, Torrey emends *ᵓt* to *zᵓt*. For *ᵓlh*, Torrey reverses the order of the letters and reads instead *hᵓl* 'the [one] God'. Torrey then reads *hᵓl* as the subject of 14c (*yhwh ᵓhbw*), which he finds metrically unsatisfactory. (It is not a "satisfactory three-beat line." However, it should be noted on this point that Torrey's concern for the three-beat line is sporadic and inconsistent. His methodology in this regard is highly subjective.) His translation of 14bc is: "What one among them foretold this? The One God, Yahwe [sic], loves him. . . ."

As indicated above, the object of the verb is understood to be the future events, especially the advent of Cyrus. The following lines somewhat clarify the phrase "these (things)."

48:14c. *yhwh ᵓhbw* "Yahweh-loves-him"

The LXX omits Yahweh and translates *ᵓhb* as a participle, 'loving (you) . . . ' instead of as a pf. verb. 1QIsa[a] reads *ᵓwhby*, which could be

137. On the occurrence of prose particles in poetry, see Andersen and Forbes, "Prose Particle," 165–83; and D. N. Freedman, "Another Look at Biblical Hebrew Poetry," in *Directions in Biblical Hebrew Poetry* (ed. Elaine R. Follis; JSOTSup 40; Sheffield: JSOT Press, 1987) 11–28. In the chapters under consideration (46–48) the sign of the definite direct object is used only twice: here and in 47:14. The frequency of occurrence of all the prose particles in chap. 48 is 2.642% (Andersen and Forbes, "Prose Particle," 174). These consist of six occurrences of the definite article between vv. 1–6. The relative pronoun *ᵓšr* does not occur. Freedman considers that "practically everything with a reading of 5% or less will be poetry" ("Another Look," 13). While there should be no question that this chapter is poetry, based on the evidence of the prose-particle count as well as other considerations, there is no convincing argument to explain why the prose particles are used on these rare occasions. As Andersen and Forbes indicate, while it is generally known that Hebrew poetry makes sparse use of prose particles, "the reason for this fact is not understood" ("Prose Particle," 167).

translated as the participle form 'my loved one'. 1QIsa[a], however, does not omit Yahweh, as the LXX does, and there are other changes in this verse in 1QIsa[a] that further complicate matters. Duhm, Skinner, and others, under the influence of the LXX, translate 'My friend shall perform his purpose'. The title "my friend" is used of Abraham (see 41:8), but most (except for Torrey) consider the reference in 48:14 to be to Cyrus.

Levy translates 'the beloved of the Lord', literally 'Yahweh-loves-him'. He reads this as a symbolic name and cites other symbolic names in Isaiah (7:3, 8:1) and Hosea (1:6, 9).[138] Muilenburg also prefers this reading and comments on the frequency of such compound titles in the ancient Near East, especially for royal figures. He cites the Cyrus cylinder, in which Cyrus is referred to as "Cyrus . . . whose rule Bel and Nebo love . . ." and a line in the Esarhaddon prism, "'Builder of the temple' he called my name."

As discussed above, naming is an important motif in this passage, and the appearance of yet another unusual name, while surprising (or "awkward" or "harsh"), should not be considered antithetical to the development of the poem.[139] North is disturbed by the statement that Yahweh loves Cyrus and tries to avoid seeing it in the text.[140] His position on the matter is striking in its internal contradiction. He says: "If we keep MT we must bracket 14b as a later expansion. But it looks basically original, not the kind of marginal comment that a scribe would dare to invent." North seems caught in a trap of his own making. He reads the text as it stands and reads it correctly.

It should be remembered that the references to Cyrus throughout DI are striking and perhaps were considered scandalous by the poet's audience. The reference to Cyrus as "the anointed" in Isa 45:1 is another example of what might be considered an awkward or shocking title. To emend a passage for reasons of harshness or awkwardness seems to subvert the very purpose of the line. The idea of Cyrus as one whom Yahweh loves and uses for his purposes, as messiah, is harsh or unusual and awkward. We should not expect the poet to soften this idea; in fact, the harshness or awkwardness is just what we might expect.

48:14c. *ḥpṣ* "purpose"

The idea that Yahweh's purpose or pleasure will be accomplished has been stated in 46:10 (see discussion, pp. 60–62). There Yahweh was to call

138. Stuhlmueller adds to this list the symbolic names in Isa 1:26 and 7:14 (*Creative Redemption*, 158 n. 526).

139. See Muilenburg, Levy, and Skinner.

140. The statement seems to put Cyrus on the same level as Abraham, and it seems to North to be more intimate a term than "shepherd," which is used in 44:28.

a bird of prey from the east, a man of his counsel, to accomplish his purpose. In 44:28 Yahweh says of Cyrus, "He is my shepherd; he will fulfill (*šlm*) my purpose (*ḥpṣ*)." In 48:14 also, the idea is that the one whom Yahweh loves is Cyrus, and he will accomplish Yahweh's purpose. The only other place the noun *ḥpṣ* appears in chaps. 40–55 is 53:10, where it is the servant in whose hands the purpose of Yahweh will prosper. In chaps. 46, 48, and 53, it is be noted that the name or identity of the one who will do this is not specifically mentioned. Whybray suggests that the reason for the oblique reference in chap. 48 is that "possibly too obvious a reference to him may have been dangerous at some points."[141]

48:14d. *bbbl wzrᶜw kśdym*
"against Babylon and Chaldea is his arm"

The difficulties of 14c continue into the following line. Most commentators and translators need to add a preposition and/or a verb, in order to make sense of the line. The LXX reads "on the seed of the Chaldeans," eliminating the 3 m. s. suffix on *zrᶜ* and reading it in construct with *kśdym*, adding the preposition *b-* and reading *zrᶜ* as 'seed' instead of 'arm'. Duhm and Skinner adopt this emendation. The NEB and Herbert, apparently reading *zrᶜ* as the verb from the root 'to scatter, sow', translate 'the Chaldeans shall be scattered'.

The targum inserts a verb, 'shall reveal', and Slotki's translation is apparently informed by this. He reads 'show his arm on the Chaldeans'. Others read *ᶜśh* from line c as a double-duty verb governing both *ḥpṣw* (line c) and *zrᶜw* (line d). But, as Wade observes, the zeugma is "rather violent."

Torrey excises the references to Babylon and Chaldea in chaps. 40–55 and reads simply, "he executes his pleasure and his might." McKenzie sees some credibility in Torrey's excision because, "in the references to Cyrus the purpose of Yahweh is not directed to Babylon and the Chaldeans." Further, McKenzie sees "no significance in itself" in the fall of Babylon, except as "an exhibition of Yahweh's judgment." He goes on to say further that this line betrays an inconsistency on the part of the prophet, though he admits that a rigorous consistency is not necessary and that it is "not impossible" for the prophet to have written this line.

141. The noun *ḥpṣ* is related to a number of other nouns in the Bible, but in reference to Yahweh it occurs only in Isaiah 40–55 and Judg 13:23. In the latter passage, Samson's mother states that it was not "Yahweh's pleasure to kill us," even though she and her husband had spoken with an angel of the Lord and asked his name. This is one of a number of times in which rare words or unusual combinations in Isaiah 40–55 also appear in the Samson stories. The significance of this phenomenon is unclear but bears further investigation.

Such an opinion does not recognize the importance of chaps. 46 and 47 to the development of the prophet's message. Babylon and the gods of Babylon are doomed to go into exile. The contrast of the fate of the Babylonians to that of Jacob/Israel is essential to the prophet's work. Throughout DI Cyrus is portrayed as the one who will accomplish God's purpose, beginning with 41:2ff., where Cyrus comes from the east, defeating kings and nations before him. Clifford especially emphasizes the importance of the downfall of Babylon as more than "an exhibition of God's judgment."[142] The downfall of Babylon is a mirror image of and complement to the success of Zion. McKenzie has woefully understated the importance of the references to Babylon here and in the rest of chaps. 40–55.

Delitzsch's translation differs from the others' in that he considers *zrᶜ* to be the subject, not the object, of the phrase (with the verb understood from 14c). He translates: "He whom Jehovah loveth will accomplish his will upon Babylon, and his arm (accomplish it) upon the Chaldeans." He objects that to read 'arm' as the object of the verb 'accomplish' is "quite unintelligible" (McKenzie makes a similar observation). Delitzsch (and later North) also rightly observes the phenomenon of the double-duty preposition, though he does not call it that and uses as an example of this usage the function of *lmᶜn* in lines 9a and b.

Another difficulty translators have with 14cd is the division of the lines. The RSV demonstrates one method of division, reading three lines:

yhwh ᵓhbw	The Lord loves him;
yᶜśh ḥpṣw bbbl	he shall perform his purpose on Babylon,
wzrᶜw kśdym	and his arm shall be against the Chaldeans.

The NEB divides 14cd into two lines, the first a very long line ending with "against Babylon," the second a short line ending with "and the Chaldeans shall be scattered."

yhwh ᵓhbw yᶜśh ḥpṣw bbbl
wzrᶜw kśdym

BHS divides 14cd as follows:

yhwh ᵓhbw yᶜśh ḥpṣw
bbbl wzrᶜw kśdym

Most translations divide 14cd into three lines, as in RSV, or into two lines, as does BHS. The JB is an example:

142. Clifford, *Fair Spoken and Persuading: An Interpretation of Second Isaiah* (New York: Paulist, 1984) 46.

"My beloved" will perform my pleasure
with Babylon and the offspring of the Chaldeans.

However, especially in the case of those who agree with BHS, these translations place the preposition *bbbl* in the second line, divided from the verb *yʿśh*, creating an awkward situation.

1QIsa[a] (which departs from the MT on a number of points in v. 14 and in North's opinion "makes 'pie' of the text") omits the conjunction on *zrʿw* and reads *bbbl zrʿw kśdyym.* One ordinarily finds 1QIsa[a] adding conjunctions rather than omitting them, so the absence here of the conjunction is worth noting.

Reading with 1QIsa[a] can clarify a number of questions regarding this text. First, there is no need to emend by adding a verb or to read *ʿśh* as the unfelicitous double-duty verb. The two lines are independent clauses, not dependent, as most read. I read line 14d as a nonverbal clause, the subject of which is "his arm" (i.e., "his might") and the predicate the prepositional phrases "against Babylon, against Chaldea." The *bet* is an adversative and serves a double-duty function for both Babylon and Chaldea, as observed earlier by Delitzsch and North.[143] The noun also serves double duty for both predicates. Freedman's suggestion is that *bbbl* and *kśdym* form a broken construct chain ("Babylon of the Chaldeans") on the same pattern as "Ur of the Chaldeans" in Genesis.[144] Ezek 23:15 has a similar phrase, *bny bbl kśdym.* The sense of the verse would be "his arm will accomplish his purpose against Babylon of the Chaldeans."

The figure of the arm of Yahweh in Isaiah 51 is used by Frank Cross as an example of the combination of historical and mythological elements in Second Isaiah. The battle at creation is conflated with the Exodus-Conquest motif. This union of history and myth was used to formulate an eschatology based on the analogy of old things with new things.[145] In chap. 48 the figure of the arm of Yahweh only alludes to what is more fully developed elsewhere in chaps. 40–66. However, this too is placed within the contexts of creation (vv. 13ab and 16bc) and history (with the references to Cyrus, Babylon, and the Chaldeans in vv. 14cd and 15bc).

48:15a. ***ʾny ʾny dbrty ʾp-qrʾtyw*** **"I, I spoke; indeed, I called him"**

The repetition of the pronoun *ʾny* and the use of *ʾp* (see above at 46:11, pp. 64–65, for a discussion of this adverb) serve to add emphasis.

143. See also Williams, *Hebrew Syntax*, §242 / p. 44.
144. D. N. Freedman, personal correspondence.
145. Cross, *Canaanite Myth*, 136–37, 174.

Muilenburg considers this verse to be an answer to the question posed in line 14b ("Who among them declares these?").

dbrty . . . qrʾtyw . . . hbyʾtyw . . . hṣlyḥ

"I spoke . . . I called him . . . I brought him . . . he prospered . . ."

Muilenburg also points to the four verbs in v. 15, which also add emphasis. North refers to the four verbs as "emphatic and swiftly moving" and sees all of these techniques as characteristic of DI. This technique has been discussed above in 46:4 (pp. 39–40), where the author piles verb upon verb, and in 46:5 (pp. 42–43), where there is a similar profusion of verbs. (In those cases, the poet used the first person pronoun and the particle *ʾp* for further emphasis.)

The four verbs are repeated in a pattern similar to that of 46:11; in three of the four verbs are repeated from 46:11. There Yahweh was going to accomplish his purpose (*ḥpṣ*) by calling (*qrʾ*) a bird of prey from the east. There he stated: *ʾp-dbrty ʾp-ʾbyʾnh*. In 48:15 the same verbs, *qrʾ*, *dbr*, and *bwʾ*, are used, though in this verse the poet uses all perfect verbs, unlike the variation between perfect and imperfect in 46:11. In both cases *dbrty* is used absolutely, with no object indicated. The following verbs, *dbrty, qrʾtyw* and *hbyʾtyw*, have 3 m. s. suffixes, referring to the one whom Yahweh called and brought. Here, as in 46:11, Cyrus's advent is attributed to Yahweh's activity.

hṣlyḥ drkw **"his way prospered greatly"**

Many versions, including the LXX, the targum, and the Syriac, read the first person here: "I made his way prosperous." The NEB translates, "Wherever he goes he shall prosper"; the JPSV reads, "He shall succeed in his mission"; and the *Hiphil* of *ṣlḥ* is translated causatively in BDB.[146] However, Freedman suggests the *Hiphil* here is not transitive or causative but intensive or internal.[147] In fact, such usage can be seen in Isa 55:11,[148] in Ps 1:3,[149] and in Judg 18:5. In Judges the subject is *drk*, just as it is in Isa 48:15.

It is not necessary to emend with the LXX here. The idea in 48:15, as in the other texts, is that it is through the agency of Yahweh, especially his speaking, that fruitful action is accomplished. Reading with the MT, the pattern that emerges is three first singular pf. verbs followed by a 3 s. pf. verb. The first three describe Yahweh's action; the fourth is the result of Yahweh's action. The notion that Yahweh speaks and acts and that things happen is a key motif in this poem and in chaps. 40–55 as a whole. This is

146. BDB 852.

147. D. N. Freedman, personal correspondence.

148. "(My word) will prosper greatly in the thing for which I sent it."

149. "Everything he (it) does is very successful."

one of the proofs for the exiles in Babylon that their faith ought not to falter. Yahweh, unlike the gods of the Babylonians, is active on behalf of his people.

48:16a. *qrbw . . . šmᶜw . . .* "Draw near . . . hear . . ."

The m. pl. imperative is resumed, as in vv. 1 and 14 above. As noted in v. 14 above, the affinity with legal language is obvious in the imperatives that summon the audience to assemble and to pay attention.[150] While line 16a contains two imperatives, it is a short line with only seven syllables. The two imperatives are grammatically parallel, but the line stands alone, without any corresponding adjacent parallel. The emphasis is on the message that follows.

48:16b. *lʾ mrʾš bstr dbrty*
"not from the very first did I speak in hiding"

Two phrases bear further examination here: the expressions 'from the very first' (*mrʾš*) and 'in hiding' (*bstr*). Regarding the latter, a similar phrase appears in 45:19: *lʾ bstr dbrty*, which the RSV renders, 'I did not speak in secret'. Both of these passages are commonly interpreted to mean that Yahweh has always spoken out openly and clearly.[151] However, this does not seem to be the case in Isaiah 48, where Yahweh specifically refers to secret things he refused to reveal to Israel (see 48:7–8). This passage, as well as others that describe God's secrecy, must be examined to determine what point the poet is making by putting this claim in the mouth of Yahweh. The word order here should be noted. The emphasis in 45:19 is on the denial of secrecy, the assertion of openness. Here, an additional word has been added to the phrase; *lʾ* precedes *mrʾš*, 'not from the first'. The word order seems to emphasize that even from the very first God spoke openly.

The adverbial *bstr* is often used in the Bible to indicate immoral behavior. For example, David's taking of Bathsheba and slaying of Uriah (2 Sam 12:12) was done *bstr*; the worship of idols or enticement to worship idols *bstr* is condemned in Deut 13:7 and 27:15; the cowardly behavior of Zedekiah is done *bstr* in Jer 37:17 and 38:16.[152] The passage in Isa 48:6 can be an indication that Yahweh does *not* speak in such a manner.

150. Westermann, *Isaiah 40–66: A Commentary* (trans. D. M. G. Stalker; OTL; Philadelphia: Westminster, 1969) 200; however, Melugin, reads v. 16 as a disputation meant to authenticate the prophet's mission (*Formation*, 200).

151. See R. N. Whybray, for example, *Isaiah 40–66* (NCB; London: Marshall, Morgan & Scott/Grand Rapids, Mich.: Eerdmans, 1981) 111, 132.

152. An exception to such use of this expression may be Prov 21:14, where the giving of a gift *bstr* seems to be a prudent move done in order to avert anger.

There is, however, another use of the expression *bstr* that may be pertinent here. Scholars frequently point to similarities between the language and thought of Ps 81:13–16 and Isa 48:18–19.[153] A comparison that seems to have gone unmentioned is that between Ps 81:8 and the passage in question. In Ps 81:8 God describes the time when he did not know Israel. They were a people in distress and, hearing their call, he answered them "from/in the secret place of thunder" (*bstr rʿm*).[154] Ps 18:12 and Job 22:14 both describe Yahweh's presence as hidden in the darkness of clouds. In Job 22 Eliphaz chides Job for charging that God is hidden by the clouds and cannot see the affairs of people on earth. In each of these passages, Yahweh is described as hidden in the clouds. In both Psalms 18 and 81, Yahweh speaks from his hiding place in the clouds.

Elsewhere in Isaiah 40–55 there are indications that Yahweh was considered distant, or unseeing, a God who ignored his people. In 40:27 Israel protests that "my way is hidden [root *str*] from the Lord." In 45:15 someone, perhaps the nations, asserts that Yahweh is a God who hides (*msttr*) himself. The meaning of the assertion in 48:16b could be that from the very beginning, God was aware of the affairs of people, a defense against the accusation made in 40:27. The ways of people were not hidden from God by the clouds, as Job 22 claims. God was not in a hiding place, unaware of his creation, outside the reach of his people. The idea seems to be (especially when read in conjunction with 16c) that God was always present, always aware, never in hiding. This contradicts the idea in Psalm 81 that there was a time when Israel was unknown to God, and that God spoke to Israel from his hiding place of thunder. According to Melugin the manner of speaking in 48:16 is through the prophetic word.[155]

Much controversy exists about the precise identification of the expression *mrʾš* 'from the very ⟨rst' and similar expressions referring to the first and the last: *rʾšwn*, *mršqt*, *mʾz*, and others.[156] Some suggest that it refers generally to the remote past or to the events of the exodus and the conquest.[157] Stuhlmueller tries to show that, especially in 40:12–31, it does not refer to the first creation, but to Yahweh's present lordship of the universe.[158] However, in 40:21 *mrʾš* is parallel to *mwsdwt hʾrṣ* ('the founda-

153. For a discussion of this, see below (p. 229).

154. See Dahood, *Psalms I*, 265, for the translation of *b-* as 'from'.

155. Melugin, *Formation*, 139.

156. See Stuhlmueller, *Creative Redemption*, 286, for a chart of these words and their distribution.

157. E. J. Kissane, *The Book of Isaiah* (Dublin: Browne & Nolan, 1943) 2.17, 139–40; J. Fischer, *Das Buch Isaias übersetzt und erklärt* (2 vols.; Die Heilige Schrift des Alten Testaments; Bonn: Hanstein, 1937–39) 2.38.

158. Stuhlmueller, *Creative Redemption*, 147–48.

tions of the earth'). In 48:16a *mrʾš* can be interpreted by the corresponding expression *mʿt hywth* 'from the time it happened', referring to the time of creation (see below, line 16c).

The poem states in a number of ways that God has been closely involved with directing activities relating to his people from the very beginning. Those who read 48:16b as an indication that God has hidden nothing from his people, he has never been secretive with them, have ignored the rest of the poem. Throughout this poem Yahweh has stated that there are a number of things that have been hidden from his people. However, even though God has not revealed everything to his people, this does not mean that he has not been with them from the beginning. Indeed, he has spoken openly with them whenever he spoke (see Levy's interpretation of 16bc below).

48:16c. *mʿt hywth šm ʾny*
"from the time it happened, there I was"

Scholars point out that there is no antecedent to the pronoun suffix 'it', and a number of possibilities are suggested. Muilenburg finds it "obscure," but goes on to say that "the reference is doubtless to what was spoken from the beginning." Pieper says 'it' is "the Cyrus matter" of vv. 14 and 15. Levy summarizes the meaning of lines 16a–c: Not from the beginning, when the project of crossing the desert was first initiated, have I spoken in a manner that was secretive or mysterious. I have been aware of it and its consequences, and have informed you of them.

Levy also compares 48:16c with Prov 8:27, where Wisdom says with regard to God's creating of the heavens *šm ʾny* 'there I was'. Skinner says that the pronoun cannot refer to the world or the creation, because they would need to be expressed. He thinks that the implied antecedent "must be . . . the purpose of Jehovah against Babylon." The beginning would therefore be the origin of revelation or of the series of prophecies which are now being fulfilled. However, the world and the creation are specifically mentioned in 13ab, and the pronoun refers to *ʾrṣ* of 13a. In view of the fact that the entire section (vv. 12–16) has several examples of merismus (first and last, earth and heavens) that function to express totality,[159] I interpret here not an allusion to Cyrus or the exodus, but another reference to the totality of Yahweh's involvement and power from the beginning of creation. The sevenfold repetition of the personal pronoun *ʾny* in this section is yet another way that the author expresses the universality of Yahweh's authority. It is not out of order to understand 'the beginning' in this passage as the time of creation. The non-specific nature of the suffix 'it'

159. Watson, *Classical Hebrew Poetry*, 321–24.

may have been intentional, to allow the reader to entertain a number of possible antecedents.

48:16de. *wʿth . . . wrwḥw* "And now . . . his spirit"

The line has vexed scholars over the ages, because of the abrupt change in subject. Many commentators suggest that it is a gloss or an interpolation. However, as Herbert indicates, the problematic nature of the passage hardly makes it suitable as a gloss.

Translators have rendered the passage in various ways:

RSV	And now the Lord God has sent me and his Spirit.
JPSV	And now the Lord God has sent me, endowed with His spirit.
JB	And now the Lord Yahweh, with his spirit, sends me.
NEB	Not included in the text; offered in a footnote.
Volz	And now I send him on his way.
Kissane	And now I Jahweh have sent deliverance.
Levy	And now the Lord God hath sent me, and his spirit hath filled me.

The RSV and JPSV translate "the Lord God" as subject and the speaker and "his spirit" as objects of the act of sending. The JB reads with the Vulgate and targum, seeing both Yahweh and his spirit as subject. The NEB, with Duhm and others, considers the passage to be out of place. Volz emends, deleting "Lord Yahweh," based on the LXX and an Arabic manuscript, and reading the *ʾalep* of *ʾdny* as the first person subject of *šlḥny.* He also reads *lʾrḥw* for *rwḥw,* saying that *lamed* and *ʾalep* are frequently obliterated in manuscripts. Kissane adopts some of Volz's emendations but for 'spirit' reads 'deliverance', based on Exod 8:11, where the feminine noun *rwḥh* is translated 'respite, relief'. According to Kissane, this reading "gives the required antithesis between chastisement and deliverance," therefore completing the prophet's argument. Levy adds *mlʾny* because "the abrupt ending of the verse seems to imply that a word has fallen out."

Volz's suggestions are the least probable. There is no textual evidence that any letters were omitted, and his suggestion that the *ʾalep* of *ʾdny yhwh* should be attached to the verb calls into question his reading with the Vulgate and Arabic versions that "Lord Yahweh" is omitted. Kissane further complicates an already-difficult passage, though he seems to read correctly that *wʿth* indicates a concluding summation to what has preceded.

Against the rendering of the JB, in which "his spirit" is read as subject along with "Yahweh," Delitzsch, Skinner and Levy point out that never in the Old Testament is such a distinction made between Yahweh and his spirit. The spirit is nowhere mentioned as one who sends the prophets.

Any idea of the connection of the spirit with prophecy is rare in the preexilic prophets (Whybray) and is more characteristic of later prophecy such as Zechariah (see, e.g., Zech 4:6 and 7:12).

Levy's addition to the text is based on his opinion that this addition would "remove the difficulty of interpretation." This does nothing, however, to answer the problem of the abrupt change in speaker from Yahweh to some unnamed person.

The speaker has been variously identified as the prophet, the servant, Cyrus, or the editor who added these words as a gloss. Clifford believes that this is the second time the prophet has modestly referred to himself, the first being Isa 40:6. Just as Yahweh spoke publicly about the first things, now a word will be spoken by a spirit-filled individual. Gitay also sees this assertion as an announcement that the prophet will announce new things in public.[160] He sees it as fitting the claim above that the new development was not revealed to Israel in advance. Delitzsch sees reference to the servant here and feels that this passage is an introduction to chap. 49, where the servant speaks his own words.

Another first-person speaker who is sent (*šlḥ*) and who has the spirit (*rwḥ*) upon him is the prophet in 61:1.[161] The prophet there is sent to proclaim a message, and here in 48:16 the sense is similar. After the exclamation *wᶜth*, an announcement of some magnitude can be expected, perhaps a message antithetical to what has preceded.[162] It appears to be a parenthetical aside of the prophet. This is also an example of enjambment.

48:17a–e. *gʾlk . . . ʾlhyk . . . mlmdk . . . mdrykk*
"your redeemer . . . (etc.)"

The use of the singular suffix ending is noteworthy. Whybray observes that this section (vv. 17–19) is different from vv. 12–16 by virtue of the singular address. However, this observation is incorrect. Verse 12 is an address in the singular, not the plural. It is only in lines 14ab and 16a that there is a plural form of address. This phenomenon of alternating between singular and plural has been noted above.

yhwh gʾlk qdš yśrʾl . . . yhwh ʾlhyk . . .
"Yahweh, your redeemer, the holy one of Israel . . . Yahweh, your God"

Yahweh is identified here by several names, continuing the important theme of naming that pervades the poem. Muilenburg points to the familiar juxtaposition of the terms *Redeemer* and *Holy One*, which also

160. Gitay, *Prophecy and Persuasion*, 220.

161. The spirit also rests on the servant in 42:1, so that he may establish justice in the earth.

162. See Muilenburg.

appeared in 47:4 (as well as in 49:7 and 54:5). The arrangement of these names, however, is not identical. Isa 47:4 reads, "Our redeemer—Yahweh of Hosts is his name—is the Holy One of Israel." In chap. 48 the word order is reversed. We can read, "Yahweh Our Redeemer, the Holy One of Israel," though the RSV divides 48:17 into two separate lines:

> Thus says the Lord,
> Our Redeemer, the Holy One of Israel.

The poet uses these combinations several times but does not seem bound to any fixed order. In fact, the opposite seems to be the case. The poet eschews fixed formulas when it comes to these names, and seems to prefer variety. Other names by which Yahweh has been identified in this poem include Yahweh without any qualifiers (1d), the God of Israel (occurs twice, in 1e and 2b), Yahweh of Hosts (2c), and Lord Yahweh (16d). Only once does the poet repeat a title, the God of Israel (1e and 2b).

mlmdk . . . mdrykk **"who teaches you . . . who leads you"**

A familiar technique of the poet is to identify Yahweh through his activities, expressed in a series of participles; here is another example of this technique. The concept of Yahweh as a teacher is more familiar in the later books, according to Whybray. The idea of teaching and being taught is infrequent in Isaiah 40–55, but whenever it is used, Yahweh is the teacher. In 50:4 the servant is helped by God to become like those who are taught. In 54:13 all the sons of Israel will be taught by Yahweh. In 48:17 also, Yahweh acts as teacher, as one who makes Israel to walk in the way it should walk. The only other use of this root in chaps. 40–55 is 40:14, where Yahweh questions any suggestion that he needs to be taught to walk on the path of righteousness—"Who taught [Yahweh] the path of righteous; who taught him knowledge?"

The two participles *mlmdk* and *mdrykk* are parallel to one another grammatically and lexically. The two lines, 17d and 17e, are parallel in meaning, but the infinitive *lhwᶜyl* is balanced in the next line by the preposition + noun *bdrk* and the impf. 2 m. s. verb *tlk*. The repetition of the root *drk* here is also to be noted. This partially contributes to the feature of assonance with the repetition of the letter *kap* in all three words of 17e. Another possible example of assonance is in the repetition of *mem* and *lamed* in 17c.

lhwᶜyl **"to profit"**

The root *yᶜl* 'to confer or gain profit, benefit' is always used with a negative or in questions implying negativity.[163] It is commonly used to refer to false gods who are of no benefit (see Isa 44:9, 10 and Jer 2:8). In

163. BDB 418; see North, who points to a few exceptions, in Isa 47:12 and Job 30:13.

47:12 above, Babylon was taunted with words that had a sense of irony: "Perhaps you will be able to profit; perhaps you will inspire awe." It is clear that Babylon will be able to do neither.[164] In 48:17, with Yahweh as the teacher, the prospect of gaining benefit or profit is a positive one; the sense is that Yahweh is doing this "for your advantage." Elsewhere, the poet has continually pointed to the foolishness of idols and their inability to do anything at all to aid their subjects. The word 'profit' may be used intentionally as another way to contrast Yahweh's actions on behalf of his people to the actions of those who are of no profit, those who can confer no benefit, the gods of the other nations.

The idea that Yahweh shows his people the way in which they are to walk is another way of saying that people are to keep the commandments (see Ps 119:35). Muilenburg relates "the way" to Israel's proper conduct and her observance of Yahweh's torah. That Yahweh's teaching was not observed is lamented in the following lines.

48:18a. *lwʾ* "If only"

The particle *lwʾ* can be used in an optative sense, to express a wish or to state a case that has not been or is not likely to be achieved.[165] Williams refers to the latter as conditional.[166] It is used to introduce unreal conditions, either in the past, present, or future. The optative can be used with the perfect verb to refer to the past or with the imperfect to indicate a hope for the future. In 48:18a it is used with a perfect verb and alludes to the fact that in the past, Israel did not hearken to God's commands.

hqšbt . . . wyhy . . . lʾ ykrt . . .

"you had hearkened . . . it would have been . . . it will not be cut off"

In line 18a the verb is *hqšbt*, a perfect verb, expressing a wish for the past: "If only you had hearkened. . . ." GKC indicates that here and in Isa 63:19 the particle *lwʾ* is used "to express a wish that something expected in the future may already have happened."[167] This curious expression points to problems that translators have with the tenses of the verbs that follow. Some translators read all the verbs as if they were imperfect and express a hope for the future. For example Westermann translates:

> O that you would hearken to my commandments!
> Then your peace would be like a river . . .
> Their name would never be cut off or destroyed from before me.

164. See above, chap. 47, for a discussion of this (p. 139).
165. BDB 530; GKC §151e/p. 477.
166. Williams, *Hebrew Syntax* §459 / p. 75.
167. GKC §151e / p. 477.

Clifford, the NAB and the JPSV also translate all the verbs in the future tense. While three of the verbs are in the past tense (*hqšbt* of 18a in the perfect and the *waw*-consecutive *wyhy* of 18b and 19a), the final two verbs are imperfect (*ykrt* and *yšmd*). These translators have attempted to normalize the text and read the entire passage as an impassioned wish for the future. Kissane supports this interpretation, arguing that, if the last line were to be translated in the past, it would mean that Israel's name had been cut off. This, says Kissane, would be inconsistent with v. 9 above, where Yahweh withholds his anger so as to avoid cutting off Israel. Kissane does not entertain the possibility of translating the imperfect verbs of 19c as future.

Other translations, of which the JB is representative (see also the RSV), read all the verbs as expressing wishes about the past:

> If only you had been alert to my commandments
> Your happiness would have been like a river. . . .
> Never would your name have been cut off or blotted out before me.

Here the verbs (perfect, imperfect, and *waw*-consecutive) are read as expressing unrealized wishes about the past.

Delitzsch repoints *wyhy*, not reading it as a *waw*-consecutive, so that only 18a expresses a past wish; the following lines describe what Israel could be like in the present. North, like Delitzsch, reads v. 18a as expressive of a past wish, but unlike Delitzsch, he reads *wyhy* as pointed in the MT. These lines, vv. 18b and 19a, refer to the past, when Israel might have achieved a state of peace and prosperity but did not. Reading these lines as referring to the future would suggest that there is no longer any hope for Israel, but North feels that 19c and 19d are a message of assurance and hope for the future.

It is the last argument, that of North, that has the most to recommend it, though Delitzsch's reading also has merit. There is no difficulty in reading *hqšbt* as a perfect verb, expressing an unrealized wish about the past. Much of the poem is directed to Israel, who has been recalcitrant from the very first. Reading the verbs in 18b and 19a as references to the past would indicate a reference to the exile: because Israel did not hearken to God's commands, she did not live in peace or see her children multiply. Reading *wyhy* as a simple imperfect, with Delitzsch, would not effect a change in meaning. The poet could be referring to the present status of the exiles in Babylon and explaining how Israel had come to be in such a state.

The imperfect verbs of 19c are to be read as a promise of God that the people (their name) will not be cut off or destroyed. This is in much the same vein as 9c. There, God promised not to cut off the people, in spite of their rebellious behavior. In 19c, as in 9c, there do not seem to be any conditions to what God will do in the future.

Many similarities have been noted between Isa 48:18–19 and Ps 81:13–16.[168] Both contain a similar wish: that the people would hearken or listen (Psalm 81 has the infinitive absolute of *šmᶜ*, while Isaiah 48 has the perfect of *qšb*). Psalm 81 adds the wish that Israel would "walk in my ways." Isa 48:17 had previously stated that God would make his people walk in the way he would show them.

There are "remarkably close" parallels, as Westermann has indicated. Both passages describe what happens when Israel hearkens to God's commands. Ps 81:14ff. promises that enemies will be conquered, those who hate Yahweh will "cringe before him," and that Yahweh will feed his people with fine food. Isa 48:18ff. describes the results in a symbolic fashion, using similes and metaphors to describe the results. Israel's peace and righteousness will be like "The River," like the waves of the sea; her descendants will be as numerous as the grains of sand.[169] One of the differences between Psalm 81 and the verses in Isaiah 48 is that the wishes of Psalm 81 are expressed in the imperfect (except for the infinitive absolute *šmᶜ*)[170] and refer to wishes for the future, while in Isaiah 48 these were unrealized hopes about Israel's past.

B. Anderson differentiates between Psalm 81 and Isaiah 48 in that the psalm is "addressed to the cultic situation of the *present*, appealing for a covenant renewal now which could affect God's future action"; second Isaiah, on the other hand, has taken this promise of blessing "out of the context of covenant renewal in the present" and refers it to behavior in the past that led to the catastrophe of the exile. He sees it as a reference to irrevocable acts of the past that "prompt an expression of divine anguish about what might have been." Anderson also emphasizes that Israel's future salvation does not depend on the renewal of the covenant or on a change in their behavior, but rather, the grounds for Israel's hope comes from God's faithfulness, above and beyond the terms of the Mosaic Covenant.[171] This is why Second Isaiah emphasizes instead the unilateral covenants with Noah in 54:7–10 and David in 55:3–5.

A perplexing feature about both of these poems is the alternation between singular and plural forms and the shift between second- and third-, or first- and third-person references. Dahood explains the shift in Ps 81:16

168. See B. W. Anderson, "Exodus and Covenant in Second Isaiah and the Prophetic Tradition," in *Magnalia Dei: The Mighty Acts of God (G. E. Wright Volume)* (ed. F. M. Cross, Werner Lemke, and Patrick D. Miller Jr.; Garden City: Doubleday, 1976) 339–60; C. Westermann, *Isaiah 40–66*; idem, "Jesaja 48," 356–66.

169. For a discussion of these images, see below (pp. 230–34).

170. But see Dahood (*Psalms II*, 266), who reads it as an imperfect.

171. Anderson, "Exodus and Covenant in Second Isaiah," 341–55.

from third-person subject and object to first-person verb and second-person object as an example of "court style." He does not have a satisfactory explanation for the other phenomenon but notes that its recurrence throughout the psalm should caution against reading textual corruption.

mṣwty **"my commands"**

McKenzie reads *mṣwty* as a reference to God's teaching in covenant law and compares it to the teaching of Deuteronomy. Scullion also finds similarities between the sentiments of v. 18 and Deuteronomy 28. But Clifford translates 'my authoritative words' and sees a special nuance in the word, as used in DI. He translates the root √*ṣwh* in 48:5 as 'directed' ('my statue directed it') but in 45:12 as 'command' ('its hosts are under my command'). Special meaning is given to this word, according to Clifford, because the prophet avoids references to the Mosaic Covenant.[172] The sense intended by the prophet is "to give authoritative direction."

This is the only occurrence of the noun *mṣwh* in Isaiah 40–66. In fact, elsewhere in Isaiah (29:13 and 36:27, the only two other occurrences in the whole of Isaiah) it does not refer to God's commands but to those of humans. It would be hard to demonstrate that the poet is using deuteronomic phraseology in 48:18 based on a single occurrence of the root in chaps. 40–55. Clifford's precise definition of the word also goes beyond what can be demonstrated from DI. The sense is that the people should obey God's commands.

48:19b. ***mʿtyw*** **"its grains"**

The word is a *hapax legomenon.* The root *mʿh* is compared with the late-Hebrew use of *mʿwt,* meaning 'tiny weights, small coins' (Levy), 'kernel' (Skinner), or '[melon] seed'.[173] Some consider the suffix to refer back to "the sea" and translate 'like its bowels', presumably to signify "multitude" by all the things within the sea. Delitzsch says that it is impossible to see why the interior of the sea would be referred to as *mʿwt* instead of *mʿym* if this were the intention. The LXX reading, "like the dust of the earth," in addition to the Vulgate, supports the reading 'grains'. Delitzsch and Torrey point to the obvious paronomasia between *mʿyk* (1QIsa^{a} does not have *mʿyk*) and *mʿtyw* (see above, line 1c, pp. 170–71, for a similar play on the words *mʿh* and *my*).

172. Anderson (ibid., 341), finds no clear allusions to Moses, the Sinai theophany, the Decalogue, or a conditional covenant in Second Isaiah. In fact, he states, "Nowhere does Second Isaiah place any stress upon the Mosaic covenant" (p. 340).

173. BDB 589.

48:18b–19b. ***knhr . . . kgly . . . kḥwl . . . kmᶜtyw***
"like a river . . . like waves . . . like sand . . . like its grains"

Following the line that expressed the wish that Israel had hearkened to God's commands is a series of similes that describe what might have happened to Israel. Four lines make up the series of similes, and these lines betray a remarkably uniform structure, with both grammatical and semantic parallelism.

Each line-pair begins with *wyhy,* followed by the object of the comparison (*kap* + noun), and then the subject of the comparison (noun + 2 m. s. suffix). In the second line of each line-pair, the order is reversed, forming a chiasm: it begins with subject (noun + 2 m. s. suffix) and follows with the object (*kap* + noun):

wyhy knhr šlwmk	Then it would have been like-The-River your-peace
wṣdqtk kgly hym	and-your-righteousness like-the-waves-of The-Sea.
wyhy kḥwl zrᶜk	Then it would have been like-the-sand your-seed
wṣʾṣʾy mᶜyk kmᶜtyw	and-the-issue-of your-loins like-its-grains.

On the level of the word, the words of lines 18b–19b are semantically or lexically parallel with one another (River // waves of The Sea; peace // righteousness; sand // its grains; seed // issue from loins). Grammatical parallelism is also present on the level of the word: *knhr* and *kḥwl* are morphologically equivalent, as are *šlwmk* and *zrᶜk.* The pattern of parallelism on the level of the word could be described as follows:

(Then it would have been) like-The-River your-peace	a	b
and-your-righteousness like-the-waves-of The-Sea.	b′	a′
(Then it would have been) like-the-sand your-seed	c	d
and-the-issue-of your-loins like-its-grains.	d′	c′

On the level of the line, a different pattern of parallelism can be seen, and the relationships between the individual line-pairs and the larger unit of the four lines have a pattern different from that described above. The first line-pair uses images of water and the word-pair peace/righteousness as items of comparison. The second line-pair employs a different image, that of grains of sand compared with descendants. On the level of the line, the lexical parallelism would be described as an aa′/bb′ pattern:

Then it would have been like-The-River your-peace	a
and-your-righteousness like-the-waves-of The-Sea.	a′
Then it would have been like-the-sand your-seed	b
and-the-issue-of your-loins like-its-grains.	b′

Another way to describe the relationship between the line-pairs is in terms of syntax. This pattern can be described as follows:

V / prep. + obj. / subj. + 2 m. s. suffix a
subj. + 2 m. s. suffix / prep. + obj. b
V / prep. + obj. / subj. + 2 m. s. suffix a
subj. + 2 m. s. suffix / prep. + obj. b

There is some variation in the second line of each pair (18c and 19b). In 18c and 19b both subjects ('righteousness' and 'issue of loins') are modified by the addition of a 2 m. s. suffix. However, in 18c it is the object of the simile ('like the waves of the sea') that has the form m. pl. construct + noun; in 19b it is the subject ('issue of your loins') that is a m. pl. construct + noun. At the same time that these lines reveal a very uniform structure and a high degree of parallelism, the poem avoids exact parallels by varying the grammatical pattern slightly.[174] The stress and syllable count of the lines are almost identical.

The word-pairs used by the poet here in 48:18–19 have a traditional ring. However, again, there is some variation and divergence from the expected patterns. Common in Biblical Hebrew and in Ugaritic is the word-pair *ym* and *nhr.* The pair in 48:18, however, is in the reverse order and is between *nhr* and *gly hym.* Dahood also cites the combination *ṣdq/šlwm* as a parallel word-pair occurring in Biblical Hebrew and in personal names in Ugaritic.[175] Again, the pairs are in reverse order in 48:18. A more familiar combination is that of *ṣdq/mšpṭ,* which appears in Amos 5:24 in another simile involving the figure of cresting waters and flowing streams.

The pairing of *ḥwl* ('sand') and *mʿtyw* ('its grains') is unique to this verse. A more common combination in the Bible is the phrase *kḥwl hym* 'like the sands of the sea', part of the figure of the promise of Abraham's descendants (see Gen 32:13). Thus we can read 'sand' to be an elliptical expression for 'sands of the sea' and the pronoun in 'its grains' to refer to the sea or the river.

Zrʿ is paired with *ṣʾṣʾ* in both Isaiah and Job.[176] The parallelism between *zrʿ* and *ṣʾṣʾ* in Isa 44:3 is used in a promise of Yahweh to Jacob. God promises to pour his spirit on Jacob's descendants, his blessing upon his issue. A further similarity between Isa 48:18–19 and 44:3 is the use of the figure of flowing water. In 44:3–4 water will be poured on the dry ground, and the fruitfulness of the people is described as being like amply watered grass and willows.

174. See M. O'Connor, *Hebrew Verse Structure* (Winona Lake, Ind.: Eisenbrauns, 1980) 88ff., for a discussion of the various levels of parallelism in Hebrew poetry.

175. Dahood, *Psalms III,* 450, 455.

176. *Ṣʾṣʾ* only occurs in these two books of the Bible.

The images in vv. 18 and 19 are connected in some way with water: the river (which many associate with The River, the Euphrates), the sea, the sands and grains (of the seashore). The simile that compares the descendants of Israel to the sand is a familiar one and easy to comprehend. The descendants are like the sands, in that they are numerous, too numerous to be counted.

The other simile, "river" / "waves of the sea," is not as obvious. Part of the problem is due to the subjects—*šlwm* and *ṣdqh*.[177] Both of these nouns are evocative of a number of interpretations. Some examples of translations of the two nouns include: 'prosperity/success' (NEB), 'happiness/integrity' (JB), 'well-being/prosperity' (Levy), and the like. As Scullion and others have indicated, the words *ṣdq*/*ṣdqh* in Second Isaiah have a variety of nuances. But a further difficulty with this simile is in the figures "river" and "waves of the sea." Scullion interprets the figures to be indicative of strength. Israel's welfare will be "like the strongly-flowing Tigris or Euphrates, and not like a Palestinian wadi, her prosperity like the waves of the sea, ever rolling in, as one can observe from any elevated point near the Mediterranean coast." Others interpret the figure as one indicating dependability, as of the perennial stream, the Euphrates, in contrast to the undependability of the Palestinian wadi (e.g., Skinner, Wade, and others).

Most scholars place Second Isaiah in Babylon, preaching to the exiles there, and perhaps this is the reason for their explanation of this figure. However, it is not necessary to look to the rivers of the Mesopotamian Valley to understand this simile. The word *nhr* is not restricted to reference to the Tigris and/or Euphrates Rivers. Furthermore, Scullion's explanation has the reader overlooking the Mediterranean coastland as well as the Mesopotamian Valley, which stretches the imagination.

Another way that this figure can be understood is as a reference to the wadis in Palestine, which some read as a figure of undependability. In his analysis of Psalm 126, Dahood discusses two similes for the restoration of Zion.[178] When Yahweh restored Zion, the people became like the "sands of the sea," like "torrents in the Negev" (v. 4).[179] The very feature of the

177. Beuken discusses the connection between *šlwm* and *ṣdq*/*ṣdqh* in Isaiah 54 ("Isaiah LIV," 61–63). In 54:14 *ṣdqh* is parallel to *šlwm* and to *nḥlh*. The "field of meaning" of the word *ṣdqh* includes a "state of peace, well-being and prosperity," but also has "cosmic dimensions." Beuken also states that *ṣdqh* with a suffix referring to Israel rather than to God occurs only in two places—48:18 and 54:17. The significance of this is that "it shows to what extent this city [the city personified in chap. 54] will be the concentration of God's creative activity" (p. 62).

178. Dahood, *Psalms III*, 216–21.

179. See Dahood's commentary (ibid.) on the problematic *kḥlmym* of Ps 126:1.

wadi that some see as negative is interpreted as a positive figure by Dahood:

> The period of the rains is particularly glorious in the Negeb, the arid district to the south of Judah, where the brooks are dried up all summer long. Thus the sand suggested by the term Negeb refers back to *ḥwl*, "sands" of vs. 1. When the winter rains come, the desert rejoices and blossoms like a rose (cf. Isa xxxv).

A similar figure, used to describe Israel's prosperity (*šlm*), appears in Isa 66:12. There are two more similes using the figure of water, *knhr* ('like a river') and *knḥl* ('like a stream'). The figure of a stream that is 'overflowing' (*šwṭp*) especially evokes the ideas to which Dahood has referred. It must be allowed that this symbolic language is evocative of a number of possible figures, from the dependability and predictability of a river, the power of the waves of the sea, to the periodic and spectacular occurrences of the winter rains in a wadi.

48:19cd. ***lʾ-ykrt . . . mlpny***

This is an example of enjambment. While there is an internal parallel formed between the two imperfects *lʾ ykrt* and *lʾ yšmd* ('it will not be cut off' and 'it will not be destroyed') in the first half of the line-pair, the second half of the line-pair is made up of the subject of the two verbs and a prepositional phrase. Thus the two lines form one sentence: "His name will not be cut off or destroyed from my presence." Neither of the adjacent lines is parallel to this sentence.

48:19d. ***šmw*** **"his name"**

The LXX reads 'your [masculine singular] name', the reading preferred by Duhm, Muilenburg, and others. But as mentioned above, such emendation does little to solve the overall problem of changes of person in the poem. The importance of the *name* and *naming* is a motif in the poem, and in line 19d the promise is that his name (Jacob/Israel's) will not be cut off or destroyed.[180]

48:20ab. ***ṣʾw mbbl*** **"Go forth from Babylon!**
brḥw mkśdym **Flee from Chaldeans!"**

The lines are short, two-stress lines, five syllables each, and are parallel to one another semantically as well as grammatically. The imperative of *yṣʾ* is parallel with the imperative of *brḥ*. The prepositional phrase *mbbl* is par-

180. There is a possibility that the word *šmw* is linked to 16de above and is another statement of the prophet about himself.

allel with *mkśdym.* The short lines and the repetition of imperatives (six in all) in v. 20 give a sense of urgency.

Whybray comments on the note of haste implied by the use of *brḥ*, as does North. North and Muilenburg both draw attention to the similarities of this verse with Jer 51:6. Muilenburg suggests the possibility that Jeremiah may be based on Second Isaiah.[181] North interprets Isa 48:20 in the light of the Jeremiah passage ("Flee from the midst of Babylon . . . do not be destroyed in her punishment") and interprets this as a warning to the exiles. If they do not hurry out of Babylon, they will suffer the same fate, destruction, that will come upon the city. Begrich and Melugin find similarities between these instructions and the warning given to Lot by the angels, in Gen 19:17, that he was to take his family and flee for his life.

Whybray, while noting the haste implied in the command to flee, does not see any note of fear or confusion.[182] Most other scholars, unlike North, read the lines as a jubilant cry of celebration rather than a warning. The command to "go forth from Babylon, flee from Chaldea" receives a number of different interpretations from commentators. Whybray compares the form of the lines to a military order of withdrawal of troops, as in 1 Kgs 12:16, "To your tents, O Israel!" McKenzie reads the lines as a summons from the prophet, "speaking in his own name." Muilenburg reads it as an impassioned song that draws imagery from the Exodus. For Westermann it is a summons to go forth, which anticipates the actual event itself. Wade's opinion is that Babylon has already been captured, and the people are now being exhorted to return home. Almost all commentators (except for North), however, are agreed that a similar call to depart is repeated in Isa 52:11–12. There Israel is to depart, but not in haste and not in flight, in contrast to the departure from Egypt at the time of the Exodus. In 52:11–12 the departure is portrayed as a solemn procession, in which the people are to purify themselves and to bear the vessels with them as they depart. Isa 35:8–10 and 51:9–11 have the same theme and depict a note of triumph and jubilation.

The following lines of 48:20–21 support the notion that what is being described is a procession rather than a flight from possible destruction. Of special note is the line immediately following 20ab, "In a ringing voice declare." The singing of songs appears in 42:10–12, 52:8, and 54:1, and the context is one of joy. Millar considers the new songs sung in Second Isaiah

181. Whether DI is dependent on the oracles in Jeremiah 50–51 or vice versa, has not been determined. However, the similarities between the two bear further investigation, with regard to literary techniques, motif and theme, as well as the question of dating.

182. See also Delitzsch. *Brḥ* means to depart with the rapidity of flight, not literally to flee.

to be announcements that Jerusalem's warfare was ended, and he sees a similar motif in Isa 24:14. These also may be allusions to shouts of victory after success in battle.[183]

48:20c–g. ***hgydw . . . hšmyʿw . . . hwṣyʾwh . . . ʾmrw***

Following the two imperatives urging Israel to flee are four imperatives (three *Hiphil,* one *Qal*) commanding Israel to call out and declare a message to the ends of the earth. The first two lines of v. 20 are short lines of equal length and are parallel. Lines 20 c–g reflect a different sort of parallelism.

c In a ringing voice declare—
d Announce this—
e Send it forth to the end of the earth—
f Say: "Yahweh redeems
g his servant Jacob!"

Arranged in this manner, the first four lines have imperatives relating to the notion of declaration: *ngd, šmʿ, yṣʾ, ʾmr.* The lines are not strictly parallel, as were the previous two, but are complementary. Each of the lines defines the announcement with a feature not found in the others. It could be said that each line has an element that serves a double-duty function for one or more of the other lines.

Line 20c tells how the announcement is to be done: "in a loud voice." Line 20d has the object *zʾt*: "announce *this*". Line 20e tells where the message is to be announced: "to the end of the earth." And 20fg is the message to be announced.[184]

The lines are of uneven length, both regarding stress and syllable count:

	syllable count	stress
ṣʾw mbbl	5	2
brḥw mkśdym	5	2
bqwl rnh hgydw	7	3
hšmyʿw zʾt	4	2
hwṣyʾwh ʿd-qṣh hʾrṣ	8/9	3
ʾmrw gʾl yhwh	6	3
ʿbdw yʿqb	4	2

183. Millar, *Isaiah 24–27,* 112–15. The author of chaps. 24–27 is a disciple of Isaiah who shared his vision for the reconstruction of Israel.

184. This is similar to the situation in 40:1–11, in which there is a buildup about who is to give the message, to whom it is delivered, and so forth, until the very end, where the message "Behold your God!" is spelled out.

In the last two lines, there is another example of enjambment, with the sentence running over into the following line. Several such examples are found within this chapter. The entire verse is united by the repetition of imperatives, urging Israel to leave Babylon and proclaim a message of salvation.

48:21ab. *wlʾ ṣmʾw bḥrbwt hwlykm*
"And they did not thirst when in the waste places he led them"

The term *ḥrbh* in Isaiah 40–55 usually refers to the ruins or waste places of the destroyed cities.[185] This is not the usual term used to describe the wilderness in the wanderings after the Exodus experience. Many commentators see allusions in vv. 20–21 to the first Exodus. The word *ḥrbh* calls to mind not only the wilderness wanderings, but the present state of the ruins of the countryside of Judah as well.

Another example of ellipsis is present in this line.[186] In prose one would expect the conjunction *ky* or *ʾšr* 'when'. Some early commentators were not aware of this feature. Delitzsch, for instance, translates:

> And they thirsted not:
> He led them through dry places;
> he caused water to trickle out of rocks for them.

As in 20fg, 21ab can be read as one long line of 4 stresses and 11 syllables, or two short lines of 2 stresses each with a combination of 4 and 7 syllables. The compound sentence is yet another example of enjambment.

48:21c–e. *mym . . . mym*

The lyrical nature, imagery, and artistry of these verses have been acknowledged by numerous commentators. To North it is "an exquisitely wrought poem." Delitzsch refers to the "palindromic repetition" of *mym* at the beginning and ending of the section. Torrey speaks of the dramatic qualities of the writer and the "extraordinary vividness of his imagination." Alter offers these verses as an example of the elegance of DI's poetry. It is both the structure and the imagery that give this section the quality of elegance.

Alter describes the parallelism and the way it works to structure the poem.[187] One of the ways that parallelism works to develop meaning, according to Alter, is that the second line (verset) often heightens or intensifies

185. See 44:26, "ruins of Jerusalem"; 49:19, "your cities and your ruins"; 52:9, "ruins of Jerusalem"; see, however, 51:3, where the word is parallel with *mdbr* and *ʿrbh*.

186. Torrey cites Isa 51:1 as a similar example.

187. Alter, *Art of Biblical Poetry*, 20.

or specifies the meaning of the first line.[188] He refers to this as an explanatory chain. In vv. 20–21, the chain operates to make the meaning of each succeeding line more specific and definite.

> What does it mean that God "redeemed" Israel (first verset)? They were not thirsty in the desert (second verset). How could they not have been thirsty?—because He made water flow from a rock (third verset). How did he make water flow from a rock?—by splitting it so that the water gushed forth (fourth verset).[189]

It should be noted that Alter reads this section as beginning in 20fg, which can be read as part of a unit with 20a–e, the series of imperatives discussed above. However, he says that "the verset in question 'hovers' between the two lines [20e and 21a], serving a double function. . . ."[190] North understands the development of this section, especially 21c–e, as Alter does, though he describes the function of the *waw*-consecutive, rather than the function of the parallels. He translates: "He made water flow out of the rock for them, by splitting the rock so that water gushed out." He explains: the *waw*-consecutive, *wybq*ᶜ, "is explicative of, not subsequent to, 'he made water flow.' " The second *waw*-consecutive, *wyzbw*, expresses the logical consequences of what precedes.

The "palindromic repetition" to which Delitzsch refers is an example of an envelope, in which the word *mym*, a palindrome, appears at the beginning of 21c and the end of 21e. In addition to the envelope formed by the repetition of *mym*, the repetition of *ṣwr* 'rock' is also noted. Two of the verbs, *nzl* and *zwb*, are synonyms. They are another example of intensification of meaning in parallelism discussed by Alter and Kugel. The first verb used, *nzl*, has the meaning 'flow, trickle, drop, distil'.[191] Isa 45:8, for instance, speaks of the skies trickling and the clouds dripping (*nzl*) righteousness. The second verb, *zwb*, has the meaning 'flow, gush'.[192] In Ps 78:20 *zwb* is parallel with *šṭp* 'overflow'. While *nzl* has the sense of gently dripping or trickling waters, *zwb* intensifies the idea. The waters do not just trickle from the rock, they gush out. The specification of meaning in the relationship between the *Hiphil* of *nzl* 'he made flow' and *bq*ᶜ 'he struck' is observed by Alter. The relationship between the various elements of the lines is complex and subtle. The parallelism can be described in several ways and affects the sense of the lines so that they can be understood in several different ways.

188. See also the discussion of 13ab above (pp. 210–12).
189. Alter, *Art of Biblical Poetry*, 20.
190. Ibid., 215–16 n. 17.
191. BDB 633.
192. BDB 264.

Inclusio often acts as a structuring, as well as a rhetorical, feature to link together two parts of a line or a larger section of a poem. However, 21ab can also be read as part of the section, since the verb *ṣmʾ* 'thirst' begins the theme carried through to the last line. As Alter has shown, the section can also be seen to incorporate the previous line.

There is no certain way to scan these lines. North sees the possibility of reading the stress count for v. 21 as either 2:2/3:3,

wlʾ ṣmʾw : bḥrbwt hwlykm 2:2
mym mṣwr hzyl lmw : wybqʿ-ṣwr wyzbw mym 3:3

or, with Köhler, as having a 2:2/2:2/2:2 pattern,

wlʾ ṣmʾw : bḥrbwt hwlykm 2:2
mym mṣwr : hzyl lmw 2:2
wybqʿ-ṣwr : wyzbw mym 2:2

The count of 3:3 seems strained. The latter pattern, as read by Köhler, describes the text more accurately.

Lines 21ab and 21c are alike in that there is no intralinear parallelism in either line. Both are long sentences, again examples of enjambment. Lines 21de are an example of ab/a′b′ parallelism. These two short lines are grammatically parallel. The verses are tied together by the theme of the abundance of waters. Within chaps. 40–55 (41:18, 43:20, and 49:10), the theme of waters in the wilderness is used and often recalls the Exodus tradition. The idea of water coming from a rock calls to mind the incidents at Kadesh in Num 20:10, and at Massah and Meribah (Exod 17:6), where Moses (and Aaron), calling together the rebellious people, caused water to gush from a rock. These events are celebrated in Ps 78:15, 20, and 105:41. The language is similar in all of these passages.[193]

The lines in 48:21 recall both events in the distant past when God sustained his rebellious people in the wilderness with water, and foretell events to come in the not-too-distant future when Jacob/Israel will again be sustained by God in the wilderness. This time, they will not be attempting to escape from an enemy but will be returning home to Zion. The verbs describing these events are perfects and *waw*-consecutives and are translated as past tense. This form, according to Westermann, is unique to DI. He calls it an "'eschatological' hymn of praise," because it assumes that God's final act of redemption has already taken place.

193. A similar incident occurs in Judg 15:19 where God splits (*bqʿ*) a hollow place, and water comes out, in order to slake Samson's thirst.

48:22. "There is no peace, says Yahweh, for the wicked."

Most commentators consider this line to be a gloss, saying that it is not related to the context and concluding that it is "taken from" Isa 57:21, which is similar, though not identical:[194] "There is no peace, says my God (*ʾlhy*), for the wicked."[195] The line functions here as an editorial insertion, a divider, marking an end to this portion of the prophet's message. Levy cites Krauss's opinion that this verse functions to divide chaps. 40–66 into "three equal scrolls, each of seven [sic] chapters" (the division is nine, not seven).[196] Commentators have also noticed similarities with the very end of the book, 66:24. The same condemnation of the wicked occurs there. Instead of *ršʿym*, the people are called *pšʿym*. Both expressions occur throughout the book of Isaiah. Lack shows connections between chaps. 1 and 66, especially with regard to the theme of sinners and the judgment to come upon them.[197]

In contrast to the general assessment of this verse, Torrey says that it "sums up a large portion of the preceding discourse. . . . This poem ends with the same note with which it began." Delitzsch also interprets the line in this context to be a "divine utterance, which pierces the conscience like the point of an arrow" and brings this ninth prophecy to a close. The godless are excluded from the coming salvation. Kaufmann considers the division original, and sees it as organically related to the prophetic composition. Each of the closing chapters (48, 57, and 66) has a similar structure, including castigation and consolation.[198]

Structure

Introductory Notes

Of the three chapters under consideration, chap. 48 is by far the most complicated to analyze. Elliger calls it "a problem child [Schmerzenskind] of criticism."[199] The difficulties of the text are evident in the great number

194. Skinner and Muilenburg.

195. Freedman cites the combination *yhwh* in 48:22 and *ʾlhy* in 57:21 as a good case of the breakup of a stereotyped expression (personal correspondence).

196. This may be an attempt to break up the book into roughly equivalent units: 40–48 has 2,678 words, 49–57 has 2,086, and 58–66 has 2,358 (Freedman, personal correspondence).

197. Lack, *Symbolique*, 140.

198. Y. Kaufmann, *The Babylonian Captivity and Deutero-Isaiah* (New York: Union of American Hebrew Congregations, 1970) 61–62.

199. *Deuterojesaja in seinem Verhältnis zu Tritojesaja* (BWANT 4/11; Stuttgart: Kohlhammer, 1931) 185.

of variants and emendations, both ancient and modern. Contradictions and/or tensions within the text have perplexed scholars for ages, and the unity of the passage is repeatedly called into question. The most obvious tensions are: the shifts between second and third person and between singular and plural addresses to Jacob/Israel; the assurances of salvation and the harsh accusations of the very people to whom salvation is promised; the assertion that there were hidden things that God did not make known to Jacob/Israel "until today" and the claim that God never spoke in secret; and the presence of single lines within the text that appear to be unrelated to their context.

A solution to these difficulties was proposed by B. Duhm in 1892. Duhm's thesis was that there was a division in the book of Isaiah, not only between chaps. 1–39 and 40–66, but also between 40–55 and 56–66, and that the latter chapters were from a later period. He further proposed that certain portions of 40–55, especially the servant songs, were also from this later period. Portions of chap. 48 were also attributed to a later hand by virtue of their "harshness." Since that time there has been a widespread tendency among DI scholars to characterize the message of DI as one of salvation and comfort and to exclude or attribute to another hand material that has a negative tone or seems to subvert the theme of salvation. Westermann's treatment of chap. 48 follows the same lines as Duhm's.

Elliger's work is a good example of this tendency to attribute material to a later hand. He attributes so much material to Trito-Isaiah that no identifiable figure stands out from the shreds of material that remain as Second Isaiah. While his commentary on Second Isaiah was not completed and does not include a detailed commentary on the chapters in question, he offered his opinion on chap. 48 in another work.[200] There he suggested, along with Duhm and many others, that chap. 48 could best be understood if the so-called harsh utterances were attributed to Trito-Isaiah and that what remained was the work of Second Isaiah.[201]

A similar criterion for dividing the text is put forth by Whybray. He refers to the "abrupt alternations of mood" or "tenor." He contrasts the "somber" portrayals, the "tone of divine grief and regret," and the "denunciatory material" to the mood of encouragement and the proclamation of salvation.

These scholars divide the text based on considerations of theme or content. Another approach was taken by Begrich, who directly addressed the problem of the shift between singular and plural in the text (in vv. 1–11)

200. Elliger, *Deuterojesaja in seinem Verhältnis.*

201. See appendix 1 for an example of the way 48:1–11 would look if the "inauthentic" material were excised.

and attempted to make divisions between those sections that used the singular and those that used the plural. His divisions in no way resembled the divisions made by those who considered content the main item of consideration. He was left with two sections, neither of which could stand alone as a coherent piece.[202]

Melugin and Schoors take issue with those who make divisions based on content alone and claim to take a strictly form-critical approach to the text. Schoors is especially critical of Elliger, charging that he does not make clear which criteria are to be used to distinguish the work of a compiler from an original author. Melugin and Schoors classify vv. 1–11 as a disputation speech-form, though Melugin adds that there are also elements of prophetic invective, and etiological narrative. In fact Melugin states that "there is no life setting for this speech-form in Israel's oral tradition" and that "it is a free creation of Deutero-Isaiah."[203] Both of these scholars, once they have made their tentative suggestions regarding the form of the passage, base their firmest conclusions regarding the unity of the passage on content and the way the content of this section is different from the content of the passages that precede and follow.

The criteria used by Schoors to dissect this passage are worth closer examination, especially in view of his criticism of the vagueness of Elliger's criteria. Schoors eliminates line 1c because it interrupts the 3+3 rhythm and because the descent from Judah is mentioned. Since descent from Judah occurs only once in DI, it can be omitted. The words *ʾmt* and *ṣdqh* of 1f do not occur with the same meaning in DI, they are negative, their existence causes rhythmic disharmony, and therefore they can be omitted. Schoors finds the repetitions in v. 2 "annoying" and "redundant" and slightly different in meaning from v. 1. They are excised, thus making the phrase *the God of Israel* of v. 2 a "superficial repetition." The presence of several *hapax legomena* in Isaiah 40–55 is also reason to excise. The accusation against Israel that it sinned from the beginning is also more fitting to Trito-Isaiah, according to Schoors, even though he admits the authenticity of 42:27: "Your first father sinned. . . ." In spite of Schoors's protestations against the negative verses in the passage, he admits in the end that God "addresses Israel reproachfully" in order to assert that he is the sole ruler of history.[204]

202. J. Begrich, *Studien zu Deuterojesaja* (BZAW 77; repr. ed.; Munich: Kaiser, 1963) 169ff.

203. Melugin, *Formation*, 41.

204. A. Schoors, *I Am God Your Savior: A Form Critical Study of the Main Genres of Is XL–LV* (VTSup 24; Leiden: Brill, 1973) 278–92.

Such criteria are woefully inadequate to justify dissecting a text. To claim that an "interruption of rhythm" or lack of harmony in rhythm is a sign of an intrusive verse is to claim that the rules of rhythm for Hebrew poetry are known quite well and that these rules allow no divergences. This of course is far from the case.[205]

To excise words that the poet has never used before puts interpreters in immediate peril of excising everything from the beginning of the book, since the occurrence of each new word would face the charge of "never used before, therefore not authentic." Furthermore, omitting words because they are "annoying" or "redundant" could lead to all sorts of manipulations of the biblical text. Some may wish to eliminate certain of the commandments and part or all of Job 38–41, because they are "annoying." The genealogical tables from Genesis and many of the preexilic prophets could be considered both annoying and redundant.

To eliminate words because of repetition would eliminate much of the poetic technique of DI and much of biblical poetry in general. Schoors's omission from the text of words used with different meanings also betrays an ignorance of the use of this as a poetic device in DI. Not only are Schoors's criteria subjective and idiosyncratic, but they betray little appreciation for the subtleties of poetic technique. Schoors, like Duhm more than a half-century before him, can also be considered "an outstanding representative of the surgical school of Hebrew poetry."[206]

A useful part of Schoors's analysis of this section is one of his many tables, in which he shows how various form critics divide or attempt to disentangle the text of Second Isaiah.[207] Schoors compares the views of seven scholars regarding which verses of 48:1–11 are later additions.[208] The chart shows that there is little consensus on the matter; the only agreement seems to be that in some way or another, vv. 1–11, or what is left of them, are a unit. Claims that form criticism has a more objective stance toward the text, or that the methodology is more consistent are belied by the kinds of results that this methodology yields.[209] Agreement is rarely achieved on the limits of short units. More often it is only the longer units about which agreement can be reached.

205. See Gray's criticism of this approach, especially as it is practiced by Duhm (G. B. Gray, *The Forms of Hebrew Poetry* [ed. D. N. Freedman; New York: KTAV, 1972] 228ff.).

206. D. N. Freedman, "Pottery, Poetry, and Prophecy: An Essay on Biblical Poetry," *Pottery, Poetry and Prophecy* (Winona Lake, Ind.: Eisenbrauns, 1980) 34.

207. Schoors, *I Am God*, 285, table VII.

208. Marti, Köhler, Mowinckel, Volz, Elliger, Begrich, and Westermann.

209. See Rolf Knierim, "Old Testament Form Criticism Reconsidered," *Int* 27 (1973) 435–68.

Of Duhm's analysis of this chapter, Scullion says that his interpretation "has been followed by virtually every commentator since [1892]."[210] Actually, there are a number of scholars who do not agree that a later hand was responsible for the "harsh" passages. These include C. C. Torrey (1928), J. Muilenburg (1956), M. Haran (1963), P. Bonnard (1972), Y. Gitay (1981), R. Clifford (1984), and to some extent J. McKenzie (Melugin considers chap. 48 to be a redactional unit, though he does divide the text into separate units based on form-critical considerations). It is to their analyses that I now turn.

Muilenburg is the champion of the thesis that DI is composed of long units, and he considers chapter 48 to be a single literary piece. However, even before Muilenburg's commentary on Second Isaiah, Torrey took issue with Duhm and proposed that the whole of chap. 48 was a unit. "There is no reason to doubt the integrity of the poem." He disagreed with Duhm's treatment, saying that vv. 1–11 is "thoroughly homogeneous" and charging that Duhm had a fundamental misconception of the message of the prophet. Torrey's reasons for reading the chapter as a single literary piece were based on considerations of internal structure and theme and a comparison of the structure and ideas of the passage with the composition and thought of DI in the rest of the book. Internally, the chapter is characterized from beginning to end by the note of rebuke. The fact that "in all its parts it contains the emphatic declaration that Israel, although the chosen people, is unworthy" is a sign of unity for Torrey. The reproachful tone continues throughout vv. 12–22, as well as pervading 1–11. The theme of the polemic against idolatry also runs throughout the poem (vv. 5, 13, and 14), as does the prophet's view of the course of history.

Torrey also interprets the poem's unity by comparing it with other similar sections of DI. He calls it a "counterpart of chapter 43," and he relates it also to chap. 41, in that it sums up what he calls the prophet's "Great Argument" from history.[211] God, and only God, is in control of events of history from the distant past into the future and has had a plan from the very beginning. Torrey, like a number of other scholars, considers this chapter to be a recapitulation of much of DI's thought in previous chapters. It adds no new features.

Chapter 48 is like the previous thought of DI in chaps. 42–46 in that it denounces the people for their faithlessness and wickedness. Harsh tones are not just a part of chap. 48; they run throughout DI's message.[212] Cen-

210. J. J. Scullion, *Isaiah 40–66* (OTM; Wilmington: Michael Glazier, 1982) 60.

211. C. C. Torrey, *The Second Isaiah: A New Interpretation* (Edinburgh, T. &. T. Clark, 1928) 67ff.

212. Torrey sees chaps. 56–66 as part of the work of DI, and he also compares these chapters with chap. 48. It will be recalled that Elliger especially attributed the harsh sections of chap. 48 to the author of 56–66.

sures and calls to repentance are fitting when spoken to people who are living in less than ideal conditions (his thesis is that the message is delivered to people in the fifth century). Torrey retains the harsh passages that are spread throughout DI's prophecy and finds them to be appropriate and necessary, given the imperfect condition and prospects of the audience to which he spoke.

The strength of Torrey's argument is that he does not need to dissect the text (except for his removal of references to Babylon/Chaldea) in order to make sense of it. He also shows the relationship between the harsh passages and those that proclaim salvation in his analysis of the first verses of the poem. These, he says, "give both sides" of the picture: "the heritage of Israel and its forfeiture of its right." He does not see the prophet as a Pollyanna, proclaiming peace when there is no peace. He allows for tension within the text between the saving power of God and the intransigency of God's people.

Muilenburg, like Torrey, sees the poem in chap. 48 as a summation of the thought of the previous chapters. Key ideas that are repeated are the argument from history and prophecy and the relationship of the former things to the new things. He too refers to the relationship between the actual situation of the audience (according to Muilenburg and most commentators, against Torrey, the audience is the exiles in Babylon) and the problems of divine providence and judgment. He characterizes the theology of the poem as "of the first importance" and almost without rival.

Muilenburg's assessment is a good example of what he later describes as rhetorical criticism. Clues to the unity of the poem are found in: (1) the repetition of key words; (2) the position of the words; and (3) the strophic structure of the poem. The key words singled out by Muilenburg are: the verb *to hear,* and the words *call, speak, declare, Jacob,* and *name.* The poem has two major divisions (1–11 and 12–21), consisting of four strophes in each with a prevailing meter of 3+3, and a concluding lyrical finale in vv. 20–21 with a 2+2 meter. Verse 22 is considered to be a later addition.

Section I (vv. 1–11)	*Section II (vv. 12–21)*
1–2	12–13
3–5	14–15
6–8	16–17
9–11	18–19

His analysis of overall unity and of the major divisions of the poem is more convincing than his strophic analyses. Even so, one of the strong points of his analysis is that there is consistency between content and form in the strophic divisions, unlike the treatment of Clifford (see below, pp. 248–49). Muilenburg stressed the importance of strophic analysis for understanding the text in his presidential address to the Society of Biblical Literature in 1968. He spoke of a strophe as a well-defined cluster of bicola or tricola that possesses its own identity, integrity, and structure, or "a series of bicola or tricola with a beginning and ending, possessing unity of thought and structure."[213] Strophes may (but need not) have the same number of lines in a given poem.

Strophes can be most easily recognized (1) when they close with a refrain or when the poem is an alphabetic acrostic. Other ways to determine the limits of a strophe are listed by Muilenburg. Another is (2) the presence of turning points, breaks or shifts. These can be changes of speaker or addressee, or of motif or theme. (3) Particles are also found at strategic locations, at the beginning or the end of a strophe. (4) Vocatives function as dividers of strophes as do (5) rhetorical questions. Finally, (6) the threefold repetition of a keyword within a strophe functions as an indication of the limits of a section within a poem.

For Muilenburg, the presence of the key word is a unifying factor not only for the strophe, but for the entire poem. This is the most convincing aspect of his analysis of chap. 48. His strophic analysis of the poem in the *Interpreter's Bible* is not as well developed as is his later thinking on the matter in his 1968 address. In my analysis of Isaiah 48, I have used the more finely nuanced observations of Muilenburg from his 1968 address.

Haran takes up the matter of divisions within the text and refers to the literary form of chaps. 40–48 as "very loose." He acknowledges that the prophecies are composed of short sections. However, he does not see these short sections as independent units, as do the form critics. He calls them "paragraphs of larger prophecies, that is, strophes of more comprehensive literary wholes." One of the ways the strophes are linked to one another is by the use of obvious connecting words, such as *but now, but you, thus says the Lord, remember this*, and the like. Sometimes passages are joined "by a vague associative link" or even by an "abrupt turn in staccato manner."[214] He admits that it is often difficult to tell where a chain of short sections ends and where another begins—that is, what makes up a complete poem.

Haran speaks of dividing chaps. 40–48 into ten separate poems,[215] which he calls "consecutive cycles," based on the existence of certain components within the poems. These components are: (1) the admonition to "fear not"; (2) proclamations of the unity and uniqueness of God; (3) "proofs" of the truth of the God of Israel from cosmogony and from

213. J. Muilenburg, "Form Criticism and Beyond," *JBL* 88 (1969) 12.

214. Haran, "Literary Structure," 128–29.

215. The ten separate poems of chaps. 40–48 are: chap. 40; 41:1–20; 41:21–42:17; 42:18–43:10; 43:11–44:5; 44:6–28; chap. 45; 46:1–11; (47); and 48:1–16a.

the activities of Cyrus; (4) proof from prophecy; (5) scenes of justice in which God addresses the nations; (6) the main component, the pivot that connects the strophes, which is the concept of *rʾšnwt-ḥdšwt.*

While Haran lists these components in a general way, he fails to show specifically how each is developed within the individual poems and even admits "that the sum of the components is only optimal, and here and there some of them may be missing."[216] His approach is vague; his methodology lacks clarity and precision. One strength of his approach is that he sees the interdependence of short units on one another. A weakness is the nebulous nature of the criteria used to judge the connections. It is no surprise that he criticizes Muilenburg's approach as being "too schematic and punctilious."[217] However, it is this very attention to detail, missing from Haran's analysis, that could have improved his arguments.

Bonnard's approach to the text is similar to Muilenburg's, though he finds the alternation between reprimand and encouragement to be discordant. He feels that in comparison with chaps. 46 and 47, chap. 48 represents a much less coherent development. He is critical, however, of those who find numerous glosses and interpolations within the text, saying that "leur chirurgie reste problematique." Like Muilenburg, Bonnard considers the repetition of certain words in different strophes to be a factor that unites them. He admits that even though the chapter may resemble a mosaic rather than a fresco by its loose development, nonetheless, the mosaic is well made, and the different pieces carefully fashioned.

Gitay uses the system and principles of classical and new rhetoric to demonstrate his position on the organization of the addresses of Second Isaiah. Though Gitay protests that an appropriate literary method should "not force its principles on the text, but, rather, the nature of the material should be taken into account by the method,"[218] he himself applies the rules of classical rhetorical theory to the text of Second Isaiah. The fatal flaw in Gitay's analysis is that he takes for granted that there is an intrinsic connection between classical rhetoric and the poetry of chaps. 40–48. Nowhere does he demonstrate the validity of this connection. He even admits that DI was not a student of classical rhetoric but goes on to force these principles upon the text.

While at times his discussions of individual items within the text can be illuminating, he often takes a circuitous route to explain a rather straightforward technique or device. For instance, he uses Cicero's definition of

216. Haran, "Literary Structure," 131.

217. Ibid., 131 n. 2.

218. Gitay, *Prophecy and Persuasion*, 26.

metaphor to explain how the metaphors in 48:4 work.[219] To discuss the function of onomatopoeia, he calls this device by its Latin name, *nominatio*, and refers his readers to a definition by Dionysius of Halicarnassus.[220]

Gitay identifies 48:1–22 as being a discourse divided into five parts: (1) introduction, vv. 1–2; (2) thesis, vv. 3–11; (3) refutation, vv. 12–15; (4) confirmation, vv. 16–19; (5) epilogue, vv. 20–22. While his analysis of the rhetorical argument is weak, he uses other methods to support his thesis of the unity of the text. The repetition of key words or phrases in significant locations is one of those methods. *Šmʿw zʾt* of v. 1 reappears in v. 16 and also in altered form in v. 20. The name *Jacob* appears in the beginning and end of the poem. The word *name* appears throughout the poem (in vv. 2, 9, and 19). His analysis of the significance of the switch from third to second person between vv. 2 and 3 is mentioned above (p. 247). However, he fails to show any integral connection between the prophet's message and the system of classical rhetoric.[221]

R. Clifford, like Gitay, considers chap. 48 to be one of a number of speeches of DI. Unlike Gitay, Clifford takes his clues for the organization of the text from the text itself, rather than applying an arbitrary system from the outside. Formal indicators pointing to unity include: the repetition of key words, such as the root *šmʿ*; the significant distribution of key words throughout the poem (for instance the word *qrʾ*, with human beings as subject, appears later on in a contrasting usage, with God as subject); strophic patterning—the use of parallel sections within the poem (vv. 1–11 is approximately the same length as vv. 12–21); and the development of each large section following the same pattern. In addition, Clifford appeals to the logical development of the poem as a whole for evidence of its unity.

Clifford divides the text into the following strophes (as in my discussion on chap. 46 above, Clifford does not specifically identify these sections as strophes or stanzas):

Section I (vv. 1–11)	*Section II (vv. 12–21)*
1–2	12–15
3–8	16–19
9–11	20–21

He compares the development of the two large sections of the poem in the following way:

219. Ibid., 224.

220. Ibid., 225. In this case he labels the wordplay in 48:19 as onomatopoeia but fails to demonstrate how the word *mʿh* sounds like the action it signifies.

221. Ibid., 217–18.

1–2	*Jacob is called to hear*	12ab	*Jacob called to hear*
3–8	*divine word* always accompanies *divine deed*	12c–13	link between *divine word* and *deed*
		14–16	new deed is Cyrus's mission
9–11	*persistence of divine purpose,* intent on good in spite of Israelite obstinacy	17–19	*persistence of divine purpose*

It should be noted that the strophic divisions in the poem do not follow the divisions of thought as outlined above. Clifford does not discuss the reason for the strophic division that he makes. In the case of the first major section, it appears that the reason for the division is the development of thought; in the second section the divisions may have been made on formal grounds.

Though Clifford has been influenced somewhat by the methodology of Muilenburg, he often diverges from Muilenburg's division of the text, and this is true in his analysis of chap. 48. Both of them see two major divisions, the first ending after v. 11, but Muilenburg sees four strophes in each division while Clifford sees three. Another difference between Clifford's analysis and Muilenburg's is that Clifford incorporates vv. 20–21 into the body of the poem. Muilenburg calls it the ninth strophe, "a lyrical finale," and it stands outside the two major divisions of the poem.

There is wide agreement among scholars that there is a major division in the chapter after verse 11. I agree with Muilenburg and Clifford that this is a division within a single poem, not a mark of two (or more) literary units. In my analysis below, I shall examine the microstructure of the two main sections of the poem and then the structure of the poem as a whole, including the relationship between the main divisions.

BHK and BHS record paragraphing divisions in the MT as follows: after vv. 2, 11, and 22, the MT has closed sections; the open section is at the end of v. 16. 1QIsa^{a} has short divisions after vv. 2, 9, and 16, and a long division after v. 11. Except for the division after v. 9, these divisions support my analysis.

Structure of Individual Sections: Microstructure, First Main Division

Section I (vv. 1–2). The first section begins with an imperative, summoning Jacob to hear, and continues with a description of the names of Jacob/Israel. The section is composed of nine lines. Of these lines, three have no parallel within the section: lines 1a, 1f, and 2c. Of the remaining lines, 1b–1e have an AB/A′B′ pattern, and 2a and 2b are parallel. Line 1f has double duty function, because it can be read with both the previous and the following lines. The first and last lines of the section stand out from the rest of the line-pairs, the imperative of 1a serving as an opening line, the line with the name of Yahweh serving to close the section.

The first and last lines of this section are distinctive also by way of the syllable count. These two lines are short with respect to syllables: line 1a has 6 syllables; 2c has 7. The intervening lines have between 8 and 11 syllables. The predominant number of stresses is 3 per line, which is typical of the poem.

Distinctive features of section I include, in addition to the above structural elements, the repetition of key words *šm* 'name' three times and *qr*ʾ 'call' twice, and the presence in almost every line of a specific name of either God or Israel. All of these elements work together to form a tightly knit, well-formed section.

The names in the section are:

1a	Jacob	1f	(no name)
b	Israel	2a	Holy city
c	Judah	b	God of Israel
d	Yahweh	c	Yahweh Sabaoth
e	God of Israel		

It can be seen that four of the names are names of Jacob/Israel, four are names of God. The line without a name is significant because it characterizes how Israel uses of all of the names. As Torrey has pointed out, the chapter begins with a note of rebuke and casts a shadow on all of the claims made by Israel: their calling on the name of Yahweh or the holy city, or remembering or leaning on the God of Israel. The reasons for this rebuke are not clearly stated. However, the same doubt about the integrity of the people is found in 46:8 and 12. The transgression in chap. 46 is the making and worshiping of idols. This is also a problem in chap. 48. The feature of naming is also important in chap. 47, where the names claimed by Babylon are taken away one by one.

Another device in the structuring of these lines is the repetition of the *Niphal* form. There are two *Niphal* participles and two *Niphal* perfect verbs. The participial forms are at the beginning (lines 1b and 1d), and the perfect verbs are at the end (lines 2a and 2b). Besides the 2 m. pl. imperative that begins the poem, the remaining six verbs are third plural.

In section I there are several elements that Muilenburg identifies as marking the limits of a given strophe. The presence of vocatives and the threefold repetition of key words both can identify the limits of a given strophe. The poem begins with a vocative, and there are several threefold repetitions within the section; the key word *name* and the name *Israel* appear at the beginning, middle, and end of the section. This is a closely knit section, or strophe, yet the repeated words and forms are used with slight modifications to lend variety to the passage.

Section II (vv. 3–5). After the summons and description of the audience that is summoned in section I, the actual address begins with Yahweh speaking in the first person. This use of the first-person verb to indicate that Yahweh now speaks makes a clear break from the previous section. Section II is composed of 10 lines, one more than the previous section. The stress pattern is regular, with 3 stresses per line throughout, except for a shorter line in the middle (4c), which has only 2 stresses. The syllable count varies from shorter lines in the middle (4bc and 5a) with only 6 syllables to longer lines at the beginning and end of the section.

The section begins with 2 line-trios and ends with 2 line-pairs. The second line-trio modifies both the preceding and following lines (see notes on text above, pp. 181–82).

Key words repeated in section II are the verbs *ngd, šmʿ, ʿśh, bwʾ*, and the adverb *mʾz*, which appears twice and occupies an important place in the section. This section emphasizes the fact that Yahweh told (declared, announced, acted, and brought forth) things "from time past," before they happened, and then caused them to happen. Lines 3ab and 5ab repeat the combinations *ngd/mʾz/šmʿ* 'from time past I declared . . . I announced. . . .' Lines 4abc and 5cd explain the reasons Yahweh told things before they happened: because Israel was stubborn (4abc) and because Israel might have attributed to her idols the things that happened (5cd). The line-trios and line-pairs are joined together by this pattern: the first of each line-trio and line-pair explains what Yahweh did; the second of each line-trio and line-pair gives the reason. The relationship between the line-trios and line-pairs can be described as an AB/A′B′ pattern.

Another element uniting the lines is the repetition of the 1st-person form of the verb six times,[222] as well as four nouns with 1st-person suffixes. The emphasis is on Yahweh's actions. Lines 3abc have three first singular verbs. Lines 4abc have only one 1st-person suffix (Yahweh says, "I know"). This line-trio shifts to put the focus on 'you' (*ʾth*) and repeats the 2 m. s. suffix twice. Lines 5ab return to the first singular, with two more verbs in the 1st person.

The final lines, 5cd, have first singular suffixes; however, this is not Yahweh, but Israel, speaking about its idols and molten images and falsely attributing Yahweh's actions to the idols. Notice the repetition of the verb *ʿśh* here. There is a fear that Israel may think that the subject of *ʿśh* is its idols, rather than Yahweh.

222. *Mdʿty*, an infinitive construct, clearly has verbal force.

The repetition of the 1st-person form has a powerful effect and can be compared to a similar phenomenon in section VI, which repeats the first-person pronoun ten times. In section II the repetition of the first-person form occurs ten times; three of these refer to the people speaking of their idols. The remaining seven are the direct speech of Yahweh.

The shift in speaker, from Yahweh to Israel, is a fitting conclusion to this section. The reason for Yahweh's concern is Israel's stubbornness. The stubbornness of Israel described in the first half of the strophe is more fully explained in the last half. It is not just an inability or refusal to trust or believe that God can deliver them from their oppressors. This passage speaks of an almost casual profusion of idols and defines Israel's sinfulness as the possibility that Israel may attribute to these many idols actions that are really to be attributed to Yahweh.

Section III (vv. 6–8). Yahweh resumes his address to the people with the second-person verb *šm*^{c}*t* 'you heard'. There is repeated emphasis on the second person: "you heard," "(you) see," "you!", "you declare." Yahweh is not just asking the people to hear, as in the previous section. In the form of a question, he asks if they cannot declare what they have heard. This can be interpreted either as a rhetorical question or a challenge that Israel is perhaps unable to meet.

While the first line-pair (6ab) represents a break in the development from the previous section, it also acts as a bridge, or link, by referring to what Israel has heard (in the previous lines). Muilenburg calls 6a–c a "superb transition." Parunak refers to the joining together of successive sections by what he calls "transitional techniques." In this case, the key word *šm*^{c} acts as a link between the two sections.

Section III is composed of 11 lines. Lines 6a–7b make up three line-pairs, followed by a single line, which has no parallel. The section ends with two more line-pairs, 8a–d. The stresses vary between 3 and 4. The first line is short with respect to syllables, having 6/7 in all. The syllable count of the remaining lines is between 8 and 10.

The theme of this section is developed by the repetition of the key words *m*^{c}*th/*^{c}*th* ('now') and *yd*^{c}, as well as the profusion of 2 m. verb forms and suffixes. The emphasis in the section is on what Israel does; the previous section stressed Yahweh's action.

Here, as in the previous section, the *Hiphil* of *šm*^{c} in the first person refers to Yahweh's claim that he announces certain things. Unlike the previous section, in which Yahweh announced *r*$^{\supset}$*šnwt* ('first things') before they happened, in this section Yahweh declares that he announces *ḥdšwt* ('new things') as they happen, not before they occur.

While Yahweh's announcement is an important element of the section, what is more important, by virtue of the repetition of the 2 m. endings, is Israel's behavior.

6d	you did not know them	A
7b	you did not hear them	B
7c	lest you say, "I knew them"	A
8a	you did not hear	B
	you did not know	A
8b	your ear did not open	C

The purpose of Yahweh's announcement of new things "only now" is to prevent Israel from claiming to have known them beforehand. The presence of the single line (7c) in the middle of the section draws attention to this purpose.

The section concludes with Yahweh's declaration that he always knew of Israel's treachery and rebellious nature and with a contrast between Yahweh and Israel. Israel did not know or hear, but Yahweh did know all along about Israel.

Sections II and III (vv. 3–8). Muilenburg divides vv. 3–8 into two separate sections, considering the major feature of division to be the topics of the former things in the first section and the new things in the latter. Clifford, on the other hand, emphasizes the unity of vv. 3–8. They emphasize the link between the divine word and the divine action, whether it is in the past or the present. Clifford's interpretation seems somewhat forced. However, he does highlight a real unity between the two sections. A comparison of the key words in each section and a discussion of the overall structure of the two sections better demonstrates this unity than Clifford's thematic or topical summary.

Elements that divide section III from section II include the following. In section II, Yahweh claimed that he told about things *before* they happened. In section III, Yahweh claims that he did not tell about things *until the time* they happened. Section III thus develops an idea that is in direct contrast to the previous section. This contrast is made by the repetition of certain key words from the previous section, as well as the use of the word *ᶜth*, which contrasts *mᵓz*, and *ḥdšwt*, which is in contrast with *rᵓšnwt.*

I have discussed the contrasting elements between the two sections: the first things versus the new things; time past versus "only now"; God's announcement of things to Israel before they happen versus God's announcement of things at the time they happen; Israel's knowledge of those things versus Israel's ignorance. Elements that are identical or similar in the two sections will now be discussed.

In both sections God announces (*Hiphil* of *šm*^{c}) things to Israel (3a and 6c). In both sections there is a fear that Israel will say something that she is not supposed to say; lines 5c and 7c begin with the same words, "lest you say. . . ." In both sections the treachery and stubbornness of Israel are known to God (4a–c, *md*^{c}*ty* and 8cd, *yd*^{c}*ty*). The last idea, that God always knew, comes at the beginning and the end of the two sections, forming an *inclusio.* The key word *yd*^{c} is also used of Israel in these sections, but it always occurs with a negative. Thus a further contrast is formed, between God who knows and Israel who does not.

The contrasts developed in vv. 3–8 have perplexed scholars. On the one hand, Yahweh makes announcements to prevent Israel from attributing God's actions to another. On the other hand, Yahweh does *not* make prior announcements of his actions to prevent Israel from knowing them. Lack advises accepting this as a paradox, without trying to interpret away apparent contradictions.[223] Taking the verses together, they can be read as a comprehensive plan to involve Israel in a sort of catch-22. Because God can and has announced events beforehand, Israel cannot attribute God's actions to some other deity. Because God does not announce certain things beforehand, Israel cannot claim prior knowledge and perhaps assert itself as independent of God. Whatever claims Israel might make regarding the course of events, whether in the past or the present, these assertions about God's knowledge and Israel's lack of knowledge should be able to take care of any contingency.

There is a clear division between the larger section consisting of vv. 3–8 and the section that follows, vv. 9–11, because of the repetition of the theme of God's knowledge of Israel's treachery in vv. 4 and 8, which forms an *inclusio.*

Section IV (vv. 9–11). In an impassioned outburst, God promises to save his people from annihilation by withholding the anger he experiences because of their rebellious behavior. There are eight lines in this section: 9ab, a line-pair, followed by 9c, a single line with no parallel; 10ab, a line-pair followed by a line-pair, 11a and 11c, that is divided by another single line with no parallel. The single lines are short with respect to syllable count: 9c has 6/7 and 11b has 4; the remaining lines have from 7 to 10 syllables each.

Most striking in this section is the resumed repetition of the first-person forms. The first-person form of the verb and first-person suffixes occur twelve times within these lines; the distribution is six first-person verbs and

223. See Lack's discussion in *Symbolique,* 197.

six suffixed nouns or particles. The threefold repetition of the phrase *lmᶜn/ lmᶜny* 'for the sake of'/'for my sake' is striking. In fact, Muilenburg titles this section "for my own sake." As stated above, the expression is more fully stated in line 9a: "for my name's sake." The focus has returned to Yahweh and his name and what he has done and will do.

There is an alternation between imperfect and perfect verbs that forms an ABA pattern in the lines. The section begins and ends with a pair of imperfect verbs; in between these is a line-pair composed of perfect verbs. Yahweh alternates in this passage between describing his actions in the present (he will refrain from cutting off his people, and he will give his glory to no one) and those in the past (he refined and tested his people).

There is a sense of unreality or disbelief about what is occurring in Section IV. The brief but powerful outburst of line 11b expresses this well. After the lengthy treatment of Israel's evils in the previous verses, God nonetheless promises to withhold his anger from them. The only reason for God to restrain himself from destroying his people and to act (*ᶜśh*) is for his name's sake, so that no one else will be glorified. This was also the reason (above in lines 5cd) for God's announcement and enactment of the first things, so that idols and images would not be credited with doing them (*ᶜśh*).

Microstructure, Second Main Division

Section V (vv. 12–13). The second main division begins in a manner identical to the first, with an imperative and two vocatives (Jacob and Israel), summoning the people to "hear!" The introduction is followed by a description. In section I it was a description of Israel and its various names. Here, however, it is God who is described. Eight lines make up section V, which has 4 line-pairs. The stress and syllable count are shorter than the previous sections of the poem. There are 3 lines with 2 stresses (12b, 12d, and 13d); the syllable count varies between 5 and 8 for these lines.

Features that unite this section are the repetition of *ᵓny* (four times) and 1st-person suffixes (four times) and the *inclusio* or envelope structure formed by the root *qrᵓ* at the beginning and end of the section. The description of God begins and ends with two participles of the root *qrᵓ*. God "names" Jacob/Israel and "calls" the heavens and the earth. The claims that God is the first and the last as well as the combination of the naming of Israel and the call to heaven and earth give this section a cosmic scope. Muilenburg sees this strophe as uniting history and creation by the framing device of the root *qrᵓ*. It also focuses on the nature of God by the repetition of *ᵓny*.

Section VI (vv. 14–16). After the summons and description, God again addresses the audience. Unlike the first major division of the poem, this one includes a number of imperatives (lines 14a and 16a), which repeatedly call Israel to hear and to gather together. These additional imperatives add a note of urgency: the audience must listen to what God has to say. The imperatives are connected by alliteration and repetition: *qbṣw* (14a) and *qrbw* (16a) are related and *šmᶜ* of 14a is repeated in 16a. The stress count varies. Lines 15b and 16e are short, with only 2 stresses. These two lines have an unusual number of syllables: the first, 14a, is long, with 11 syllables; 15b is short, with only 4.

There is some disagreement about the limits of section VI. Muilenburg places vv. 14–15 in a single unit by virtue of the sequence: imperative and address, direction question, central disclosure, and theocentric conclusion, which is an emphatic answer to the question. Verse 16, in his schema, starts a new section. Clifford's division reflects his ambiguity about the strophic structure of this part of the poem. He considers vv. 12–15 to be one strophe, but when he describes the development of the poem by content, he divides the lines differently: lines 12ab are a summons to hear, 12c–13d connect divine word and deed, and vv. 14–16 speak of the new deed as the mission of Cyrus.

Form-critical considerations shed no light on the question of the limits of the sections here. Köhler, Volz, and Mowinckel combine vv. 12–16 into a unit. Westermann, too, sees 12–16 as a unit by showing the relationship between 46:3–13, 48:1–11, and 48:12–16.[224] Each of the passages has the same pattern: (1) summons to hear, with an address to Israel; (2) God makes a proclamation and gives effect to it; (3) the call of Cyrus. However, in his commentary, Westermann makes a different division, including v. 17 in the unit with vv. 12–16. He does rearrange the lines somewhat to fit his scheme of a trial speech with a supplement, that of God the redeemer.

One of the factors causing difficulties is the sentence in lines 16de: "And now Yahweh has sent me and his spirit." Many consider this to be a gloss, and the reason for its presence here is unclear. Another factor is the use of imperatives calling Israel to hear and to draw near in v. 16a. We would usually expect imperatives to begin a new section or strophe. Muilenburg does read the imperative in 16a as the sign of a new strophe. However, the oracular *kh-ʾmr yhwh* of v. 17 would also usually be considered the beginning of a strophe. Muilenburg believes that "possibly something has fallen out of the text at this point," in which case v. 17 would "introduce a new strophe." However, he sees 16–17 as forming one strophe.

224. C. Westermann, *Sprache und Struktur der Prophetie Deuterojesajas* (CTM 11; Stuttgart: Calwer, 1981) 68–73.

The obvious division at v. 17 and the presence of the three (or four) imperatives calling Israel to gather are factors in favor of dividing at the end of v. 16. The most important factor, which tips the balance in favor of this division, is the presence throughout vv. 14–16 of the plural forms and the change to the singular in v. 17.

Section VII (vv. 17–19). The announcement of an oracle by the familiar formula *kh-ʾmr yhwh* opens this new strophe. Verse 17 also marks a new development in the poem by introducing names of Yahweh not used previously in this poem, the names redeemer and Holy One of Israel. In v. 12 Yahweh described himself as first and last, creator of heaven and earth. Here the description emphasizes God's concern for his people by use of the term *redeemer*, as well as by a series of participles portraying God as teacher and leader. This section has 12 lines, with 5 line-pairs and (a feature that is typical of this poem) two single lines without immediate parallels, lines 17c and 18a. The end of the section, 19cd, is one long sentence. The lines are not a parallel line-pair but must be divided because of the number of stresses and syllables: the stress pattern is 3+2 (as in the first lines of the section, 17ab), and the syllable count is 9 and 6.

I connect v. 17 with 18 and 19 as part of one section because v. 17 announces the oracle and describes the oracle-giver, and vv. 18–19 contain the oracle. Problems with this section were described above (pp. 227–34).

Section VIII (vv. 20–21). A joyful call to flee from Babylon and a vivid description of the return, in imagery drawn from the Exodus, close the poem. Muilenburg describes the stress count as 2+2, which would make a total of 13 lines. This arrangement of lines shows a very regular stress count, as well as a very short syllable count in each line.

20a	*ṣʾw mbbl*	2+3	= 5	2
20b	*brḥẁ mkśdym*	2+3	= 5	2
20c	*bqwl rnh hgydw*	2 + 2 + 3	= 7	2/3
20d	*hšmyʿw zʾt*	3+1	= 4	2
20e	*hwṣyʾwh ʿd-qṣh hʾrṣ*	3/4 + 1 + 2 + 2	= 8/9	3
20f	*ʾmrw gʾl yhwh*	2 + 2 + 2	= 6	3
20g	*ʿbdw yʿqb*	2+2	= 4	2
21a	*wlʾ ṣmʾw*	2+3	= 5	2
21b	*bḥrbwt hwlykm*	3/4 + 3	= 6/7	2
21c	*mym mṣwr*	1/2 + 2	= 3/4	2
21d	*hzyl lmw*	2+2	= 4	2
21e	*wybqʿ-ṣwr*	3+1	= 4	2
21f	*wyzbw mym*	4 + 1/2	= 5/6	2

Muilenburg's arrangement of lines shows a very unusual syllable count compared to the rest of the poem. The average number of syllables per line for the whole poem is between 7.5 and 7.8. An arrangement of section VIII that reflects the prevailing 2+2 stress count shows an average syllable count of between 5.07 and 5.46, well below the average of the rest of the poem. A shortcoming of this arrangement is that is does not properly outline the relationship of line-pairs at the very end of the poem. It is clear that *mym mṣwr hzyl lmw* (21cd) is parallel and forms a chiasm with *wybqʿ-ṣwr wyzbw mym* (21ef).

Lines 21ab can also be scanned as one long line rather than two non-parallel lines, but in this case, there are equally good reasons for reading them as 2 lines: to avoid a very large uncharacteristic syllable count and to maintain the prevailing stress count of 2 stresses per line. The very last part of v. 20 can also be read as either 1 or 2 lines. The advantage of reading it as 2 lines is that the prevailing stress pattern is maintained. However, if we read it as one long line, we reflect the fact that it is not a parallel line-pair but rather one long sentence, of which there are several in the poem. The possibilities, then, are to scan the section with as few as 9 lines or as many as 13.

An alternative arrangement to Muilenburg's is as follows:

20a	*ṣʾw mbbl*	2 + 3	= 5	2
20b	*brḥw mkśdym*	2 + 3	= 5	2
20c	*bqwl rnh hgydw*	2 + 2 + 3	= 7	3
20d	*hšmyʿw zʾt*	3 + 1	= 4	2
20e	*hwṣyʾwh ʿd-qṣh hʾrṣ*	3/4 + 1 + 2 + 2	= 8/9	3
20f	*ʾmrw gʾl yhwh ʿbdw yʿqb*	2 + 2 + 2 + 2 + 2	= 10	5
21a	*wlʾ ṣmʾw bḥrbwt hwlykm*	2 + 3 + 3/4 + 3	= 11/12	4
21b	*mym mṣwr hzyl lmw*	1 + 2 + 2 + 2	= 7	4
21c	*wybqʿ-ṣwr wyzbw mym*	3 + 1 + 4 + 1/2	= 9/10	4

The virtues of this arrangement are that it reflects the parallelism of 21bc, and it shows that 20f and 21a are both long lines without any internal parallelism. The syllable count, while long in the second half of the section, is not out of line when compared with the rest of the poem. The only real difficulty with this arrangement is the long, 5-stress line, 20f. The symmetry of construction is apparent, whether a line is measured as 4 stresses or is separated into 2 lines of 2 stresses each. In this case, stress-counting is not the definitive factor in determining line length, though it can be helpful in other cases, as shown above. Both arrangements of section VIII have merit. Here it is impossible to determine the limits of the line with precision.

This section is divided into two parts: the first is a series of imperatives that urge Israel to leave Babylon and to tell all the earth that Yahweh has redeemed his servant Jacob. The second section recaptures a scene of the Exodus from Egypt in order to portray this new exodus from Babylon. Muilenburg refers to these lines as "a closing lyrical finale." The tone is joyful, positive, and hopeful.

The final line is best understood as a line inserted to serve as a divider. It is one of the three such dividers or closing statements in chaps. 40–66 that serve to divide these chapters into three equal sections of nine chapters each. It is not part of the poem and is not included in the analysis of the structure.

Structure of the Poem: Macrostructure

Views about the overall unity of this poem were given above in the introductory notes (pp. 240–44). Though many scholars believe the chapter is a mosaic of individual and originally unrelated pieces, this is not universally held. Those who consider it to be a single poem point to the following unifying elements:

1. The presence of key words throughout the poem[225]
2. The tone of rebuke throughout[226]
3. Themes such as the argument from history and prophecy, the relationship of the former things to the new things, or the link between word and deed
4. Significant distribution of certain words[227]
5. The presence of parallel sections[228]

The two large divisions (vv. 1–11 and 12–20) are parts of a larger whole, and all of the above serve to show the relationship between these two large divisions.

225.

Key Word	*Verse*
šmʿ:	1, 3, 5, 6, 7, 8, 12, 13, 16, 20
qrʾ:	1, 2, 8, 12, 13, 16, 15
ngd:	3, 5, 6, 14, 20
yʿqb:	1, 12, 20
šm:	1, 2, 9, 19
ʿṣwh:	5, 18
ʿśh:	3, 5, 11, 14
yṣʾ:	1, 3, 19, 20 (2x)
zʾt:	1, 16, 20.

226. Verses 1f, 4–5, 7c–8, 9–10, 18–19, and 22.

227. E.g., the use of *qrʾ* with human beings as subject and later God as subject.

228. Verses 1–11 balance 12–21.

The analysis of chap. 48 above has also shown the pervasive presence of the first-person forms: 10 times in section II, 3 times in section III, 12 times in section IV, 8 times in section V, 10 times in section VI, and 3 times in section VII. The only sections that do not have such forms are the first and the last. These 2 sections frame the poem and form a large envelope around the remaining 6 sections.

The first section introduces the chapter with the imperative to Jacob/Israel to hear. The chapter ends with more commands in the closing section, this time to flee, go out from Babylon, and to announce, declare, send out, and say all the things that Yahweh has announced and that make up the body of the poem. The relationship between the first and last sections is highlighted by the contrasting commands: v. 1 calls Jacob/Israel to "hear this!" (*šmᶜw-zᵓt*); v. 20 has the same phrase, but the verb is *Hiphil*, "make this known!" (*hšmyᶜw zᵓt*). Israel is a listener in the beginning but in the end is to be a proclaimer. The passivity of Israel ("they came forth from Judah") in the first section is contrasted with the more active "go forth from Babylon" in the last. In both, the root *yṣᵓ* is used. The phrase *house of Jacob* 'is mirrored in *his servant Jacob*. In the two verses a contrast can be seen in the different names by which Jacob is identified. These *inclusios* are powerful unifying features in the poem.

Both major divisions of the poem have sections containing passionate exclamations from Yahweh that express his anger and anguish because of the people's refusal to follow his commands.[229] Israel's treachery threatens to cause another break in its relationship with God. Those scholars who would eliminate any harsh utterances in order to see in DI's message "salvation and nothing but salvation" completely miss the poignancy of these outbursts from God.[230] The poem maintains a level of intensity throughout by contrasting what Israel ought to be with what Israel is. Israel is not a community that needs to hear only sentiments of encouragement and confidence. There is much about the community and audience of DI that has not been investigated adequately. This poem, as well as the others studied, points to a more complicated situation than has generally been admitted.

The perplexing shifts between singular and plural have been mentioned in the notes on the text and translation. It has been shown that neither piecemeal nor wholesale emendations can solve the problem of these shifts. In fact, it may be that these shifts serve to unite the poem by their ubiquity. No attempt to divide passages on the basis of the shifts has been successful.

229. Verses 9–11 and 18–19.

230. Westermann, *Isaiah 40–66*, 199.

Clifford has pointed out that vv. 1–11 and 12–22 make parallel statements and are approximately equal in length of line. In support of his comparison of the two main divisions of the poem is the following analysis of the sections according to syllable and stress patterns. The sections are remarkably similar, almost equal in length:

	First Division	*Second Division*
Syllables	304–16	304–13
Stresses	117–18	119–22
Lines	38	44

While precise delineation of the individual lines is difficult and uncertain, the overall structure of the two main divisions according to the measure of syllables and stresses is another convincing sign of unity.

Summary

The purposes of this study were to test the theory that each of the chapters is a unified literary work, to discover more about the poetic techniques and devices used by DI, and to see how the poetry of DI is related to other Biblical Hebrew poetry.

A close study of the chapters has shown each one of them to be a well-constructed poem. Many devices and techniques have been used by the poet. These include: paronomasia, alliteration and assonance, double-duty modifiers (suffixes, whole words, or entire phrases), rhetorical questions, particles for emphasis, homonyms, litotes, gapping (forward and backward), envelope construction and *inclusio*, distant or discontinuous parallelism, antithetic parallelism, repetitive parallelism, and enjambment. The poet has employed a variety of structuring techniques to join line to line, to join line-pairs or line-trios to one another, and to relate the larger sections or strophes to one another within the poem.

The author is an artist and poet of great skill and uses familiar devices such as parallelism and chiasm in new and creative ways, showing a sophistication and subtlety that has often been overlooked. The poet transforms and transcends many conventional techniques. The fact that the poet frequently gives new twists to old devices has not been adequately recognized by form-critical scholars.

The form-critical approach, which looks for conventional and typical genres in a given work is inadequate for analyzing the poetry of DI. It does not bring the correct tools or methodology to a study of this inventive and imaginative thinker. Some scholars who have studied this poet from such a perspective do acknowledge the creativity of the poet but still claim to be able to make decisions about "original units" based on genre. None has proven that the poet restricted himself to one genre per poem. In fact, some (e.g., Melugin) see combinations of genres. However, when form critics look only for genres as markers of division, they fail to see other elements that unite serve to unite a variety of genres, or traces of genres, into a larger whole.

Certain verses referred to by form critics as polemics against idols are considered secondary or inauthentic, as are other verses that are harshly critical of Jacob/Israel. However, this study has shown that both the polemic against idols or idolatry and the so-called "harsh" passages are integral to both chapters 46 and 48. The passages in which the people are criticized for being stubborn and far from justice, that is, rebels, are related to the theme of idolatry. While many scholars look upon the polemic against idols as mocking the foolish Babylonians for their worship of mere wood and metal objects, in these two poems it is a far more serious matter. The charges of idolatry are directed at Jacob/Israel. It is the Israelites, not the Babylonians, who are criticized for making and worshiping idols. DI is not addressing his message to the Babylonians, nor is he concerned with their future. This poet is concerned that the exiles might once again jeopardize their chance to escape from oppression, just as they did at Mt. Sinai by their lack of true righteousness and their making and worshiping idols.

In addition to the proscription of idolatry pervading chapters 46 and 48, another theme is present in all of the poems. The emphasis on Yahweh as the only God is an integral part of each of the chapters studied. Yahweh is the only one who was present in the beginning to control events of history, who continues to exercise sole control of events, and who can by speaking bring future events into existence. Yahweh's sway over creation is contrasted in chaps. 46 and 48 with the theme of the helplessness of idols; in chap. 47 Babylon's impotence is the foil to Yahweh's might. The repeated uses of the first-person forms in chapters 46 and 48 are striking and serve to draw attention to Yahweh's position.

Each of the three poems portrays a procession: the Babylonian gods walk into exile, carried on the backs of beasts; virgin daughter Babylon proceeds from her throne down to earth, crossing rivers into humiliating defeat; Jacob/Israel's future flight from Babylon is pictured in terms of the first Exodus, when the people were led through the desert and fortified with life-giving water. This theme of procession is introduced in the prologue to chaps. 40ff., with the description of the way through the wilderness. It is used later in a fuller description of the liberation from captivity (another poem of some length) in 51:9–52:2. The descent and exile of Babylon are contrasted with the ascent and liberation of Jacob/Israel.

While there are several similarities among the poems in Isaiah 46–48, there are also differences in structure. Chapter 46 is a classic example of a nonalphabetic acrostic poem, with 22 units and a syllable and stress pattern of 8+8=16 and 3+3=6. This is the standard structure of alphabetic and nonalphabetic acrostics, as described by Freedman. Chapter 47 has a different structure. It does not reflect the standard meter of 8+8=16 and 3+3=6, as chap. 46 does. Rather, it is an example of a poem written in the so-called Qinah meter, which has a pattern of 8+5(7+6)=13 and 3+2=5. In this respect it is similar to the poems in Lamentations 1–4, in which the prevailing pattern of stresses is 3+2, with an average syllable count of 13. Chapter 48 has a prevailing stress pattern of 3 per line, with syllables averaging around 15 per line. This chapter is most remarkable in the overall balance of syllables (a total of 608 syllables) in each major section (304 syllables per section). Such findings would seem to point to quantity as a factor in the composition of Hebrew poetry.

A number of basic issues in Second Isaiah research now deserve further examination based on the findings of this book. Isa 44:9–20, the long section on the construction and worship of idols, is usually assumed to be prose. But given my findings on the anti-idolatry poems in chapters 46 and 48, as well as the BHS arrangement of these verses as poetry, this assumption must be challenged. My methodology could be used to good effect. Other poems in DI should be studied to see whether or not they have structures similar to chapters 46–48. The relationship between chapters 45–55 and 56–66 should be studied, especially regarding the harsh criticisms of the people of the community. It may be that the links between the chapters are stronger than they are generally thought to be and that it is not necessary to propose different authors for the sections.

The personification of Babylon as a virgin daughter is one of many personifications employed by DI. All of these figures (the servant, virgin daughter Babylon, daughter Jerusalem, messenger Zion, the vindicator coming from Edom, mother Jerusalem) should be studied more closely to see how they are used in individual poems by the poet and how they function in the overall work. Such studies might be helpful in shedding light on the meaning and function of the servant figure who has received so much attention over the centuries, during which the servant's identity was the predominant issue rather than his metaphorical function within the complete poem. More work on the Babylonian setting of DI would prove fruitful. What kinds of processions would the exiles in Babylon have viewed, and what are the details of these processions? Was DI influenced by the forms of Babylonian literature, and to what extent? How do the hymns to Babylonian gods compare to those in DI? These questions remain for another day.

Appendix 1

Divisions Indicated in the Masoretic Text and 1QIsa^a

Chapter 46 is divided from chapter 45 by a large space, but it does not begin a new line, as do the other poems in this study. *Q* indicates a large space between verses. *QQ* indicates the beginning of a new line in 1QIsa^a. The symbol ^̲ indicates presence of *ʾatnaḥ*, and פ and ס indicate a *petuḥah* and *setumah*, respectively.

Chapter 46

I					
	1a	krʿ bl qrs nbw			
	1b	hyw ʿṣbyhm			
	1c	lḥyh wlbhmh	^̲		
	1d	nśʾtykm ʿmwswt			
	1e	mśʾ lʿyph			
	2a	qrsw krʿw yḥdw			
	2b	lʾ yklw mlṭ mśʾ	^̲		
	2c	wnpšm bšby hlkh		MT ס	*QQ*
II					
	3a	šmʿw ʾly byt yʿqb			
	3b	wkl-šʾryt byt yśrʾl	^̲		
	3c	hʿmsym mny-bṭn			
	3d	hnśʾm mny-rḥm			
	4a	wʿd-zqnh ʾny hwʾ			
	4b	wʿd-śybh ʾny ʾsbl	^̲		
	4c	ʾny ʿśyty wʾny ʾśʾ			
	4d	wʾny ʾsbl wʾmlṭ		MT ס	*Q*
III					
	5a	lmy tdmywny wtšww	^̲		
	5b	wtmšlwny wndmh			
	6a	hzlym zhb mkys			
	6b	wksp bqnh yšqlw	^̲		
	6c	yśkrw ṣwrp wyʿśhw ʾl			

	6d	ysgdw ᵓp-yšthww		
	7a	yśᵓhw ᶜl-ktp ysblhw		
	7b	wynyḥhw tḥtyw wyᶜmd		
	7c	mmqwmw lᵓ ymyš	^	
	7d	ᵓp-yṣᶜq ᵓlyw wlᵓ yᶜnh		
	7e	mṣrtw lᵓ ywšyᶜnw	MT ס	*Q*
IV				
	8a	zkrw-zᵓt whtᵓššw	^	
	8b	hšybw pwšᶜym ᶜl-lb		*Q*
	9a	zkrw rᵓšnwt mᶜwlm	^	
	9b	ky ᵓnky ᵓl wᵓyn ᶜwd		
	9c	ᵓlhym wᵓps kmwny		
	10a	mgyd mrᵓšyt ᵓḥryt		
	10b	wmqdm ᵓšr lᵓ-nᶜśw	^	
	10c	ᵓmr ᶜṣty tqwm		
	10d	wkl-ḥpṣy ᵓᶜśh		
	11a	qrᵓ mmzrḥ ᶜyṭ		
	11b	mᵓrṣ mrḥq ᵓyš ᶜṣtw	^	
	11c	ᵓp-dbrty ᵓp-ᵓbyᵓnh		
	11d	yṣrty ᵓp-ᵓᶜśnh	MT ס	*QQ*
V				
	12a	šmᶜw ᵓly ᵓbyry lb	^	
	12b	hrḥwqym mṣdqh		
	13a	qrbty ṣdqty lᵓ trḥq		
	13b	wtšwᶜty lᵓ tᵓḥr	^	
	13c	wntty bṣywn tšwᶜh		
	13d	lyśrᵓl tpᵓrty	MT ס	*QQ*

Chapter 47

I				
	1a	rdy wšby ᶜl-ᶜpr		
	1b	btwlt bt-bbl		
	1c	šby-lᵓrṣ ᵓyn-ksᵓ		
	1d	bt-kśdym	^	
	1e	ky lᵓ twsypy yqrᵓw-lk		
	1f	rkh wᶜngh		
	2a	qḥy rḥym		
	2b	wṭḥny qmḥ		
	2c	gly ṣmtk		
	2d	ḥśpy-šbl		
	2e	gly-šwq		

	2f	ʿbry nhrwt		
	3a	tgl ʿrwtk		
	3b	gm trʾh ḥrptk	^	
	3c	nqm ʾqḥ		
	3d	wlʾ ʾpgʿ ʾdm	MT ס	*Q*
	4a	gʾlnw yhwh ṣbʾwt šmw	^	
	4b	qdwš yśrʾl		*Q*
II				
	5a	šby dwmm wbʾy bḥšk		
	5b	bt-kśdym	^	
	5c	ky lʾ twsypy yqrʾw-lk		
	5d	gbrt mmlkwt		
	6a	qṣpty ʿl-ʿmy		
	6b	ḥllty nḥlty		
	6c	wʾtnm bydk	^	
	6d	lʾ-śmt lhm rḥmym		
	6e	ʿl-zqn hkbdt ʿlk mʾd		
	7a	wtʾmry lʿwlm		
	7b	ʾhyh gbrtʿd	^	
	7c	lʾ-śmt ʾlh ʿl-lbk		
	7d	lʾ zkrt ʾḥryth	MT ס	*Q*
III				
	8a	wʿth šmʿy-zʾt ʿdynh		
	8b	hywšbt lbṭḥ		
	8c	hʾmrh blbbh		
	8d	ʾny wʾpsy ʿwd	^	
	8e	lʾ ʾšb ʾlmnh		
	8f	wlʾ ʾdʿ škwl		
	9a	wtbʾnh lk šty-ʾlh		
	9b	rgʿ bywm ʾḥd		
	9c	škwl wʾlmn ktmm	^	
	9d	bʾw ʿlyk		
	9e	brb kšpyk		
	9f	bʿṣmt ḥbryk mʾd		
	10a	wtbṭḥy brʿtk		
	10b	ʾmrt ʾyn rʾny		
	10c	ḥkmtk wdʿtk		
	10d	hyʾ šwbbtk	^	
	10e	wtʾmry blbk		
	10f	ʾny wʾpsy ʿwd		
	11a	wbʾ ʿlyk rʿh		
	11b	lʾ tdʿy šḥrh		

	11c	wtpl ʿlyk hwh		
	11d	lʾ twkly kprh	^	
	11e	wtbʾ ʿlyk ptʾm		
	11f	šwʾh lʾ tdʿy		
IV				
	12a	ʿmdy-nʾ bḥbryk		
	12b	wbrb kšpyk		
	12c	bʾšr ygʿt mnʿwryk	^	
	12d	ʾwly twkly hwʿyl		
	12e	ʾwly tʿrwṣy		
	13a	nlʾyt brb ʿṣtyk	^	
	13b	yʿmdw-nʾ wywšyʿk		
	13c	hbrw šmym		
	13d	hḥzym bkwkbym		
	13e	mwdyʿm lḥdšym		
	13f	mʾšr ybʾw ʿlyk		
V				
	14a	hnh hyw kqš		
	14b	ʾš śrptm		
	14c	lʾ-yṣylw ʾt-npšm		
	14d	myd lhbh	^	
	14e	ʾyn-gḥlt lḥmm		
	14f	ʾwr lšbt ngdw		
	15a	kn hyw-lk ʾšr ygʿt	^	
	15b	sḥryk mnʿwryk		
	15c	ʾyš lʿbrw tʿw		
	15d	ʾyn mwšyʿk	MT ס	*QQ*

Chapter 48

I				
	1a	šmʿw-zʾt byt-yʿqb		
	1b	hnqrʾym bšm yśrʾl		
	1c	wmmy yhwdh yṣʾw	^	
	1d	hnšbʿym bšm yhwh		
	1e	wbʾlhy yśrʾl yzkyrw		
	1f	lʾ bʾmt wlʾ bṣdqh		
	2a	ky-mʿyr hqdš nqrʾw		
	2b	wʿl-ʾlhy yśrʾl nsmkw	^	
	2c	yhwh ṣbʾwt šmw	MT ס	*Q*
II				
	3a	hrʾšnwt mʾz hgdty		
	3b	wmpy yṣʾw wʾšmyʿm	^	

	3c	ptʾm ʿśyty wtbʾnh		
	4a	mdʿty ky qšh ʾth	^	
	4b	wgyd brzl ʿrpk		
	4c	wmṣḥk nḥwšh		
	5a	wʾgyd lk mʾz		
	5b	bṭrm tbwʾ hšmʿtyk	^	
	5c	pn-tʾmr ʿṣby ʿśm		
	5d	wpsly wnsky ṣwm		
III				
	6a	šmʿt ḥzh klh		
	6b	wʾtm hlwʾ tgydw	^	
	6c	hšmʿtyk ḥdšwt mʿth		
	6d	wnṣrwt wlʾ ydʿtm		
	7a	ʿth nbrʾw wlʾ mʾz		
	7b	wlpny-ywm wlʾ šmʿtm	^	
	7c	pn-tʾmr hnh ydʿtyn		
	8a	gm lʾ-šmʿt gm lʾ ydʿt		
	8b	gm mʾz lʾ-ptḥh ʾznk		
	8c	ky ydʿty bgwd tbgwd		
	8d	wpšʿ mbṭn qrʾ lk		
IV				
	9a	lmʿn šmy ʾʾryk ʾpy		
	9b	wthlty ʾḥṭm-lk	^	
	9c	lblty hkrytk		*Q*
	10a	hnh ṣrptyk wlʾ bksp	^	
	10b	bḥ[n]tyk bkwr ʿny		
	11a	lmʿny lmʿny ʾʿśh		
	11b	ky ʾyk yḥl	^	
	11c	wkbwdy lʾḥr lʾ-ʾtn	MT ס	*QQ*
V				
	12a	šmʿ ʾly yʿqb		
	12b	wyśrʾl mqrʾy	^	
	12c	ʾny-hwʾ ʾny rʾšwn		
	12d	ʾp ʾny ʾḥrwn		
	13a	ʾp-ydy ysdh ʾrṣ		
	13b	wymyny ṭpḥh šmym	^	
	13c	qrʾ ʾny ʾlyhm		
	13d	yʿmdw yḥdw		
VI				
	14a	hqbṣw klkm wšmʿw		
	14b	my bhm hgyd ʾt-ʾlh	^	
	14c	yhwh ʾhbw yʿśh ḥpṣw		
	14d	bbbl wzrʿw kśdym		

	15a	ᵓny ᵓny dbrty			
	15b	ᵓp-qrᵓtyw	^		
	15c	hbyᵓtyw whṣlyḥ drkw			
	16a	qrbw ᵓly šmᶜw-zᵓt			
	16b	lᵓ mrᵓš bstr dbrty			
	16c	mᶜt hywth šm ᵓny			
	16d	wᶜth ᵓdny yhwh			
	16e	šlḥny wrwḥw		MT פ	*Q*
VII					
	17a	kh-ᵓmr yhwh gᵓlk			
	17b	qdwš yśrᵓl	^		
	17c	ᵓny yhwh ᵓlhyk			
	17d	mlmdk lhwᶜyl			
	17e	mdrykk bdrk tlk			
	18a	lwᵓ hqšbt lmṣwty	^		
	18b	wyhy knhr šlwmk			
	18c	wṣdqtk kgly hym			
	19a	wyhy kḥwl zrᶜk			
	19b	wṣᵓṣᵓy mᶜyk kmᶜtyw	^		
	19c	lᵓ-ykrt wlᵓ-yšmd			
	19d	šmw mlpny			*Q*
VIII					
	20a	ṣᵓw mbbl			
	20b	brḥw mkśdym			
	20c	bqwl rnh hgydw			
	20d	hšmyᶜw zᵓt			
	20e	hwṣyᵓwh ᶜd-qṣh hᵓrṣ	^		
	20f	ᵓmrw gᵓl yhwh			
	20g	ᶜbdw yᶜqb			
	21a	wlᵓ ṣmᵓw			
	21b	bḥrbwt hwlykm			
	21c	mym mṣwr hzyl lmw	^		
	21d	wybqᶜ-ṣwr			
	21e	wyzbw mym			
	22	ᵓyn šlwm ᵓmr yhwh lršᶜym		MT ס	

Appendix 2

So-Called Original of 48:1–11 after Removal of Secondary Harsh Passages

1 Hear this, O house of Jacob,
the ones calling themselves by the name Israel
and from the waters of Judah they came forth;
the ones swearing by the name of Yahweh,
and the God of Israel they invoke.
3 The first things from time past I declared
and from my mouth they went forth and I announced them.
Suddenly I acted and they came.
5 (And I declared it to you from time past,
before it came I announced it to you,)
6 (You heard, now see it all!
and you, won't you declare?)
I announced to you new things only now
and secret things, and you did not know them.
7 (Now they are created and not in time past;
not before today, and you did not hear them)
8 (No, you did not hear; no, you did not know,
no, in time past your ear did not open.)
11 For my sake, for my sake I act.
and my glory to another I will not give.

Note: Material in parentheses indicates further excisions, mostly by Begrich, but also some by Marti and Kohler.

Bibliography

Achtemeier, E. *The Community and Message of Isaiah 56–66.* Minneapolis: Augsburg, 1982.

Ackroyd, P. R. *Exile and Restoration.* Old Testament Library. Philadelphia: Westminster, 1968.

_______. "The History of Israel in the Exilic and Post-Exilic Periods." Pp. 320–50 in *Tradition and Interpretation: Essays by Members of the Society for Old Testament Study.* Edited by G. W. Anderson. Oxford: Clarendon, 1979.

_______. "Interpretation of the Babylonian Exile: A Study of 2 Kings 20, Isaiah 38–39." *Scottish Journal of Theology* 27 (1974) 329–52.

Albright, W. F. *Yahweh and the Gods of Canaan: A Historical Analysis of Two Contrasting Faiths.* Garden City, New York: Doubleday, 1968; Reprint, Winona Lake, Indiana: Eisenbrauns, 1978.

Alonso Schökel, L. *Estudios de poetica Hebrea.* Barcelona: Juan Flors, 1963.

_______. "Hermeneutical Problems of a Literary Study of the Bible." Pp. 1–15 in *Congress Volume: Edinburgh, 1974.* Vetus Testamentum Supplements 28. Leiden: Brill, 1975.

Alter, Robert. *The Art of Biblical Poetry.* New York: Basic Books, 1985.

Alter, Robert, and F. Kermode. *The Literary Guide to the Bible.* Cambridge, Massachusetts: Harvard University Press, 1987.

Althann, R. "*Yom* 'Time' and Some Texts in Isaiah." *Journal of Northwest Semitic Languages* 11 (1983) 3–8.

Andersen, Francis I. *The Sentence in Biblical Hebrew.* Janua Linguarum, Series Practica 235. The Hague: Mouton, 1974.

Andersen, Francis I., and A. Dean Forbes. " 'Prose Particle' Counts of the Hebrew Bible." Pp. 165–83 in *The Word of the Lord Shall Go Forth: Essays in Honor of David Noel Freedman in Celebration of His Sixtieth Birthday.* Edited by Carol L. Meyers and M. O'Connor. Winona Lake, Indiana: Eisenbrauns, 1983.

Andersen, Francis I., and D. N. Freedman. *Hosea: A New Translation with Introduction and Commentary.* Anchor Bible 24. Garden City, New York: Doubleday, 1980.

Anderson, Bernhard W. "Exodus and Covenant in Second Isaiah and Prophetic Tradition." Pp. 339–60 in *Magnalia Dei: The Mighty Acts of God* (Essays on the Bible and Archaeology in Memory of G. Ernest Wright). Edited by Frank Moore Cross, Werner E. Lemke, and Patrick D. Miller Jr. Garden City, New York: Doubleday, 1976.

———. "The New Frontier of Rhetorical Criticism: A Tribute to James Muilenburg." Pp. ix–xvii in *Rhetorical Criticism: Essays in Honor of James Muilenburg.* Edited by J. J. Jackson and M. Kessler. Pittsburgh Theological Monograph Series 1. Pittsburgh: Pickwick, 1974.

Auffret, P. *The Literary Structure of Psalm 2.* Translated by D. J. A. Clines. Journal for the Study of the Old Testament Supplement Series 3. Sheffield: JSOT Press, 1977.

———. *La Sagesse à bati sa maisson: études de structures litteraires dans l'AT et specialement dans les Pss.* Fribourg: Éditions Universitaires / Göttingen: Vandenhoeck & Ruprecht, 1982.

Baltzer, D. *Ezechiel und Deuterojesaja.* Beihefte zur Zeitschrift für die alttestamentliche Wissenschaft 121. Berlin: de Gruyter, 1971.

Baltzer, K. "Liberation from Debt Slavery after the Exile in Second Isaiah and Nehemiah." Pp. 477–84 in *Ancient Israelite Religion: Essays in Honor of Frank Moore Cross.* Edited by P. D. Miller, P. D. Hanson, and S. D. McBride. Philadelphia: Fortress, 1987.

Banwell, B. O. "A Suggested Analysis of Isaiah xl.–lxvi." *Expository Times* 76 (1964–65) 166.

Barr, James. "Reading the Bible as Literature." *Bulletin of the John Rylands University Library of Manchester* 56 (1973) 10–33.

Barthes, R., et al., editors. *Structural Analysis and Biblical Exegesis: Interpretational Essays.* Translated by A. Johnson. Pittsburgh Theological Monograph Series 3. Pittsburgh: Pickwick, 1974.

Beeston, A. F. L. "Hebrew *šibbolet* and *šobel* (Is 47,2)." *Journal of Semitic Studies* 24 (1979) 175–77.

Begrich, J. *Studiën zu Deuterojesaja.* Beihefte zur Zeitschrift für die alttestamentliche Wissenschaft 77. Berlin: de Gruyter, 1938. Reprint, Munich: Chr. Kaiser, 1963.

Berlin, Adele. *The Dynamics of Biblical Parallelism.* Bloomington: Indiana University Press, 1985.

———. "Motif and Creativity in Biblical Poetry." *Prooftexts* 3 (1981) 231–41.

Best, T. F. *Hearing and Speaking the Word: Selections from the Works of James Muilenburg.* Chico, California: Scholars Press, 1984.

Beuken, W. A. M. "Isaiah LIV: The Multiple Identity of the Person Addressed." *Oudtestamentische Studiën* 19 (1974) 28–70.

———. *Jesaja.* Series de Prediking van het Oude Testament. Nijkerk: Callenbach, 1979.

Bickerman, Elias. "The Diaspora: The Babylonian Captivity." Pp. 342–58 in *The Cambridge History of Judaism,* volume 1: *Introduction: The Persian Period.* Edited by W. D. Davies and Louis Finkelstein. Cambridge: Cambridge University Press, 1984.

Blank, Sheldon H. *Prophetic Faith in Isaiah.* Detroit: Wayne State University Press, 1958.

———. "Irony by Way of Attribution." *Semitics* 1 (1970) 1–6.

______. "Studies in Deutero-Isaiah." *Hebrew Union College Annual* 15 (1940) 1–46.

Blau, J. "*Hōbərē šāmājim* (Jes xlvii 13) = Himmelsanbeter?" *Vetus Testamentum* 7 (1957) 183–84.

Blenkinsopp, J. *A History of Prophecy in Israel.* Philadelphia: Westminster, 1983.

Boadt, L. "Intentional Alliteration in Second Isaiah." *Catholic Biblical Quarterly* 45 (1983) 353–63.

______. "Isaiah 41:8–13: Notes on Poetic Structure and Style." *Catholic Biblical Quarterly* 35 (1973) 20–34.

Boer, P. A. H., de. "The Counsellor." Pp. 42–71 in *Wisdom in Israel and in the Ancient Near East* (Harold Henry Rowley Festschrift). Vetus Testamentum Supplements 3. Leiden: Brill, 1955.

Bonnard, P.-E. *Le second Isaïe, son disciple et leur éditeurs, Isaïe 40–66* Paris: Gabalda, 1972.

Bright, John. *A History of Israel.* 3d ed. Philadelphia: Westminster, 1981.

Brown, F., S. R. Driver, and C. A. Briggs. *A Hebrew and English Lexicon of the Old Testament.* Oxford: Clarendon, 1907.

Budde, K. "Das hebräische Klagelied." *Zeitschrift für die alttestamentliche Wissenschaft* 2 (1882) 1–52.

______. "Ein altehebräisches Klagelied." *Zeitschrift für die alttestamentliche Wissenschaft* 3 (1883) 299–306.

______. "Die hebräische Leichenklage." *Zeitschrift des deutschen Palästina-Vereins* 6 (1883) 180–94.

______. "Zum hebräischen Klagelied." *Zeitschrift für die alttestamentliche Wissenschaft* 12 (1892) 31–37, 261–75.

Burrows, Millar, editor. *The Dead Sea Scrolls of St. Mark's Monastery,* volume 1: *The Isaiah Manuscript and the Habakkuk Commentary.* New Haven, Connecticut: American Schools of Oriental Research, 1950.

Casanowicz, I. M. *Paronomasia in the Old Testament.* Boston: Norwood, 1894.

Cassuto, U. "On the Formal and Stylistic Relationship between Deutero-Isaiah and Other Biblical Writers." Pp. 141–77 in *Biblical and Oriental Studies, Volume 1: Bible.* Translated by Israel Abrahams. Jerusalem: Magnes, 1973.

Ceresko, Anthony R. "The Function of Chiasmus in Hebrew Poetry." *Catholic Biblical Quarterly* 40 (1978) 1–10.

______. "A Poetic Analysis of Ps 105, with Attention to Its Use of Irony." *Biblica* 64 (1983) 20–46.

______. "A Rhetorical Analysis of David's 'Boast' (1 Samuel 17:34–37) Some Reflections on Method." *Catholic Biblical Quarterly* 47 (1985) 58–74.

______. "The A:B::B:A Word Pattern in Hebrew and Northwest Semitic with Special Reference to the Book of Job." Pp. 73–88 in *Ugarit-Forschungen* 7. Neukirchen-Vluyn: Neukirchener Verlag, 1975.

Cheyne, T. K. *The Prophecies of Isaiah: A New Translation with Commentary and Appendices.* 5th ed. rev. 2 volumes. London: Kegan Paul, Trench, 1889.

Childs, Brevard S. *The Book of Exodus: A Critical, Theological Commentary.* Old Testament Library. Philadelphia: Westminster, 1974.

Christensen, Duane L. "The Acrostic of Nahum Once Again: A Prosodic Analysis of Nahum 1,1–10." *Zeitschrift für die alttestamentliche Wissenschaft* 99 (1987) 409–15.

———. "The Acrostic of Nahum Reconsidered." *Zeitschrift für die alttestamentliche Wissenschaft* 87 (1975) 17–30.

———. "Anticipatory Paronomasia in Jonah 3:7–8 and Genesis 37:2." *Revue Biblique* 90 (1983) 261–63.

———. "Janus Parallelism in Gen. 6:3." *Hebrew Studies* 27 (1986) 20–24.

———. "Narrative Poetics and the Interpretation of the Book of Jonah." Pp. 29–48 in *Directions in Biblical Hebrew Poetry.* Edited by E. Follis. Journal for the Study of the Old Testament Supplement Series 40. Sheffield: JSOT Press, 1987.

———. "Prose and Poetry in the Bible. The Narrative Poetics of Deuteronomy 1,9–18." *Zeitschrift für die alttestamentliche Wissenschaft* 97 (1985) 179–89.

———. *Transformation of the War Oracle in Old Testament Prophecy: Studies in the Oracles against the Nations.* Harvard Dissertations in Religion 3. Missoula, Montana: Scholars Press, 1975.

Clements, R. E. "Beyond Tradition-History: Deutero-Isaianic Development of First Isaiah's Themes." *Journal for the Study of the Old Testament* 31 (1985) 95–113.

Clifford, Richard J. *Fair Spoken and Persuading: An Interpretation of Second Isaiah.* New York: Paulist, 1984.

———. "Cosmogonies in the Ugaritic Texts and in the Bible." *Orientalia* 53 (1984) 183–201.

———. "In Zion and David a New Beginning: An Interpretation of Psalm 78." Pp. 121–41 in *Traditions in Transformation: Turning Points in Biblical Faith* (Frank Moore Cross Festschrift). Edited by Baruch Halpern and Jon D. Levenson. Winona Lake, Indiana: Eisenbrauns, 1981.

———. "Rhetorical Criticism in the Exegesis of Hebrew Poetry." Edited by P. Achtemeier. Pp. 17–28 in *Society of Biblical Literature Seminar Papers,* 1980. Chico, California: Scholars Press, 1980.

———. "The Function of the Idol Passages in Second Isaiah." *Catholic Biblical Quarterly* 42 (1980) 450–64.

Clines, D. J. A., D. M. Gunn, and A. J. Hauser, editors. *Art and Meaning: Rhetoric in Biblical Literature.* Journal for the Study of the Old Testament Supplement Series 19. Sheffield: JSOT Press, 1982.

Clines, D. J. A. *I, He, We and They: A Literary Approach to Isaiah 53.* Journal for the Study of the Old Testament Supplement Series 1. Sheffield: JSOT Press, 1976.

______. "The Parallelism of Greater Precision." Pp. 77–100 in *Directions in Biblical Hebrew Poetry.* Edited by E. Follis. Journal for the Study of the Old Testament Supplement Series 40. Sheffield: JSOT Press, 1987.

Coggins, R. J. *Samaritans and Jews.* Atlanta: John Knox, 1975.

Cohen, Chayim. "The 'Widowed City.'" *Journal of the Ancient Near Eastern Society of Columbia University* 5 (The Gaster Festschrift; 1973) 75–81.

Collins, Terence. *Line-Forms in Hebrew Poetry: A Grammatical Approach to the Stylistic Study of the Hebrew Prophets,* Studia Pohl: Series Maior 7. Rome: Pontifical Biblical Institute, 1978.

Condamin, A. *Le livre de'Isaïa: traduction critique avec notes et commentaire.* Paris: Victor Lecoffre, 1905.

Conrad, Edgar W. "The 'Fear Not' Oracles in Second Isaiah." *Vetus Testamentum* 34 (1984) 129–52.

______. "The Community as King in Second Isaiah." Pp. 99–112 in *Understanding the Word: Essays in Honor of Bernhard W. Anderson.* Edited by James T. Butler, E. Conrad, and B. C. Ollenburger. Journal for the Study of the Old Testament Supplement Series 37. Sheffield: JSOT Press, 1985.

______. *Fear Not Warrior: A Study of 'al tira' Pericopes in the Hebrew Scriptures.* Brown Judaic Studies. Chico, California: Scholars Press, 1985.

______. "Second Isaiah and the Priestly Oracle of Salvation." *Zeitschrift für die alttestamentliche Wissenschaft* 93 (1981) 234–46.

Coogan, M. D. "A Structural and Literary Analysis of the Song of Deborah." *Catholic Biblical Quarterly* 40 (1978) 143–66.

Crenshaw, J. L. "*YHWH Ṣ^eba^ʾôt Š^emô*: A Form-Critical Analysis." *Zeitschrift für die alttestamentliche Wissenschaft* 81 (1969) 156–75.

Cross, Frank Moore, Jr. *Canaanite Myth and Hebrew Epic: Essays in the History of the Religion of Israel.* Cambridge: Harvard University Press, 1973.

______. "The Council of Yahweh in Second Isaiah." *Journal of Near Eastern Studies* 12 (1953) 274–77.

______. "New Directions in the Study of Apocalyptic." *Journal for Theology and the Church* 6 (1969) 157–65.

______. "Studies in the Structure of Hebrew Verse: The Prosody of Lamentations 1:1–22." Pp. 129–55 in *The Word Shall Go Forth: Essays in Honor of David Noel Freedman in Celebration of His Sixtieth Birthday.* Edited by Carol L. Meyers and M. O'Connor. Winona Lake, Indiana: Eisenbrauns, 1983.

Culley, R. C. *Oral Formulaic Language in the Biblical Psalms.* Toronto: University of Toronto Press, 1967.

Dahood, Mitchell. "A New Metrical Pattern in Biblical Poetry." *Catholic Biblical Quarterly* 29 (1967) 574–79.

———. *Psalms I: 1–50.* Anchor Bible 16. Garden City, New York: Doubleday, 1965.

———. *Psalms II: 51–100.* Anchor Bible 17. Garden City, New York: Doubleday, 1968.

———. *Psalms III: 101–150.* Anchor Bible 17A. Garden City, New York: Doubleday, 1970.

———. "Some Ambiguous Texts in Isaiah." *Catholic Biblical Quarterly* 20 (1958) 41–49.

Dahood, Mitchell, and Tadeusz Penar. "Ugaritic-Hebrew Parallel Pairs." Pp. 71–382 in *Ras Shamra Parallels,* volume 1. Edited by Loren R. Fisher. Analecta Orientalia 49. Rome: Pontifical Biblical Institute, 1972.

Darr, Katheryn Pfisterer. "Like Warrior, like Woman: Destruction and Deliverance in Isaiah 42:10–17." *Catholic Biblical Quarterly* 49 (1987) 560–71.

Daube, D. *The Sudden in Scripture.* Leiden: Brill, 1964.

Davies, W. D., and L. Finkelstein, editors. *The Cambridge History of Judaism,* volume 1: *Introduction: The Persian Period.* Cambridge: Cambridge University Press, 1984.

Delitzsch, Franz. *Biblical Commentary on the Prophecies of Isaiah,* volume 2. Reprinted, Grand Rapids, Michigan: Eerdmans, 1949.

Dillmann, August. *Der Prophet Jesaia.* Kurzgefasstes exegetisches Handbuch zum Alten Testament. Leipzig: S. Hirzel, 1890.

Dion, P. "The 'Fear Not' Formula and Holy War." *Catholic Biblical Quarterly* 32 (1970) 565–70.

Dohmen, Ch. "Ein kanaanäischer Schmiedeterminus (*NSK*)." *Ugarit-Forschungen* 15 (1983) 39–42. Neukirchen-Vluyn: Neukirchener Verlag, 1983.

Donner, H., and W. Röllig. *Kanaanäische und aramäische Inschriften.* Wiesbaden: Harrassowitz, 1962.

Driver, G. R. "Linguistic and Textual Problems: Isaiah XL–LXVI." *Journal of Theological Studies* 36 (1935) 399.

———. "Isaiah 6:1: 'His Train Filled the Temple.'" Pp. 87–96 in *Near Eastern Studies in Honor of William Foxwell Albright.* Edited by Hans Goedicke. Baltimore: Johns Hopkins University Press, 1971.

Duhm, B. *Das Buch Jesaia.* 3d ed. Handbuch zum Alten Testament 3/1. Göttingen: Vandenhoeck & Ruprecht, 1914.

Eaton, J. H. *Festal Drama in Deutero-Isaiah.* London: SPCK, 1979.

Ellenbogen, M. *Foreign Words in the Old Testament: Their Origin and Etymology.* London: Luzac, 1962.

Elliger, K. *Deuterojesaja.* Biblischer Kommentar: Altes Testament 12/1. Neukirchen-Vluyn: Neukirchener Verlag, 1978.

_______. *Deuterojesaja in seinem Verhältnis zu Tritojesaja.* Beiträge zur Wissenschaft vom Alten und Neuen Testament 4/11. Stuttgart: Kolhammer, 1933.

Elliger, K., and W. Rudolph, editors. *Biblia Hebraica Stuttgartensia.* Stuttgart: Deutsche Bibelstiftung, 1977.

Erlandsson, Seth. *The Burden of Babylon: A Study of Isaiah 13:2–14:23.* Coniectanea Biblica: Old Testament Series 4. Lund: CWK Gleerup, 1970.

Even-Shoshan, A., editor. *A New Concordance of the Bible.* Jerusalem: Kiryat-Sepher, 1983 [Hebrew].

Fensham, F. Charles. "Widow, Orphan, and the Poor in Ancient Near Eastern Legal and Wisdom Literature." *Journal of Near Eastern Studies* 21 (1962) 129–39.

Fichtner, J. "Jahves Plan in der Botschaft des Jesaja." *Zeitschrift für die alttestamentliche Wissenschaft* 64 (1951) 16–33.

Fischer, J. *Das Buch Isaias übersetzt und erklärt.* 2 volumes. Die Heilige Schrift des Alten Testaments. Bonn: Hanstein, 1937–1939.

Fishbane, Michael. *Biblical Interpretation in Ancient Israel.* Oxford: Clarendon, 1985.

_______. *Text and Texture: Close Readings of Selected Biblical Texts.* New York: Schocken, 1979.

Fitzgerald, Aloysius. "*BTWLT* and *BT* as Titles for Capital Cities." *Catholic Biblical Quarterly* 37 (1975) 167–83.

_______. "The Interchange of *L, N,* and *R* in Biblical Hebrew." *Journal of Biblical Literature* 97 (1978) 481–88.

_______. "The Mythological Background for the Presentation of Jerusalem as Queen and False Worship in the Old Testament." *Catholic Biblical Quarterly* 34 (1972) 302–16.

Fohrer, Georg. *Das Buch Jesaja, 3: Kapitel 40–66.* Zürcher Bibelkommentar. Zürich: Zwingli, 1965.

Follis, Elaine R., editor. *Directions in Biblical Hebrew Poetry.* Journal for the Study of the Old Testament Supplement Series 40. Sheffield: JSOT Press, 1987.

_______. "The Holy City as Daughter." Pp. 173–84 in *Directions in Biblical Hebrew Poetry.* Edited by Elaine R. Follis. Journal for the Study of the Old Testament Supplement Series 40. Sheffield: JSOT Press, 1987.

Frankfort, H. *Kingship and the Gods: A Study of Ancient Near Eastern Religion as the Integration of Society and Nature.* Preface by S. N. Kramer. Chicago: University of Chicago Press, 1978.

Freedman, David Noel. "The Aaronic Benediction (Numbers 6:24–26)." Pp. 229–42 in *Pottery, Poetry, and Prophecy: Collected Essays on Hebrew Poetry.* Winona Lake, Indiana: Eisenbrauns, 1980.

———. "Acrostic Poems in the Hebrew Bible: Alphabetic and Otherwise." *Catholic Biblical Quarterly* 48 (1986) 408–31.

———. "Acrostics and Metrics in Hebrew Poetry." Pp. 51–76 in *Pottery, Poetry, and Prophecy: Collected Essays on Hebrew Poetry.* Winona Lake, Indiana: Eisenbrauns, 1980.

———. "Another Look at Biblical Hebrew Poetry." Pp. 11–28 in *Directions in Biblical Hebrew Poetry.* Edited by Elaine R. Follis. Journal for the Study of the Old Testament Supplement Series 40. Sheffield: JSOT Press, 1987.

———. "The Broken Construct Chain." *Biblica* 53 (1972) 534–36.

———. "Discourse on Prophetic Discourse." Pp. 141–58 in *The Quest for the Kingdom of God: Studies in Honor of George E. Mendenhall.* Edited by H. B. Huffmon, F. A. Spina, and A. R. W. Green. Winona Lake, Indiana: Eisenbrauns, 1983.

———. "Mistress Forever": A Note on Isaiah 47,7." *Biblica* 51 (1970) 538.

———. "Pottery, Poetry, and Prophecy: An Essay on Biblical Poetry." Pp. 1–22 in *Pottery, Poetry, and Prophecy: Collected Essays on Hebrew Poetry.* Winona Lake, Indiana: Eisenbrauns, 1980.

———. "Prolegomenon." Pp. 23–50 in *Pottery, Poetry, and Prophecy: Collected Essays on Hebrew Poetry.* Winona Lake, Indiana: Eisenbrauns, 1980.

———. "The Refrain in David's Lament over Saul and Jonathan." Pp. 115–26 in *Ex Orbe Religionum: Studia Geo Widengren Oblata* 1. Leiden: Brill, 1972.

———. "Strophe and Meter in Exodus 15." Pp. 187–228 in *Pottery, Poetry, and Prophecy: Collected Essays on Hebrew Poetry.* Winona Lake, Indiana: Eisenbrauns, 1980.

———. "The Structure of Isaiah 40:1–11." Pp. 167–93 in *Perspectives on Language and Text: Essays Presented in Honor of Francis I. Andersen's Sixtieth Birthday, July 28, 1985.* Edited by E. W. Conrad and E. G. Newing. Winona Lake, Indiana: Eisenbrauns, 1987.

———. "The Twenty-Third Psalm." *Michigan Oriental Studies in Honor of George G. Cameron.* Edited by Louis L. Orlin, et al. Ann Arbor: Department of Near Eastern Studies, University of Michigan, 1976.

Freedman, David Noel, and Chris Franke-Hyland. "Psalm 29: A Structural Analysis." *Harvard Theological Review* 66 (1973) 237–56.

Fretheim, Terence E. *The Suffering of God: An Old Testament Perspective.* Overtures to Biblical Theology 14. Philadelphia: Fortress, 1984.

Garr, W. R. "The Qinah: A Study of Poetic Meter, Syntax and Style." *Zeitschrift für die alttestamentliche Wissenschaft* 95 (1983) 54–75.

Geller, Stephen A. "The Dynamics of Parallel Verse: A Poetic Analysis of Deut 32:6–12." *Harvard Theological Review* 75 (1982) 35–56.

———. "Theory and Method in the Study of Biblical Poetry." *Jewish Quarterly Review* 73 (1982) 65–77.

Geller, Stephen A., Edward L. Greenstein, and Adele Berlin. *A Sense of Text: The Art of Language in the Study of Biblical Literature.* Jewish Quarterly Review Supplement: 1982. Philadelphia: Dropsie College, 1983.

Gelston, A. "Some Notes on Second Isaiah." *Vetus Testamentum* 21 (1971) 517–27.

Gevirtz, S. *Patterns in the Early Poetry of Israel.* Studies in Ancient Oriental Civilization 32. Chicago: University of Chicago Press, 1963.

Gileadi, A. *The Apocalyptic Book of Isaiah: A New Translation with Interpretive Key.* Provo, Utah: Hebraeus, 1982.

Ginsberg, H. L. "The Arm of YHWH in Isaiah 51–63 and the Text of Isa 53 10–11." *Journal of Biblical Literature* 77 (1958) 152–56.

Gitay, Yehoshua. "Deutero-Isaiah: Oral or Written?" *Journal of Biblical Literature* 99 (1980) 185–97.

_______. *Prophecy and Persuasion: A Study of Isaiah 40–48.* Forschung zur Theologie und Literatur 14. Bonn: Linguistica Biblica, 1981.

Glück, J. J. "Assonance in Ancient Hebrew Poetry: Sound Patterns as a Literary Device." Pp. 69–84 in *De Fructu Oris Sui: Essays in Honour of Adrianus van Selms.* Edited by I. H. Eybers et al. Pretoria Oriental Series 9. Leiden: Brill, 1971.

_______. "Paronomasia in Biblical Literature." *Semitics* 1 (1970) 50–78.

Goldingay, John. *God's Prophet, God's Servant: A Study in Jeremiah and Isaiah 40–55.* Exeter: Paternoster, 1984.

Good, E. W. *Irony in the Old Testament.* Philadelphia: Westminster, 1965. Reprint, Sheffield: Almond, 1981.

Gordon, Cyrus. H. *Ugaritic Literature: A Comprehensive Translation of the Poetic and Prose Texts.* Scripta Pontificii Instituti Biblici 98. Rome: Pontifical Biblical Institute, 1949.

Gottwald, Norman K. *The Hebrew Bible: A Socio-Literary Introduction.* Philadelphia: Fortress, 1985.

Graffy, Adrian. *A Prophet Confronts His People: The Disputation Speech in the Prophets.* Analecta Biblica 104. Rome: Pontifical Biblical Institute, 1984.

Gray, George Buchanan. *The Forms of Hebrew Poetry.* London and New York: Hodder and Stoughton, 1915. Reprint, The Library of Biblical Studies. New York: KTAV, 1972.

Greenspahn, F. E. *Hapax Legomena in Biblical Hebrew.* Chico, California: Scholars Press, 1984.

Greenwood, David. "Rhetorical Criticism and *Formgeschichte*: Some Methodological Considerations." *Journal of Biblical Literature* 89 (1970) 418–26.

Gressman, H. "Die literarische Analyse Deuterojesajas." *Zeitschrift für die alttestamentliche Wissenschaft* 34 (1914) 254–97.

Gruber, M. I. "The Motherhood of God in Second Isaiah." *Revue biblique* 90 (1983) 351–59.

Guillaume, A. *Prophecy and Divination.* New York: Harper Bros., 1938.

Guillet, Jacques. "La polémique contre les idols et le serviteur de Yahve." *Biblica* 40 (1959) 428–34.

Gunkel, Hermann. "Die Propheten als Schriftsteller und Dichter." Pp. 34–70 in *Die Propheten.* Göttingen: Vandenhoeck & Ruprecht, 1923. Reprint, "The Prophets as Writers and Poets." Pp. 22–73 in *Prophecy in Israel: Search for an Identity.* Edited by David L. Petersen. Issues in Religion and Theology 10. Philadelphia: Fortress / London: SPCK, 1987.

———. *The Legends of Genesis: The Biblical Saga and History.* Translated by W. H. Carruth. New York: Schocken, 1901.

Gunn, D. "Deutero-Isaiah and the Flood." *Journal of Biblical Literature* 94 (1975) 493–508.

Gunn, Giles. "Threading the Eye of the Needle: The Place of the Literary Critic in Religious Studies." *Journal of the American Academy of Religion* 43 (1975) 183–84.

Habel, N. "Appeal to Ancient Tradition as a Literary Form," *Zeitschrift für die alttestamentliche Wissenschaft* 88 (1975) 253–72.

Hallo, W. "Cult Statue and Divine Image: A Preliminary Study." Pp. 1–17 in *Scripture in Context II: More Essays on the Comparative Method.* Edited by W. W. Hallo, J. C. Moyer, and L. G. Perdue. Winona Lake, Indiana: Eisenbrauns, 1983.

Hanson, P. D. *The Dawn of Apocalyptic: The Historical and Sociological Roots of Jewish Apocalyptic Eschatology.* Rev. ed. Philadelphia: Fortress, 1979.

Haran, Menaḥem. *Between Riʾshonot (Former Prophecies) and Ḥadashot (New Prophecies) A Literary Historical Study in the Group of Prophecies Isaiah XL–XLVIII.* Jerusalem: n. p., 1963 [Hebrew].

———. "The Literary Structure and Chronological Framework of the Prophecies in Is. xl–xlviii." Pp. 127–53 in *Congress Volume: Bonn, 1962.* Vetus Testamentum Supplements 9. Leiden: Brill, 1963.

Harner, P. *Grace and Law in Second Isaiah: "I Am the Lord."* Lewiston: Edwin Mellen, 1988.

———. "The Salvation Oracle in Second Isaiah." *Journal of Biblical Literature* 88 (1968) 418–34.

Hayes, John H. "The History of the Form-Critical Study of Prophecy." Pp. 60–99 in *Society of Biblical Literature 1973 Seminar Papers 1.* Edited by George MacRae. Cambridge, Massachusetts: Society of Biblical Literature, 1973.

———. "The Usage of Oracles against Foreign Nations in Ancient Israel." *Journal of Biblical Literature* 87 (1968) 81–92.

Hayes, John H., and Stuart A. Irvine. *Isaiah, The Eighth Century Prophet: His Times and His Preaching.* Nashville: Abingdon, 1987.

Hengel, Martin. *Judaism and Hellenism: Studies in Their Encounter in Palestine during the Early Hellenistic Period.* 2 volumes. Translated by John Bowden. Philadelphia: Fortress, 1974.

Herbert, A. S. *The Book of the Prophet Isaiah: Chapters 40–66.* Cambridge Bible Commentary on the Old Testament. Cambridge: Cambridge University Press, 1975.

Hillers, D. *Lamentations: A New Translation.* Anchor Bible 7A. Garden City, New York: Doubleday, 1972.

Hoffman, Hans Werner. "Form-Funktion-Intention." *Zeitschrift für die alttestamentliche Wissenschaft* 82 (1970) 341–46.

Hoffman, Y. "The Root QRB as a Legal Term." *Journal of Northwest Semitic Languages* 10 (1982) 67–73.

Holladay, W. L. *The Architecture of Jeremiah 1–20.* Lewisburg, Pennsylvania: Bucknell University Press, 1976.

Hollenberg, D. E. "Nationalism and 'the Nations' in Isaiah xl–lv." *Vetus Testamentum* 19 (1967) 23–36.

Holmgren, Fredrick. *With Wings as Eagles: Isaiah 40–55.* New York: Scholars Press, 1973.

Hrushovski, Benjamin. "The Meaning of Sound Patterns in Poetry." *Poetics Today* 2 (1980) 39–56.

Huey, F. B., and B. Corley. *A Student's Dictionary for Biblical and Theological Studies.* Grand Rapids, Michigan: Zondervan, 1983.

Hurvitz, Avi. "The History of a Legal Formula, *kōl ašer ḥāpēṣ ᶜāśā.*" *Vetus Testamentum* 32 (1982) 265–67.

Irwin, W. *Isaiah 28–33: A Translation and Philological Commentary.* Biblica et Orientalia 30. Rome: Pontifical Biblical Institute, 1977.

Janssen, Enno. *Juda in der Exilszeit: Ein Beitrag zur Frage der Entstehung des Judentums.* Forschungen zur Religion und Literatur des Alten und Neuen Testaments 69. Göttingen: Vandenhoeck & Ruprecht, 1956.

Janzen, J. G. "Another Look at *Yaḥalipu Koaḥ* in Isaiah xl,i." *Vetus Testamentum* 33 (1983) 428–34.

Jensen, J. *Isaiah 1–39.* Old Testament Message 8. Wilmington, Delaware: Michael Glazier, 1984.

_______. *The Use of tôrâ by Isaiah: His Debate with the Wisdom Tradition.* Washington, D.C.: Catholic Biblical Association, 1973.

_______. "Yahweh's Plan in Isaiah and in the Rest of the Old Testament." *Catholic Biblical Quarterly* 48 (1986) 443–55.

Jones, D. R. "The Tradition of the Oracles of Isaiah of Jerusalem." *Zeitschrift für die alttestamentliche Wissenschaft* 67 (1955) 226–46.

Kapelrud, Arvid S. "The Date of the Priestly Code (P)." *Annual of the Swedish Theological Institute* 3 (1964) 58–64.

_______. "The Main Concern of Second Isaiah." *Vetus Testamentum* 32 (1982) 50–59.

Kaufmann, Yehezkel. *The Babylonian Captivity and Deutero-Isaiah.* New York: Union of American Hebrew Congregations, 1970.

Kautzsch, E., editor. *Gesenius' Hebrew Grammar.* Translated by A. E. Cowley. 2d Eng. ed. Oxford: Clarendon, 1910.

Kay, W. *The Holy Bible,* volume 5: *Isaiah, Jeremiah, Lamentations.* Edited by F. C. Cook. New York: Charles Scribners Sons, 1909.

Kessler, Martin. "An Introduction to Rhetorical Criticism of the Bible: Prolegomena." *Semitics* 7 (1980) 1–27.

______. "A Methodological Setting for Rhetorical Criticism." Pp. 1–19 in *Art and Meaning: Rhetoric in Biblical Literature.* Edited by David J. A. Clines, David M. Gunn, and Alan J. Hauser. Journal for the Study of the Old Testament Supplement Series 19. Sheffield: JSOT Press, 1982.

Kikawada, I. "Some Proposals for the Definition of Rhetorical Criticism." *Semitics* 5 (1977) 67–91.

Kissane, Edward J. *The Book of Isaiah,* volume 2. Dublin: Browne & Nolan, 1943.

Klein, Ralph W. *Israel in Exile: A Theological Interpretation.* Overtures to Biblical Theology. Philadelphia: Fortress, 1979.

Knierim, R. "Old Testament Form Criticism Reconsidered." *Interpretation* 27 (1973) 435–68.

Knight, G. A. F. *Deutero-Isaiah: A Theological Commentary on Isaiah 40–55.* New York: Abingdon, 1965.

Koch, L. *The Prophets,* volume 2: *The Babylonian and Persian Periods.* Translated by M. Kohl. Philadelphia: Fortress, 1982.

Köhler, Ludwig. *Deuterojesaja stilkritisch untersucht.* Beihefte zur Zeitschrift für die alttestamentliche Wissenschaft 37. Giessen: Alfred Töpelmann, 1923.

König, Ed. *The Exiles' Book of Consolation.* Edinburgh: T. & T. Clark, 1899.

______. *Das Buch Jesaja.* Gütersloh: n. p., 1926.

Kraft, C. F. *The Strophic Structure of Hebrew Poetry.* Chicago: University of Chicago Press, 1938.

Krašovec, J. *Antithetic Structure in Biblical Hebrew Poetry.* Vetus Testamentum Supplements 35. Leiden: Brill, 1984.

______. "Merism-Polar Expressions in Biblical Hebrew." *Biblica* 64 (1983) 231–39.

Kselman, John S. "Design and Structure in Hebrew Poetry." Pp. 1–16 in Society of Biblical Literature Seminar Papers, 1980. Edited by P. Achtemeier. Chico, California: Scholars Press, 1980.

______. "Psalm 3: A Structural and Literary Study." *Catholic Biblical Quarterly* 49 (1987) 572–80

______. "'Why Have You Abandoned Me?' A Rhetorical Study of Psalm 22." Pp. 179–98 in *Art and Meaning: Rhetoric in Biblical Literature.* Edited by D. J. A. Clines, D. M. Gunn, and Alan J. Hauser. Journal for the Study of the Old Testament Supplement Series 19. Sheffield: JSOT Press, 1982.

Kugel, James L. *The Idea of Biblical Poetry.* New Haven: Yale University Press, 1981.

______. "On the Bible and Literary Criticism." *Prooftexts* 1 (1981) 217–34.

______. "Some Thoughts on Future Research into Biblical Style: Addenda to the Idea of Biblical Poetry." *Journal for the Study of the Old Testament* 28 (1984) 107–17.

Kuhn, G. "Babulwn." Pp. 512–14 in *Theologisches Wörterbuch zum Neuen Testament,* volume 1. Edited by G. Kittel and G. Friedrich. Stuttgart: Kohlhammer, 1933.

Kuntz, K. "The Contribution of Rhetorical Criticism to Understanding Isaiah 51:1–16." Pp. 140–71 in *Art and Meaning: Rhetoric in Biblical Literature.* Edited by D. J. A. Clines, D. M. Gunn, and Alan J. Hauser. Journal for the Study of the Old Testament Supplement Series 19. Sheffield: JSOT Press, 1982.

Kutscher, E. Y. *The Language and Linguistic Background of the Isaiah Scroll (1QIsa[a]).* Leiden: Brill, 1974.

Labuschagne, C. J. "The Emphasizing Particle *gam* and Its Connotations." Pp. 193–203 in *Studia Biblica et Semitica in Honor of T. C. Vriezen.* Edited by Willem Cornelis van Unnik and A. S. van der Woude. Wageningen: H. Veenman, 1966.

______. *The Incomparability of Yahweh in the Old Testament.* Leiden: Brill, 1966.

Lack, R. *La symbolique du livre d'Isaïe: Essai sur l'image littéraire comme élément de structuration.* Analecta Biblica 59. Rome: Pontifical Biblical Institute, 1973.

Leene, Henk. "Isaiah 46.8: Summons to Be Human?" *Journal for the Study of the Old Testament* 30 (1984) 111–21.

Levy, Reuben. *Deutero-Isaiah: A Commentary, Together with a Preliminary Essay on Deutero-Isaiah's Influence on Jewish Thought.* London: Oxford University Press, 1925.

Lewy, J. "The Late Assyro-Babylonian Cult of the Moon and Its Culmination at the Time of Nabonidus." *Hebrew Union College Annual* 19 (1945–46) 405–89.

Liebreich, L. J. "The Compilation of the Book of Isaiah." *Jewish Quarterly Review* 46 (1956) 121–22.

Lisowsky, G. *Konkordanz zum hebräischen Alten Testament.* 2d ed. Stuttgart: Deutsche Bibelgesellschaft, 1981.

Longman, T. "A Critique of Two Recent Metrical Systems." *Biblica* 63 (1982) 230–54.

Loretz, Oswald. "Mesopotamische und ugaritisch-kanaanäische Elemente im Prolog des Buches Deuterojesaja (Jes 40,1–11)." *Orientalia* 53 (1984) 284–96.

Lowth, Robert. *Isaiah: A New Translation, with a Preliminary Dissertation and Notes,* volume 2. 3d ed. London: J. Nichols, 1795.

Ludwig, Theodore M. "The Traditions of Establishing the Earth in Deutero-Isaiah." *Journal of Biblical Literature* 92 (1973) 345–51.

Lundy, F. "Poetry and Parallelism: Some Comments on James Kugel's *The Idea of Biblical Poetry.*" *Journal for the Study of the Old Testament* 28 (1984) 61–87.

Luyster, Robert. "Wind and Water: Cosmogonic Symbolism in the Old Testament." *Zeitschrift für die alttestamentliche Wissenschaft* 93 (1981) 1–9.

McKane, W. *Prophets and Wise Men.* Studies in Biblical Theology 44. London: SCM, 1965.

McKenzie, J. *Second Isaiah.* Anchor Bible 20. Garden City, New York: Doubleday, 1967.

Mandelkern, S. *Veteris Testamenti concordantiae Hebraicae atque Chaldaicae.* Reprint, Tel Aviv: Schocken, 1968.

Marti, D. Karl. *Das Buch Jesaja.* Tübingen: Mohr, 1900.

Martin-Achard, R. "Esaïe 47 et la tradition prophétique sur Babylone." Pp. 83–105 in *Prophecy: Essays Presented to Georg Fohrer on His Sixty-Fifth Birthday, 6 September 1980.* Edited by J. A. Emerton. Beihefte zur Zeitschrift für die alttestamentliche Wissenschaft 150. Berlin: de Gruyter, 1980.

———. *A Light to the Nations: A Study of the Old Testament Conception of Israel's Mission to the World.* Edinburgh: Oliver and Boyd, 1962.

Melamed, E. "Break-up of Stereotype Phrases as an Artistic Device in Biblical Poetry." Pp. 115–21 in *Studies in Bible.* Edited by Chaim Rabin. Scripta Hierosolymitana 8. Jerusalem: Magnes, 1961.

Melugin, Roy F. "Muilenburg, Form Criticism, and Theological Exegesis." Pp. 91–99 in *Encounter with the Text: Form and History in the Hebrew Bible.* Edited by Martin J. Buss. The Society of Biblical Literature Semeia Supplements. Philadelphia: Fortress / Missoula, Montana: Scholars Press, 1979.

———. "Deutero-Isaiah and Form Criticism." *Vetus Testamentum* 21 (1971) 326–27.

———. "The Conventional and the Creative in Isaiah's Judgment Oracles." *Catholic Biblical Quarterly* 36 (1974) 307–10.

———. *The Formation of Isaiah 40–55.* Beihefte zur Zeitschrift für die alttestamentliche Wissenschaft 141. Berlin: de Gruyter, 1976.

Mendenhall, G. E. *The Tenth Generation: The Origins of the Biblical Tradition.* Baltimore: Johns Hopkins University Press, 1973.

Merendino, Rosario Pius. *Der Erste und der Letzte: Eine Untersuchung von Jes 40–48.*" Vetus Testamentum Supplements 31. Leiden: Brill, 1981.

Mettinger, Tryggve N. D. *A Farewell to the Servant Songs: A Critical Examination of an Exegetical Axiom.* Lund: CWK Gleerup, 1983.

———. "The Elimination of a Crux? A Syntactic and Semantic Study of Isaiah xl 18–20." Pp. 77–83 in *Studies on Prophecy: A Collection of Twelve Papers.* Vetus Testamentum Supplements 26. Leiden: Brill, 1974.

Millar, William R. *Isaiah 24–27 and the Origin of Apocalyptic.* Missoula, Montana: Scholars Press, 1976.

Miller, J. M., and John H. Hayes. *A History of Ancient Israel and Judah.* Philadelphia: Westminster, 1986.

Miller, John W. "Prophetic Conflict in Second Isaiah: The Servant Songs in the Light of Their Context." Pp. 77–85 in *Wort, Gebet, Glaube: Walter Eichrodt zum 30. Geburtstag.* Edited by J. J. Stamm. Abhandlungen zur Theologie des Alten und Neuen Testaments 59. Zürich: Theologischer Verlag, 1970.

Miller, P. "The Divine Council and the Prophetic Call to War." *Vetus Testamentum* 18 (1968) 100–107.

_______. "Fire in the Mythology of Canaan and Israel." *Catholic Biblical Quarterly* 27 (1965) 256–61.

_______. "Meter, Parallelism and Tropes: The Search for Poetic Style." *Journal for the Study of the Old Testament* 28 (1984) 99–106.

_______. "Studies in Hebrew Word Patterns." *Harvard Theological Review* 73 (1980) 79–90.

_______. "Synonymous-Sequential Parallelism in the Psalms." *Catholic Biblical Quarterly* 61 (1980) 256–60.

Miller, P., and J. J. M. Roberts. *The Hand of the Lord: A Reassessment of the "Ark Narrative" of I Samuel.* Baltimore: Johns Hopkins University Press, 1977.

Morgenstern, Julian. *The Message of Deutero-Isaiah in Its Sequential Unfolding.* Hebrew Union College Annual 29–30 (1958–1959). Reprint, Cincinnati: Hebrew Union College Press, 1961.

Mowinckel, Sigmund. "Cult and Prophecy (1922)." Pp. 74–98 in *Prophecy in Israel: Search for an Identity.* Edited with introduction by David L. Petersen. Issues in Religion and Theology 10. Philadelphia: Fortress / London: SPCK, 1987.

_______. *He That Cometh.* Nashville: Abingdon, 1954.

_______. "Die Komposition des deuterojesajanischen Buches." *Zeitschrift für die alttestamentliche Wissenschaft* 49 (1931) 87–112.

Muilenburg, James. "Form Criticism and Beyond." *Journal of Biblical Literature* 88 (1969) 1–18.

_______. "The Book of Isaiah: Chapters 40–66." Pp. 381–773 in *Interpreter's Bible,* volume 5. New York: Abingdon, 1956.

_______. "Hebrew Rhetoric: Repetition and Style." Pp. 97–111 in *Congress Volume: Copenhagen, 1953.* Vetus Testamentum Supplements 1. Leiden: Brill, 1953.

_______. "The Literary Character of Isaiah 34." *Journal of Biblical Literature* 59 (1940) 339–65.

_______. "Modern Issues in Biblical Studies: The Gains of Form Criticism in Old Testament Studies." *Expository Times* 71 (1960) 229–33.

Naidoff, Bruce D. "The Rhetoric of Encouragement in Isaiah 40:12–21: A Form Critical Study." *Zeitschrift für die alttestamentliche Wissenschaft* 93 (1981) 62–75.

_______. "The Two-Fold Structure of Isaiah xlv 9–13." *Vetus Testamentum* 31 (1981) 180–85.

North, C. R. *The Second Isaiah.* Oxford: Clarendon, 1964.

———. "The 'Former Things' and the 'New Things' in Deutero-Isaiah." Pp. 111–26 in *Studies in Old Testament Prophecy: Presented to Professor Theodore H. Robinson.* Edited by H. H. Rowley. Edinburgh: T. & T. Clark, 1950.

———. *The Suffering Servant in Deutero-Isaiah.* 2d ed. London: Oxford University Press, 1956.

O'Connor, M. *Hebrew Verse Structure.* Winona Lake, Indiana: Eisenbrauns, 1980.

Oded, B. "Judah and the Exile." Pp. 435–88 in *Israelite and Judean History.* Edited by John H. Hayes and J. Maxwell Miller. London: SCM, 1977.

Odendaal, Dirk H. *The Eschatological Expectation of Isaiah 40–66 with Special Reference to Israel and the Nations.* Biblical and Theological Studies. Philadelphia: Presbyterian and Reformed, 1970.

Ogden, Graham S. "Moses and Cyrus: Literary Affinities between the Priestly Presentation of Moses in Exodus vi and the Cyrus Song of Isaiah xliv 24–xlv 13." *Vetus Testamentum* 28 (1978) 195–203.

Olley, J. W. "Notes on Is 32:1; 45:19, 21 and 63:1." *Vetus Testamentum* 33 (1983) 446–53.

Olmstead, A. T. *History of the Persian Empire.* Chicago: University of Chicago Press, 1948.

Oppenheim, A. Leo. *Ancient Mesopotamia: Portrait of a Dead Civilization.* Revised and completed by Erica Reiner. Chicago: University of Chicago Press, 1977.

Orelli, C. von. *The Prophecies of Isaiah.* Edinburgh: T. & T. Clark, 1889.

Pallis, S. A. *The Babylonian Akitu Festival.* Historisk-filolgiske Meddelelser 12. Copenhagen: Bianco Lunos, 1926.

Parunak, H. Van Dyke. "Oral Typesetting: Some Uses of Biblical Structure." *Biblica* 62 (1981) 153–68.

———. "Transitional Techniques in the Bible." *Journal of Biblical Literature* 102 (1983) 525–48.

Paul, Shalom M. "Deutero-Isaiah and Cuneiform Royal Inscriptions." *Journal of the American Oriental Society* 88 (1968) 180–86.

Payne, D. F. "Characteristic Word Play in 'Second-Isaiah': A Reappraisal." *Journal of Semitic Studies* 12 (1967) 207–29.

Petersen, David L. *Late Israelite Prophecy: Studies in Deutero-Prophetic Literature and in Chronicles.* Society of Biblical Literature Monograph Series 23. Missoula, Montana: Scholars Press, 1977.

Pieper, August. *Isaiah II.* Translated by Erwin E. Kowalke. 1919. Reprint, Milwaukee: Northwestern, 1979.

Plamondon, Paul-Henri. "Le Deutero-Isaïe: De la multiplicite de genres littéraires a l'unite d'un discours." *Laval Théologique et Philosophique* 39 (1983) 171–93.

Polan, G. *In the Ways of Justice toward Salvation: A Rhetorical Analysis of Isaiah 56–59.* New York: Peter Lang, 1986.

Preuss, H. D. *Deuterojesaja: Eine Einfuhrung in seine Botschaft.* Neukirchen-Vluyn: Neukirchener Verlag, 1976.

______. *Verspottung fremder Religionen im Alten Testament.* Beiträge zur Wissenschaft vom Alten und Neuen Testament 12. Stuttgart: Kohlhammer, 1971.

Rabban, N. *Second Isaiah: His Prophecy, His Personality and His Name.* Jerusalem: Kiryat-Sepher, 1971 [Hebrew].

Rabinowitz, J. "A Note on Isa 46,4." *Journal of Biblical Literature* 73 (1954) 237.

Rahlfs, A., editor. *Septuaginta.* Stuttgart: Württembergische Bibelanstalt, 1935.

Rignell, L. *A Study of Isaiah, Ch 40–55.* Lund: CWK Gleerup, 1955.

Robertson, David. *The Old Testament and the Literary Critic.* Guides to Biblical Scholarship. Philadelphia: Fortress, 1977.

Robinson, H. W. "The Council of Yahweh." *Journal of Theological Studies* 45 (1944) 151–57.

Rosenbloom, Joseph R. *The Dead Sea Isaiah Scroll: A Literary Analysis.* Grand Rapids, Michigan: Eerdmans, 1970.

Roth, W. M. W. "For Life, He Appeals to Death (Wis 13:18) A Study of Old Testament Idol Parodies." *Catholic Biblical Quarterly* 37 (1975) 21–47.

Saggs, H. W. F. *The Encounter with the Divine in Mesopotamia and Israel.* London: Athlone Press, 1978.

______. *The Greatness That Was Babylon.* New York: New American Library, 1962.

Sasson, J. M. "Word Play in Gen 6:8–9." *Catholic Biblical Quarterly* 37 (1975) 165–66.

______. "Wordplay in the OT." Pp. 968–70 in *Interpreter's Dictionary of the Bible,* supplementary volume. Edited by Keith Crim et al. Nashville: Abingdon, 1976.

Sawyer, John F. A. "A Change of Emphasis in the Study of the Prophets." Pp. 233–49 in *Israel's Prophetic Traditions: Essays in Honour of Peter R. Ackroyd.* Edited by R. Coggins, Anthony Phillips, and Michael Knibb. Cambridge: Cambridge University Press, 1982.

Saydon, P. "Assonance in Hebrew as Means of Expressing Emphasis." *Biblica* 36 (1955) 36–50; 287–304.

Schmitt, J. J. "The Gender of Ancient Israel." *Journal for the Study of the Old Testament* 26 (1983) 115–26.

Schoors, A. *I Am God Your Savior: A Form Critical Study of the Main Genres of Is XL–LV.* Vetus Testamentum Supplements 24. Leiden: Brill, 1973.

______. "Two Notes on Isaiah xl–lv." *Vetus Testamentum* 21 (1971) 503–5.

Schrader, E. *The Cuneiform Inscriptions and the Old Testament.* 2 volumes. Translated by O. C. Whitehouse. London: Williams and Norgate, 1885–1888.

Scullion, John J. *Isaiah 40–66.* Old Testament Message. Wilmington, Deleware: Michael Glazier, 1982.

———. "Ṣedeq-Ṣedaqah in Isaiah cc. 40–66 with Special Reference to the Continuity in Meaning between Second and Third Isaiah." *Ugarit-Forschungen* 3 (1971) 335–48.

Simon, W. E. *A Theology of Salvation: A Commentary on Isaiah 40–55.* London: S.P.C.K., 1953.

Skinner, J. *The Book of the Prophet Isaiah: Chapters XL–LXVI.* 2d ed. The Cambridge Bible for Schools and Colleges. Cambridge: Cambridge University Press, 1915.

Slotki, I. W. *Isaiah: Hebrew Text and English Translation with an Introduction and Commentary.* London: Soncino, 1949.

Smart, J. D. *History and Theology in Second Isaiah: A Commentary on Isaiah 35, 40–66.* Philadelphia: Westminster, 1965.

Smith, Morton. *Palestinian Parties and Politics That Shaped the Old Testament.* New York: Columbia University Press, 1971.

Smith, S. *Babylonian Historical Texts Relating to the Capture and Downfall of Babylon.* London: Methuen, 1924.

———. *Isaiah Chapters XL–LV: Literary Criticism and History.* London: Oxford University Press, 1944.

Spykerboer, H. C. *The Structure and Composition of Deutero-Isaiah with Special Reference to the Polemic against Idolatry.* Frankener, Netherlands: Rijksuniversitet te Groningen, 1976.

Stinespring, W. F. "No Daughter of Zion." *Encounter* 26 (1965) 133–41.

Stoebe, Hans Joachim. "Überlegungen zu Jesaja 40,1–11." *Theologische Zeitschrift* 40 (1984) 104–13.

Stuhlmueller, Carroll. *Creative Redemption in Deutero-Isaiah.* Analecta Biblica 43. Rome: Pontifical Biblical Institute, 1970.

———. "Deutero-Isaiah: Major Transitions in the Prophet's Theology and in Contemporary Scholarship." *Catholic Biblical Quarterly* 42 (1980) 1–29.

———. "'First and Last' and 'Yahweh-Creator' in Deutero-Isaiah." *Catholic Biblical Quarterly* 29 (1967) 495–511.

Stummer, F. "Einige keilschriftliche Parallelen zu Jes. 40–66." *Journal of Biblical Literature* 45 (1926) 171–89.

Thomas, D. Winton. "Isaiah XLIV.9–20: A Translation and Commentary." Pp. 319–30 in *Hommages a André Dupont-Sommer.* Edited by A. Caquot and M. Philonenko. Paris: Adrien Maisonneuve, 1971.

———. "The Sixth Century BC: A Creative Epoch in the History of Israel." *Journal of Semitic Studies* 6 (1961) 33–46.

Thompson, R. Campbell, editor. *The Reports of the Magicians and Astrologers of Nineveh and Babylon in the British Museum,* volume 2. London: Luzac, 1900.

———. *Semitic Magic.* London: Luzac, 1908.

Torrey, C. C. *The Second Isaiah: A New Interpretation.* Edinburgh: T. & T. Clark, 1928.

Tromp, N. J. *Primitive Conceptions of Death and the Netherworld in the Old Testament.* Biblica et Orientalia 21. Rome: Pontifical Biblical Institute, 1969.

Trudinger, P. " 'To Whom Then Will You Liken God?' (Is xl 18–20)." *Vetus Testamentum* 17 (1967) 220–25.

Ullendorf, E. "Ugaritica Marginalia II." *Journal of Semitic Studies* 7 (1962) 339–51.

Van Winkle, D. W. "The Relationship of the Nations to Yahweh and to Israel in Isaiah lx–lv." *Vetus Testamentum* 35 (1985) 446–58.

Vincent, J. M. *Studiën zur literarischen Eigenart und zur geistigen Heimat von Jesaja, Kap 40–55.* Berne: Peter Lang, 1977.

Volz, D. Paul. *Jesaia II übersetzt und erklärt.* Kommentar zum Alten Testament 9. Leipzig: Scholl, 1932.

Wade, G. W. *The Book of the Prophet Isaiah with Introduction and Notes.* Westminster Commentaries. London: Methuen, 1911.

Waldow, H. E. von. "The Message of Deutero-Isaiah." *Interpretation* 22 (1968) 259–87.

Walsh, Jerome P. "The Case for the Prosecution: Isa 41:21–42:17." Pp. 101–18 in *Directions in Biblical Hebrew Poetry.* Edited by E. Follis. Journal for the Study of the Old Testament Supplement Series 40. Sheffield: JSOT Press, 1987.

Watson, Wilfred G. W. *Classical Hebrew Poetry: A Guide to Its Techniques.* Journal for the Study of the Old Testament Supplement Series 26. Sheffield: JSOT Press, 1984.

_______. "Gender-Matched Synonymous Parallelism in the Old Testament." *Journal of Biblical Literature* 99 (1980) 321–41.

_______. "The Pivot Pattern in Hebrew, Ugaritic and Akkadian Poetry." *Zeitschrift für die alttestamentliche Wissenschaft* 88 (1976) 239–53.

Watters, William R. *Formula Criticism and the Poetry of the Old Testament.* Beihefte zur Zeitschrift für die alttestamentliche Wissenschaft 138. Berlin and New York: de Gruyter, 1976.

Watts, J. D. W. *Isaiah 34–66.* Word Biblical Commentary. Waco, Texas: Word, 1987.

Webster, Edwin C. "A Rhetorical Study of Isaiah 66." *Journal for the Study of the Old Testament* 34 (1986) 93–108.

Weiss, M. *The Bible from Within: The Method of Total Interpretation.* Jerusalem: Magnes, 1984.

Welch, J., editor. *Chiasmus in Antiquity: Structures, Analyses, Exegesis.* Hildesheim: Gerstenberg, 1981.

_______. "Chiasmus in Ugaritic." *Ugarit-Forschungen* 6 (1974) 421–36.

Westermann, Claus. *Basic Forms of Prophetic Speech.* Translated by H. C. White. Philadelphia: Westminster, 1967.

_______. *Isaiah 40–66: A Commentary.* Translated by D. M. G. Stalker. Old Testament Library. Philadelphia: Westminster, 1969.

_______. "Jesaja 48 und die 'Bezeugung gegen Israel.'" Pp. 356–66 in *Studia Biblica et Semitica: Theodoro Christiano Vriezen Dedicata.* Edited by W. C. van Unnik and A. S. van der Woude. Wageningen: H. Veenman en Zonen, 1966.

———. *Sprache und Struktur der Prophetie Deuterojesajas.* Calwer Theologische Monographien 11. Stuttgart: Calwer, 1981.

Westhuizen, J. P. van der. "Assonance in Biblical and Babylonian Hymns of Praise." *Semitics* 7 (1980) 81–101.

Whedbee, J. W. *Isaiah and Wisdom.* Nashville: Abingdon, 1971.

White, J. B. "Universalization of History in Deutero-Isaiah." Pp. 179–95 in *Scripture in Context: Essays on the Comparative Method.* Edited by Carl D. Evans, William W. Hallo, and John B. White. Pittsburgh Theological Monograph Series 34. Pittsburgh: Pickwick, 1980.

Whitley, Charles Francis. *The Exilic Age.* Philadelphia: Westminster, 1957.

Whybray, R. N. *Isaiah 40–66.* New Century Bible. London: Marshall, Morgan & Scott/Grand Rapids, Michigan: Eerdmans, 1981.

———. *The Heavenly Counsellor in Isaiah xl 13–14.* London: Cambridge University Press, 1971.

———. *The Second Isaiah.* Old Testament Guides. Sheffield: JSOT Press, 1983.

———. "Two Recent Studies on Second Isaiah." *Journal for the Study of the Old Testament* 34 (1986) 109–17.

Wiklander, Bertil. *Prophecy as Literature: A Text-Linguistic and Rhetorical Approach to Isaiah 2–4.* Coniectanea Biblica, Old Testament Series 22. Uppsala: CWK Gleerup, 1984.

Wilkie, J. M. "Nabonidus and the Later Jewish Exiles." *Journal of Theological Studies* 11 (1951) 36–44.

Williams, J. G. "Irony and Lament: Clues to Prophetic Consciousness." *Semeia* 8 (1977) 51–74.

Williams, Ronald J. *Hebrew Syntax: An Outline.* 2d ed. Toronto: University of Toronto Press, 1976.

Williamson, H. G. M. "A Reconsideration of *ᶜzb* in Biblical Hebrew." *Zeitschrift für die alttestamentliche Wissenschaft* 97 (1985) 74–85.

———. "A Response to A. G. Auld." *Journal for the Study of the Old Testament* 27 (1983) 33–39.

Willis, John T. "Alternation (ABA′B′) Parallelism in the Old Testament Psalms and Prophetic Literature." Pp. 49–76 in *Directions in Biblical Hebrew Poetry.* Edited by E. Follis. Journal for the Study of the Old Testament Supplement Series 40. Sheffield: JSOT Press, 1987.

Wilson, Andrew. *The Nations in Deutero-Isaiah: A Study on Composition and Structure.* Lewiston, New York: Andrew Mellen, 1986.

Wilson, R. "A Progress Report or an Obituary?" *Interpretation* 30 (1976) 71–74.

———. *Prophet and Society in Ancient Israel.* Philadelphia: Fortress, 1980.

Wohl, H. "A Note on the Fall of Babylon." *Journal of the Ancient Near Eastern Society of Columbia University* (1969) 28–38.

Young, Edward J. *The Book of Isaiah,* volume 1. The New International Commentary on the Old Testament. Grand Rapids, Michigan: Eerdmans, 1965.

Zimmerli, W. *I Am Yahweh.* Translated by D. W. Stott. Atlanta: John Knox, 1982.